THE MARGINS OF DISCRETION IN TRANSNATIONAL ADMINISTRATIVE ACTS

This book analyses the expulsion of delinquent foreigners and their exclusion from the territory through a comparative lens.

The book begins with a vertical perspective, focusing on the effects of European standards on the law of expulsion and entry bans in Germany and the Netherlands, and the law regulating deportation from the United Kingdom. It explores how these countries use their margin of discretion, granted by European law, to solve the societal, political and legal challenges that are posed by delinquent foreigners. Moreover, it highlights the similarities, convergences and differences between these countries' approaches to the topic.

Subsequently, the book adopts a horizontal perspective by focusing on the effects of national decisions on other states, thereby addressing transnational administrative acts. National expulsion decisions and entry bans can be given effect throughout European countries, with the consequence that other states are in principle obliged to enforce them by refusing foreigners access to their territory. This obligation arises despite the fact that expulsion decisions and entry bans are adopted on the basis of diverging national provisions. Even though the margin of discretion of national decision makers has already been limited, the remaining differences call for further recommendations, which are put forward in this book.

The Margins of Discretion in Transnational Administrative Acts

Expulsion Decisions and Entry Bans Following a Criminal Conviction

Kathrin Hamenstädt

•HART•

OXFORD • LONDON • NEW YORK • NEW DELHI • SYDNEY

HART PUBLISHING
Bloomsbury Publishing Plc
Kemp House, Chawley Park, Cumnor Hill, Oxford, OX2 9PH, UK
1385 Broadway, New York, NY 10018, USA
29 Earlsfort Terrace, Dublin 2, Ireland

First published in Great Britain 2022

A catalogue record for this book is available from the British Library.

Library of Congress Cataloging-in-Publication Data

Names: Hamenstädt, Kathrin, author.

Title: The margins of discretion in transnational administrative acts : expulsion decisions and entry bans following a criminal conviction / Kathrin Hamenstädt.

Description: Oxford ; New York : Hart, 2022. | Based on author's thesis (doctoral - Universiteit Maastricht, 2015) issued under title: The margins of discretion in European expulsion decisions. | Includes bibliographical references and index.

Identifiers: LCCN 2021060695 (print) | LCCN 2021060696 (ebook) | ISBN 9781509925988 (hardback) | ISBN 9781509959006 (paperback) | ISBN 9781509926008 (pdf) | ISBN 9781509925995 (EPub)

Subjects: LCSH: Deportation—Europe. | Noncitizen criminals—Legal status, laws, etc.—Europe. | Administrative discretion—Europe. | Deportation—Great Britain. | Deportation—Germany. | Deportation—Netherlands. | Noncitizen criminals—Legal status, laws, etc.—Great Britain. | Noncitizen criminals—Legal status, laws, etc.—Germany. | Noncitizen criminals—Legal status, laws, etc.—Netherlands.

Classification: LCC KJC6050 .H36 2022 (print) | LCC KJC6050 (ebook) | DDC 342.408/3—dc23/eng/20220204

LC record available at https://lccn.loc.gov/2021060695

LC ebook record available at https://lccn.loc.gov/2021060696

ISBN: HB: 978-1-50992-598-8
ePDF: 978-1-50992-600-8
ePub: 978-1-50992-599-5

Typeset by Compuscript Ltd, Shannon
Printed and bound in Great Britain

ACKNOWLEDGEMENTS

Without the inspiration, support, and encouragement of many wonderful people who have accompanied me on my way and who believe in me, this book would not exist.

I am deeply grateful to my *Doktormütter*, Hildegard Schneider and Elise Muir, for their constructive ideas and advice, their invaluable comments and questions, their incredible enthusiasm and contagious motivation, and for their continuous support, during my time as a PhD researcher at Maastricht University and later in my life.

Die Entstehung dieses Buches hat sehr von den Tagungen und Kolloquien des Netzwerks Migrationsrecht und dem Austausch mit den Netzwerksmitgliedern profitiert. Bedanken möchte ich mich insbesondere bei Jürgen Bast für seine konstruktiven Anregungen und für seine Unterstützung.

Ein herzliches Dankeschön gilt Imke Baasen, Sara Berendsen, Silke Böttcher, Anke Bohm, Andrea Broderick, Julia Cordes, Mark Dawson, Juliane von Eitzen, Sabine Gorn, Marieke Heers, Felicitas Kaape, Nina Lück, Ewan McGaughey, Inga Owesen, Eva Pils, Mark Provera, Farrah Raza, Juana Remus, Sabrina Röttger-Wirtz, Markus Schlaab, Mareike Schmidt, Peter Schmidt, Caroline Schrakamp, Martina Summer-Kutmon, Pierre Thielbörger, Maria Tzanakopoulou und Ermioni Xanthopoulou für ihre Freundschaft und dass sie mich auf dieser Reise begleitet haben.

Besonders bedanken möchte ich mich bei meinen Eltern und bei meinem Bruder Ulrich, die immer für mich da waren, mich unterstützt und mir zur Seite gestanden haben. Vielen lieben Dank!

Kathrin Hamenstädt

CONTENTS

PART II
THE EFFECTS OF EUROPEAN LAW ON EXPULSION DECISIONS TAKEN AT THE NATIONAL LEVEL

TABLE OF CASES

EU Case Law

EFTA Court Case Law

ECHR Case Law

National Case Law

Germany

The Netherlands

United Kingdom

United States

TABLE OF LEGISLATION

EU Legislation

Council of Europe

International Treaties/Conventions

National Legislation

Germany

The Netherlands

Primary Legislation

Delegated Legislation

United Kingdom

Introduction

Before focusing on the structure, purpose and aim of the analysis in the present book, some general remarks will provide an overview of the area under scrutiny and highlight its intricacies and inherent challenges. The book's focus rests on the margin of discretion in transnational administrative acts and more specifically on expulsion decisions and entry bans following a criminal conviction.

The freedom of states to expel foreigners is not absolute and is circumscribed by the rules of international law, in particular human rights law.[1] Several regional human rights instruments, such as the African Charter on Human and Peoples' Rights,[2] the American Convention on Human Rights,[3] the European Convention on Establishment[4] and the Charter of Fundamental Rights of the European Union (CFR or 'the Charter'),[5] have constrained states' power to expel foreigners from their territory. While a reference to expulsion is lacking in the European Convention on Human Rights (ECHR), it contains an absolute prohibition of torture, inhuman or degrading treatment or punishment,[6] thereby barring expulsions that would precipitate the risk of such a treatment. In addition to these limitations, several instruments ban collective or mass expulsions,[7] provide for procedural safeguards in the context of expulsion[8] and afford guarantees to specific groups of migrants, such as refugees or migrant workers.[9]

[1] See International Law Commission, Draft Articles on the Expulsion of Aliens, with Commentaries (2014) UN Doc A/69/10, draft Article 3.

[2] Article 12(4) African Charter on Human and Peoples' Rights (Nairobi, 27 June 1981) (ACHPR).

[3] Article 22(6) American Convention on Human Rights (San José, 22 November 1969) (ACHR).

[4] Article 3 European Convention on Establishment, and Protocol thereto, ETS no 19 (Paris, 13 December 1955). Originally, Article 4 of Protocol 4 to the ECHR (full citation below n 7) contained provisions on individual expulsions which were abandoned as provisions regarding individual expulsion are already contained in the European Convention on Establishment. For further information see Explanatory Report to Protocol No 4 to the Convention for the Protection of Human Rights and Fundamental Freedoms, securing certain rights and freedoms other than those already included in the Convention and in the first Protocol thereto, ETS no 46 (Strasbourg, 16 September 1963) nos 31–34.

[5] Article 19(2) Charter of Fundamental Rights of the European Union [2012] OJ C 326/391 (CFR).

[6] Article 3 Convention for the Protection of Human Rights and Fundamental Freedoms (Rome, 4 November 1950) (ECHR).

[7] Article 12(5) ACHPR; Article 22(9) ACHR; Article 26(2) Arab Charter on Human Rights (Tunis, 22 May 2004); Article 25(4) Commonwealth of Independent States Convention on Human Rights and Fundamental Freedoms (Minsk, 26 May 1995); Article 4 of Protocol No 4 to the Convention for the Protection of Human Rights and Fundamental Freedoms, securing certain rights and freedoms other than those already included in the Convention and in the first Protocol thereto, as amended by Protocol No 11, ETS no 46 (Strasbourg, 16 September 1963); Article 19(1) CFR; ILC, Draft Articles on the Expulsion of Aliens, draft Article 9.

[8] Article 1 of Protocol No 7 to the Convention for the Protection of Human Rights and Fundamental Freedoms, as amended by Protocol No 11, ETS no 117 (Strasbourg, 22 November 1984) and Article 13 International Covenant on Civil and Political Rights (New York, 16 December 1966).

In principle, expulsions and deportations may be directed against nationals,[10] but a number of states have subscribed to the prohibition of expulsion of nationals,[11] which underlines a general perception that nationals' membership and presence on the national territory is unconditional.[12] The Court of Justice of the European Union (CJEU) has repeatedly highlighted nationals' absolute security of residence by stating that public policy and public security exceptions allow Member States to adopt 'measures which they cannot apply to their own nationals, inasmuch as they have no authority to expel the latter from the territory or to deny them access thereto'.[13] Even though nationals normally enjoy an absolute security of residence, they can be deprived of their nationality by way of denaturalisation, which turns them into expellable foreigners.[14] However, the 2014 International Law Commission's Draft Articles on the Expulsion of Aliens provide in Article 8 that 'A State shall not make its national an alien, by deprivation of nationality, for the sole purpose of expelling him or her'.[15]

While penal provisions apply to nationals and foreigners alike and both groups can be subject to criminal convictions, some penal provisions apply exclusively to foreigners. Immigration-related offences, such as entering the national territory without the requisite permission,[16] can only be committed by foreigners, as nationals' residence is unconditional. Foreigners can consequently be punished for a behaviour that would not constitute a crime if it were attributable to a national. This difference increases the number of punishable offences that can be committed by foreigners and might result in a distorted perception of the crimes committed by them. Even though some crime statistics, for instance the German police crime statistic, clearly distinguish between criminal offences and immigration-related offences,[17] which might counteract this risk to some extent, this distinction generally does not seem to attract much attention.

[9] Article 22 International Convention on the Protection of the Rights of All Migrant Workers and Their Families (New York, 18 December 1990); Article 32 Convention relating to the Status of Refugees (Geneva, 28 July 1951).

[10] W Kälin, 'Aliens, Expulsion and Deportation' in R Wolfrum (ed), *The Max Planck Encyclopedia on Public International Law* (2008–) § 2, www.opil.ouplaw.com/view/10.1093/law:epil/9780199231690/law-9780199231690-e745.

[11] Article 22(5) ACHR; Article 3 of Protocol 4 ECHR.

[12] B Anderson, M Gibney and E Paoletti, 'Citizenship, Deportation and the Boundaries of Belonging' (2011) 15 *Citizenship Studies* 547, 555.

[13] Joined Cases C-115/81 and 116/81 *Adoui and Cornuaille* ECLI:EU:C:1982:183, [1982] ECR I-01655, para 7; Case C-348/96 *Calfa* ECLI:EU:C:1999:6, [1999] ECR I-00011, para 20; Case C-100/01 *Oteiza Olazabal* ECLI:EU:C:2002:712, [2002] ECR I-11000, para 40.

[14] *K2 v UK* App no 42387/13 (ECHR, 07 February 2017); L Zedner, 'Citizenship Deprivation, Security and Human Rights' (2016) 18 *European Journal of Migration and Law* 222; T Choudhury, 'The Radicalisation of Citizenship Deprivation' (2017) 37 *Critical Social Policy* 225.

[15] Adopted by the International Law Commission at its sixty-sixth session, in 2014, and submitted to the General Assembly (A/69/10).

[16] See, for instance, s 95(1) no 3 Gesetz über den Aufenthalt, die Erwerbstätigkeit und die Integration von Ausländern im Bundesgebiet (Aufenthaltsgesetz – AufenthG) of 25 February 2008, Federal Law Gazette Part I 162, last amended on 9 July 2021, Federal Law Gazette Part I 2467 ('Residence Act').

[17] Bundesministerium des Innern, für Bau und Heimat, 'Polizeiliche Kriminalstatistik 2018 Ausgewählte Zahlen im Überblick' (Innenminister Konferenz 2019) 9, 10, 11, 13, 23, 24, 26, 27, 30, 31, 33,

The law on expulsion constitutes a further distinguishing factor between nationals and foreigners. Both foreigners and nationals can be imprisoned, but only foreigners can be expelled. The provisions on expulsion mark their addressees as outsiders and non-members,[18] as aliens who do not belong to the polity and can therefore be removed in case they misbehave. The enforcement of an expulsion decision by way of deportation highlights foreigners' wrongdoing, putting the wrongdoers and their crimes in the spotlight, whereas the same attention is normally not given to nationals' wrongdoing. Expulsion excludes foreigners from society, ostracises them and underpins the alleged threat their presence poses to society. It helps support the narrative of 'the criminal migrant', who continues to be a danger to society even after being released from prison, which simultaneously serves as a justification to impose and increase control measures on foreigners.

The law on expulsion constitutes a mirror of society as it reflects the attitude of nationals towards non-nationals. It sheds light on the preparedness of the host country's society to accept responsibility for the misconduct of foreigners, who often slipped into criminality and became criminals in the host country. States should accept responsibility for 'their' criminals, especially if they grew up and were socialised in that state, even if they hold a foreign passport. However, Duff observes that there is 'a persistent tendency, among both politicians and theorists, to talk about crime and criminality in the third person: about what "we" … should do about "them" – those who do or might break the law'.[19] Given that criminals are already considered outsiders, this applies all the more to criminals with a foreign passport. The tendency of states and societies to distance themselves from criminals with a foreign passport is reflected by their lack of preparedness to accept responsibility. This is illustrated by the non-binding recommendations of the Committee of Ministers of the Council of Europe. In 2000 the Committee of Ministers adopted a recommendation on long-term residents' security of residence,[20] which called for three categories of foreigners to be exempted from expulsion. These categories comprised, first, foreigners with more than 20 years of residence;[21] second, long-term resident immigrants who have reached the age of 18, if they were born on the territory of the Member State or were admitted before the age of 10 and have been lawfully and habitually resident there;[22] and third, foreigners who are minors.[23] Contracting States refrained from converting this recommendation

www.bmi.bund.de/SharedDocs/downloads/DE/publikationen/themen/sicherheit/pks-2018.pdf?__blob=publicationFile&v=3.

[18] PH Schuck, 'The Transformation of Immigration Law' (1984) 84 *Columbia Law Review* 1.

[19] A Duff, 'Inclusion and Exclusion: Citizens, Subjects and Outlaws' (1998) 51 *Current Legal Problems* 241, 243.

[20] Council of Europe, Committee of Ministers, Recommendation Rec (2000)15, concerning the security of residence of long-term migrants, adopted on 13 September 2000 at the 720th meeting of the Ministers' Deputies.

[21] ibid, no 4(b).

[22] ibid, no 4(c).

[23] ibid, no 4(c).

into a legally binding instrument, which underpins their lack of willingness to accept responsibility for delinquent foreigners, even though these foreigners have often grown up and/or lived in their societies for decades, and should therefore be considered the states' 'own criminals'. Interestingly, the Netherlands even reversed its previous stance. Until 2012 Dutch law afforded several categories of long-term resident foreigners (categories resembling those listed in the recommendation of the Council of Europe) an absolute protection against expulsion. This protection covered foreigners who had resided in the Netherlands for more than 20 years and foreigners who were born in the Netherlands or had lawfully resided there before the age of 10 and had been resident for more than 15 years.[24] In 2012 this protection was abolished,[25] which, again, highlights the lack of preparedness of societies, not only in the Netherlands, to accept responsibility for their 'own criminals'. Judge Turković aptly notes in her dissenting opinion in the *Ndidi* case that

> [a]t a time when Europe is coping with the serious problems which partially originate in a poor record in terms of integration efforts, especially with regard to second-generation migrants, it is of utmost importance to balance wisely society's impulse to attach greater weight to the public interest than to private and family life claims under Article 8 of the Convention.[26]

Next to being a mirror of society, the provisions on expulsion reflect the *zeitgeist* as they echo society's reaction to socio-political developments. The likelihood of an expulsion generally increases the more severe the crime and the higher the prison sentence imposed on the foreigner. Apart from this general rule, the provisions on expulsion list crimes that are considered to pose a particularly serious threat to society at a given time and which normally constitute a response to specific events or developments. This is demonstrated by the evolution of the German provisions on expulsion over the last 30 years and by the developments in other states. The 1990 Foreigner Act stipulated that a foreigner shall normally be expelled if s/he commits drug-related crimes, namely crimes covered by the Narcotics Act,[27] thereby reflecting the seriousness attached to the threat posed by drugs. The 2004 German Residence Act completely revised the provisions but retained this ground for expulsion. It added, however, in response to the growth of terrorist networks and the attacks of 9/11, a novel ground of expulsion, that is, membership of a terrorist organisation.[28] This ground has also been retained, albeit in a modified

[24] Article 3.86(7)(c) and Article 3.86(8)(b) Vreemdelingenbesluit 2000 (Vb 2000) of the version that entered into force on 1 April 2001; Article 3.86(10b) and (11b) Vb 2000 of the version of the Vreemdelingenbesluit 2000 which was applicable on 18 April 2012.

[25] By the 'Besluit van 26 maart 2012, houdende wijziging van het Vreemdelingenbesluit 2000 in verband met aanscherping van de glijdende schaal', Official Gazette of the Kingdom of the Netherlands 2012, 158.

[26] *Ndidi v UK* App no 41215/14 (ECHR, 14 September 2017), dissenting opinion of Judge Turković, para 7.

[27] Gesetz zur Neuregelung des Ausländerrechts of 9 July 1990, Federal Law Gazette Part I 1354, s 47(2) no 2 ('Foreigner Act').

[28] Residence Act 2004, Federal Law Gazette 2004 Part I 1950, s 54 no 5.

form, in the current version of the German Residence Act. In 2007 three new grounds for expulsion were inserted into the Residence Act,[29] which reflect the public debate about foreigners' integration into society. According to the explanatory memorandum to the legislative proposal, these grounds target actions that have an adverse effect on an individual's integration.[30] In 2015 the German law on expulsion was completely revised to ensure compatibility with the ECHR and to reflect the changes that had been precipitated by case law.[31] To that end, the new system requires a balancing process between the interests of the individual and the interest of the state in every decision concerning expulsion.[32] To guide the decision-making process, the newly established system contains a non-exhaustive list of interests and provides for a specific weight that has to be attached to the interests of the foreigner and the interests of the state respectively.[33] The state's interest in expelling the foreigner shall, for example, carry particularly great weight if the foreigner has been sentenced to at least one year's imprisonment for an offence against another person's sexual self-determination.[34] This ground was only incorporated into the statutory provisions in March 2016.[35] According to the explanatory memorandum, it constitutes a reaction to the incidents on the night of New Year's Eve 2015,[36] during which several women were sexually assaulted in Cologne. The law establishing this new ground for expulsion and containing amendments of the Residence Act and the Asylum Act is titled 'Law on the simplified expulsion of delinquent foreigners and the extended exclusion of delinquent asylum seekers from asylum procedures'.[37]

The title of the law seems to reflect a trend also visible in several other states to seek to rid themselves quickly of unwanted foreigners. This trend is demonstrated by the 'hostile environment' policy in the United Kingdom,[38] and by the legislative developments in the Netherlands. In the Netherlands, the coalition agreement

[29] Residence Act, version applicable on 28 August 2007, s 55(2) nos 9, 10, 11; Gesetz zur Umsetzung aufenthalts- und asylrechtlicher Richtlinien der Europäischen Union of 19 August 2007, Federal Law Gazette Part I 1970.

[30] Gesetzentwurf der Bundesregierung, 'Entwurf eines Gesetzes zur Umsetzung aufenthalts- und asylrechtlicher Richtlinien der Europäischen Union' (2007) Bundestagdrucksache 16/5065 at 183.

[31] Gesetz zur Neubestimmung des Bleiberechts und der Aufenthaltsbeendigung of 27 July 2015, Federal Law Gazette Part I 1386, 1392–94.

[32] Residence Act, s 53(1).

[33] ibid, ss 54, 55.

[34] ibid, s 54(1) no 1a.

[35] Gesetz zur erleichterten Ausweisung von straffälligen Ausländern und zum erweiterten Ausschluss der Flüchtlingsanerkennung bei straffälligen Asylbewerbern of 11 March 2016, Federal Law Gazette Part I 394.

[36] Gesetzentwurf der Fraktionen der CDU/CSU und SPD 'Entwurf eines Gesetzes zur erleichterten Ausweisung von straffälligen Ausländern und zum erweiterten Ausschluss der Flüchtlingsanerkennung bei straffälligen Asylbewerbern' (2016) Bundestagsdrucksache 18/7573 at 5.

[37] Above n 35.

[38] For further information regarding the notion of 'hostile environment' see B Bowling and S Westenra, '"A Really Hostile Environment": Adiaphorization, Global Policing and the Crimmigration Control System' (2020) 24 *Theoretical Criminology* 163, 179, note 1; L Waite, 'Asylum Seekers and the Labour Market: Spaces of Discomfort and Hostility' (2017) 16 *Social Policy & Society* 669, 673.

of 2010 explicitly stated that delinquent foreigners have to be removed from the Netherlands as quickly as possible and stipulated that the cabinet must tighten the so-called *glijdende schaal*.[39] The *glijdende schaal* determines the protection against expulsion depending on the duration of the foreigner's residence in relation to the crime committed and the prison sentence imposed. The coalition agreement was implemented in 2012 and resulted, among other legislative amendments, in the above-mentioned abolition of the absolute protection against expulsion that was previously afforded to certain categories of long-term resident foreigners. Whether the measures instituted by the legislative amendments in the United Kingdom, Germany and the Netherlands are effective instruments, or whether they are primarily symbol politics designed to demonstrate the state's determination to fight crime and to protect its citizens by rigorously expelling unwanted migrants, is a different question. The (forceful) removal of foreigners will not only depend on the legal provisions in place in the expelling state, it will also be determined by the willingness of the home state or a third state to accept the person. In 2020 Lutz pointed out that 'today's real problem of EU return policy is not the regulatory aspect of issuance or recognition of return decisions but rather the enforcement angle (ie identification and documentation)'.[40] In addition, Covid-19 and the political situation in receiving states has had a considerable impact on EU Member States' possibility to remove delinquent foreigners from their territory.

Expulsion decisions are normally categorised as administrative acts, with the consequence that the expulsion and removal of delinquent foreigners following their criminal conviction does not infringe the prohibition of double punishment (*ne bis in idem*).[41] Nonetheless, the legal classification does not necessarily reflect the perception of expelled foreigners. As early as in 1926 a US court held:

> At any rate we think it not improper to say that deportation under the circumstances would be deplorable. Whether the relator came here in arms or at the age of ten, he is as much our product as though his mother had borne him on American soil. He knows no other language, no other people, no other habits, than ours; he will be as much a stranger in Poland as any one born of ancestors who immigrated in the seventeenth century. However heinous his crimes, deportation is to him exile, a dreadful punishment, abandoned by the common consent of all civilized peoples.[42]

Not only does this statement acknowledge society's responsibility for the foreigner's conduct by stating that 'he is as much our product as though his mother had borne him on American soil', it also highlights the impact of an expulsion on the individual. Foreigners often experience expulsion or deportation as tantamount

[39] Rijksoverheid, 'Vrijheid en verantwoordelijkheid, Regeerakkoord VVD-CDA', 30 September 2010, www.rijksoverheid.nl/documenten/rapporten/2010/09/30/regeerakkoord-vvd-cda24.

[40] F Lutz, 'Prologue: The Genesis of the EU's Return Policy' in M Moraru, G Cornelisse and P De Bruycker (eds), *Law and Judicial Dialogue on Return of Irregular Migrants from the European Union* (Oxford, Hart Publishing, 2020) 10.

[41] Article 50 CFR.

[42] 13 F.2d 630 (1926) *United States ex rel. Klonis v. Davis*, 13 F.2d 630, 630 (2d Cir. 1926) (L Hand J).

to criminal punishment.[43] Some foreigners, especially those who were born and raised in the 'host' state and who lack links with their country of nationality, perceive banishment as the most severe form of punishment.[44] Apart from individual perceptions, the legal classification of expulsion as a non-punitive and administrative measure also raises doubts.[45] Bowling and Westenra point out that deportation 'parallels the use of imprisonment for criminal citizens but is a more far-reaching method of social exclusion and incapacitation'.[46] Similarly, Kanstroom argues that deportation is a form of punishment.[47] It becomes indistinguishable from the assessments that are routinely made by criminal law as it reflects a judgement about the 'moral worth of individual conduct'.[48] Indeed, doubts regarding the classification of an expulsion decision as an administrative act arise against the background of considerations which originate in penology and which are also invoked in the context of expulsion. The first consideration is the isolation of the foreigner from the general public,[49] which reflects the 'incapacitating function' of expulsion.[50] Even though the rationale of isolation only applies to the expelling state's society and not to the receiving society, isolation and incapacitation are firmly rooted in punitive theories and pursue the aim of special prevention. The second consideration is that of deterrence vis-à-vis other foreigners.[51] The purpose of deterrence is also firmly rooted in punitive theories and pursues the aim of general prevention. Since expulsion is based on considerations originating in penology, it is not clear why an expulsion does not amount to punishment.

Apart from these valid concerns, the expulsion of delinquent foreigners who have served their prison sentence also calls into question the effectiveness of criminal punishment.[52] Criminal punishment serves the aim of rehabilitating the criminal offender, among other objectives. Expulsion, on the other hand, normally

[43] Bowling and Westenra, 'A Really Hostile Environment' 167; J Wegner, 'Die Behandlung straffällig gewordender Einwanderer im neuen Ausweisungsrecht' (1993) 46 *Die Öffentliche Verwaltung* 1031, 1032; S Turnbull and I Hasselberg, 'From Prison to Detention: The Carceral Trajectories of Foreign National Prisoners in the United Kingdom' (2017) 19 *Punishment & Society* 135, 143, 147.

[44] W Meyer, 'Die Ausweisung nach dem Ausländergesetz in der Rechtsprechung des Bundesverwaltungsgerichts' (1984) *Neue Zeitschrift für Verwaltungsrecht* 13; K Sieveking, 'Security of Residence and Expulsion: The German Experience' in E Guild and P Minderhoud (eds) *Security of Residence and Expulsion* (The Hague, Kluwer Law International, 2001) 109; C Mielitz, 'Die aufenthaltsrechtlichen Rechtsfolgen der Ausweisung' (2009) 29 *Zeitschrift für Ausländerrecht und Ausländerpolitik* 264.

[45] Schuck, 'The Transformation of Immigration Law' 24–27.

[46] Bowling and Westenra, 'A Really Hostile Environment' 167.

[47] D Kanstroom, 'Deportation, Social Control, and Punishment: Some Thoughts about Why Hard Laws Make Bad Cases' (2000) 113 *Harvard Law Review* 1890, 1893–94.

[48] Schuck, 'The Transformation of Immigration Law' 26.

[49] S Legomsky, 'Ausweisung und Abschiebung straffälliger Ausländer. The Expulsion of Criminal Aliens' in K Hailbronner and E Klein (eds), *Einwanderungskontrolle und Menschenrechte – Immigration Control and Human Rights, Beiträge anlässlich des Symposiums am 29–30 Juni 1998 in Potsdam* (Heidelberg, C.F. Müller Verlag, 1999) 164.

[50] Kanstroom, 'Deportation, Social Control, and Punishment' 1894.

[51] ibid; Legomsky, 'Ausweisung und Abschiebung straffälliger Ausländer' 164.

[52] Turnbull and Hasselberg, 'From Prison to Detention' 150.

requires that the foreigner's presence or conduct poses a threat to the 'host' state's public policy or public security. If the aim of rehabilitation were achieved, the foreigner would no longer pose a threat and expulsion following release from prison would neither be necessary nor possible.

Focus of the Book

The focus of this book rests on the margin of discretion in transnational administrative acts and more specifically on expulsion decisions and entry bans following a criminal conviction. The notion of expulsion has no single meaning as it has been defined in various ways.[53] Even though the EU Commission's Glossary defines 'expulsion' as the 'removal of a third-country national',[54] this notion is not confined to third-country nationals as it is also used in the context of EU citizens.[55] The International Law Commission's Memorandum on the Expulsion of Aliens provides that expulsion 'may be understood as referring to the exercise of the right or power of a State to require an alien to leave its territory when his or her continuing presence is contrary to the interests of the territorial State'.[56] Moreover, the memorandum states that a 'State usually exercises this right or power in the form of a decision or order issued by the appropriate judicial or administrative body in accordance with its national law'.[57] This understanding of the notions of expulsion and expulsion decision is applied in this book and both notions will at times be used interchangeably. Moreover, the International Law Commission's memorandum provides that a 'distinction may be drawn between the notion of expulsion … and the notion of deportation as referring to the enforcement of the decision or order'.[58] Similarly, Kälin states that 'there is a clear tendency to call expulsion the legal order to leave the territory of a State, and deportation the actual implementation of such order in cases where the person concerned does not follow it voluntarily'.[59] This distinction between expulsion and deportation will subsequently be applied as far as possible, though the primary focus will remain

[53] cf International Law Commission, Expulsion of Aliens: Memorandum by the Secretariat, UN Doc A/CN.4/565 of 10 July 2006 61; European Commission, 'Expulsion' (Glossary of the EU Commission) www.ec.europa.eu/home-affairs/what-we-do/networks/european_migration_network/glossary_search/expulsion_en.

[54] European Commission, 'Expulsion'.

[55] See Article 28 of Directive 2004/38/EC of the European Parliament and of the Council of 29 April 2004 on the right of citizens of the Union and their family members to move and reside freely within the territory of the Member States amending Regulation (EEC) No 1612/68 and repealing Directives 64/221/EEC, 68/360/EEC, 72/194/EEC, 73/148/EEC, 75/34/EEC, 75/35/EEC, 90/364/EEC, 90/365/EEC and 93/96/EEC [2004] OJ L 158/77 ('Citizenship Directive'), which is titled 'protection against expulsion'.

[56] International Law Commission, Expulsion of Aliens: Memorandum by the Secretariat, para 67.

[57] ibid.

[58] ibid, para 91.

[59] Kälin, 'Aliens, Expulsion and Deportation'.

on expulsions or expulsion decisions, which are understood as legal orders that oblige the foreigner to leave the state's territory.

The right of states to decide on the admission and presence of foreigners on their territory is an attribute of their sovereignty.[60] The freedom to expel and forcefully remove foreigners from their national territory emanates from this sovereignty and is firmly rooted in international law.[61] Consequently, states seek to maintain this power, as illustrated by the legal position of EU citizens in other EU Member States. Even though 'Union citizenship is destined to be the fundamental status of nationals of the Member States, enabling those who find themselves in the same situation to enjoy the same treatment in law irrespective of their nationality',[62] EU citizens can still be subject to expulsion from the 'host' Member State, whereas nationals of the respective Member State are exempt from expulsion. This underpins that even in an 'ever closer union among the peoples of Europe'[63] with common values[64] and a Charter of Fundamental Rights, states are determined to retain and assert their power to expel EU citizens as an expression of their sovereignty.

Even though national expulsion decisions and entry bans can only be issued by national authorities and are solely enforceable on the territory of the respective state, they can be given a European dimension by entering an alert into the Schengen Information System (SIS). The SIS relies on mutual recognition and enables the exchange of information and the sharing of data between the participating states. A national entry ban that has been given European effect by the entry of an alert into the SIS constitutes a transnational administrative act that must, in principle, be enforced by all participating states in the same way as an act of their own national authorities. Consequently, a foreigner in respect of whom a national authority entered an alert into the SIS for the purpose of refusing entry will be refused entry to the entire Schengen territory, unless an exception applies.

The research herein consists of two tiers. In a first step, it addresses the effects of the European level on the national level, and in a second step the effects of the national level on the European level. Using this two-tiered approach, the book's first focus rests on the margin of discretion granted by the European level to the national level, hence to national decision makers. To that end, it outlines the standards set by the European law and assesses how this margin is used at the national level. It examines the legislative, administrative and judicial approaches to expulsion decisions and entry bans in the UK, the Netherlands and Germany. It identifies the commonalities and differences between these approaches and assesses whether the national provisions and their application stay within, or risk overstepping, the margin of discretion granted by the European level.

[60] ibid; Schuck, 'The Transformation of Immigration Law' 1, 6.

[61] E Pistoia, 'The Unbearable Lightness of a Piecemeal Approach. Moving Public Policy or Public Security Offenders in Europe' (2014) 20 *European Public Law* 745, 747.

[62] Case C-184/99 *Grzelczyk* ECLI:EU:C:2001:458, [2001] ECR I-06193, para 31.

[63] See Article 1 Treaty on European Union (TEU).

[64] Article 2 TEU.

The book's second focal point rests on transnational administrative acts and addresses the horizontal dimension of national expulsion decisions and entry bans by examining their impact on other EU Member States. National expulsion decisions and entry bans against delinquent foreigners are adopted on the basis of national provisions which are not identical. National provisions differ as European standards leave a margin of discretion to the national legislatures. The European instruments that facilitate the entry of an alert into the SIS for the purpose of refusing a third-country national entry, which are the Return Directive[65] and the SIS Regulation,[66] both grant a margin of discretion to the Member States. Given the discretion granted by European provisions, national alerts entered into the SIS can differ. Despite these differences, national decisions leading to SIS alerts must be recognised and enforced by other states, unless an exception applies. Mutual recognition of possibly diverging decisions can be problematic in light of the repercussions on individuals affected by these decisions, and in light of their effects on the common European approach to migration.

Both focal points are connected to each other by the margin of discretion granted by the European level to the national level regarding the issuance of expulsion decisions and the imposition of entry bans. The lesser the margin of discretion granted by the European level to the national level, the greater the level of compliance with the European requirements that is required, which does not necessarily reflect national requirements and policy choices. Conversely, a broader margin of discretion granted by the European level to the Member States puts them in a position to pursue their national policies and priorities to a greater extent. This, in turn, can lead to greater differences between expulsion decisions and entry bans in the assessed states, differences that have implications for the horizontal effect, hence the obligation to mutually recognise these expulsion decisions and entry bans.

The margin of discretion has different manifestations, three types of which are relevant in the context of this book. First, there is the margin granted by the European level to the national level, which is, in the context of the ECHR, often referred to as the margin of appreciation, and which determines the degree of influence of the European level on the national level. The second margin describes the discretion granted by the national legislature to national decision makers (that is, administrative authorities and courts), which enables them to conduct a balancing process, to take the particulars of the individual case into account and to incorporate the requirements established by European law and case law into the

[65] Directive 2008/115/EC of the European Parliament and of the Council of 16 December 2008 on common standards and procedures in Member States for returning illegally staying third-country nationals [2008] OJ L 348/98 ('Return Directive').

[66] Regulation (EU) 2018/1861 of the European Parliament and of the Council of 28 November 2018 on the establishment, operation and use of the Schengen Information System (SIS) in the field of border checks, and amending the Convention implementing the Schengen Agreement, and amending and repealing Regulation (EC) No 1987/2006 [2018] OJ L 312/14 ('SIS II Regulation').

decision-making process. The third margin of discretion refers to that granted to administrative authorities vis-à-vis administrative courts, which limits the scope of judicial scrutiny regarding decisions taken by administrative authorities.

The three states examined herein the United Kingdom, the Netherlands and Germany provide an interesting comparison as the Netherlands and Germany are civil law jurisdictions and participate in the Schengen Agreement, whereas the United Kingdom is a common law jurisdiction and is outside the Schengen Area, though it participates in certain aspects of the Schengen Agreement.

Moreover, these states have different statutory frameworks in place to terminate lawful residence and to declare a foreigner *persona non grata*. Germany installed a layered system of expulsion in 1990 and kept this system,[67] albeit with a series of amendments and revisions,[68] until 2015. Depending on the seriousness of the foreigner's offence or the length of the prison term, the German law on expulsion provided for three different types of expulsion decisions: mandatory expulsion, expulsion as a rule, and expulsion following a balancing process between the interests of the foreigner and the interests of the state. Most problematic and debated was the provision on mandatory expulsion (section 53 Residence Act), which prescribed an expulsion decision if the foreigner was convicted of a specific offence or sentenced to a certain duration of imprisonment. This provision was fraught with problems as the legislature did not grant a margin of discretion to the decision maker and thereby forestalled an assessment of the facts of the individual case and a balancing process. The automatic link between a criminal conviction and the expulsion decision was not only incompatible with the requirements of EU law, and therefore inapplicable to EU citizens and other groups of foreigners covered by EU law, it was also incompatible with Article 8 ECHR as it barred the decision maker from taking the individual's private and family life into account. The provision on mandatory expulsion left the administration and the judiciary with the impossible task of adhering to the obligations under the ECHR on the one hand, and applying a binding Act of Parliament on the other. This system was revised in 2015, and the new provisions on expulsion entered into force in January 2016.[69] The new provisions prescribe a balancing process between the interests of the foreigner and the interests of the state, thereby ensuring compliance with ECHR standards.[70]

[67] Foreigner Act, Federal Law Gazette Part I 1354.

[68] For example, Gesetz zur Änderung des Strafgesetzbuches, der Strafprozeßordnung und anderer Gesetze (Verbrechensbekämpfungsgesetz) of 28 October 1994, Federal Law Gazette Part I 1386; Gesetz zur Steuerung und Begrenzung der Zuwanderung und zur Regelung des Aufenthalts und der Integration von Unionsbürgern und Ausländern (Zuwanderungsgesetz) of 30 July 2004, Federal Law Gazette Part I 1950; Gesetz über den Aufenthalt, die Erwerbstätigkeit und die Integration von Ausländern im Bundesgebiet1) (Aufenthaltsgesetz – AufenthG) of 25 February 2008, Federal Law Gazette Part I 162.

[69] Gesetz zur Neubestimmung des Bleiberechts und der Aufenthaltsbeendigung of 27 July 2015, Federal Law Gazette Part I 1386.

[70] Residence Act, ss 53–55.

In the Netherlands, the Vreemdelingenwet 2000 grants discretion to administrative authorities and is further specified by the Vreemdelingenbesluit 2000 and the Vreemdelingencirculair 2000. The Vreemdelingenwet 2000 distinguishes between the termination of lawful residence after a criminal conviction and the declaration of a foreigner as *persona non grata* by an *ongewenstverklaring* or an *inreisverbod*, which both have their own framework of assessment. The termination of lawful residence after a criminal conviction is further specified by the sliding scale,[71] which determines the foreigner's protection against expulsion by relating the duration of the foreigner's lawful residence to the seriousness of the criminal offence.[72] The protection provided for by the sliding scale has been continuously reduced.

In contrast to the current German and Dutch system, the United Kingdom prescribes automatic deportation in section 32 of its Borders Act.[73] Section 33 Borders Act provides for exceptions to accommodate, for instance, the requirements of the ECHR and the Geneva Refugee Convention.[74] Nonetheless, the concept of automatic deportation, which exhibits parallels to the abolished German provision on mandatory expulsion, is problematic as it does not provide for a level playing field between the interests of the foreigner against the interests of the state, but places greater emphasis on the state's interests by demanding deportation.

The comparison between these three countries is insightful, as their treatment of long-term resident foreigners differs. In the United Kingdom, Commonwealth citizens and citizens of the Republic of Ireland are exempted from deportation, subject to certain conditions.[75] While Germany never provided for an absolute protection against expulsion, the Netherlands originally provided that two categories of long-term resident foreigners could not lose their residence permits due to a criminal conviction.[76] This absolute protection was abolished when the sliding scale was tightened in 2012.[77] Interestingly, there seems to be a convergence between the German and Dutch rules. While the initial rigidity of the German system could not be maintained, the Dutch system became increasingly stricter in order to remove delinquent foreigners more easily.[78]

[71] Article 3.86 Besluit van 23 november 2000 tot uitvoering van de Vreemdelingenwet 2000 ('Vreemdelingenbesluit 2000'), Official Gazette of the Kingdom of the Netherlands 2000, 497.

[72] The sliding scale takes into account the duration of the lawful stay, the seriousness of the committed offence, the maximum imprisonment which can be imposed and the imposed prison term, see H Oosterom-Staples, 'Naar een Europese glijdende openbare ordeschaal voor het personenverkeer' (2012) 18 *Nederlands tijdschrift voor Europees recht* 265.

[73] UK Borders Act 2007.

[74] ibid, s 33(2).

[75] Immigration Act 1971, s 7.

[76] See Chapter 6.

[77] By the 'Besluit van 26 maart 2012, houdende wijziging van het Vreemdelingenbesluit 2000 in verband met aanscherping van de glijdende schaal', Official Gazette of the Kingdom of the Netherlands 2012, 158. The version of the Vreemdelingenbesluit 2000 applicable as of 1 July 2012 no longer mentions these categories.

[78] M Stronks, 'Een bijna ongebreidelde beteugeling van de tijd, Een analyse van aanscherpingen van de glijdende schaal' (2013) 34 *Nederlands Juristenblad* 2306, 2312 points out that the emphasis on the

Finally, the status of both EU law and the ECHR differs in the three countries under scrutiny. In contrast to the Netherlands, which is a monist country, the United Kingdom and Germany are dualist countries. While both the Netherlands and Germany are bound by EU law, the United Kingdom has left the European Union.

The assessment carried out herein is intended to highlight the similarities and differences between these different national systems. The differences between Germany and the Netherlands are particularly relevant as both countries apply the Return Directive and the SIS Regulation and can thereby create transnational administrative acts by entering an alert into the SIS. Being outside the Schengen Area, the United Kingdom takes part in some of the provisions of the Schengen *acquis*. However, it participates in neither the Return Directive nor the SIS Regulation.

Structure of the Book

The book is divided into three parts and is structured as follows. The first part is titled 'European law' and addresses the European level, comprising both EU law and the ECHR. It provides an overview of the criteria established at the European level for the termination of lawful residence of foreigners after a criminal conviction, thus establishing the foundations for the assessment of the national level, which is conducted in the second part.

Chapter 1 focuses on expulsions in light of EU law and introduces the relevant legal instruments and CJEU case law regarding the termination of lawful residence on grounds of public policy or public security. The groups of foreigners covered by EU law are addressed in order, based on the extent of protection they enjoy, starting with the group of EU citizens and their (third-country national) family members who can rely on the Citizenship Directive,[79] who benefit from the most far-reaching protection against expulsion. The focus rests, next to EU citizens, on Turkish nationals covered by the EEC–Turkey Association Agreement, and long-term resident third-country nationals covered by Directive 2003/109/EC ('LTR Directive').[80]

Chapter 2 examines expulsions in light of the ECHR and the European Court of Human Rights' (ECtHR) case law. It explores the requirements established by the ECHR and focuses on the right to respect for private and family life enshrined

fight against crime among foreigners became explicit in 2002 and has been a distinctive focus of the foreigner policy since 2010.

[79] See above n 55.

[80] Council Directive 2003/109/EC of 25 November 2003 concerning the status of third-country nationals who are long-term residents [2003] OJ L 16/44 amended by Directive 2011/51/EU of 11 May 2011 amending Council Directive 2003/109/EC to extend its scope to beneficiaries of international protection [2011] OJ L 132/1 ('LTR Directive').

in Article 8. It provides an overview of the ECtHR's case law regarding the principle of proportionality, the margin of appreciation granted to the contracting states and the criteria established by the ECtHR for assessing whether the interference with private or family life is necessary in a democratic society. Next to these criteria, the question of whether a specific weight can or should be attached to the respective criteria is discussed.

Chapter 3 addresses the CFR and briefly assesses the right to respect for private and family life (Article 7), the rights of the child (Article 24) and the right to an effective remedy and to a fair trial (Article 47).

Chapter 4 summarises the differences between the EU level and the Council of Europe and concludes the first part.

The second part of the book focuses on the effects of European law on decisions on expulsion and entry bans taken at the national level, and analyses the national implementation of the margin of discretion that is granted by the European level. It explores the national approaches to expulsion decisions and entry bans in two civil law jurisdictions and the approach taken to expulsion in one common law jurisdiction, and examines the margin of discretion granted by the national legislature to administrative authorities and courts. It addresses the extent to which national provisions on expulsion and entry bans and their application remain within the margin of discretion granted by the European level, while highlighting the differences and commonalities between the approaches in the United Kingdom, the Netherlands and Germany.

Chapter 5 addresses the legal framework in Germany and provides a comprehensive overview of the new German provisions on expulsion and the provisions on entry bans. The main focus rests on the margin of discretion granted by the legislature to the administrative authorities and courts. This chapter compares the newly adopted system of expulsion with its predecessor, which was in place from 1990 to 2015, and explores their underlying rationales. It critically assesses whether the new system remedies the problems of the old system and emphasises the improvements that have been made, while highlighting problems that require further attention.

Chapter 6 focuses on the Netherlands and introduces the Dutch rules regulating the termination of lawful residence after a criminal conviction and the requirements for declaring a foreigner *persona non grata*. It assesses the implementation of the European requirements, the margin of discretion granted by the national legislature to the administrative authorities and the margin of discretion of administrative authorities vis-à-vis administrative courts. It introduces the sliding scale, which relates the duration of the foreigner's lawful residence to the crime committed and the prison term imposed, and highlights the amendments that have been undertaken in recent years.

The focus of Chapter 7 rests on the United Kingdom and outlines the key features of the system of deportation. It critically assesses section 32 of the UK Borders Act 2007, which provides for automatic deportation, and addresses the margin of discretion granted by the legislature to the Secretary of State to determine whether the deportation of a foreigner is conducive to the public good. It highlights the factors that are taken into consideration when balancing the interests of the foreigner against the public interest in deporting the foreigner and the weight that is attached to these factors.

Chapter 8 focuses on comparing the different systems by juxtaposing them and identifying their commonalities and differences. The comparison serves a double purpose. First, it helps to identify the weaknesses and advantages of the respective systems. Second, the differences between the German and the Dutch systems are relevant for the third part, which focuses on transnational administrative acts.

The third part of the book focuses on transnational administrative acts and thereby on the horizontal effects of national expulsion decisions and entry bans that have been given a European dimension through the entry of an alert into the SIS. Notwithstanding the undisputable advantages that arise out of transnational administrative acts, mutual recognition of possible diverging national decisions also engenders disadvantages. The aim of this part is to introduce the different forms of transnational administrative acts, to address their emergence, advantages and disadvantages, and to suggest measures to remedy the existing problems that are inherent in the assessed transnational administrative acts.

Chapter 9 addresses different modes of administrative decision making and the concept of transnational administrative acts. Subsequently, it introduces the Return Directive and the SIS Regulation, which can give European effect to national expulsion decisions and entry bans. It discusses the concepts of mutual trust and mutual recognition, which are foundational mechanisms of both legal instruments, and the requirements for entering an alert into the SIS. These requirements simultaneously demarcate the margin of discretion granted to national authorities to pursue their national policies when attaching a European dimension to their decisions.

Chapter 10 discusses national expulsion decisions and entry bans and explores the implementation of these European instruments at the national level. It recalls the differences between Germany and the Netherlands regarding the criteria for terminating lawful residence after a criminal conviction, and carves out the differences regarding the requirements for adopting a national entry ban, for entering an alert into the SIS, and the duration of such an alert. The differences between Germany and the Netherlands are relevant given that alerts entered into the SIS must be recognised, in principle, by all other Schengen states. The differences between these two countries point to a need for change.

Chapter 11 discusses options to remedy the problems inherent in the SIS. Among other things, it addresses the need for and the likelihood of harmonisation of the criteria for adopting expulsion decisions and entry bans at the national level and the tightening of the criteria for entering an alert into the SIS respectively, while acknowledging that full harmonisation supplants mutual recognition.

The margin of discretion becomes relevant in all three parts. The first part addresses the margin of discretion granted by the European level to the national level by outlining the standards set by EU law and the ECHR. The second part explores national legislation against the background of European standards and assesses whether national legislation remains within the margin of discretion set by the European level. Moreover, it addresses the margin of discretion granted by the national legislature to the administration and courts when issuing or reviewing expulsion decisions. The third part addresses the margin of discretion granted by European instruments to national decision makers to attach European effect to national expulsion decisions and entry bans. Even though asylum seekers and refugees can also be subject to expulsion decisions, they are excluded from the scope of this book.

By way of disclaimer, it should be noted that, due to Covid-19 and its impact on mobility and access to libraries, the choice of sources has been impaired.

PART I

European Law

European Union law and the ECHR establish several criteria with which national decisions have to comply, thereby determining the margin of discretion granted to the Member States. The more specific the European criteria are, the smaller the state's margin of discretion or appreciation. Chapter 1 addresses the EU law requirements for the expulsion of EU citizens, Turkish citizens and third-country nationals covered by the Long-Term Residence Directive on grounds of public policy and public security. Chapter 2 focuses on the implications of expulsion decisions for the right to respect for one's private and family life and analyses Article 8 ECHR and the ECtHR's case law. Chapter 3 addresses the right to respect for private and family life in Article 7 CFR,[1] the rights of the child in Article 24 CFR, and the right to an effective remedy and to a fair trial in Article 47. Chapter 4 summarises the differences between the EU level and the Council of Europe and concludes this first part. The analysis begins with EU law, which grants a stronger protection against expulsion compared to the ECHR and enjoys supremacy vis-à-vis the law of the Member States.

[1] Charter of Fundamental Rights of the European Union [2012] OJ C 326/391.

1

Expulsions in Light of EU Law

Expulsion decisions can only be taken at the national level as a European authority with the power to expel foreigners from the territory of the European Union does not exist. Nonetheless, EU law plays a crucial role at the national level as it prescribes the requirements Member States have to comply with if they wish to expel foreigners who are covered by EU law. Even though the analysis focuses mainly on the expulsion of third-country nationals on grounds of public policy or public security, it is necessary to first introduce the rules that apply to EU citizens. The first judgments of the CJEU on expulsion, in which the Court interpreted the concepts of public policy or public security, concerned nationals of the Member States. Therefore, the analysis begins with EU, European Economic Area (EEA) and Swiss citizens and their family members, who are granted the strongest protection against expulsion (Section I), and proceeds with Turkish nationals, who are covered by the EEC–Turkey Association Agreement and Decision 1/80 (Section II). Subsequently, long-term resident third-country nationals are addressed, whose protection against expulsion is governed by the LTR Directive (Section III).[2] It can be questioned whether the distinction between Turkish nationals and long-term resident third-country nationals is still pertinent, given that the rules governing their protection against expulsion have been approximated. However, to trace the evolution of the interpretation of the provisions that determine Turkish nationals' and long-term resident third-country nationals' protection against expulsion, both groups will be discussed separately. Moreover, it is important to note that the notion of 'third-country national' is not homogeneous as it comprises groups of people whose rights are determined by different legal regimes. The applicable legal regime is not static but is determined by different factors, such as the passage of time or a change of the marital or civil status of a person. The need for a distinction between the different groups of third-country nationals is also underpinned by Article 3(1) of Directive 2008/115/EC ('Return Directive')[3] as well as by Article 2(6) of the Schengen

[2] Council Directive 2003/109/EC of 25 November 2003 concerning the status of third-country nationals who are long-term residents [2003] OJ L 16/44 amended by Directive 2011/51/EU of 11 May 2011 amending Council Directive 2003/109/EC to extend its scope to beneficiaries of international protection [2011] OJ L 132/1.

[3] Directive 2008/115/EC of the European Parliament and of the Council of 16 December 2008 on common standards and procedures in Member States for returning illegally staying third-country nationals [2008] OJ L 348/98 ('Return Directive').

Borders Code,[4] which exempt third-country family members of EU citizens who are covered by the Citizenship Directive from their scope. Not only is the group of third-country nationals heterogeneous, the notions of public policy and public security have not been defined exhaustively and the meaning that has been attached to these notions can differ depending on the context as well as the legal instrument they stem from.[5] Finally, this chapter addresses other groups of third-country nationals (Section IV) followed by a summary and conclusion (Section V).

I. Expulsions of EU Citizens, EEA and Swiss Nationals and their Family Members

While EU Member States are barred from expelling their own citizens,[6] they can issue expulsion decisions against foreigners, including EU, EEA and Swiss citizens.

A. EU Citizens

The right of Member States to issue expulsion decisions against EU citizens is subject to restrictions as expulsions constitute a limitation of EU citizens' free movement rights. EU citizens enjoy equal treatment with nationals of the respective Member State in several areas,[7] but unlike nationals they do not enjoy an absolute right of residence as Article 21(1) Treaty on the Functioning of the European Union (TFEU) provides that their free movement right is subject to limitations and conditions. The capacity of EU Member States to expel EU citizens who are not nationals highlights the weakness of EU citizenship and marks their status as foreigners.

i. Directive 2004/38/EC

Directive 2004/38/EC ('Citizenship Directive') further specifies the rights and limitations contained in the TFEU. Chapter VI (Articles 27–33) establishes the

[4] Regulation (EU) 2016/399 of the European Parliament and of the Council of 9 March 2016 on a Union Code on the rules governing the movement of persons across borders (Schengen Borders Code) [2016] OJ L 77/1 (Schengen Borders Code).

[5] See J Chlebny, 'Public Order, National Security and the Rights of Third-Country Nationals in Immigration Cases' (2018) 20 *European Journal of Migration and Law* 115, 119.

[6] Case C-348/96 *Calfa* ECLI:EU:C:1999:6, [1999] ECR I-00011, para 20.

[7] See Article 24(1) of Directive 2004/38/EC of the European Parliament and of the Council of 29 April 2004 on the right of citizens of the Union and their family members to move and reside freely within the territory of the Member States amending Regulation (EEC) No 1612/68 and repealing Directives 64/221/EEC, 68/360/EEC, 72/194/EEC, 73/148/EEC, 75/34/EEC, 75/35/EEC, 90/364/EEC, 90/365/EEC and 93/96/EEC [2004] OJ L 158/77 ('Citizenship Directive').

'restrictions on the right of entry and the right of residence on grounds of public policy, public security or public health' and (partially) codifies the CJEU's case law. The Citizenship Directive replaces several other Directives, among them Directive 64/221/EEC.[8] The latter Directive obliged the expelling Member State to consider neither the foreigner's duration of residence on its territory nor the level of integration, a shortcoming which was criticised by Guild.[9] The Citizenship Directive contains more detailed requirements and provides for a stronger level of protection. Article 27 sets out the general requirements and clarifies that measures taken on grounds of public policy or public security cannot serve economic ends.[10] It stipulates that measures have to comply with the principle of proportionality and 'shall be based exclusively on the personal conduct of the individual concerned'.[11] Moreover, Article 27(2) provides that 'previous criminal convictions … [shall] not in themselves constitute grounds for taking such measures'.[12] The provision precludes considerations that are based on general preventive grounds[13] and requires that the 'personal conduct of the individual concerned must represent a genuine, present and sufficiently serious threat affecting one of the fundamental interests of society',[14] a requirement that codifies the CJEU's case law.[15] Further requirements are contained in Article 28(1), which stipulates that the duration of the individual's stay on the territory of the host Member State, his/her age, state of health, family and economic situation, social and cultural integration into the host Member State, and the extent of his/her links with the country of origin must be considered before an expulsion decision is taken.

Article 28(2) and (3) of the Citizenship Directive provide for three different stages of protection against expulsion depending on the length of the foreigner's residence. The first stage covers EU citizens and their family members who have resided on the territory of the Member State for less than five years. They can be expelled on grounds of public policy, public security or public health, whereas an expulsion decision on grounds of public health can only be taken in the first three months of arrival.[16] The second stage of protection is codified by Article 28(2)

[8] Council Directive 64/221/EEC of 25 February 1964 on the co-ordination of special measures concerning the movement and residence of foreign nationals which are justified on grounds of public policy, public security or public health [1964] OJ 56/850.

[9] E Guild, 'Security of Residence and Expulsion of Foreigners: European Community Law' in E Guild and P Minderhoud (eds), *Security of Residence and Expulsion* (The Hague, Kluwer Law International, 2001) 66.

[10] Article 27(1), second sentence Citizenship Directive.

[11] Article 27(2) Citizenship Directive. The requirement that the measure shall be exclusively based on personal conduct was already contained in Article 3(1) Directive 64/221/EEC.

[12] This requirement was already contained in Article 3(2) Directive 64/221/EEC.

[13] Article 27(2), second subparagraph, second sentence Citizenship Directive. See also Case C-67/74 *Bonsignore* ECLI:EU:C:1975:34, [1975] ECR 00297, para 7.

[14] Article 27(2), second subparagraph first sentence Citizenship Directive.

[15] *Calfa*, para 21; Case C-30/77 *Bouchereau* ECLI:EU:C:1977:172, [1977] ECR 01999, para 35; Case C-36/75 *Rutili* ECLI:EU:C:1975:137, [1975] ECR 01219, para 28.

[16] Article 29(2) Citizenship Directive.

and concerns EU citizens and their family members who have obtained the right of permanent residence, which is acquired after five years of lawful and continuous residence.[17] Individuals who are covered by Article 28(2) cannot be expelled 'except on serious grounds of public policy or public security'. Finally, Article 28(3) provides that an expulsion decision may not be taken against an EU citizen who has resided in the Member State for the previous 10 years[18] or who is a minor[19] 'except if the decision is based on imperative grounds of public security'. Even though Article 28(3)(a) of the Citizenship Directive only stipulates that the EU citizen must 'have resided in the host Member State for the previous ten years' and does not refer to the right of permanent residence, the CJEU held in the joined cases of *B* and *Franco Vomero* that the acquisition of the right of permanent residence, which is a requirement for the protection granted by Article 28(2), also constitutes a prerequisite for invoking the protection of Article 28(3)(a) of the Citizenship Directive.[20] The Court based its reasoning on the wording and structure of Article 28 and the context of Article 28(3)(a).[21]

Interestingly, the first two stages of protection refer to public policy and/or public security, whereas the third stage only lists public security as a ground for expulsion. Moreover, the strongest protection against expulsion is not available to third-country national family members of EU citizens as Article 28(3) only refers to EU citizens. Barnard noted in 2007 with regard to the very strict requirements that are established by Article 28 that a 'migrant EU citizen is treated like a national in all but name'.[22] The legislative history of the Citizenship Directive, however, casts doubts on whether Member States were willing to grant such a strong position to EU citizens.

The Commission originally proposed to afford an absolute protection against expulsion to EU citizens and their family members, who have acquired the right of permanent residence, and to family members who are minors.[23] This absolute protection against expulsion was almost unanimously rejected by the Council[24] as Member States sought to retain the possibility to expel EU citizens whom they deem a threat to their public policy or public security. Moreover, a control

[17] Article 16(1) Citizenship Directive.

[18] Article 28(3)(a) Citizenship Directive.

[19] Article 28(3)(b) Citizenship Directive.

[20] Joined Cases C-316/16 and C-424/16 *B* and *Franco Vomero* ECLI:EU:C:2018:256, [2018], para 61.

[21] *B* and *Franco Vomero*, paras 48 and 50.

[22] C Barnard, *The Substantive Law of the EU, The Four Freedoms*, 2nd edn (Oxford, OUP, 2007) 468.

[23] COM(2001) 257 final, Proposal for a European Parliament and Council Directive on the right of citizens of the Union and their family members to move and reside freely within the territory of the Member States, Article 26(2).

[24] Common Position (EC) No 6/2004 of 5 December 2003 adopted by the Council, acting in accordance with the procedure referred to in Article 251 of the Treaty establishing the European Community, with a view to adopting a directive of the European Parliament and of the Council on the right of citizens of the Union and their family members to move and reside freely within the territory of the Member States amending Regulation (EEC) No 1612/68 and repealing Directives 64/221/EEC, 68/360/EEC, 72/194/EEC, 73/148/EEC, 75/34/EEC, 75/35/EEC, 90/364/EEC, 90/365/EEC and 93/96/EEC [2004] OJ C 54 E/12, p 32.

mechanism proposed by the European Parliament, which envisaged that Member States shall notify the Commission of all expulsion decisions directed against EU citizens and their family members, was also rejected.[25]

ii. The Court's Interpretation of the Concepts of Public Policy and Public Security

In contrast to Directive 64/221/EEC, the Citizenship Directive requires a distinction between the notion of public policy and the notion of public security[26] but refrains from providing an exact definition thereof, which is unsurprising, given that they are designed to cover a broad range of situations, thus requiring flexibility.[27] Public policy and public security are notions of Union law and must be interpreted autonomously,[28] nonetheless they must be interpreted in a restrictive manner[29] as they limit the freedoms provided for by the Treaty.

a. The Concept of Public Policy

The concept of public policy was first addressed by the Court in the *van Duyn* case,[30] which concerned the refusal of leave to enter by the United Kingdom to a Dutch member of the Church of Scientology. The Court limited Member States' interpretational sovereignty by stating that the concept of public policy 'must be interpreted strictly, so that its scope cannot be determined unilaterally by each Member State without being subject to control by the institutions of the Community'.[31] Simultaneously the Court acknowledged that

> the particular circumstances justifying recourse to the concept of public policy may vary from one country to another and from one period to another and it is therefore

[25] Committee on Citizens' Freedoms and Rights and Justice and Home Affairs of the European Parliament, European Parliament legislative resolution on the proposal for a European Parliament and Council Directive on the right of citizens of the Union to and their family members to move and reside freely within the territory of the Member States, PE 319.238, A5-0009/2003 of 23 January 2003, Article 25(5a).

[26] Article 28(3) only permits expulsion on grounds of public security.

[27] M Schmid-Drüner, *Der Begriff der öffentlichen Sicherheit und Ordnung im Einwanderungsrecht ausgewählter EU-Mitgliedstaaten* (Baden-Baden, Nomos, 2007) 398.

[28] W Frenz, 'Differenzierter Ausweisungsschutz von Unionsbürgern nach dem Urteil Tsakouridis' (2011) *Zeitschrift für Ausländerrecht und Ausländerpolitik* 174.

[29] See also COM(2009) 313 final, Communication from the Commission to the European Parliament and the Council on guidance for better transposition and application of Directive 2004/38/EC on the right of citizens of the Union and their family members to move and reside freely within the territory of the Member States, p 10.

[30] Case C-41/74 *van Duyn* ECLI:EU:C:1974:133, [1974] ECR 01337.

[31] ibid, para 18. Subsequently the Court repeated elements of this statement in *Rutili*, para 27; *Calfa*, para 23; Joined Cases C-482/01 and C-493/01 *Orfanopoulos/Olivieri* ECLI:EU:C:2004:262, [2004] ECR I-05257, para 64; Case C-441/02 *Commission v Germany* ECLI:EU:C:2006:253, [2006] ECR I-03449 ('*Commission v Germany 2006*'), para 34; Case C-503/03 *Commission v Spain* ECLI:EU:C:2006:74, [2006] ECR I-01097, para 45 ('*Commission v Spain 2006*'); Case C-50/06 *Commission v The Netherlands* ECLI:EU:C:2007:325, [2007] ECR I-04383, para 42 ('*Commission v The Netherlands 2007*');

> necessary … to allow the competent national authorities an area of discretion within the limits imposed by the Treaty.[32]

The Court's judgment in the *van Duyn* case was contentious as it appeared to allow Member States to adopt repressive measures against nationals of other states for a conduct that, if exercised by nationals of the expelling state, did not give rise to any restrictions.[33] In later judgments the Court clarified that the Treaty obliges Member States to refrain from discriminating against nationals of other Member States and from applying any arbitrary distinction disadvantaging them.[34] Consequently, the Court stated that an expulsion of a national of another Member State cannot be based on a conduct which is said to be contrary to public policy if the same conduct does not give rise to repressive measures intended to combat such behaviour when nationals of the expelling state engage in it.[35] Unfortunately the Court did not specify what kind of repressive measure would have to be taken in relation to the nationals of the expelling Member State.[36]

In later judgments the Court confirmed that there is 'no uniform set of values' that justifies a limitation of free movement rights on grounds of public policy[37] and that Member States essentially retain the freedom to determine the requirements of public policy and public security in accordance with their national needs.[38] Nevertheless, the Court kept reiterating that the public policy exception must be interpreted strictly[39] and its interpretation cannot be determined unilaterally by each Member State.[40]

The CJEU refined the requirements for Member States' recourse to public policy by stipulating that, in addition to the disruption of the social order which is inherent in every breach of the law,[41] it is necessary that the presence of the foreigner[42] or his conduct forms a 'genuine and sufficiently serious threat affecting

N Fennelly, 'The European Union and Protection of Aliens from Expulsion' (1999) 1 *European Journal of Migration and Law* 313, 320.

[32] *van Duyn*, para 18.

[33] ibid, para 23. See also C Barnard, *The Substantive Law of the EU*, 6th edn (Oxford, OUP, 2019) 479; E Guild, 'Restrictions on the Right of Entry and the Rights of Residence on Grounds of Public Policy, Public Security, or Public Health' in E Guild, S Peers and J Tomkin (eds), *The EU Citizenship Directive, A Commentary*, 2nd edn (Oxford, OUP, 2019) 260, 261.

[34] Joined Cases C-115/81 and 116/81 *Adoui/Cornuaille* ECLI:EU:C:1982:183, [1982] ECR 01665, para 9; Case C-268/99 *Jany* ECLI:EU:C:2001:616, [2001] ECR I-08615, para 60; Case C-100/01 *Oteiza Olazabal* ECLI:EU:C:2002:712, [2002] ECR I-10981.

[35] *Adoui/Cornuaille*, paras 8, 9; *Oteiza Olazabal*, para 42.

[36] H Oosterom-Staples, 'Adjudicating the External Schengen Border' in K Groenendijk, E Guild and P Minderhoud (eds), *In Search of Europe's Borders* (The Hague, Kluwer Law International, 2002) 239.

[37] *Jany*, para 60.

[38] *Rutili*, para 26; Case C-33/07 *Jipa* ECLI:EU:C:2008:396, [2008] ECR I-05157, para 23; Case C-430/10 *Gaydarov* ECLI:EU:C:2011:749, [2011] ECR I-11637, para 32; Case C-434/10 *Aladzhov* ECLI:EU:C:2011:750, [2011] ECR I-11659, para 34.

[39] *Calfa*, para 23.

[40] See, eg, *Jipa*, para 23.

[41] *Bouchereau*, para 35.

[42] *Rutili*, para 28.

one of the fundamental interests of society',[43] a requirement which has been codified almost identically in Article 27(2) of the Citizenship Directive.

The requirement in the Citizenship Directive that 'justifications that are isolated from the particulars of the case or that rely on considerations of general prevention shall not be accepted'[44] has been interpreted by the Court to exclude systems that mandatorily require expulsion. Moreover, the Court clarified that any application of a national provision requiring the authorities to order an expulsion where the individual has been sentenced to a specific length of prison term or for a specific offence is barred by Union law.[45] Any provision which 'makes it possible to establish a systematic and automatic connection between a criminal conviction and a measure ordering expulsion'[46] and does not take the personal conduct of the individual into account must be considered incompatible with Union law.[47]

b. The Concept of Public Security

Even though the concept of public security is often used in conjunction with the concept of public policy, the former has a narrower and separate scope of application. The concepts of public policy and public security are said to protect different interests and are not congruent. The structure of Article 28 of the Citizenship Directive illustrates the narrower scope of the concept of public security. Unlike Article 28(1) and (2), which refer to public policy and public security, Article 28(3) refers only to public security and omits any reference to public policy.

The European Commission called for Member States to 'define clearly the protected interests of society, and make a clear distinction between public policy and public security. The latter cannot be extended to measures that should be covered by the former'.[48] Similarly Advocate General (AG) Bot noted that 'the two concepts are therefore not the same and although any conduct which creates a threat to public security by definition disturbs public policy, the opposite is not true, even if, once known, the act committed may give rise in public opinion to an emotion which reflects the disturbance caused by the offence'.[49]

The CJEU repeatedly stated that only Articles 36, 45, 52, 346 and 347 TFEU[50] provide for public security derogations and that these articles 'deal with exceptional

[43] *Bouchereau*, para 35; *Orfanopoulos/Olivieri*, para 66; *Commission v Germany 2006*, para 74; *Commission v Spain 2006*, para 46; *Commission v The Netherlands 2007*, para 43.

[44] Article 3(2) of Directive 64/221/EEC; Article 27(2) Citizenship Directive.

[45] *Orfanopoulos/Olivieri*, paras 71, 91, 93; *Commission v The Netherlands*, para 44.

[46] *Commission v The Netherlands*, para 51.

[47] *Orfanopoulos/Olivieri*, paras 70, 71.

[48] COM(2009) 313 final, p 10; COM(2008) 840 final, Report from the Commission to the European Parliament and the Council on the application of Directive 2004/38/EC on the right of citizens of the Union and their family members to move and reside freely within the territory of the Member States, p 8.

[49] Case C-348/09 *P.I.* ECLI:EU:C:2012:123, [2012], Opinion of AG Bot, para 38.

[50] Articles 30, 39, 46, 296 and 297 Treaty establishing the European Community.

and clearly defined cases'. They have a limited character and therefore 'do not lend themselves for a wide interpretation'.[51] In cases unrelated to expulsion, the Court stated that the concept of public security requires 'a genuine and sufficiently serious threat to a fundamental interest of society'[52] but it refrained from providing an exhaustive definition of this notion.[53] Moreover, the Court clarified that public security refers to the Member State's internal and external security.[54] A state's internal security covers the existence of the country's institutions, its essential public services and the survival of its population.[55] Its external security is closely interwoven with the security of the international community as a whole; it is nearly impossible to assess the security of a state isolated from the security of the international community.[56] Therefore, the Court asserted that the security of the state may also be affected by a risk of a serious disturbance to its foreign relations or to the peaceful coexistence of nations.[57]

Regarding the intensity of scrutiny a state would be subjected to in relation to its recourse to the notion of public security, the Court held, as with the concept of public policy, that the scope and the concept of public security 'cannot be determined unilaterally by each Member State without any control of the Community institutions'.[58] It clarified that it can exercise control over Member States and examine whether their measures serve the aim of protecting public security and whether they constitute an appropriate and necessary instrument to achieve this aim.[59] On the other hand, the CJEU acknowledged that Member States have discretion to adopt measures which they regard as necessary for the maintenance of their public security.[60] Regarding cases concerning expulsion, it was not until the *Tsakouridis* case[61] that the Court clarified the content of the notion of public security in terms of Article 28(3) of the Citizenship Directive.[62]

[51] Case C-222/84 *Johnston* ECLI:EU:C:1986:206, [1986] ECR 01651, para 26; Case C-414/97 *Commission v Spain* ECLI:EU:C:1999:417, [1999] ECR I-05585, para 21; Case C-186/01 *Dory* ECLI:EU:C:2003:146, [2003] ECR I-02479, para 31.

[52] Case C-483/99 *Commission v France* ECLI:EU:C:2002:237, [2002] ECR I-04781, para 48.

[53] H Oosterom-Staples, 'Naar een Europese glijdende openbare ordeschaal voor het personenverkeer' (2012) 18 *Nederlands Tijdschrift voor Europees Recht* 266 points out that the examples given by the CJEU are not exhaustive.

[54] Case C-367/89 *Aimé Richardt and Les Accessoires Scientifiques SNC* ECLI:EU:C:1991:376, [1991] ECR I-04621, para 22 (with regard to Article 36 TFEU); Case C-83/94 *Leifer* ECLI:EU:C:1995:329, [1995] ECR I-03231, para 26; Case C-273/97 *Sirdar* ECLI:EU:C:1999:523, [1999] ECR I-07403, para 17; Case C-423/98 *Albore* ECLI:EU:C:2000:401, [2000] ECR I-05965, para 18; Case C-285/98 *Kreil* ECLI:EU:C:2000:2, [2000] ECR I-00069, para 17.

[55] Case C-72/83 *Campus Oil Limited* ECLI:EU:C:1984:256, [1984] ECR 02727, para 34.

[56] *Leifer*, para 27.

[57] Case C-70/94 *Fritz Werner Industrie-Ausrüstungen GmbH* ECLI:EU:C:1995:328, [1995] ECR I-03189, para 27; *Leifer*, para 28.

[58] *Commission v France*, para 48; Joined Cases C-331/16 and C-366/16 *K.* and *H.F.* ECLI:EU:C:2018:296, [2018], para 40.

[59] *Sirdar*, para 28.

[60] *Leifer*, para 35.

[61] Case C-145/09 *Tsakouridis* ECLI:EU:C:2010:708, [2010] ECR I-11979.

[62] G Anagnostaras, 'Enhanced Protection of EU Nationals Against Expulsion and the Concept of Internal Public Security: Comment on the PI Case' (2012) 37 *EL Rev* 627, 632.

Tsakouridis Case

The *Tsakouridis* case revolved around the question of whether dealing in narcotics as part of an organised group is covered by the notion of public security. AG Bot argued that public security is not 'to be interpreted exclusively in a narrow sense' and does not only refer 'to the protection of a Member State or its institutions'.[63] He contended that public security also covers 'serious threats to a fundamental interest of society such as the values essential to the protection of its citizens characterised by that state by means of the offences it establishes for their protection'.[64]

The Court pointed to the devastating effects of crimes linked to drug trafficking and referred to Council Framework Decision 2004/757/JHA.[65] It highlighted the first recital of the Preamble, which lists the threats resulting from drugs, in particular the 'threat to health, safety and the quality of life' of EU citizens and the threat to 'the legal economy, stability and security of the Member States'.[66] The Court considered that trafficking in narcotics as part of an organised group is not necessarily excluded from the concept of public security[67] as drug trafficking 'could reach a level of intensity that might directly threaten the calm and physical security of the population as a whole or a large part of it'.[68] Finally, the Court stated that 'Article 28(3) of Directive 2004/38, … must be interpreted as meaning that the fight against crime in connection with dealing in narcotics as part of an organised group is capable of being covered by the concept of "imperative grounds of public security"'[69] and left the final decision to the Member States.

P.I. Case

The *P.I.* case concerned an Italian citizen who had resided for more than 10 years in Germany before he was given a custodial sentence of seven years and six months for sexual assault, sexual coercion and rape of a minor. The offences took place between 1990 and 2001 and the victim was the daughter of his former partner, who was eight years old when the offences commenced.[70] Germany sought to expel him and the question arose whether his conduct was covered by the notion of imperative grounds of public security in terms of Article 28(3) of the Citizenship Directive. This time, AG Bot took a different approach and stated that the concept of public security is not automatically triggered by a violation of the law.

[63] Case C-145/09 *Tsakouridis* ECLI:EU:C:2010:322, [2010] ECR I-11979, Opinion of AG Bot, para 55.

[64] ibid, para 97.

[65] Council Framework Decision 2004/757/JHA of 25 October 2004 laying down minimum provisions on the constituent elements of criminal acts and penalties in the field of illicit drug trafficking [2004] OJ L 335/8.

[66] *Tsakouridis*, para 46.

[67] ibid, para 45.

[68] ibid, para 47.

[69] ibid, para 56.

[70] Case C-348/09 *P.I.* ECLI:EU:C:2012:300, [2012], para 10. For further information regarding the facts and the judgment see Oosterom-Staples, 'Naar een Europese glijdende openbare ordeschaal voor het personenverkeer' 267, 268.

It rather requires, said AG Bot, that the criminal conduct is 'particularly serious in principle and also in its effect' and that it must 'go beyond the individual harm caused to the victim or victims'.[71] In AG Bot's opinion the offences committed by P.I. did not involve the same kind of threat as described by the CJEU in *Tsakouridis*. AG Bot stated that if the offences committed by P.I. were considered to constitute a threat to public security, this would 'amount to acknowledging that only the objective seriousness of a criminal offence, determined by the penalties incurred or imposed for it, may constitute justification of an expulsion measure on grounds of public security'.[72] Even though AG Bot did not consider P.I.'s behaviour to be covered by the notion of public security, but by the notion of public policy, he reached the conclusion that P.I. could not rely on the protection of Article 28(3) of the Citizenship Directive. He argued that Article 28(3) contains a presumption of integration and that this presumption was rebutted in P.I.'s case by the facts themselves.[73] He stated that P.I.'s conduct 'constitutes a serious disturbance of public policy, shows a total lack of desire to integrate into the society'[74] and consequently P.I. could not enjoy the protection against expulsion provided for by Article 28(3).

Even though the Court did not follow the AG's approach, it weakened P.I.'s protection against expulsion by different means. The Court based its argument on Article 83(1) TFEU, which refers to sexual exploitation of children as one of the areas of particularly serious crimes with a cross-border dimension.[75] In addition, it relied on Directive 2011/93 concerning the combating of sexual abuse and sexual exploitation of children and child pornography.[76] The Court invoked the first recital of the Preamble, which emphasises that sexual abuse and sexual exploitation of children constitute serious violations of fundamental rights, and Article 3 of that Directive, which sets out the punishment for these offences.[77] The CJEU did not decide whether P.I.'s conduct constituted an imperative ground of public security. It rather stated 'that it is open to the Member State' to consider criminal offences such as those referred to in Article 83(1) TFEU

> as constituting a particular serious threat to one of the fundamental interests of society, which might pose a direct threat to the calm and physical security of the population and thus be covered by the concept of 'imperative grounds of public security'.[78]

While affording domestic courts a margin of discretion, the Court recalled that 'the manner in which such offences were committed' must disclose 'particularly serious

[71] *P.I.*, Opinion of AG Bot, para 38.
[72] ibid, para 45.
[73] ibid, para 56.
[74] ibid, para 60.
[75] *P.I.*, para 25.
[76] Directive 2011/93/EU of the European Parliament and of the Council of 13 December 2011 on combating the sexual abuse and sexual exploitation of children and child pornography, and replacing Council Framework Decision 2004/68/JHA [2004] OJ L 335/1.
[77] *P.I.*, paras 26, 27.
[78] ibid, para 28.

characteristics, which is a matter for the referring court to determine'.[79] Moreover, the CJEU clarified that even where offences such as those committed by P.I. 'pose a direct threat to the calm and physical security of the population, that should not necessarily lead to' an expulsion.[80] The CJEU reminded the referring court of three limitations. First, the Court referred to the requirement in the second subparagraph of Article 27(2) according to which the individual's conduct 'must represent a genuine, present and sufficiently serious threat affecting one of the fundamental interests of society' and added that this 'implies, in general, the existence in the individual concerned of a propensity to act in the same way in the future'.[81] Second, the Court referred to the requirement of Article 33(2) of the Citizenship Directive, which requires a fresh assessment if two years have elapsed between the expulsion order and its enforcement.[82] Third, the Court reminded the national Court of the requirements of Article 28(1) of the Citizenship Directive.[83]

Both judgments, *Tsakouridis* and *P.I.*, received considerable criticism and triggered further questions. One main point of criticism, which has been raised by several scholars, concerns the demarcation of the concepts of public policy and public security, which is said to have been blurred by the Court.[84] Anagnostaras rightly points out that the CJEU opened up the scope of application of the concept of public security 'to some criminal activities that are also covered by public policy grounds'.[85] He argues that the Court extended the notion of imperative grounds of public security 'to ordinary criminal law offences that are allegedly characterized by an exceptional gravity given the circumstances in which they were committed'.[86] Kochenov and Pirker state that the Court watered down EU citizens' protection against expulsion and that the judgments in *Tsakouridis* and *P.I.* are a '*de facto* attack on the core of the status of EU citizenship, undermining its promise and ability to function successfully in the European legal context'.[87] Anagnostaras makes an interesting observation regarding the Court's double standard when he highlights that the Court obliges Member States to interpret the exceptions to the fundamental freedoms restrictively, while 'its own judicial pronouncements allow

[79] ibid.

[80] ibid, para 29.

[81] ibid, para 30.

[82] ibid, para 31.

[83] ibid, para 32.

[84] Among many others see L Azoulai and S Coutts, 'Restricting EU Citizens' Residence Rights on Grounds of Public Security. Where EU Citizenship and the AFSJ Meet: P.I.' (2013) 50 *CML Rev* 568; D Kostakopoulou-Douchery and N Ferreira, 'Testing Liberal Norms: The Public Policy and Public Security Derogations and the Cracks in European Union Citizenship' (2014) 20 *Columbia Journal of European Law* 173; E Pistoia, 'The Unbearable Lightness of a Piecemeal Approach. Moving Public Policy or Public Security Offenders in Europe' (2014) 4 *European Public Law* 754.

[85] Anagnostaras, 'Enhanced Protection of EU Nationals' 633.

[86] ibid, 630, 634.

[87] D Kochenov and B Pirker, 'Deporting the Citizens within the European Union: A Counter-Intuitive Trend in Case C-348/09, P.I. v Oberbürgermeisterin der Stadt Remscheid' (2013) 19 *Columbia Journal of European Law* 369, 388.

national authorities to make extensive reliance on them in order to introduce additional barriers to the free movement of persons'.[88] The unclear distinction between the 'elusive concepts'[89] of public policy and public security and the broad interpretation given to the notion of public security are capable of increasing the number of cases that may be covered by the notion of public security. The expansion of the scope of application of this concept increases Member States' discretion to expel EU citizens after 10 years of residence and thereby weakens the latter's protection.

Second, the lack of clarity regarding crimes that can be covered by the concept of public security is problematic and needs further clarification by the Court, as demonstrated by two diverging interpretations of the Court's judgments. Oosterom-Staples refers to the Court's *P.I.* judgment, arguing that it clarifies in plain language that Article 28(3) of the Citizenship Directive, and thereby public security, can be invoked if the EU citizen is convicted of one of the crimes listed in Article 83(1) TFEU,[90] hence crimes that have a cross-border dimension. She states that this conclusion implicitly follows from the *Tsakouridis* judgment.[91] Anagnostaras, by contrast, referring to the same judgment, points out that illicit drug trafficking is listed by Article 83(1) TFEU and highlights that 'this argument was never invoked in Tsakouridis where the emphasis was placed exclusively on the social and economic consequences'.[92] Indeed, the Court could have referred to Article 83(1) TFEU in the *Tsakouridis* case but chose – intentionally or unintentionally – to refrain from any reference to this provision. In light of these different interpretations, the Court has to answer the question whether all crimes, or only some of the crimes that are listed in Article 83(1) TFEU, can be considered to pose a threat to public security. Moreover, the Court needs to clarify whether crimes other than those that are listed in Article 83(1) TFEU are capable of constituting such a threat.

Third, there seems to be a differentiation regarding, on the one hand, the seriousness of the offence or the way in which it was committed and, on the other hand, the nature of the offence or the object of the threat. Several authors point out that it seems that it is not the offence or the nature of the grounds invoked (whether the survival of the state or its institutions is threatened) that matters, but rather their imperative character.[93] They criticise this approach and highlight that it is questionable whether such a reading reflects the intention of the legislature. Kostakopoulou and Ferreira argue that if the legislature wished to put the

[88] Anagnostaras, 'Enhanced Protection of EU Nationals' 634.

[89] P Koutrakos, 'Public Security Exceptions and EU Free Movement Law' in P Koutrakos, N Nic Shuibhne and P Sypris (eds), *Exceptions from EU Free Movement Law* (Oxford, Hart Publishing, 2016) 202.

[90] Oosterom-Staples, 'Naar een Europese glijdende openbare ordeschaal voor het personenverkeer' 268, 271.

[91] ibid, 268.

[92] Anagnostaras, 'Enhanced Protection of EU Nationals' 635.

[93] ibid, 636; Oosterom-Staples, 'Naar een Europese glijdende openbare ordeschaal voor het personenverkeer' 270.

emphasis on the seriousness of the offence rather than on the nature of the offence, Article 28(3) of the Citizenship Directive would read 'imperative grounds of public policy or public security'.[94] However, it is unlikely that the Member States are opposed to these judgments as the Court's interpretation of the notion of public security extends the competences of the Member States, as rightly noted by Anagnostaras.[95]

iii. *Further Limitations of EU Citizens' Protection against Expulsion*

After the *P.I.* judgment, the Court further upheld its restrictive interpretation of EU citizens' protection against expulsion in the *M.G.* judgment and the *B* and *Franco Vomero* judgment.

a. *M.G.* Judgment

The *M.G.* judgment primarily concerned the calculation of the 10-year period of Article 28(3)(a) of the Citizenship Directive. The Court consolidated its previously established approach by revisiting the AG's suggestion to link EU citizens' protection against expulsion to their integration in the host society.

The Portuguese national M.G. entered the United Kingdom in April 1998 and was convicted and subsequently sentenced to a 21-month prison term in 2009.[96] In July 2010 the Secretary of State ordered her deportation on grounds of public policy and public security. The referring English court asked the CJEU how the 10-year period of Article 28(3)(a) of the Citizenship Directive was to be calculated, whether the period spent in prison interrupts the period of residence, and whether it made a difference that the Union citizen accrued 10 years of residence prior to imprisonment.

The CJEU referred to the *Tsakouridis* case[97] and stated that the '10-year period must be calculated by counting back from the date of the decision ordering that person's expulsion'.[98] Given that M.G. had already lawfully resided in the United Kingdom for the 10 years prior to her imprisonment, the method for the calculation of the 10-year period was crucial. Moreover, the Court held 'that a period of imprisonment is, in principle, capable of interrupting the continuity of the period of residence' in terms of Article 28(3)(a) of the Citizenship Directive and of 'affecting the decision regarding the grant of the enhanced protection provided for thereunder, even where the person concerned resided in the host Member State for 10 years prior to imprisonment'.[99] The 10-year residence 'may be taken

[94] Kostakopoulou-Douchery and Ferreira, 'Testing Liberal Norms' 175.
[95] Anagnostaras, 'Enhanced Protection of EU Nationals' 635.
[96] Case C-400/12 *M.G.* ECLI:EU:C:2014:9, [2014], para 13.
[97] *Tsakouridis*, para 31.
[98] *M.G.*, paras 23, 24.
[99] ibid, para 38.

into consideration as part of the overall assessment required in order to determine whether the integrating links previously forged with the Member State have been broken.'[100]

The *M.G.* judgment marks a further limitation of EU citizens' protection against expulsion, albeit by different means. While AG Bot's approach in the *P.I.* case, that is, making the EU citizen's protection by Article 28(3) of the Citizenship Directive dependent on his or her integration into the host society, was not taken up by the Court back in 2012, the CJEU revisited this approach in the *M.G.* case. When addressing the question of whether imprisonment is capable of interrupting the continuity of residence, the Court pointed out that the protection against expulsion in the Citizenship Directive is 'based on the degree of integration of the persons concerned in the host Member State'.[101] Crucially, it emphasised that the 'degree of integration … is a vital consideration underpinning both the right of permanent residence and the system of protection against expulsion'.[102]

Linking the protection against expulsion to the individual's integration, in particular if integration is conceived as a 'duty to integrate properly',[103] is highly problematic. EU citizens who pose a threat to public policy or public security and are therefore subject to an expulsion decision are not normally considered to be 'properly' integrated in the society of the host Member State. This applies all the more if integration is understood as compliance with 'the values of the society of the host Member State, as reflected in its criminal law', as was suggested in the *M.G.* case.[104] Moreover, such an understanding of integration in the context of expulsion is difficult to reconcile with the first sentence of Recital 23 of the Preamble to the Citizenship Directive. It provides that 'Expulsion of Union citizens and their family members on grounds of public policy or public security is a measure that can seriously harm persons who, … have become genuinely integrated into the host Member State'. This sentence underpins that delinquent EU citizens who are subject to expulsion can be integrated into society, and, crucially, that integration and the commission of criminal offences are not necessarily mutually exclusive. In addition, recourse to the notion of integration is not warranted by the Citizenship Directive. The wording of both the Preamble and of Article 28 refrains from requiring EU citizens' integration in order for them to enjoy protection from expulsion. Even though Article 28(1) refers to integration, it does not constitute a condition for reliance on the protection granted by the Citizenship Directive. Integration works as a constraint on the use of the public policy exception[105] by obliging

[100] ibid.

[101] ibid, para 30.

[102] ibid, para 32.

[103] N Nic Shuibhne, 'Limits Rising, Duties Ascending: The Changing Legal Shape of Union Citizenship' (2015) 52 *CML Rev* 889, 920.

[104] *M.G.*, para 31.

[105] Azoulai rightly points out that 'integration' was originally used as a qualifying criterion for protection, see L Azoulai, 'The (Mis)Construction of the European Individual, Two Essays on Union Citizenship Law' (2014) no 14 *EUI Department of Law Research Paper*, www.cadmus.eui.eu/handle/1814/33293, p 9.

Member States to take the individual's social and cultural integration into account before issuing an expulsion decision. If the level of protection against expulsion were not determined by the duration of residence, but by the individual's integration, whereby integration is understood as compliance with the values of the host Member State as expressed in its criminal law, the protection against expulsion would be reduced to absurdity. An individual who infringes criminal law and is subject to an expulsion decision could not be considered to be integrated and would therefore be excluded from the protection against expulsion. Moreover, the indeterminate notion of integration is open to interpretation, which undermines legal certainty and expands Member States' discretion to interpret the concept in light of national policies, within the limits granted by the CJEU. This could enable Member States to deny EU citizens the strong protection against expulsion that has been granted to them by the EU legislature by invoking an EU citizen's lack of integration.

Apart from these fundamental objections against the Court's recourse to the notion of integration, the *M.G.* judgment is problematic also insofar as it can be used as an instrument to annul the protection against expulsion granted after 10 years of lawful residence. The Court held that imprisonment is in principle capable of interrupting the continuity of the period of residence for the purposes of Article 28(3) of the Citizenship Directive.[106] Read in conjunction with the statement that the 10-year period must be calculated by counting back from the date of the decision ordering the person's expulsion, an EU citizen can, in principle, be stripped of the enhanced protection against expulsion by ordering a period of imprisonment preceding the actual decision to expel him or her. Even lawful residence of more than 10 years prior to imprisonment may not suffice to preserve the protection granted by Article 28(3) of the Citizenship Directive. The CJEU held in the *M.G.* case that the 10-year period of lawful residence prior to imprisonment may be taken into consideration[107] and – *argumentum e contrario* – does not have to be taken into account.

b. *B* and *Franco Vomero* Judgment

In the joined cases of *B* and *Franco Vomero*, the Court further elaborated on EU citizens' continuity of residence in case of imprisonment and clarified the requirements of the applicability of Article 28(3) of the Citizenship Directive. B had resided virtually all his life in Germany, had only rudimentary knowledge of the language of his home Member State, which he left at the age of three, and was deeply rooted in Germany.[108] In light of the strong integrative links between B and his host Member State,[109] the referring German court took the view that they

[106] *M.G.*, para 36.
[107] ibid, para 37.
[108] *B* and *Franco Vomero*, paras 12, 13, 21.
[109] ibid, para 21.

had not been broken by his imprisonment and thus continued to exist.[110] More generally, the referring German court suggested that imprisonment as a result of an offence which constitutes the basis for an expulsion 'should not, in any event, be taken into account in determining whether the integrative link has been broken, interrupting the continuity of residence in that Member State for the purposes of Article 28(3)(a)'.[111] It rightly noted that

> [o]therwise, a person sentenced to a custodial sentence of more than five years' imprisonment and who, under the applicable provisions of German law, will, in principle, still be in detention when the administrative decision determining the loss of the right of entry and residence is adopted could never benefit from the enhanced protection provided for in that provision.[112]

Interestingly, the German court's considerations and its questions for preliminary ruling suggest that it sought to apply the protection of Article 28(3) of the Citizenship Directive to the case before it, even though it could have effortlessly refused its application by referring to the CJEU's judgment in the *M.G.* case.

The CJEU did not follow the national court's suggestion that, in jurisdictions where the expulsion measure is adopted after the foreigner's imprisonment and not as an ancillary penalty to a custodial sentence,[113] the custodial sentence should not be considered when assessing whether the integrative links between the EU citizen and the host Member State have been broken. Such a statement would have required the CJEU to depart from its previous case law, given that it held in *M.G.* that imprisonment is, in principle, capable of interrupting the continuity of the period of residence for the purposes of Article 28(3) of the Citizenship Directive.[114]

Nevertheless, the CJEU accommodated the national court's considerations to a certain extent by stating that a custodial sentence cannot be considered to automatically break the EU citizen's integrative links with the host Member State, and thereby the continuity of residence for the purposes of Article 28(3) of the Citizenship Directive.[115] It held that the 10-year requirement of Article 28(3) 'may be satisfied where an overall assessment of the person's situation, … leads to the conclusion that, notwithstanding that detention, the integrative links between the person concerned and the host Member State have not been broken'.[116] This overall assessment is guided by criteria such as the solidity or strength of the integrative links forged with the host Member State, the circumstances in which that offence was committed, the nature of the offence, and the conduct of the person concerned during imprisonment.[117] Moreover, the CJEU addressed the probability of the

[110] ibid.
[111] ibid, para 22.
[112] ibid.
[113] Regarding this differentiation, see *B* and *Franco Vomero*, paras 22, 23, 77–79.
[114] *M.G.*, para 36.
[115] *B* and *Franco Vomero*, para 71.
[116] ibid, para 83.
[117] ibid, paras 72, 73, 83.

severance of ties by stating that 'the more those integrative links with that State are solid … the lower the probability that a period of detention could have resulted in those links being broken'.[118] Even though the Court allows national courts an assessment of the EU citizens' expulsion decision against the benchmark of Article 28(3) of the Citizenship Directive, notwithstanding their detention, it clarifies that the applicability of Article 28(3) of the Citizenship Directive is subject to conditions.

Where an EU citizen has been imprisoned prior to expulsion, the applicability of Article 28(3) is conditional upon the finding that residence in the host Member State has been continuous, which in turn requires that the integrative links with the State have not been severed. Whether the EU citizen's integrative links continue to exist depends on the outcome of the overall assessment that is conducted at the national level. This assessment is guided by a non-exhaustive list of criteria that has been clarified by the CJEU in the *B* and *Vomero* judgment.[119] Only if this overall assessment leads to the conclusion that the integrative links with the host Member State continue to exist can the EU citizen's residence be considered to be continuous for the purposes of Article 28(3). While the CJEU's clarification that a prison sentence does not automatically interrupt the EU citizen's continuity of residence in the host Member State is to be welcomed, the conditional applicability of Article 28(3) of the Citizenship Directive constitutes another cornerstone of the Court's restrictive case law as it equips Member States with another instrument to deny EU citizens the protection against expulsion granted to them by the Citizenship Directive.

In sum, the CJEU's reliance on the notion of integration in the *M.G.* case marks a further stage in the process of undermining EU citizens' protection against expulsion. Recourse to the open-ended and indeterminate notion of integration is problematic against the background of legal certainty, but it is also highly questionable in the context of expulsion, in particular if integration is understood as compliance with the values expressed in the criminal law of the host Member State. Such an interpretation of the notion of integration enables Member States to deny EU citizens and their third-country national family members, irrespective of the length of their residence, the protection against expulsion granted to them by the Citizenship Directive by relying on their lack of integration as evidenced by their criminal convictions.

The Court's judgment in the joined cases of *B* and *Franco Vomero* adds nuance to the *M.G.* judgment without fundamentally altering it. In *M.G.* the Court stipulated that imprisonment 'is, in principle, capable both of interrupting the continuity of the period of residence for the purposes' of Article 28(3) of the Citizenship Directive 'and of affecting the decision regarding the grant of the

[118] ibid, para 72.
[119] ibid, paras 72, 73, 83.

enhanced protection provided for thereunder'.[120] This statement directly impacts on EU citizens' possibility to rely on the enhanced protection of Article 28(3) of the Citizenship Directive and creates a strong argument for Member States to deny this protection where the EU citizen has been imprisoned. In *B* and *Franco Vomero* the Court clarified the importance of an overall assessment and emphasised that the continuity of residence, and thereby the applicability of Article 28(3), depends on the EU citizen's integrative links, an aspect that it had already raised in the *M.G.* judgment. Even though the Court provided a non-exhaustive list of criteria that guide this assessment, which has to be conducted at the national level, the Court left a considerable margin of discretion to national decision makers. This discretion gives national decision makers the possibility to deny EU citizens the protection against expulsion by reference to their lack of integration. The requirement of integration or integrative links, which constitutes a precondition for relying on Article 28(3) where the EU citizen has been imprisoned, adds another layer to the erosion of EU citizens' protection against expulsion.

iv. The Proportionality Assessment

An interference with EU citizens' rights is unlawful unless it can be justified, which requires the interference to be proportionate.[121] According to Article 27(2) of the Citizenship Directive 'measures taken on grounds of public policy or public security shall comply with the principle of proportionality and shall be based exclusively on the personal conduct of the individual concerned'. Proportionality requires the measure to be 'suitable for securing the attainment of the objective which it pursues'[122] and necessary. Necessity entails that the measure must not go beyond what is required in order to attain the objective,[123] which implies that no alternative, equally effective but less intrusive measure is available (the 'least onerous means' test).

While the proportionality assessment at EU level undoubtedly consists of the assessment of the suitability of the measure and its necessity, hence a two-stage test,[124] there is a lack of certainty as to whether the proportionality assessment comprises a third limb, the proportionality *stricto sensu*.[125] In the following sections the stages of the proportionality assessment will be discussed in the context of expulsion.

[120] *M.G.*, para 39.

[121] For an overview of the development of the principle of proportionality, see A Barak, *Proportionality: Constitutional Rights and their Limitations* (Cambridge, CUP, 2012) 175–86.

[122] Case C-55/94 *Gebhardt* ECLI:EU:C:1995:411, [1995] ECR I-04165, para 37; *Oteiza Olazabal*, para 43.

[123] ibid.

[124] T Tridimas, *General Principles of EU Law*, 2nd edn (Oxford, Oxford EU Law Library, 2006) 139.

[125] P Craig, *EU Administrative Law*, 3rd edn (Oxford, OUP, 2018) 643.

a. Suitability and Necessity

The first limb of the proportionality assessment focuses on the suitability of the measure for attaining the legitimate objective. The expulsion of a delinquent foreigner aims at averting a threat to public policy or public security and is in principle suitable. However, doubts arise in the context of EU citizens' free movement rights and the abolition of border controls in the Schengen Area. Even though an EU citizen is not allowed to return to the expelling Member State for the duration of the entry ban, compliance with re-entry bans is difficult to police.[126] Given the absence of border controls, an EU citizen could theoretically return unnoticed to the expelling state the day following his or her expulsion. Another aspect, which calls the suitability of the measure into question, is the impact of expulsion on EU citizens' social rehabilitation and resocialisation.

In his Opinion in the *Tsakouridis* case, AG Bot suggested that a Member State that wishes to expel an individual must explain precisely 'in what way the decision does not prejudice the offender's rehabilitation'.[127] AG Bot emphasised that expelled EU citizens can still exercise their free movement rights and that it is in the interest of the other Member States, and hence in the general interest, that individuals who are released from prison are not pushed back into reoffending.[128] The CJEU referred to AG Bot's Opinion and pointed out that social rehabilitation of an EU citizen in the Member State in which he or she has become genuinely integrated is not only in the interest of the individual, but also in the interest of the Union.[129] Consequently, the Court stated that the risk of compromising social rehabilitation has to be considered in the balancing process,[130] but it refrained from specifying the weight that should be ascribed to the promotion of resocialisation.

Before the *Tsakouridis* judgment, the aspect of rehabilitation had already been discussed at the national level, where it was linked to the principle of sincere cooperation (Article 4(3) TEU).[131] Given that a criminal offender's resocialisation is a common objective of the penal systems of all EU Member States, it was argued that the question of where this objective can best be attained has to be considered in the proportionality assessment.[132] Situations where the foreigner is forced to leave family and friends behind can be diametrically opposed to the aim of resocialisation. This applies in particular to EU citizens who no longer have any links with their Member State of nationality. Only if the prospect of resocialisation was more promising in the Member State of nationality could an expulsion to that

[126] Guild, 'Restrictions on the Right of Entry' 255.
[127] *Tsakouridis*, Opinion of AG Bot, para 95.
[128] ibid.
[129] *Tsakouridis*, para 50.
[130] ibid.
[131] R Gutmann, 'Anmerkung zum Urteil des Hessischen Verwaltungsgerichtshofs, Urteil vom 4.3.2002, 12 UE 200/02' (2002) 24 *Informationsbrief Ausländerrecht* 346.
[132] ibid.

state be justified.[133] If the EU citizen is likely to become a social burden for the state of nationality, an expulsion to that state would impinge on the duty of sincere cooperation.[134] The first limb of the proportionality assessment, the suitability of an expulsion, should therefore comprise an assessment of where rehabilitation can best be attained.

The second limb of the proportionality assessment addresses the necessity of the measure. In the *Tsakouridis* case the Court explicitly highlighted the need to address the measure's necessity by stating that the expulsion must be 'necessary for the protection of the interests it aims to secure, provided that that objective cannot be attained by less strict means'.[135] However, the need for a necessity assessment does not always arise, as demonstrated by the *P.I.* case, where the referring national court sought a clarification of the notion of 'imperative grounds of public security'[136] and the CJEU consequently refrained from assessing the criterion of necessity.

A less restrictive or less intrusive measure than a foreigner's expulsion is the limitation of his or her free movement rights to certain parts of the host Member State's territory. The territorial limitation of free movement rights was discussed in the *Rutili* case, which concerned an Italian citizen whose residence right in France was limited to parts of the territory. The Court stated that a foreigner's right to reside in the territory of another Member State can only be limited to certain parts of that territory if the same restrictions can be applied to nationals of that state.[137] This approach was not strictly followed by the Court as in *Oteiza Olazabal* it held that it was not necessary that the same territorial restriction be applicable to nationals.[138] Nevertheless, the Court imposed three conditions to be fulfilled to restrict a foreigner's residence to parts of the territory. First, the limitation of free movement rights must serve the aim of public policy or public security and must be based on the conduct of the individual. Second, this conduct must be serious enough to otherwise give rise to measures prohibiting him or her from residing on the territory. Third, the conduct of the person concerned must also give rise to punitive measures if effected by a national of that state.[139] Even though both judgments, *Oteiza Olazabal* and *Rutili*, addressed the limitation of free movement rights to a part of the territory, this measure was not discussed from the angle of its possibly constituting a less restrictive measure than expulsion.

[133] S Beichel, 'Das deutsche Ausweisungsrecht auf dem Prüfstand' (2002) 24 *Informationsbrief Ausländerrecht* 457, 462.

[134] Gutmann, 'Anmerkung zum Urteil des Hessischen Verwaltungsgerichtshofs' 347.

[135] *Tsakouridis*, para 49.

[136] *P.I.*, para 14.

[137] *Rutili*, para 50. Codified in Article 22 Citizenship Directive.

[138] *Oteiza Olazabal*, para 41.

[139] ibid, para 45.

b. A Third Limb – Semantics or a Real Concern?

While it is undisputed that the proportionality assessment requires an assessment of the suitability and the necessity of the measure, it is not entirely clear whether there is a third limb, that is, proportionality *stricto sensu*. Craig argues that this question is important as it 'changes the nature of the test'.[140] If a third stage did not exist, a measure could be regarded as lawful even if the burden imposed on the individual was disproportionate to the pursued objective.[141] Therefore, it is relevant to determine whether the Court also examines the expulsion measure's proportionality in the strict sense or whether it only addresses its suitability and necessity.

The Citizenship Directive sets out the requirements for terminating residence on grounds of public policy or public security and provides for a non-exhaustive list of criteria that have to be considered before an expulsion decision can be issued. Article 28(1) stipulates that 'considerations such as how long the individual concerned has resided on [the Member State's] territory, his/her age, state of health, family and economic situation, social and cultural integration into the host Member State and the extent of his/her links with the country of origin' shall be considered. This provision requires a balancing process between the interests of the individual and the interests of the Member State in order to determine whether the state's measure disproportionally encroaches upon the EU citizen's rights. This balancing process is precisely what the third limb of the proportionality test requires.

In *Tsakouridis* the Court addressed the expulsion measure's proportionality by highlighting that it has to be assessed 'whether the interference contemplated is proportionate to the legitimate aim pursued, in this case the protection of public security'.[142] The Court referred to the measure's proportionality in the strict sense by stating that a balance must be struck 'particularly between the exceptional nature of the threat to public security as a result of the personal conduct of the person concerned' and 'the risk of compromising the social rehabilitation of the Union citizen'.[143] While the Court reiterated the criteria that guide the balancing process,[144] it refrained from deciding whether the expulsion decision was proportionate and left the balancing to the referring court.[145]

In the *P.I.* case the Court pursued a similar approach in that it left the final decision to the national court. It stated that the conduct of the individual 'is capable of justifying an expulsion measure under Article 28(3)' but highlighted that the decision on expulsion 'is a matter for the referring court to determine on the basis of an individual examination of the specific case before it'.[146] The CJEU set out the

[140] Craig, *EU Administrative Law* 643.
[141] ibid, 643, 644.
[142] *Tsakouridis*, para 53.
[143] ibid, para 50.
[144] ibid, paras 50–53.
[145] ibid, para 55.
[146] *P.I.*, para 33.

considerations that have to be taken into account in the balancing process[147] but left the decision as to whether the expulsion is proportionate to the national court.

The Court's assessment often comprises the measure's suitability and necessity but does not always refer to the measure's proportionality in the strict sense. Craig observes that 'the normal judicial formulation of proportionality is cast in terms of suitability and necessity'[148] and 'that there is little evidence that the EU Courts will raise the third limb of proportionality of their own volition'.[149] Even though this might point to a two-part test, Craig argues that there are two reasons for resisting the conclusion that the proportionality assessment is a two-part test. First, he points out that in some cases the Court 'will in effect consider the third limb of the test when addressing one of the other limbs'.[150] The second reason is that the Court will explicitly address the third limb of the proportionality test 'when the applicant advances arguments in those terms'.[151]

Thus, it is not necessary either to explicitly refer to a three-stage assessment or to clearly separate the stages of assessment or to define the content of the respective stage as long as the concerns brought before the Court are addressed in the judgment. Hence, if the parties before the Court agree or if the Court finds that the measure is both suitable and necessary for attaining the pursued aim, but if it is submitted that a disproportionate weight is attached to the respective interest, the Court assesses whether the measure is disproportionate to the aim pursued.

The existence of a third limb in the proportionality test is a real concern as it can change the nature of the assessment. However, the requirement of a three-part test can also be a question of semantics as the balancing of the competing interests can also be addressed together with the first or second limb. In the context of expulsion, a balancing process is foreseen by Article 28(1) of the Citizenship Directive, which lists the relevant considerations that have to be taken into account when balancing the competing interests. The *Tsakouridis* and *P.I.* cases demonstrate that the Court can also delegate the balancing process to the national court but it will normally remind the national court of the criteria that guide this process.

v. Conclusion: Still a Strong Protection against Expulsion?

The EU legislature afforded EU citizens equal treatment with nationals in many areas of life and a strong protection against expulsion. Morano-Foadi and Andreadakis observe that there is 'a hierarchy of legal residents within the EU, with the EU citizens at the apex'.[152] Despite EU citizens' enhanced status and their

[147] ibid, paras 29–32.
[148] Craig, *EU Administrative Law* 653, 654.
[149] ibid, 654.
[150] ibid.
[151] ibid.
[152] S Morano-Foadi and S Andreadakis, 'The Convergence of the European Legal System in the Treatment of Third-Country Nationals in Europe: The ECJ and ECtHR Jurisprudence' (2011) 22 *EJIL* 1071, 1076.

strong protection, they were not put on an equal footing with nationals of the respective state, who enjoy an absolute protection against expulsion.

In the drafting process of the Citizenship Directive, the EU Commission suggested that permanently resident and minor EU citizens should be granted an absolute protection against expulsion. This suggestion was endorsed by the European Parliament, however it was subsequently rejected by the Member States. Instead, an incremental protection was introduced which links the protection against expulsion to the duration of lawful residence on the territory of the host Member State.

Expulsion decisions require a threat to public policy or public security (or public health). Public policy and public security are distinct concepts and have not been exhaustively defined, either by EU law or by the CJEU. Member States retain some discretion to determine the requirements of public policy and public security but the CJEU repeatedly asserted its control over the interpretation of these notions. In the last decade, however, the Court's control became increasingly relaxed. In the *Tsakouridis* and *P.I.* cases the Court expanded the scope of the concept of public security, thereby considerably broadening Member States' discretion to expel EU citizens after more than 10 years of lawful residence. These judgments curtailed EU citizens' protection against expulsion granted to them by the EU legislature and ultimately strengthened Member States' sovereignty. Moreover, the Court did not provide additional insights into the features of the crimes that might be covered by the concept of public security. It implicitly invited national courts to refer further preliminary questions, which give the Court the possibility to further elaborate on the notion of public security.

While Kochenov and Pirker already considered the judgments in *Tsakouridis* and *P.I.* as a '*de facto* attack on the core of the status of EU citizenship, undermining its promise and ability to function successfully in the European legal context',[153] these judgments initially could have been classed as a non-recurring development that does not generally empty the concept of EU citizenship. However, read in conjunction with the *M.G.* judgment, which continues this trend, the judgments in the *Tsakouridis* and *P.I.* cases laid the foundation for a trend of reactive judgments, which restrict and undermine EU citizens' protection against expulsion.

B. Third-country National Family Members of EU Citizens

Third-country national family members of EU citizens cannot rely on free movement rights but as family members[154] of mobile EU citizens[155] they enjoy derived rights. EU citizens have a right to be accompanied by their third-country national

[153] Kochenov and Pirker, 'Deporting the Citizens within the European Union' 388.
[154] See Article 2(2) Citizenship Directive.
[155] Article 3(1) Citizenship Directive.

family members in the host Member State,[156] and also upon return to their country of nationality, after having exercised free movement rights.[157] As the Court held in *Rendón Marín*, 'a derived right of residence of a third-country national exists, in principle, only when it is necessary in order to ensure that a Union citizen can exercise effectively his rights to move and reside freely in the European Union'.[158] Limitations on the rights of third-country national family members to accompany an EU citizen in another Member State are consequently regarded as a limitation of the rights of the latter.[159]

i. Expulsion of Third-country National Family Members of EU Citizens

Third-country national family members of EU citizens enjoy a protection against expulsion that is similar but not identical to that afforded to EU citizens. While third-country national family members can rely on Article 27 and Article 28(1) and (2) of the Citizenship Directive, Article 28(3) is not available to them as it refers exclusively to EU citizens. The strongest protection that is available to third-country national family members is Article 28(2) of the Citizenship Directive, which bars expulsion decisions 'except on serious grounds of public policy or public security'. In order for Article 28(2) to apply, the beneficiary must have acquired the right of permanent residence, which requires that the third-country national family member has 'legally resided with the Union citizen in the host Member State for a continuous period of five years'.[160]

In the *Onuekwere* case the Court addressed the question of whether time spent in prison can be taken into account for the calculation of the five-year period and ultimately answered the question in the negative. Moreover, it held that the continuity of residence was interrupted by the prison term.[161] In reaching those conclusions, the Court stated that 'The EU legislature accordingly made the acquisition of the right of permanent residence … subject to the integration of the citizen of the Union in the host Member State'.[162] A few paragraphs later the Court referred to 'the integration requirement which is a precondition for the acquisition of the right of permanent residence'.[163] Turning to the facts of the case, the Court held that Onuekwere's lack of integration was demonstrated by the rejection of or

[156] Case C-127/08 *Metock* ECLI:EU:C:2008:449, [2008] ECR I-06241, para 99.

[157] Case C-370/90 *Singh* ECLI:EU:C:1992:296, [1992] ECR I-04265, para 25; Case C-291/05 *Eind* ECLI:EU:C:2007:771, [2007] ECR I-10719. Regarding the requirements see Case C-456/12 *O. and B.* ECLI:EU:C:2014:135, [2014].

[158] Case C-165/14 *Rendón Marín* ECLI:EU:C:2016:675, [2016], para 36.

[159] Case C-157/03 *Commission v Spain* ECLI:EU:C:2005:225, [2005] ECR I-02911, para 17; Case C-40/11 *Iida* ECLI:EU:C:2012:691, [2012], para 68.

[160] Article 16(2) Citizenship Directive.

[161] Case C-378/12 *Onuekwere* ECLI:EU:C:2014:13, [2014]. For comments on the case see S Coutts, 'Union Citizenship as Probationary Citizenship: Onuekwere' (2015) 52 *CML Rev* 531.

[162] *Onuekwere*, para 24.

[163] ibid, para 30.

'non-compliance by the person concerned with the values expressed by the society of the host Member State in its criminal law'.[164]

However, the Court's approach to linking the acquisition of the right of permanent residence to the individual's integration in the host Member State is problematic. First, the notion of integration is not mentioned in Article 16 of the Directive. Second, recourse to the notion of integration considerably broadens Member States' discretion to deny third-country national family members of EU citizens the right of permanent residence and thereby the enhanced protection against expulsion of Article 28(2) of the Citizenship Directive.

Both judgments – the above-mentioned *M.G.* judgment, which concerns the interpretation of Article 28(3) of the Citizenship Directive, and the *Onuekwere* judgment, which addresses the requirements for the acquisition of the right of permanent residence – exhibit clear parallels. In both cases, which were decided on the same day, the Court reverts to the requirement of integration,[165] which constitutes a core feature of its reasoning. The importance of the notion of integration is underlined by the Court's statement that the 'degree of integration … is a vital consideration underpinning both the right of permanent residence and the system of protection against expulsion'.[166] By placing the inherently open-ended umbrella concept of integration, which can be given different meanings,[167] at the heart of both the protection against expulsion and the acquisition of the right of permanent residence, the Court undermines EU citizens' protection and that of their third-country national family members. The Court's approach is capable of enabling Member States to interpret the notion of integration in light of their national immigration policies and to limit or terminate residence rights of those EU citizens and their third-country national family members who are considered 'undesirable' migrants.

ii. Expulsion of Third-country National Carers of Minor EU Citizens

The CJEU adopted a different approach in cases concerning third-country national carers of minor EU citizens. In the cases of *Rendón Marín* and *C.S.* the third-country nationals had previous criminal convictions and were granted sole care and custody of their children.[168] The minor EU citizens had never left their Member State of nationality and were dependent on their third-country national parents.

In Mr Rendón Marín's case, his previous criminal conviction resulted in his application for a temporary residence permit being rejected[169] as the relevant

[164] ibid, paras 26, 31. See also *M.G.*, para 31.
[165] See, eg, *Onuekwere*, paras 26, 31 and *M.G.*, para 31.
[166] *M.G.*, para 32.
[167] D Thym, 'Towards a Contextual Conception of Social Integration in EU Immigration Law. Comments on P & S and K & A' (2016) 18 *European Journal of Migration and Law* 89, 106, 107.
[168] *Rendón Marín*, para 15; Case C-304/14 *C.S.* ECLI:EU:C:2016:674, [2016], para 13.
[169] *Rendón Marín*, para 18.

Spanish law prohibited the 'grant of a residence permit when the applicant has a criminal record'.[170] Mr Rendón Marín challenged the rejection of his residence permit and based his argument on the Court's judgments in the case of *Zhu and Chen* and the *Ruiz Zambrano* case. He invoked the 'substance of the rights test', established by the Court in *Ruiz Zambrano*,[171] which prohibits national measures that 'deprive those children of the genuine enjoyment of the substance of the rights attaching to the status of European Union citizen'.[172] The Court clarified in the *Derici* judgment that an EU citizen is deprived of the substance of his rights if he has 'to leave not only the territory of the Member State of which he is a national but also the territory of the Union as a whole'.[173] Mr Rendón Marín argued that Spain's refusal to grant him a residence permit 'would result in his removal … from the territory of the European Union, which the two minor children, his dependents, would have to leave as a consequence'.[174] However, unlike the third-country nationals in the cases of *Zhu and Chen* and *Ruiz Zambrano*, Mr Rendón Marín had a criminal conviction. The Court assessed the case in two stages. First, it had recourse to the Citizenship Directive, which was applicable since Mr Rendón Marín's daughter was a dual national of Poland and Spain,[175] and Article 21 TFEU. In a second step the Court addressed Article 20 TFEU.

Beginning with the assessment of the Citizenship Directive and Article 21 TFEU, the Court recalled that a third-country national who is the direct ascendant of an EU citizen having a right of residence under the Directive is covered by the Directive's definition of family member if he is 'dependent'.[176] Given that the case concerned the reverse situation, as Mr Rendón Marín provided material support to the EU citizen, he was not 'dependent'.[177] Nevertheless, since the enjoyment of a right of residence by a minor EU citizen necessarily implies that this child is accompanied by the primary carer, that carer must be allowed to reside with the child.[178] The Court stated that the Directive has 'to be interpreted as precluding, in principle, Mr Rendón Marín being refused a derived right to reside on the territory of that Member State'.[179] Subsequently, the Court addressed the protection against expulsion granted by the Citizenship Directive and assessed the denial of the derived right of residence against the benchmarks of Articles 27 and 28. The Court highlighted that EU law precludes measures based on grounds of a general preventive nature, in particular where they 'have been adopted automatically

[170] ibid, para 21.
[171] Case C-34/09 *Ruiz Zambrano* ECLI:EU:C:2011:124, [2011] ECR I-01177.
[172] ibid, para 45.
[173] Case C-256/11 *Dereci* ECLI:EU:C:2011:734, [2011] ECR I-11315, para 66. For comments see C Berneri, *Family Reunification in the EU* (Oxford, Hart Publishing, 2017) 108, 109.
[174] *Dereci*, para 66.
[175] *Rendón Marín*, paras 41–44.
[176] See Article 2(2)(d) in conjunction with Article 3(1) Citizenship Directive.
[177] *Rendón Marín*, para 50.
[178] ibid, para 51.
[179] ibid, para 53.

following a criminal conviction, without any account being taken of the personal conduct of the offender or of the danger which that person represents for the requirements of public policy',[180] and noted that Spanish legislation contained such an automatism.[181]

Turning to the second limb of the assessment, the interpretation of Article 20 TFEU, the CJEU recalled the 'substance of the rights' test,[182] which it had established in *Ruiz Zambrano*. The Court reasserted the derived right of residence of third-country national family members of EU citizens, even in purely internal situations, if the EU citizen was otherwise deprived of his or her rights. Nevertheless, it acknowledged Member States' need to limit this right on grounds of public policy or public security and stated that such a limitation would be consistent with EU law if it was 'founded on the existence of a genuine, present and sufficiently serious threat to the requirements of public policy or of public security, in view of the criminal offences committed by a third-country national'.[183] In both parts of the assessment the Court underlined the need for a balance to be struck between the genuine enjoyment of the substance of EU citizens' rights on the one hand and Member States' possibility to interfere with the derived right of residence of a third-country national carer of an EU citizen on grounds of public policy or public security. Moreover, the Court emphasised the need to assess the denial of a residence permit in light of Article 7 of the Charter and Article 24(2),[184] and highlighted that an automatic rejection of a right of residence due to a previous criminal conviction is incompatible with the requirements of EU law.

The *C.S.* case concerned a third-country national who was liable to be deported from the United Kingdom as a result of her criminal conviction. Her son, of whom C.S. had sole custody and who held British nationality, had never left the United Kingdom. Consequently, the Citizenship Directive was inapplicable and the Court's assessment focused on Article 20 TFEU. Recalling the 'substance of the rights'[185] test and the derived right of residence of third-country national family members of EU citizens, the Court turned to the possibility of limiting the derived right on grounds of public policy or public security. Even though the Court avoided mentioning Article 27 and 28 of the Citizenship Directive, which were inapplicable, it recalled the principles that are codified in these articles and that were established in earlier judgments. The Court stated that Member States' recourse to public policy grounds requires 'a genuine, present and sufficiently serious threat affecting one of the fundamental interests of society'.[186] Moreover, the Court referred to the 'length and legality' of residence, 'the nature and gravity of

[180] ibid, para 61.
[181] ibid, para 63.
[182] ibid, para 74.
[183] ibid, para 84.
[184] ibid, paras 66, 81.
[185] *C.S.*, para 26.
[186] ibid, para 38; see Article 27(2) Citizenship Directive.

the offence committed, the extent to which the person concerned is currently a danger to society, the age of the child at issue and his state of health, as well as his economic and family situation'.[187] The Court's statement that any conclusion 'cannot be drawn automatically on the basis solely of the criminal record of the person concerned'[188] resembles Article 27(2) of the Citizenship Directive, which provides that 'Previous criminal convictions shall not in themselves constitute grounds for taking such measures'. Moreover, the Court noted that the relevant national legislation seems to establish a 'systematic and automatic link between the criminal conviction of the person concerned and the expulsion measure applicable to him'[189] and clarified that 'the mere existence of a criminal record cannot, by itself, justify an expulsion decision'.[190] The Court emphasised, as it did in *Rendón Marín*, the need to take Article 7 and Article 24(2) of the Charter into account.[191] It concluded that a Member State may adopt an expulsion decision in exceptional circumstances, provided that this decision complies with the criteria that have been established by the Court.[192]

iii. Conclusions

Rendón Marín and *C.S.* concern delinquent third-country nationals who are the sole carers of minor EU citizens who have never left their country of nationality. Even though the static minor EU citizens have not committed any crime, they would be forced to leave their Member State of nationality and the territory of the EU if their delinquent third-country national carer were denied a residence permit and expelled respectively. These cases resemble the *Ruiz Zambrano* constellation but differ from it in that the third-country national carer committed a criminal offence and that Mr Rendón Marín's daughter held dual nationality. The Court, aware of the conflict between, on the one hand, Member States' needs to respond to public policy or public security threats, and, on the other hand, the right of EU citizens to remain in the territory of the EU, balances these competing interests by allowing Member States to revert to restrictive measures by limiting third-country nationals' residence rights. At the same time the Court acknowledges that these measures affect the minor EU citizen and that they must therefore be reserved as a last resort. Therefore, the Court requires a thorough scrutiny against the benchmarks of the principles that are codified in Articles 27 and 28(1) of the Citizenship Directive. These requirements were applied by the Court either explicitly (*Rendón Marín*) or impliedly (*C.S.*) as the Citizenship Directive was inapplicable in the latter case.

[187] *C.S.*, para 42.
[188] ibid, para 41.
[189] ibid, para 44.
[190] ibid, paras 40–42, 44.
[191] ibid, paras 36, 48, 49.
[192] ibid, para 50.

In both cases the CJEU left the actual balancing process between the interests of the foreigner and the interests of the Member State to national courts. In *C.S.*, however, the Court determined the weight that has to be attached to the interests of the foreigner in the balancing process by stating that 'in exceptional circumstances a Member State may adopt an expulsion measure'.[193] Nevertheless, the Court stressed in both instances that EU law bars an automatic link between a criminal conviction and an expulsion decision,[194] and refusal to grant a residence permit,[195] respectively. Simultaneously, the Court pointed out that the national provisions in question seemed to be based on such an automatism.[196] The high threshold for Member States to revert to an expulsion decision against a third-country national carer of a minor EU citizen is likely to be influenced by the fact that the EU citizen, who has not committed any crime, would be forced to leave the territory of the EU. In that regard, both cases might not be representative of 'classic' expulsion decisions against third-country nationals.

C. Agreement on the European Economic Area (EEA) and the EC–Swiss Agreement

Nationals of Norway, Iceland, Liechtenstein and Switzerland benefit from the provisions of the EEA[197] and the EC–Swiss Agreement[198] respectively. This group of third-country nationals derives more rights from these agreements than from the LTR Directive,[199] and their status is comparable to that of EU citizens. Regarding EEA nationals, Article 28 of the EEA Agreement provides that the rights to accept offers of employment, to move freely and to reside in the territory of another state for the purpose of employment are subject to 'the limitations justified on grounds of public policy, public security or public health'. Annex V to the EEA Agreement refers to the free movement of workers and determines the scope of application of Article 28 of the EEA Agreement. Among other legislative acts, it refers to the Citizenship Directive and provides that 'this act, as adapted for the purposes of the Agreement shall apply, as appropriate, to the fields covered by this Annex'. In the *Wahl* case,[200] which concerned the refusal of entry of a Norwegian Hells Angels member to Iceland, the EFTA Court had recourse to Article 27 of the

[193] ibid.
[194] ibid, para 44.
[195] *Rendón Marín*, para 87.
[196] *C.S.*, para 43; *Rendón Marín*, para 63.
[197] Agreement on the European Economic Area [1994] OJ L 1/3.
[198] Agreement between the European Community and its Member States, of the one part, and the Swiss Confederation, of the other, on the free movement of persons [2002] OJ L 114/6.
[199] S Boelaert-Suominen, 'Non-EU Nationals and Council Directive 2003/109/EC on the Status of Third-Country Nationals Who Are Long-Term Residents: Five Paces Forward and Possibly Three Paces Back' (2005) 42 *CML Rev* 1037, 1038.
[200] Case E-15/12 *Wahl* [2013] OJ C 309/6.

Citizenship Directive and the interpretation given to the notions of public policy and public security by the CJEU.[201]

Regarding Swiss nationals, Article 5 of Annex I to the EU–Swiss Agreement[202] stipulates that the rights granted under this Agreement can only be restricted by measures 'which are justified on grounds of public order, public security or public health'. Moreover, Article 16(2) of the Swiss Agreement provides that 'insofar as the application of this Agreement involves concepts of community law, account shall be taken of the relevant case law of the Court of Justice of the European Communities prior to the date of its signature'. On the basis of the latter provision it is argued that, in the application of Article 5 of Annex I of the Agreement, an expulsion decision can only be issued if it could also be issued against an EU citizen.[203]

D. Conclusions

In the 1960s Member States enjoyed a considerable discretion to expel nationals of other Member States as Directive 64/221/EEC contained few and relatively basic safeguards against expulsion. It provided for the prohibition on invoking public policy or public security grounds to serve economic ends,[204] the requirement that 'previous criminal convictions shall not in themselves constitute grounds' for taking the measures provided for by the Directive,[205] and the obligation to base a decision exclusively on the personal conduct of the individual.[206] Starting in the 1970s, when the first cases addressing the termination of residence of nationals of other Member States on grounds of public policy and public security came before the CJEU, the Court enhanced the protection against expulsion. It limited Member States' discretion by defining, refining and advancing the safeguards provided for in Directive 64/221/EEC. The Court required, for example, that the 'personal conduct of the individual concerned must represent a genuine, present and sufficiently serious threat affecting one of the fundamental interests of society'[207] and established the prohibition of expulsion decisions based on general preventive grounds.[208] Oosterom-Staples argued that the Court 'has placed the individual's

[201] See in particular ibid, paras 83, 85, 86, 89.

[202] Agreement between the European Community and its Member States, of the one part, and the Swiss Confederation, of the other, on the free movement of persons [2002] OJ L 114/6.

[203] V Westphal, 'Das Freizügigkeitsabkommen zwischen der EG, ihren Mitgliedstaaten und der Schweiz' (2002) 24 *Informationsbrief Ausländerrecht* 333.

[204] Article 2(2) of Directive 64/221/EEC.

[205] Article 3(2) of Directive 64/221/EEC.

[206] Article 3(1) of Directive 64/221/EEC.

[207] *Bouchereau*, para 35; *Rutili*, para 28, which is now codified in Article 27(2), second subparagraph first sentence Citizenship Directive.

[208] *Bonsignore*, para 7, which is now codified in Article 27(2), second subparagraph, second sentence Citizenship Directive.

fundamental rights that have been accorded to him or her by the Community Treaty itself above a Member State's interest in maintaining law and order within its territory'.[209]

Many of the safeguards that were established by the Court have been codified in the Citizenship Directive, with the result that EU citizens and their family members enjoy a very strong protection against expulsion. The protection granted by Articles 27 and 28 of the Directive contains three basic lines. First, Article 27 of the Citizenship Directive contains the general principles, such as the principle of proportionality,[210] and 'prohibitions', such as the prohibition on basing an expulsion decision on general preventive grounds[211] or invoking public policy or public security to serve economic ends.[212]

Second, the interests that have to be taken into consideration in the balancing process, such as the duration of the EU citizen's lawful residence in the host Member State and his or her age, family and economic situation, are listed in Article 28(1) of the Citizenship Directive.

Finally, Article 28 of the Citizenship Directive provides for a layered protection against expulsion, depending on the duration of lawful residence of EU citizens and their family members in the host Member State. This incremental protection attaches a specific weight to the interests of the individual, for instance by barring an expulsion decision against an EU citizen who has resided in the host Member State for 10 years, except if the decision is based on imperative grounds of public security, as provided by Article 28(3)(a).

It is remarkable that the Court continuously developed and extended EU citizens' protection by restricting Member States' powers to expel them. After the codification of its case law in the Citizenship Directive, however, the Court has been more hesitant and has even seemed to reverse its previous approach. In this regard, Meduna observes that the Court 'has not only abandoned its vision for EU citizenship spelt out in *Grzelczyk* and the key legal principles of its pre-2004 case law, it has also dismantled the … protection against expulsion'.[213] Indeed, the Court's case law regarding the expulsion of EU citizens and their family members corresponds to Member States' increasing focus on security concerns, their repeated emphasis on the need to strengthen immigration controls and their assertion of sovereignty by expelling foreigners – including EU citizens and their third-country national family members – they deem a threat to their public policy or security. Even though the EU legislature granted EU citizens with at least 10 years of lawful residence on the territory of the host Member States a considerably

[209] Oosterom-Staples, 'Adjudicating the External Schengen Border' 244.
[210] Article 27(2) Citizenship Directive.
[211] Article 27(2) Citizenship Directive.
[212] Article 27(1) Citizenship Directive.
[213] M Meduna, '"Scelestus Europeus Sum": What Protection against Expulsion Does EU Citizenship Offer to European Offenders?' in D Kochenov (ed), *EU Citizenship and Federalism: The Role of Rights* (Cambridge, CUP, 2017) 404.

enhanced protection by barring expulsion decisions except on imperative grounds of public security, the CJEU watered down this high threshold.

The Court's judgments in *Tsakouridis* and *P.I.* are exemplary in this respect. In *Tsakouridis* the Court held that dealing in narcotics as part of an organised group is capable of being covered by the notion of public security. Similarly, the Court stated in the *P.I.* case that the Member State could consider the crimes committed by P.I. (the continuous sexual abuse and rape of a minor) to be covered by the concept of imperative grounds of public security. While both cases concern crimes that are undoubtedly covered by the notion of public policy, it is questionable whether they also fall within the scope of the narrower notion of public security, which had previously been interpreted, in cases unrelated to expulsion, to cover threats to the internal or external security of the State.[214]

In *Tsakouridis* and *P.I.* the CJEU broadened the scope of application of the notion of public security, thus blurring the distinction between the more general concept of public policy and the narrower concept of public security. Moreover, it shifted a crucial element of its own interpretational sovereignty to the Member States and increased their discretion to revert to restrictive measures at the expense of EU citizens, even though the EU legislature afforded them an enhanced protection against expulsion after 10 years of lawful residence.

This development was continued, albeit by different means, in the *M.G.* case, where the Court linked an EU citizen's protection against expulsion to her integration in the host Member State. The Court emphasised that the 'degree of integration … is a vital consideration underpinning both the right of permanent residence and the system of protection against expulsion'.[215] Reliance on the requirement of integration is highly problematic for reasons that have been outlined above. The integration requirement was also invoked in the *Onuekwere* case, which, even though it concerned the acquisition of the right of permanent residence by a third-country national family member of an EU citizen, has direct repercussions on the protection against expulsion for third-country national family members of EU citizens. Article 28(2) of the Citizenship Directive provides for the strongest form of protection against expulsion available to this category but it is only available to those who have acquired the right of permanent residence. Denying third-country national family members the right of permanent residence simultaneously excludes them from the scope of protection of Article 28(2). The implications of the requirement of integration for the acquisition of the right of permanent residence ultimately also affect EU citizens' protection against expulsion, as demonstrated by the joined cases of *B* and *Franco Vomero*, where the Court held that the right of permanent residence is a prerequisite for EU citizens' reliance on Article 28(3)(a) of the Citizenship Directive.[216] This leads

[214] *P.I.*, para 14; *Tsakouridis*, para 21.
[215] *M.G.*, para 32.
[216] *B* and *Franco Vomero*, para 49.

to situations where EU citizens with more than 10 years of lawful residence, who have either not acquired or have lost the right of permanent residence, are barred from relying on the protection against expulsion provided for by Article 28(3) of the Citizenship Directive. Given that they are also barred from invoking Article 28(2) of the Citizenship Directive, which explicitly requires the right of permanent residence, these EU citizens fall back on the protection provided for by Article 27 and Article 28(1). This protection was available to them on the day they entered the territory of the host Member State. However, even though the legal framework is the same as on the day of entry, the balancing process between the interests of the individual and the interests of the state would be different after several years of residence as the duration of residence, the individual's integration into the host Member State and other factors have to be considered.

The Court's judgments in *Rendón Marín* and *C.S.*, which concern delinquent third-country national carers of minor EU citizens, deviate from the reasoning in previous judgments as they do not follow the rationale of restricting EU citizens' protection against expulsion and strengthening Member States' discretion to expel unwanted foreigners. Both judgments are remarkable as the Court brings these cases into the scope of EU law and thereby exempts them from national immigration law, even though the minor EU citizens had never left their Member State of nationality. Moreover, the CJEU imposes clear limits on Member States' capacity to terminate the residence of third-country national carers of minor EU citizens. While the Court allows these measures, it simultaneously clarifies that an expulsion decision and a refusal to issue a residence permit, respectively, are measures of last resort as the departure of the third-country parent implies that the minor EU citizens would be forced to leave the territory of the EU. These cases resemble the *Ruiz Zambrano* constellation, with the difference that in *Rendón Marín* and *C.S.* the third-country national parent had a criminal conviction. These judgments may have been influenced by the relatively specific pattern and the fact that the minor EU citizens had not committed any crime but would be deprived of the substance of the rights attached to EU citizenship if obliged to follow their third-country national carers and leave the EU. The *Rendón Marín* case and the *C.S.* judgment do not seem to be representative of the more recent case law on expulsion, which places Member States' sovereignty over the rights of EU citizens.

II. Expulsion of Turkish Nationals

The EEC–Turkey Association Agreement was signed in 1963.[217] It aims at strengthening trade and economic relations between the parties to the agreement,

[217] Adopted by the Council Decision of 23 December 1963 on the conclusion of the Agreement establishing an Association between the European Economic Community and Turkey [1964] OJ 3685/64 ('Association Agreement').

the promotion of Turkey's economic development, and the improvement of the level of employment and the living conditions of the Turkish people.[218] With a view to ensuring the implementation and progressive development of the Association, the Association Agreement provides that the parties shall meet in a Council of Association which shall act within the powers conferred upon it by the Agreement.[219] This Council adopted several decisions, among them Decision 1/80.

Council Decision 1/80 addresses work-related legal issues of Turkish workers and their family members and does not explicitly refer to a right of residence. Nevertheless, the right to employment would be thwarted if a concomitant right of residence were not guaranteed. Therefore, the CJEU held that the right of residence is the 'corollary of the right to have access to the employment market and to take up employment'[220] and specified this so-called 'implied right to residence'[221] in a series of judgments.[222]

A. Public Policy Exception, Article 14(1) of Decision 1/80

Turkish nationals who are covered by Article 6 or 7 of Decision 1/80 can lose their right of residence on three grounds,[223] one of them being the public policy exception of Article 14(1) of Decision 1/80.[224] Article 14(1) provides that the 'previous sections shall be applied subject to the limitations justified on grounds of public policy, public security or public health'. In *Nazli* the Court interpreted the public policy exception of Article 14(1) and held that 'reference should be made to the interpretation given to that exception in the field of freedom of movement for

[218] Article 2(1) Association Agreement.

[219] Article 6 Association Agreement.

[220] Case C-329/97 *Ergat* ECLI:EU:C:2000:133, [2000] ECR I-01487, para 45.

[221] A Steinebach and L Güneş, 'Prekärer Aufenthaltsstatus? Ausweisungsschutz von Unionsbürgern und Drittstaatsangehörigen in der EU – ein Überblick' (2010) *Zeitschrift für Ausländerrecht und Ausländerpolitik* 97, 98; P Boeles, 'Residence Rights of Turkish Nationals under the Association Agreement' in P Boeles, M den Heijer, G Lodders and K Wouters (eds), *European Migration Law*, 2nd edn (Cambridge, Intersentia, 2014) 97, 98; K Hailbronner, 'Neue Entwicklungen im Personenverkehr für Unionsbürger und Angehörige assoziierter Staaten' (2002) *Zeitschrift für Ausländerrecht und Ausländerpolitik* 11; K Hailbronner, 'Ausweisung und Abschiebung straffälliger Ausländer, The Expulsion of Criminal Aliens' in K Hailbronner and E Klein (eds), *Einwanderungskontrolle und Menschenrechte – Immigration Control and Human Rights, Beiträge anläßlich des Symposiums am 29.30. Juni 1998 in Potsdam* (Heidelberg, C.F. Müller Verlag, 1999) 178.

[222] Case C-340/97 *Nazli* ECLI:EU:C:2000:77, [2000] ECR I-00957, para 28; Case C-237/91 *Kus* ECLI:EU:C:1992:527, [1992] ECR I-06781, paras 29, 30; Case C-192/89 *Sevince* ECLI:EU:C:1990:322, [1990] ECR I-03461, para 29; Case C-434/93 *Ahmet Bozkurt* ECLI:EU:C:1995:168, [1995] ECR I-01475, para 28.

[223] For further information see N Tezcan-Idriz, 'Free Movement of Persons Between Turkey and the EU: To Move or Not to Move? The Response of the Judiciary' (2009) 46 *CML Rev* 1625, 1658; regarding family members of Turkish nationals see pp 1660–61.

[224] K Dienelt, 'Die Aufenthaltsrechtliche Bedeutung des Diskriminierungsverbots nach Art. 37 des Zusatzprotokolls' (2003) *Neue Zeitschrift für Verwaltungsrecht* 54, 56 argues that Article 37 of the Additional Protocol to the Association Agreement contains an inherent protection against expulsion which is independent from Article 6 or Article 7 of Decision 1/80.

workers who are nationals of a Member State of the Community'.[225] Moreover, the Court repeatedly stipulated that decisions based on Article 14(1) of Decision 1/80 require that the personal conduct of the individual concerned poses a present, genuine and sufficiently serious threat to a fundamental interest of society.[226] A measure based on Article 14(1) of Decision 1/80 may therefore only be taken 'if the personal conduct of the person concerned indicates a specific risk of new and serious prejudice to the requirements of public policy'.[227] In addition, the Court clarified that expulsion decisions cannot be based on general preventive grounds.[228]

This 'parallel interpretation' or analogous application is justified, the Court stated, as the wording of Article 14 of Council Decision 1/80 and the wording of the Treaty provision are almost identical.[229] These Treaty provisions were specified by Directive 64/221/EEC. When this Directive was repealed by the Citizenship Directive, the question arose whether the parallel interpretation is also justified with regard to the Citizenship Directive, which provides in Article 38(3) that 'references made to the repealed provisions and Directives shall be construed as being made to this Directive'.

B. Analogous Application of the Provisions Applicable to EU Citizens

In the *Ziebell* case the CJEU was asked whether the protection against expulsion granted to EU citizens after 10 years of lawful residence (Article 28(3)(a) of the Citizenship Directive) can be applied, by analogy, to Turkish citizens covered by the EEC–Turkey Association Agreement.

Prior to the *Ziebell* case it was disputed whether the layered protection against expulsion that is provided for by Article 28 of the Citizenship Directive was primarily a manifestation and expression of the principle of proportionality and was therefore also applicable to Turkish citizens,[230] or whether it was a specific characteristic of the concept of EU citizenship.[231]

[225] *Nazli*, para 56.

[226] Case C-303/08 *Bozkurt* ECLI:EU:C:2010:800, [2010] ECR I-13445, para 61; Case C-371/08 *Ziebell* ECLI:EU:C:2011:809, [2011] ECR I-12735, para 82.

[227] Case C-325/05 *Derin* ECLI:EU:C:2007:442, [2007] ECR I-06495, para 74; Case C-383/03 *Dogan* ECLI:EU:C:2005:436, [2005] ECR I-06237, para 24.

[228] *Dogan*, para 24; *Nazli*, para 63.

[229] *Bozkurt*, para 55; Case C-349/06 *Polat* ECLI:EU:C:2007:581, [2007] ECR I-08167, para 30; Case C-136/03 *Dörr* and *Ünal* ECLI:EU:C:2005:340, [2005] ECR I-04759, para 63.

[230] Boeles, 'Residence Rights of Turkish Nationals under the Association Agreement' 110; R Gutmann, 'Die neue Unionsbürger-Richtlinie 2004/38/EG und ihr Verhältnis zu Art. 14 Abs. 1 ARB 1 /80' (2005) 27 *Informationsbrief Ausländerrecht* 401, 402; R Marx, 'Aktuelle Entwicklungen im gemeinschaftsrechtlichen Ausweisungsschutz' (2007) 27 *Zeitschrift für Ausländerrecht und Ausländerpolitik* 142, 147; Steinebach and Güneş, 'Prekärer Aufenthaltsstatus?' 99, 101.

[231] K Hailbronner, 'Einreise und Aufenthalt türkischer Staatsangehöriger im Assoziationsrecht EWG-Türkei – Anmerkungen zur Rechtsprechung des EuGH' (2011) *Zeitschrift für Ausländerrecht und Ausländerpolitik* 322, 326.

The Court conducted a comparison 'between the objective pursued by the Association Agreement and the context of which it forms a part' and the Citizenship Directive.[232] To that end, it recalled the wording of Article 2(1) of the Association Agreement, which aims to promote the 'continuous and balanced strengthening of trade and economic relations'. Moreover, it considered the wording and purpose of other provisions of the Association Agreement and Decision 1/80, its own case law, and the AG's opinion,[233] and concluded that 'the purpose underpinning that association is solely economic in nature'.[234] Turning to the Citizenship Directive, the Court stated that it is 'far from pursuing a purely economic objective'[235] as it aims to facilitate and strengthen the rights of EU citizens. Regarding the wording of the two provisions, the Court ascertained that 'the very concept of "imperative grounds" of public security as set out in Article 28(3)(a) of Directive 2004/38 … has no equivalent in Article 14(1) of Decision No 1/80'.[236] Moreover, the Court held that

> the very concept of citizenship, as it results from the mere fact that a person holds the nationality of a Member State and not from the fact that the person has the status of a worker, and which … is intended to be the fundamental status of nationals of the Member States … justifies the recognition, for Union citizens alone, of guarantees which are considerably strengthened in respect of expulsion, such as those provided for in Article 28(3)(a) of Directive 2004/38/EC.[237]

The Court made clear that EU citizens *alone* enjoy the enhanced protection against expulsion granted by Article 28(3) of the Citizenship Directive, irrespective of their economic contribution to the host Member State, and thereby underlined their special status.

Due to the substantial differences between not only the wording, but also the purpose and objective of the Association Agreement and the Citizenship Directive, the Court held that these two legal regimes cannot be considered equivalent, with the result that Article 28(3)(a) of the Citizenship Directive cannot be applied, by analogy, to situations covered by Article 14(1) of Decision 1/80.[238] Instead, the relevant legal framework, said the Court, consists of Article 12 of the LTR Directive, unless the EEC–Turkey Association provides more favourable rules.[239] The Court referred to the requirements listed in Article 12(1)–(3) of the LTR Directive and reiterated the principles that it established in previous judgments regarding the

[232] *Ziebell*, para 62.
[233] ibid, paras 63–68.
[234] ibid, para 68.
[235] ibid, para 69.
[236] ibid, para 71.
[237] ibid, para 73.
[238] ibid, paras 74, 86.
[239] ibid, para 79.

expulsion of Turkish nationals.[240] In particular the Court emphasised that the public policy exception must be interpreted strictly,[241] that expulsion decisions must comply with the principle of proportionality, respect fundamental rights, and can only be adopted if an individual assessment has been conducted that demonstrates 'that the personal conduct of the individual concerned constitutes at present a genuine and sufficiently serious threat to a fundamental interest of society'.[242] Moreover, the Court recalled that an expulsion decision 'cannot be ordered automatically on general preventive grounds following a criminal conviction'.[243]

In sum, the Court held that Article 28(3)(a) of the Citizenship Directive cannot be applied to Turkish nationals and emphasised that the relevant legal framework is Article 12 of the LTR Directive. Moreover, it confirmed that the principles it had developed in previous judgments regarding Turkish nationals' protection continue to apply. The judgment clarifies that at least the protection provided for by Article 28(3) is an expression of the special status of EU citizenship.

III. Third-country Nationals Covered by the Long-term Residence Directive

The status of a 'long-term resident' is governed by the LTR Directive[244] and shall be granted to a third-country national who has legally and continuously resided in the host Member State for five years.[245] The LTR Directive regulates neither the conditions of entry nor the right to remain in the Member State prior to the acquisition of long-term resident status. These requirements are, in principle, governed by national immigration law. Moreover, Member States can refuse to grant long-term resident status to a third-country national on grounds of public policy or public security.[246] In 2011 the scope of the Directive was extended to beneficiaries of international protection.[247]

The CJEU repeatedly held that the Directive's principal objective 'As it is apparent from recitals 4, 6 and 12 in the preamble to Directive 2003/109 … is the

[240] ibid, paras 81–84.

[241] ibid, para 81. See also *Bozkurt*, para 56.

[242] *Ziebell*, para 82.

[243] ibid, para 83.

[244] Regarding the application of the LTR Directive, see COM(2011) 585 final, Report from the Commission to the European Parliament and the Council on the application of Directive 2003/109/EC concerning the status of third-country nationals who are long-term residents.

[245] Article 4 LTR Directive.

[246] Article 6 LTR Directive.

[247] Directive 2011/51/EU of the European Parliament and of the Council of 11 May 2011 amending Council Directive 2003/109/EC to extend its scope to beneficiaries of international protection [2011] OJ L 132/1.

integration of third-country nationals who are settled on a long-term basis in the Member States'.[248] In order to advance the Directive's objective of integration, the EU legislature has granted long-term resident third-country nationals a reinforced protection against expulsion in Article 12.[249] The link between expulsion and integration is important as foreigners who do not enjoy a certain security of residence will not have an incentive to integrate into society.[250] As early as in 1994 the European Commission identified security of stay and permanent residence for all those third-country nationals satisfying stability criteria as the 'fundamental prerequisites for a successful integration'.[251] Without 'this foundation, uncertainty will pervade other aspects of the integration process'.[252] Moreover, the Commission noted that an 'immigrant's own commitment to integration depends to a large extent on whether he feels secure in his residence status'.[253]

Long-term residents enjoy a reinforced protection against expulsion, which is provided for by Article 12 of the LTR Directive. Article 12(1) states that Member States may expel a long-term resident 'solely where he/she constitutes an actual and sufficiently serious threat to public policy or public security'. Thym rightly points out that the notion of 'public policy' refers, according to the Court's settled case law, to 'any "genuine and sufficiently serious threat … affecting one of the fundamental interests of society"'[254] and that the requirement of a 'sufficiently serious threat' is therefore redundant as it is inherent in the concept of public policy.[255] Article 12(2) bars expulsion decisions based on economic considerations and mirrors Article 27(1) of the Citizenship Directive. Article 12(3) lists the factors that have to be taken into consideration before an expulsion decision can be taken and is similar to Article 28(1) of the Citizenship Directive. The EU Commission noted in 2019 that 12 Member States had not implemented all of the balancing factors provided for by Article 12(3) of the Directive.[256] Recital 16 of the Preamble to the LTR Directive clarifies that the list of balancing factors 'is based on the criteria determined by the decisions of the European Court of Human Rights'. Two opposing views were held regarding the question of whether or not this list is exhaustive.

[248] Case C-502/10 *Singh* ECLI:EU:C:2012:636, [2012], para 45; Case C-508/10 *Commission v Netherlands* ECLI:EU:C:2012:243, [2012], para 66; Case C-309/14 *CGIL* and *INCA* ECLI:EU:C:2015:523, [2015], para 21.

[249] See Recital 16 of the Preamble.

[250] K Groenendijk, 'Long-term Immigrants and the Council of Europe' in E Guild and P Minderhoud (eds), *Security of Residence and Expulsion* (The Hague, Kluwer Law International, 2001) 7.

[251] COM(94) 23 final, Communication from the Commission to the Council and the European Parliament on Immigration and Asylum Policies, para 124.

[252] ibid.

[253] ibid.

[254] D Thym, 'Directive 2003/109/EC' in K Hailbronner and D Thym (eds), *EU Immigration and Asylum Law, A Commentary*, 2nd edn (Munich, C.H. Beck, 2016) Art 12, para 4.

[255] ibid.

[256] COM(2019) 161 final, Report from the Commission to the European Parliament and the Council on the implementation of Directive 2003/109/EC concerning the status of third-country nationals who are long-term residents, p 6.

In support of the argument that the list was exhaustive,[257] a comparison between the relevant provisions of the Citizenship Directive and the LTR Directive was drawn. Article 12(3) states that 'Member States shall have regard to the following factors', whereas Article 28(1) of the Citizenship Directive, which contains a non-exhaustive list, provides that 'Member States shall take account of considerations such as …'. In light of these differences, it was held that the list in Article 12(3) is exhaustive. On the other hand, it was argued that the list in Article 12(3) is not exhaustive.[258] In support of this view, Recital 16 of the Preamble to the Directive was invoked, which refers to the ECtHR's case law. It was held that the 'additional criteria established by the case law of the Court in Strasbourg can be considered', which supports the argument of a non-exhaustive list. In *López Pastuzano* the Court held that the balancing process 'must, in particular, have regard to the elements mentioned in Article 12(3) of Directive 2003/109'[259] and thereby clarified that the list of criteria is not exhaustive. In addition, the Court provided further guidance on the interpretation of Article 12 of the LTR Directive.[260]

A. The Different Views on the Interpretation of Article 12 of the LTR Directive

Before the Court's *López Pastuzano* judgment, different views were advanced as to whether Article 12 has to be interpreted in line with the Court's case law regarding EU citizens. Lodder noted a lack of clarity in this regard, which, he said, is 'a result of disagreement among the negotiating Member States' on the approximation of long-term residents' protection to that of EU citizens.[261]

On the one hand, it was argued that the LTR Directive has to be interpreted in line with the CJEU's case law on the expulsion of EU citizens.[262] On the other hand, it was held that there is no necessity to align long-term residents' protection against expulsion to that of EU citizens.[263] In support of the former position, the legally non-binding Tampere Presidency Conclusions were cited, which are also mentioned in Recital 2 of the Preamble to the LTR Directive. The Presidency

[257] D Acosta Arcarazo, *The Long-Term Resident Status as a Subsidiary Form of EU Citizenship* (The Hague, Martinus Nijhoff, 2011) 125; Morano-Foadi and Andreadakis, 'The Convergence of the European Legal System in the Treatment of Third-country Nationals in Europe' 1078.

[258] D Thym, 'Directive 2003/109/EC', Art 12, para 9.

[259] Case C-636/16 *López Pastuzano* ECLI:EU:C:2017:949, [2017], para 27.

[260] ibid.

[261] G Lodders, 'Movement and Residence Rights of Third-Country Nationals' in P Boeles, M den Heijer, G Lodders and K Wouters (eds), *European Migration Law*, 2nd edn (Cambridge, Intersentia, 2014) 187.

[262] Marx, 'Aktuelle Entwicklungen im gemeinschaftsrechtlichen Ausweisungsschutz' 149; Acosta Arcarazo, *The Long-Term Resident Status as a Subsidiary Form of EU Citizenship* 138.

[263] C Langenfeld, 'Menschenrecht auf Aufenthalt?' in M Herdegen, H Klein, H-J Papier and R Scholz (eds), *Staatsrecht und Politik, Festschrift für Roman Herzog* (Munich, C.H. Beck, 2009) 262.

Conclusions aim at approximating the status of long-term resident third-country nationals to that of Member States' nationals, as well as at granting them rights 'which are as near as possible to those enjoyed by EU citizens'.[264] Peers argued that, in light of the Tampere principle of equality, 'the substantive protection of EC free movement law should apply to long-term residents'.[265] Moreover, he held that 'there is no express authorization in Article 12 to treat long-term residents differently from EC citizens'.[266] Similarly, Groenendijk stated that a comparison between the requirements of Article 12 of the LTR Directive and those of Articles 27(1), (2) and 28(1) of the Citizenship Directive demonstrates that the differences are minor.[267] Lodder argued that 'it seems fair to assume that Article 12 Long-Term Residence Directive aims at protection as near as possible to protection against expulsion of EU citizens who have not yet acquired a permanent status'.[268]

Inversely, those who argue that long-term residents' protection against expulsion cannot be interpreted in line with the protection that applies to EU citizens invoke two main arguments. The first argument relies on the drafting history of the LTR Directive. The wording of the original proposal of the LTR Directive was based on the wording of the provisions that apply to EU citizens and was rejected by the Council.[269] This demonstrates, Hauschild and Thym argue, that Member States did not wish to grant long-term resident third-country nationals the same protection against expulsion as EU citizens.[270] The second argument builds on the differences between the rights of third-country nationals, on the one hand, and the free movement rights that apply to EU citizens on the other. Third-country nationals are covered by the area of freedom, security and justice, which does not provide – at least not to the same extent – for a free movement right.[271] Therefore, a general equivalence of the legal status of EU citizens and third-country nationals with regard to expulsion decisions cannot be assumed.[272]

[264] Presidency Conclusions, Tampere European Council, 15 and 16 October 1999, SN 200/99, para 21.

[265] S Peers, 'Implementing Equality? The Directive on Long-term Resident Third-country nationals' (2004) 29 *EL Rev* 437, 452, 453.

[266] ibid, 452.

[267] K Groenendijk, 'Long-Term Residents' in S Peers, E Guild, D Acosta Arcarazo, K Groenendijk and V Moreno-Lax (eds), *EU Immigration and Asylum Law (Text and Commentary) Volume 2: Immigration Law*, 2nd edn (Leiden, Martinus Nijhoff Publishers, 2012) 313.

[268] Lodders, 'Movement and Residence Rights of Third-Country Nationals' 188.

[269] Thym, 'Directive 2003/109/EC', Art 12, para 2; K Hailbronner, 'Langfristig aufenthaltsberechtigte Drittstaatsangehörige' (2004) 24 *Zeitschrift für Ausländerrecht und Ausländerpolitik* 163, 166.

[270] C Hauschild, 'Neues europäisches Einwanderungsrecht: Das Daueraufenthaltsrecht von Drittstaatsangehörigen' (2003) 23 *Zeitschrift für Ausländerrecht und Ausländerpolitik* 350, 352: Thym, 'Directive 2003/109/EC', Art 12, para 2.

[271] D Thym, *Migrationsverwaltungsrecht* (Tübingen, Mohr Siebeck, 2010) 234; D Thym, 'Schutz des Aufenthalts zwischen polizeilicher Herkunft und menschenrechtlicher Neuausrichtung' in F Arndt, N Betz, A Farahat, M Goldmann, M Huber, R Keil, P Láncos, J Schaefer, M Smrkolj, F Sucker and S Valta (eds), *Freiheit – Sicherheit – Öffentlichkeit, 48. Assistententagung Öffentliches Recht* (Baden-Baden, Nomos, 2009) 234.

[272] ibid.

B. The *López Pastuzano* Judgment

In the *López Pastuzano* judgment the Court provided clarification on the interpretation of Article 12 of the LTR Directive. Mr López Pastuzano, a Colombian national, had been a long-term resident third-country national in Spain. He was sentenced to a prison term of 12 months and to another term of three months.[273] According to the referring court, Spanish law distinguishes between 'two different sets of rules relating to the administrative expulsion of a foreign national'.[274] The first type is an 'expulsion as a sanction imposed on a person committing certain administrative offences … and, [the] second, expulsion as a legal consequence stemming from a conviction for wilful misconduct to a term of imprisonment of more than one year'.[275] The Spanish statutory provision, which implements Article 12(3) of the LTR Directive, had been interpreted by the greater part of the judiciary as only covering the former type of expulsion. Consequently, it did not cover the situation of Mr López Pastuzano, who was sentenced to a prison term of more than a year. The referring Spanish court therefore sought interpretation of the notion 'decision to expel' that is contained in Article 12(3) of the LTR Directive and asked whether it must be interpreted 'as covering any administrative decision to expel, whatever its nature may be'.[276]

The CJEU rejected the differentiation between these two types of expulsion decisions by stating that it is irrelevant for the application of Article 12(3) 'whether such a measure has been delivered in the form of an administrative penalty or whether it is the result of a criminal conviction'[277] and concluded that Article 12(3) applies to 'all administrative expulsion decisions, regardless of the legal nature of that measure'.[278] In reaching this conclusion, the Court reiterated that an expulsion decision 'may not be ordered automatically following a criminal conviction, but rather requires a case-by-case assessment which must, in particular, have regard to the elements mentioned in Article 12(3)'.[279]

Moreover, the Court referred in the *López Pastuzano* judgment to two paragraphs of the *Ziebell* judgment.[280] Paragraph 82 of the *Ziebell* judgment stipulates that 'measures on grounds of public policy or public security may be taken only following a case-by-case assessment' and only if 'the personal conduct of the individual concerned constitutes at present a genuine and sufficiently serious threat to a fundamental interest of society'.[281] The same paragraph also provides

[273] *López Pastuzano*, para 7.
[274] ibid, para 10.
[275] ibid.
[276] ibid, para 14.
[277] ibid, para 26.
[278] ibid, para 29.
[279] ibid, para 27.
[280] *López Pastuzano*, para 27; *Ziebell*, paras 82, 83.
[281] *Ziebell*, para 82.

that expulsion decisions must comply with the principle of proportionality and must respect fundamental rights.[282] Paragraph 83 of the *Ziebell* judgment, cited by the Court in *López Pastuzano*, states that measures 'cannot be ordered automatically on general preventive grounds following a criminal conviction or as a means of deterring other foreign nationals from committing offences'.[283]

Even though the Court did not explicitly refer to the remaining paragraphs of the *Ziebell* judgment and the principles contained therein, the CJEU's approach demonstrates the alignment of long-term resident third-country nationals' protection against expulsion to that of Turkish citizens, which in turn reflects the foundational principles of EU citizens' protection.

The synchronisation of long-term resident third-country nationals' and Turkish nationals' protection against expulsion implies that the limits of the latter's protection also apply to long-term resident third-country nationals. As the Court clarified in the *Ziebell* judgment that the protection that is provided for by Article 28(3)(a) of the Citizenship Directive is unavailable to Turkish nationals,[284] it cannot be invoked by long-term resident third-country nationals.

IV. Other Groups of Third-country Nationals

Expulsions of third-country nationals who are not covered by a special regime are normally not assessed by the CJEU as they fall outside the scope of EU law. The protection against expulsion for these groups of third-country nationals is determined by national law and by the ECHR. However, if these nationals are subject to an entry ban according to the Return Directive or an SIS alert according to the SIS Regulation, their situation comes within the scope of application of EU law, and the CJEU has jurisdiction to interpret the SIS Regulation and the Return Directive respectively. In addition, Member States are bound by the CFR as they implement EU law.

V. Summary and Conclusions

This chapter addressed the protection against expulsion provided for by EU law. It started with EU citizens, who enjoy the most far-reaching protection against expulsion, and their third-country national family members. It outlined the protection provided for by Articles 27 and 28 of the Citizenship Directive and their interpretation by the CJEU. Article 27 contains general principles and

[282] ibid.
[283] ibid, para 83.
[284] ibid, para 86.

prohibitions that have to be observed when restricting EU citizens' free movement rights on grounds of public policy or public security. Article 28(1) lists the considerations that have to be considered when balancing the individual's interest against the Member State's interest and is informed by the criteria that have been established by the ECtHR in the context of Article 8 ECHR.[285] Article 28 of the Citizenship Directive provides for a layered protection against expulsion depending on the duration of residence: the longer EU citizens and their family members reside on the territory of the host Member State, the stronger their protection against expulsion is. The EU legislature already attaches a specific weight to the interests of the individual and the interests of the state by stipulating the grounds that can justify an expulsion. Where an EU citizen lawfully resided in the host Member State for more than 10 years, an expulsion decision can only be based on imperative grounds of public security, per Article 28(3)(a) of the Citizenship Directive. Grounds of public policy are no longer sufficient. In cases unrelated to expulsion the Court stated that public security refers to the Member State's internal and external security[286] and that a state's internal security covers the existence of the country's institutions, its essential public services and the survival of its inhabitants.[287] Even though Article 28(3) sets a high threshold for Member States to expel EU citizens, it was lowered considerably by the Court. In the *Tsakouridis* judgment the Court considered dealing in narcotics as part of an organised group capable of being covered by the notion of public security. The same approach was adopted by the Court in the *P.I.* case, which concerned sexual coercion and rape of a minor. These judgments were criticised for blurring the demarcation line between public policy and public security and led Kochenov and Pirker to brand them as a '*de facto* attack on the core of the status of EU citizenship'.[288] Both judgments undermine the strong protection that is granted to EU citizens by the EU legislature and afford Member States considerable discretion to expel EU citizens after more than 10 years of lawful residence. The Court furthered its restrictive approach in the *M.G.* case by stating that the protection against expulsion in the Citizenship Directive is 'based on the degree of integration of the persons concerned in the host Member State'.[289] Linking EU citizens' protection against expulsion to the inherently open-ended notion of integration is highly problematic. This applies in particular if integration is understood as a 'duty to integrate properly'[290] and if the breach of Member States' criminal law is considered to show a lack of integration. Given that EU citizens, who are subject to expulsion decisions on grounds of public policy or public security, have often been convicted of criminal offences,

[285] Guild, 'Restrictions on the Right of Entry' 255.
[286] *Aimé Richardt and Les Accessoires Scientifiques SNC*, para 22 (with regard to Article 36 TFEU); *Leifer*, para 26; *Sirdar*, para 17; *Albore*, para 18; *Kreil*, para 17.
[287] *Campus Oil Limited*, para 34.
[288] Kochenov and Pirker, 'Deporting the Citizens within the European Union' 388.
[289] *M.G.*, para 30.
[290] Nic Shuibhne, 'Limits Rising, Duties Ascending' 920.

such an approach would effectively hollow out their protection against expulsion. The Court's reliance on the notion of integration also became apparent in the *Onuekwere* case, which concerned the acquisition of the right of permanent residence by a third-country national family member of an EU citizen. The Court linked the acquisition of the right of permanent residence to the individual's integration in the host Member State and held that the imposition of a prison sentence demonstrates 'the non-compliance by the person concerned with the values expressed by the society of the host Member State in its criminal law'[291] and hence the individual's lack of integration. This has implications for access to the enhanced protection against expulsion afforded by Article 28(2) of the Citizenship Directive, which presupposes the right of permanent residence.

In September 2016 the CJEU took a different approach in *Rendón Marín* and *C.S.*, two cases concerning delinquent third-country national carers of minor EU citizens who had not left their Member State of nationality. In both cases the Court emphasised that EU law bars any automatism between a criminal conviction and a decision terminating residence. Even though the CJEU did not completely bar Member States from adopting expulsion decisions against the third-country national carers of minor EU citizens, it imposed several limitations. While these judgments derogate from the previously outlined cases, they do not seem to be representative due to the specificity of their fact patterns.

Turning to Turkish nationals, whose protection against expulsion is governed by Article 14 of Decision 1/80, the CJEU's *Ziebell* judgment is instructive. In judgments pre-dating *Ziebell*, the Court interpreted the concepts of public policy and public security in Article 14 of Decision 1/80 in line with the interpretation given to these concepts in the Treaty and Directive 64/221/EEC. According to the Court, this parallel interpretation was justified insofar as the wording of Article 14 of Decision 1/80 and the wording of the Treaty provisions were almost identical.[292] The Court was asked in the *Ziebell* case whether the protection of Article 28(3)(a) of the Citizenship Directive, which is afforded to EU citizens after more than 10 years of residence, can be equally applied to Turkish nationals. It answered this question in the negative and based its reasoning on the substantial differences between the objectives and wording of the two legal instruments. The Court emphasised that the fundamental status of EU citizenship justifies that EU citizens alone enjoy the enhanced protection against expulsion provided for by Article 28(3) of the Citizenship Directive.

While the CJEU stated that the relevant framework for Turkish nationals' expulsion is Article 12 of the LTR Directive, it clarified that the shift from the rules that are applicable to nationals of the Member States to the LTR Directive does not affect the previously established principles and safeguards of Turkish nationals'

[291] *Onuekwere*, para 26.

[292] *Bozkurt*, para 55; *Polat*, para 30; *Dörr* and *Ünal*, para 63; Case C-467/02 *Cetinkaya* ECLI:EU:C:2004:708, [2004] ECR I-10895, para 43; *Nazli*, para 56.

protection against expulsion.[293] Those safeguards, which were developed by the Court in analogy to the safeguards that are applicable to nationals of the Member States, continue to apply to Turkish nationals.

In December 2017 the Court provided an interpretation of Article 12 of the LTR Directive in the *López Pastuzano* judgment: it asserted that Article 12 of the LTR Directive applies to every expulsion decision against long-term resident third-country nationals, irrespective of whether the misconduct that triggered the expulsion decision is of an administrative or a criminal nature. It clarified that an expulsion may not be ordered automatically following a criminal conviction and that every expulsion decision must be preceded by a case-by-case assessment that takes factors such as those mentioned in Article 12(3) into account. While the Court did not directly refer to its case law regarding nationals of the Member States, it quoted two paragraphs of the *Ziebell* judgment,[294] which in turn mirror general principles of EU citizens' protection against expulsion that are codified in Article 27 of the Citizenship Directive. In *López Pastuzano* the Court transferred the application of these principles to long-term resident third-country nationals. The Court thereby synchronised Turkish nationals' and long-term resident third-country nationals' protection against expulsion by aligning it to the general principles that govern EU citizens' protection against expulsion. These developments are to be welcomed as they enhance Turkish nationals' and long-term resident third-country nationals' protection. Moreover, they simplify administrative processes as they ensure that the same set of fundamental principles and safeguards apply to the expulsion of EU citizens, their third-country national family members, Turkish nationals and long-term resident third-country nationals, which, in turn, enhances clarity and legal certainty.

However, in the *Ziebell* judgment the Court highlighted the limits of such parallel interpretation and clarified that EU citizenship as 'a fundamental status of nationals of the Member States … justifies the recognition, for Union citizens alone, of guarantees which are considerably strengthened in respect of expulsion, such as those provided for in Article 28(3)(a) of Directive 2004/38/EC'.[295] Consequently, neither Turkish nationals nor long-term resident third-country nationals can rely on this protection. The use of the words 'such as' might indicate that the Court could denote further provisions or safeguards that are reserved to EU citizens. At the same time this statement is remarkable against the backdrop of the CJEU's case law on EU citizens as the fundamental status of EU citizenship has not prevented the Court from curtailing the protection afforded to EU citizens by Article 28(3)(a) of the Citizenship Directive.

In sum, the CJEU's case law has precipitated a convergence of the level of protection against expulsion that is available to EU citizens and their family

[293] See *Ziebell*, paras 81–84.
[294] *López Pastuzano*, para 27; *Ziebell*, paras 82, 83.
[295] *Ziebell*, para 73.

members, Turkish nationals and long-term resident third-country nationals. On the one hand, this convergence is achieved by an improvement of the protection of Turkish nationals and long-term resident third-country nationals, who can rely on the general principles of protection against expulsion available to EU citizens. On the other hand, this convergence is achieved by reducing EU citizens' protection as the Court has undermined the protection afforded by Article 28(3) of the Citizenship Directive. Instead of extending Article 28(3) to third-country nationals, the Court clarified that it applies exclusively to EU citizens, while simultaneously eroding the protection granted by this provision.

2

Expulsion in Light of the ECHR and the ECtHR's Case Law

This chapter provides an overview of the protection against expulsion provided for by the ECHR and the ECtHR's case law. The ECHR and EU law are distinct but they have several points of correspondence as every individual who is covered by EU law can also rely on the ECHR. Conversely, not everyone who is covered by the ECHR can also rely on EU law. The previous chapter addressed different groups of foreigners based on the protection against expulsion afforded them by EU law. It started with the group that is granted the most enhanced protection against expulsion and closed with third-country nationals who are not covered by EU law. For the latter group, the ECHR often constitutes the only available protection that is provided by European law as they are barred from relying on the often more beneficial provisions of EU law.

The differences between the protections afforded by EU law and by the ECHR are illustrated by the rights of EU citizens and their protection against expulsion. Guild rightly points out that the free movement rights are the inverse of what is provided for by the Convention. The free movement rights applicable in the European Union are enforceable against the Member State(s) in a way that no Convention right, with the possible exception of Article 3 ECHR, applies.[1]

This chapter starts by briefly outlining the Council of Europe's binding and non-binding instruments that address expulsion. Next, the focus rests on the first two limbs of Article 8(1) ECHR, the right to respect for private life and the right to respect for family life. Subsequently, Article 8(2) ECHR is examined, which outlines the requirements that can justify an interference with Article 8(1) ECHR. In the context of justification, the legitimate aims of an interference, the criterion of necessity, and the factors that have been developed by the Court to guide the balancing process between the interest of the individual and the interests of the state, are discussed. Attention is paid to the value that is ascribed to the different balancing factors and to the margin of appreciation granted to the Contracting States. Finally, this chapter explores the rationale of the Court's case law by

[1] E Guild, 'Security of Residence and Expulsion of Foreigners: European Community Law' in E Guild and P Minderhoud (eds), *Security of Residence and Expulsion* (The Hague, Kluwer Law International, 2001) 65.

focusing on the burden of proof and the distinction between positive and negative obligations.

I. Binding and Non-binding Instruments

The Council of Europe has issued several legally binding and non-binding instruments that either specifically address expulsion or are relevant to the ECtHR's case law regarding expulsion.

A. ECHR and the Additional Protocols

The ECHR is binding upon 47 states in Europe. Article 1 ECHR obliges the Contracting States to secure for everyone within their jurisdiction the fundamental rights granted by the Convention. The ECHR refers neither to immigration nor to the termination of residence.[2] The right to asylum, which is provided for by the Geneva Refugee Convention, the Universal Declaration of Human Rights[3] and the CFR for instance,[4] has not been incorporated in the ECHR, nor has the principle of non-refoulement. Thym points out that the missing reference to immigration and the non-incorporation of a right to asylum reflect deliberate choices.[5]

In contrast to the ECHR, Additional Protocols No 4 and No 7 to the ECHR explicitly address expulsion, but they are only binding upon the ratifying states. Article 4 of Protocol No 4,[6] which is described as being primarily a procedural guarantee,[7] bars collective expulsion.[8] A collective expulsion is understood 'as any measure compelling aliens, as a group, to leave a country, except where such a measure is taken on the basis of a reasonable and objective examination of the particular case of each individual alien of the group'.[9] The ECtHR has repeatedly

[2] F Fritzsch, 'Die Auswirkungen des Rechtes auf Achtung des Privat- und Familienlebens auf Ausweisung und andere Rückführungsentscheidungen' (2011) 31 *Zeitschrift für Ausländerrecht und Ausländerpolitik* 297.

[3] Article 14(1) Universal Declaration of Human Rights.

[4] Article 18 Charter of Fundamental Rights of the European Union.

[5] D Thym, 'Respect for Private and Family Life under Article 8 ECHR in Immigration Cases: A Human Right to Regularize Illegal Stay?' (2008) 57 *ICLQ* 87, 103, note 65.

[6] Protocol No 4 to the Convention for the Protection of Human Rights and Fundamental Freedoms, securing certain rights and freedoms other than those already included in the Convention and in the first Protocol thereto, as amended by Protocol No 11, ETS no 46 (Strasbourg, 16 September 1963).

[7] D Sander, *Der Schutz des Aufenthalts durch Artikel 8 der Europäischen Menschenrechtskonvention* (Berlin, Duncker & Humblot, 2008) 38, 39.

[8] For further information see L Leboeuf and J-Y Carlier, 'The Prohibition of Collective Expulsion as an Individualisation Requirement' in M Moraru, G Cornelisse and P De Bruycker (eds), *Law and Judicial Dialogue on Return of Irregular Migrants from the European Union* (Oxford, Hart Publishing, 2020) 455.

[9] *Andric v Sweden* App no 45917/99 (ECHR, 23 February 1999); *Čonka v Belgium* App no 51564/99 (ECHR, 5 February 2002), para 59; *Berisha and Haljiti v 'the former Yugoslav Republic of Macedonia'* App no 18670/03 (ECHR, 18 June 2005).

stated that the purpose of Article 4 of Protocol No 4 is to prevent states from 'being able to remove certain aliens without examining their personal circumstances and, consequently, without enabling them to put forward their arguments against the measure taken by the relevant authority'.[10] The protection against collective expulsion in Article 4 of Protocol No 4 applies to all foreigners, irrespective of whether their stay is regular or irregular.[11] Article 1 of Protocol No 7[12] provides for minimum procedural safeguards against expulsion[13] but has considerable limitations as it only applies to foreigners who are legally resident in the territory of the Contracting State. The limited nature of this protection is also demonstrated by the lack of clarification regarding the level of scrutiny that has to be applied.[14] According to the non-binding Explanatory Report,[15] Article 1 of Protocol No 7 does not grant a suspensive effect in case of appeal.[16] Finally, Article 3(1) of Protocol No 4 to the ECHR prohibits the expulsion of nationals.

B. Non-binding Instruments Adopted by the Council of Europe

Three recommendations of the Council of Europe address expulsion, with two having been adopted by the Committee of Ministers and one by the Parliamentary Assembly. In 2000, three years before the Long-Term Residence Directive was adopted by the European Union, the Council of Ministers of the Council of Europe adopted Recommendation Rec(2000)15 'concerning the security of long-term migrants'.[17] It proposes that states may provide that certain groups of long-term residents should no longer be subject to expulsion.[18] Moreover, it recommends a sliding scale, which is similar to the Dutch sliding scale and to Article 28 of the Citizenship Directive. The recommended sliding scale provides that a long-term

[10] *Hirsi Jamaa and others v Italy* App no 27765/09 (ECHR, 23 February 2012), para 177; *Sharifi and others v Italy and Greece* App no 16643/09 (ECHR, 21 October 2014), para 210; *Khlaifia and others v Italy* App no 16483/12 (ECHR, 15 December 2016), para 238.

[11] *N.D. and N.T. v Spain*, App nos 8675/15 and 8697/15 (ECHR, 13 February 2020), para 185.

[12] Protocol No 7 to the Convention for the Protection of Human Rights and Fundamental Freedoms as amended by Protocol No 11, ETS no 117 (Strasbourg, 22 November 1984).

[13] I Bryan and P Langford, 'Impediments to the Expulsion of Non-Nationals: Substance and Coherence in Procedural Protection under the European Convention on Human Rights' (2010) 79 *Nordic Journal of International Law* 457, 463. For criticism see J Schwarze, 'Der Beitrag des Europarates zur Entwicklung von Rechtsschutz und Verfahrensgarantien im Verwaltungsrecht' (1993) 21 *Europäische Grundrechte-Zeitschrift* 377, 382; H Lambert, *The Position of Aliens in Relation to the European Convention on Human Rights* (Strasbourg, Council of Europe Publishing, 2007) 36.

[14] H Toner, 'Article 8 ECHR – Full Judicial Scrutiny?' (2007) 1–2 *Migrantenrecht* 48, 49.

[15] Council of Europe, Explanatory Report to Protocol No 7 to the Convention for the Protection of Human Rights and Fundamental Freedoms, ETS no 117.

[16] ibid, Article 1 para 13.2.

[17] Council of Europe, Committee of Ministers, Recommendation Rec(2000)15 concerning the security of long-term migrants, 13 September 2000.

[18] Council Recommendation Rec(2000)15, para 4(b).

resident migrant with more than five years of residence can only be expelled if s/he is sentenced to at least two years' imprisonment without suspension. After 10 years of residence, the migrant can only be expelled if sentenced to at least five years of imprisonment without suspension. After more than 20 years of residence, the migrant should no longer be expellable.[19] 'Long-term residents who were born on the territory of the Member State or admitted to the Member State before the age of ten' should 'not be expellable once they reached the age of eighteen'. Moreover, it provides that long-term resident minors may in principle not be expelled.[20] Simultaneously the recommendation seems to weaken the proposed safeguards by stating that 'each Member State should have the option to provide in its internal law that a long-term immigrant may be expelled if he or she constitutes a serious threat to national security or public safety',[21] which confirms that, even after more than 20 years of residence, a long-term resident is not safe from being expelled.

The second relevant non-binding instrument is Recommendation Rec(2002)4 'on the legal status of persons admitted for family reunification',[22] which lists the criteria that should be considered by states when expelling a family member. These criteria comprise 'the person's place of birth, his age of entry on the territory, the length of residence, his family relationships, the existence of family ties in the country of origin and the solidity of social and cultural ties with the country of origin'.[23] Moreover, 'Special consideration should be paid to the best interest of children'.

The third instrument is the Parliamentary Assembly's Recommendation 1504(2001) on the 'non-expulsion of long-term immigrants'.[24] The Parliamentary Assembly holds the view that expulsion measures against lawful long-term residents are both disproportionate and discriminatory.[25] It states that long-term residents, especially those who were born in the host country, have integrated in the host society and are 'no longer humanly or sociologically foreigners'.[26] It considers an expulsion measure against an integrated alien to be disproportionate as it has lifelong consequences for the individual, often entails a separation from the family and an uprooting from his or her environment.[27] Moreover, the recommendation underlines the discriminatory nature of expulsion measures as nationals who have

[19] ibid.

[20] Council Recommendation Rec(2000)15, para 4(c).

[21] ibid.

[22] Council of Europe, Committee of Ministers, Recommendation Rec(2002)4 on the legal status of persons admitted for family reunification, adopted by the Committee of Ministers on 26 March 2002 at the 790th meeting of the Ministers' Deputies.

[23] ibid, IV No 1.

[24] Council of Europe, Parliamentary Assembly's Committee on Migration, Refugees and Demography, Recommendation 1504, Non-expulsion of long-term immigrants, adopted by the Standing Committee, acting on behalf of the Assembly, on 14 March 2001.

[25] ibid, no 3.

[26] ibid, no 2.

[27] ibid, no 3.

committed the same offence cannot be expelled.[28] In addition, it addresses the issue of integration and notes that an insecure residence status hampers the alien's integration into the host society.[29] Finally, it criticises the lack of a clear position of the ECtHR regarding the expulsion of foreigners and calls upon the Contracting States to exempt certain categories of foreigners from expulsion and to reserve expulsion for highly exceptional cases.[30]

These three recommendations are to be appreciated as they afford non-nationals an enhanced protection against expulsion, which implies a more secure residence status, which in turn is beneficial to integration. At the same it has to be noted that these recommendations have not been put into legally binding instruments, which demonstrates that states wish to retain the power to exercise their sovereignty, including by way of expelling foreigners whom they deem a threat to their public policy or public security.

C. The European Convention on Establishment, the European Social Charter and the European Convention on Social and Medical Assistance

The 1955 European Convention on Establishment provides in Article 3(1) that 'nationals of any Contracting Party lawfully residing in the territory of another Party may be expelled only if they endanger national security or offend against *ordre public* or morality'.[31] Article 3(2) stipulates that the expellee, after two years of legal residence, shall in principle not be expelled without first being allowed to appeal against his expulsion, which gives an appeal suspensive effect.[32] According to Article 3(3), a national of any Contracting Party 'who has been lawfully residing ten years in the territory of any other Party may only be expelled for reasons of national security or if the other reasons mentioned in paragraph 1 of this article are of a particularly serious nature'.

This Convention is binding upon 12 Member States of the Council of Europe.[33] Ten of these states are EU/EEA Member States and the other two states are Turkey and the United Kingdom. The European Convention on Establishment has several flaws,[34] with the result that it does not provide for a more effective protection

[28] ibid, no 3.
[29] ibid, no 4.
[30] ibid, nos 5, 7, 10.
[31] European Convention on Establishment, ETS no 19 (Paris, 13 December 1955).
[32] K Groenendijk, 'Long-term Immigrants and the Council of Europe' in E Guild and P Minderhoud (eds), *Security of Residence and Expulsion* (The Hague, Kluwer Law International, 2001) 18.
[33] The Convention was ratified by Belgium, Denmark, Germany, Greece, Ireland, Italy, Luxembourg, the Netherlands, Norway, Sweden, Turkey and the United Kingdom.
[34] See Groenendijk, 'Long-term Immigrants and the Council of Europe' 10: 'its scope is restricted to nationals of the Member States, national immigration rules determine the content of several provisions of the Convention and there is no effective system of international supervision of its implementation'.

against expulsion than other legal instruments applicable to EU, EEA or Swiss citizens. The Association Agreement and Decision 1/80 also provide for a further-reaching protection against expulsion than the Convention on Establishment.[35] In light of the synchronisation of Turkish and long-term resident third-country nationals' protection against expulsion, the same can be said with regard to third-country nationals covered by the LTR Directive.

The European Social Charter (ESC) grants migrant workers and their families the right to protection and assistance.[36] According to Article 19(8) ESC, Contracting Parties undertake 'to secure that such workers lawfully residing within their territories are not expelled unless they endanger national security or offend against public interest or morality'.

Finally, Article 6(1) of the European Convention on Social and Medical Assistance provides that a foreigner cannot be expelled after a prolonged lawful period of residence on the sole ground that s/he is in need of social or medical assistance.[37]

The three instruments can afford some protection against expulsion but they also exhibit several limitations. In addition, the Contracting States can limit the guarantees provided for by these instruments partially due to the lack of an international authority responsible for their binding interpretation.

II. Article 8 ECHR and the ECtHR's Case Law

It is nearly impossible to provide a systematic and comprehensive overview of the Court's case law, which is highly casuistic and fact specific.[38] Nevertheless, an attempt will be made to outline the main features of the ECtHR's reasoning and the criteria that are applied in cases concerning expulsion.

The primary responsibility to ensure the compatibility of national measures with the Convention rests with the Contracting States. The ECHR and the ECtHR are said to have a subsidiary function,[39] which is also reflected in Articles 1 and 35

[35] J Bast, 'Internationalisierung und De-Internationalisierung der Migrationsverwaltung' in C Möllers, A Voßkuhle and C Walter (eds), *Internationales Verwaltungsrecht* (Tübingen, Mohr Siebeck, 2007) 298.

[36] European Social Charter, ETS no 35 (Turin, 18 October 1961).

[37] European Convention on Social and Medical Assistance, ETS no 14 (Paris, 11 December 1953).

[38] B Strieder, 'Wann "gebieten" Belange des Ausländers im Ausweisungsrecht eine Ermessensentscheidung?' (2009) 31 *Informationsbrief Ausländerrecht* 371, 376; S Zeichen, 'Ausweisungsschutz für integrierte Fremde' (2002) 57 *Zeitschrift für Öffentliches Recht* 413, 448; I Roagna, *Protecting the Right to Respect for Private and Family Life under the European Convention on Human Rights* (Strasbourg, Council of Europe, 2012) 86.

[39] M Hutchinson, 'The Margin of Appreciations Doctrine in the European Court of Human Rights' (1999) 48 *ICLQ* 638, 640; I Siess-Scherz, 'Die Bedeutung des Subsidiaritätsprinzips für den Reformprozess des EGMR' in W Karl and F Matscher (eds), *Internationale Gerichtshöfe und nationale Rechtsordnung* (Kehl am Rhein, N.P. Engel Verlag, 2005) 83; J Vondung, *Die Architektur des europäischen Grundrechtsschutzes nach dem Beitritt der EU zur EMRK* (Tübingen, Mohr Siebeck, 2012) 32; J Rubel, *Entscheidungsfreiräume in der Rechtsprechung des Europäischen Gerichtshofes für Menschenrechte und des Europäischen Gerichtshofes* (Hamburg, Verlag Dr. Kovač, 2005) 24.

of the ECHR and Article 1 of Protocol No 15 to the ECHR. Judgments of the ECtHR are binding for the state that is a party to the legal dispute (*inter partes* effect)[40] and have at least a guiding effect for the other states.[41] A general *erga omnes partes* effect of judgments was said to require a structural amendment of the architecture of the ECHR to a system comparable to the European Union.[42] The *erga omnes partes* effect of judgments was up for debate in the context of the reform of the ECtHR,[43] a process that had been precipitated by the Interlaken High Level Conference on the Future of the ECtHR. In December 2015 the Steering Committee for Human Rights presented its Report on the Longer-Term Future of the System of the European Court of Human Rights. Regarding the effects of judgments on the High Contracting Parties other than the responding party, the Steering Committee stated that it 'opposes the proposal that there should be a Convention-based legal obligation upon States Parties to abide by final judgments of the Court in cases to which they are not parties'.[44]

Despite the lack of a formal change to that effect, Vondung observes a factual *erga omnes* effect,[45] and Farahat points out that the ECtHR's case law develops 'more general human rights standards' with a view to providing 'guidance for future domestic jurisprudence and legislation within the area of the Council of Europe'.[46] She states that the Court thereby 'produces *erga omnes* effects of its judgments and enhances their effectiveness in domestic law'.[47] Similarly, Arnardóttir argues that the principle of *res interpretata*, which obliges the Contracting Parties to take account of the ECtHR's case law, creates an *erga omnes partes* effect of the Court's case law.[48]

[40] Article 46(1) ECHR.

[41] K Grupp and U Stelkens, 'Zur Berücksichtigung der Europäischen Menschenrechtskonvention bei der Auslegung deutschen Rechts' (2005) *Deutsches Verwaltungsblatt* 133, 134; G Ress, 'Wirkung und Beachtung der Urteile und Entscheidungen der Straßburger Konventionsorgane' (1996) *Europäische Grundrechte-Zeitschrift* 350; H Landau, 'Die Entwicklung der Menschenrechte in der Rechtsprechung des Bundesverfassungsgerichts und des Europäischen Gerichtshofs für Menschenrechte' (2008) *Deutsches Verwaltungsblatt* 1269, 1274.

[42] W Okresek, 'Die Umsetzung der EGMR-Urteile und ihre Überwachung' (2003) *Europäische Grundrechte-Zeitschrift* 168, 174; M Ruffert, 'Die Europäische Menschenrechtskonvention und innerstaatliches Recht' (2007) *Europäische Grundrechte-Zeitschrift* 245, 249.

[43] See OM Arnardóttir, '*Res Interpretata, Erga Omnes* Effect and Role of the Margin of Interpretation in Giving Domestic Effect to the Judgments of the European Court of Human Rights' (2017) 28 *European Journal of International Law* 819, 823.

[44] Steering Committee for Human Rights, CDDH Report on the Longer-Term Future of the System of the European Convention on Human Rights (CDDH Report), Doc CDDH(2015)R 84, Addendum I, 11 December 2015, para 64.

[45] Vondung, *Die Architektur des europäischen Grundrechtsschutzes nach dem Beitritt der EU zur EMRK* 33.

[46] A Farahat, 'Enhancing Constitutional Justice by Using External References: The European Court of Human Rights' Reasoning on the Protection Against Expulsion' (2015) 28 *Leiden Journal of International Law* 303, 320.

[47] ibid.

[48] Arnardóttir, '*Res Interpretata, Erga Omnes* Effect and Role of the Margin of Interpretation' 842, 843.

The next section focuses on Article 8 ECHR by addressing its scope and the justifications for interference listed in Article 8(2) ECHR.

A. The Scope of Article 8 ECHR and its Relevance for Expulsion

Article 8(1) ECHR provides for the right to respect for one's private and family life, home and correspondence. An expulsion mainly encroaches upon the first two limbs, which is why the focus of the following sections rests on family and private life. Even though for a long time the Court addressed family life and private life together, mainly focusing on the former, the right to respect for private life can be invoked independently from family life.

i. Right to Respect for Family Life

Initially the ECtHR had a broad understanding of the notion of family life, which was said to encompass the relationship between children and their parents, between siblings,[49] and between grandchildren and grandparents.[50] Even in cases concerning second-generation migrants who were of age, had not established a family of their own[51] and were not dependent on their parents,[52] the Court referred to the concept of family life. Later, the Court only considered the relationship between parents and their minor children to be covered by the notion of family life,[53] while in cases of grown-up children it required 'specific elements of dependency going beyond the normal affective ties'[54] for the relationship to be covered by Article 8 ECHR.[55]

For a long time, the ECtHR's main focus in expulsion cases rested on the right to respect for family life.[56] The Court's approach was criticised not only for being methodologically flawed, as situations involving migrants of full age should rather

[49] *Moustaquim v Belgium* App no 12313/86 (ECHR, 18 February 1991), para 36.

[50] *Marckx v The United Kingdom* App no 6833/74 (ECHR, 13 June 1979), para 45.

[51] See *Moustaquim v Belgium*.

[52] See *Moustaquim v Belgium*; *Bouchelika v France* App no 23078/93 (ECHR, 22 January 1997). In both cases the applicants were adults and a dependency did not exist.

[53] Zeichen, 'Ausweisungsschutz für integrierte Fremde' 427; F Fritzsch, 'Die Grenzen des völkerrechtlichen Schutzes sozialer Bindungen von Ausländern nach Art. 8 EMRK' (2010) 30 *Zeitschrift für Ausländerrecht und Ausländerpolitik* 16.

[54] *Kaftailova v Latvia* App no 59643/00 (ECHR, 22 June 2006), para 63; *Slivenko v Latvia* App no 48321/99 (ECHR, 2 October 2003), para 97; *A.W. Khan v The United Kingdom* App no 47486/06 (ECHR, 12 January 2010), para 32.

[55] B Aarrass, 'Artikel 8 EVRM als middel tegen uitzetting: de moeizame integratie van "privéleven" in migratiezaken' (2010) *Asiel & Migrantenrecht* 176, 179.

[56] *Slivenko v Latvia*, para 94. See also S Trechsel, 'Artikel 3 EMRK als Schranke der Ausweisung' in K Barwig (ed), *Ausweisung im demokratischen Rechtsstaat* (Baden-Baden, Nomos, 1996) 225, who stated in 1995 that it is not certain whether the right to private life can be invoked in expulsion decisions.

be covered by the concept of private life, but also for disadvantaging those migrants whose parents left the host country or had died.[57]

In the *Slivenko* case the Court clearly differentiated between family life and private life,[58] narrowed the scope of the notion of family life by ruling that only the core family could be covered by this concept,[59] and gave a broader and independent meaning to the concept of private life.[60] The Court's narrow understanding of the concept of family life, which in principle excludes children who have reached the age of majority, was, however, also criticised.[61]

ii. Right to Respect for Private Life

The *Slivenko* case, the judgment of which was issued in 2003, is considered to be the first case 'in which the Court acknowledged that the right to private life may have autonomous standing in cases involving the expulsion of settled migrants'.[62] Therein, the Court held that the 'network of personal, social and economic relations … make up the private life of every human being'.[63] The Court achieved this autonomous standing by introducing a new line of argument[64] and by establishing a conceptual differentiation between the right to family life and the right to private life.[65] Thym notes that the Court limited the scope of application of the concept of family life by including all wider family relationships and other social ties in the notion of private life.[66]

Subsequently, in the *Üner* judgment (2006), the ECtHR acknowledged that the expulsion of a long-term immigrant can violate Article 8 ECHR even in the absence of family ties. The Court stated that not all second-generation migrants necessarily enjoy family life and that 'the expulsion of a settled migrant constitutes an interference with his or her right to respect for private life'.[67] It clarified that Article 8 'protects the right to establish and develop relationships with other human beings and the outside world' and highlighted that 'it must be accepted that

[57] M Caroni, *Privat- und Familienleben zwischen Menschenrecht und Migration* (Berlin, Duncker & Humblot, 1999) 446.

[58] *Slivenko v Latvia*, paras 95–98.

[59] ibid, para 97.

[60] ibid; Roagna, *Protecting the Right to Respect for Private and Family Life under the European Convention on Human Rights* 82.

[61] *Slivenko v Latvia*, partly concurring and partly dissenting opinion of Judge Kovler.

[62] G Lodders, 'Movement and Residence Rights of Third-Country Nationals' in P Boeles, M den Heijer, G Lodders and K Wouters (eds), *European Migration Law*, 2nd edn (Cambridge, Intersentia, 2014) 148.

[63] ibid, para 96.

[64] See Aarrass, 'Artikel 8 EVRM als middel tegen uitzetting' 177.

[65] D Thym, 'Humanitäres Bleiberecht zum Schutz des Privatlebens?' (2007) 29 *Informationsbrief Ausländerrecht* 133, 135; D Thym, 'Menschenrecht auf Legalisierung des Aufenthalts?' (2006) *Europäische Grundrechte-Zeitschrift* 541, 542.

[66] Thym, 'Menschenrecht auf Legalisierung des Aufenthalts?' 541.

[67] *Üner v The Netherlands* App no 46410/99 (ECHR, 18 October 2006), para 59.

the totality of social ties between settled migrants and the community in which they are living constitute part of the concept of "private life" within the meaning of Article 8'.[68] Regarding the differentiation between private life and family life, the ECtHR held that 'it will depend on the circumstances of the particular case whether it is appropriate for the Court to focus on the family life rather than the private life aspect'.[69] However, in the *A.A.* judgment (2011) the Court noted that, while it

> has previously referred to the need to decide on the circumstances of the particular case whether it is appropriate to focus on 'family life' rather than 'private life', it observed that in practice the factors to be examined in order to assess the proportionality of the deportation measure are the same regardless of whether family or private life is engaged.[70]

Moreover, both rights are not mutually exclusive, which was confirmed by the Court in the *Maslov* judgment (2008) and the *Omojudi* judgment (2009), where it held that the measures complained of interfered with the settled migrants' rights to private life and family life.[71]

B. The Requirements of Justification, Article 8(2) ECHR

An interference with the right to respect for private and family life may be justified, provided that it is in accordance with the law, necessary in a democratic society and that it pursues one or more legitimate aims that are listed in Article 8(2) ECHR. While the first and the third criteria are usually unproblematic, the Court regularly addresses the second requirement in more detail.

i. *In Accordance with the Law*

The requirement that the interference be 'in accordance with the law' presupposes that the contested measure has its basis in domestic law,[72] which in turn must be accessible to the person affected by the measure. Moreover, the relevant provision must be formulated with sufficient precision in order to enable its addressees to foresee the possible consequences of their actions and to adapt their conduct accordingly.[73] The requirement of 'foreseeability' of the law does not require

[68] ibid; see also *Maslov v Austria* App no 1638/03 (ECHR, 23 June 2008), para 63; *Trabelsi v Germany* App no 41548/06 (ECHR, 13 October 2011), para 48.

[69] *Üner v The Netherlands*, para 59; *Maslov v Austria*, para 63.

[70] *A.A. v The United Kingdom* App no 8000/08 (ECHR, 20 December 2011), para 49.

[71] *Maslov v Austria*, para 64: ECtHR, *Omojudi v The United Kingdom* App no 1820/08 (ECHR, 24 November 2009), paras 37, 38.

[72] For further information see Caroni, *Privat- und Familienleben zwischen Menschenrecht und Migration* 39.

[73] *Lupsa v Romania* App no 10337/04 (ECHR, 8 June 2006), para 32; *The Association for European Integration and Human Rights and Ekimdzhiev v Bulgaria* App no 62540/00 (ECHR, 29 June 2007), para 71; *Al-Nashif v Bulgaria* App no 50963/99 (ECHR, 20 June 2002), para 119.

a detailed list of every conduct that may trigger an expulsion decision,[74] which would be impossible and impractical. Finally, the law must also 'afford a measure of protection against arbitrary interference by the public authorities with the rights secured in the Convention'.[75]

ii. Legitimate Aims

An expulsion measure that interferes with Article 8(1) ECHR must pursue a legitimate aim. Article 8(2) ECHR contains an exhaustive list of legitimate aims,[76] and makes reference to, for example, national security, public safety or the prevention of disorder and crime. Interestingly, the economic well-being of the country is listed as a legitimate aim,[77] whereas EU law prohibits a limitation of free movement rights on grounds of public policy or public security being invoked to serve economic ends.[78] They constitute autonomous notions[79] but the Court refrained from providing an abstract definition of any of these concepts.[80]

a. National Security

The lack of an abstract definition of the notion of 'national security' was addressed by the ECtHR when it held that 'threats to national security may vary in character and may be unanticipated or difficult to define in advance'.[81] Moreover, the Court stated that 'the notion of "national security" is not capable of being comprehensively defined'[82] and that 'It may, indeed, be a very wide one, with a large margin of appreciation left to the executive to determine what is in the interests of that security'.[83] However, the Court also clarified that the limits of this margin must not be stretched 'beyond its natural meaning'.[84] It reminded states that when they invoke national security they 'may not, in the name of the struggle against espionage and terrorism, adopt whatever measures they deem appropriate' and that they must install adequate and effective measures against abuse.[85] Moreover, it clarified

[74] *C.G. and others v Bulgaria* App no 1365/07 (ECHR, 4 April 2008), para 40.

[75] *Lupsa v Romania*, para 34.

[76] Sander, *Der Schutz des Aufenthalts durch Artikel 8 der Europäischen Menschenrechtskonvention* 143, 144.

[77] *Berrehab v France* App no 53441/99 (ECHR, 10 July 2003), para 26; *Rodrigues da Silva and Hoogkamer v The Netherlands* App no 50435/99 (ECHR, 31 January 2006), para 44.

[78] See Article 27(1) Citizenship Directive.

[79] T Marauhn and J Thorn, 'Privat- und Familienleben' in O Dörr, R Grote and T Marauhn (eds), *EMRK/GG Konkordanzkommentar, Volume 1*, 2nd edn (Tübingen, Mohr Siebeck, 2013) 944.

[80] P Kempees, '"Legitimate Aims" in the Case Law of the European Court of Human Rights' in P Mahoney, F Matscher, H Petzold and L Wildhaber (eds), *Protection des droits de l'homme: la perspective européenne* (Cologne, Carl Heymanns Verlag KG, 2000) 660.

[81] *C.G. and others v Bulgaria*, para 40.

[82] ibid, para 43.

[83] ibid.

[84] ibid.

[85] *Klass and Others v Germany* App no 5029/71 (ECHR, 6 September 1978), paras 49, 50.

in *Al-Nashif* that 'the individual must be able to challenge the executive's assertion that national security is at stake'.[86] Even though the Court acknowledged that the 'executive's assessment of what poses a threat to national security will naturally be of significant weight',[87] it demanded that an 'independent authority must be able to react in cases where invoking that concept has no reasonable basis in the facts or reveals an interpretation of "national security" that is unlawful or contrary to common sense and arbitrary'.[88]

Regarding drug-related crimes and national security, the ECtHR held in *C.G. and others* that a person's involvement in unlawful drug trafficking, also if committed as member of a gang, notwithstanding the 'devastating effect drugs have on people's lives', can hardly be said to be capable 'of impinging on the national security'.[89] The CJEU, by contrast, adopted a different approach in *Tsakouridis* when it held that 'the fight against crime in connection with dealing in narcotics as part of an organised group is capable of being covered by the concept of "imperative grounds of public security"'.[90] The two courts' diverging approaches might derive from the difference in wording in the instruments they interpret. While Article 8(2) ECHR refers to national security, Article 28(3) of the Citizenship Directive refers to public security. The CJEU's approach might also have been influenced by the structure of Article 28 of the Citizenship Directive, which bars expulsion of EU citizens after more than 10 years unless imperative grounds of public security can be invoked.[91] Had the CJEU reached the conclusion that Tsakouridis' crimes were covered by the notion of public policy, but not by the notion of public security, Tsakouridis could not have been expelled.

b. Public Safety, the Prevention of Disorder or Crime

Public safety has been accepted by the Court as a legitimate aim in cases concerning expulsions and has sometimes been mentioned next to the aim of prevention of disorder or crime.[92] The meaning of the notion of 'public safety' is not entirely clear.[93]

The aim of 'prevention of disorder or crime' has not been addressed by the Court in any great depth[94] but it has been accepted repeatedly in expulsion

[86] *Al-Nashif v Bulgaria*, para 124.

[87] ibid.

[88] ibid.

[89] *C.G. and others v Bulgaria*, para 43.

[90] Case C-145/09 *Tsakouridis* ECLI:EU:C:2010:708, [2010] ECR I-11979, para 56.

[91] Article 28(3)(a) Citizenship Directive; for further information see Chapter 1.

[92] *Keles v Germany* App no 32231/02 (ECHR, 27 October 2005), para 55; *Sezen v The Netherlands* App no 50252/99 (ECHR, 21 January 2006), para 41.

[93] Sander, *Der Schutz des Aufenthalts durch Artikel 8 der Europäischen Menschenrechtskonvention* 147.

[94] C Harvey, 'Promoting Insecurity: Public Order, Expulsion and the European Convention on Human Rights' in E Guild and P Minderhoud (eds), *Security of Residence and Expulsion* (The Hague, Kluwer Law International, 2001) 56.

decisions against foreign criminal offenders.[95] Disorder seems to embrace, according to Roagna, 'alarming situations derived from individual or collective conducts threatening peaceful social life'.[96] The concept of 'prevention of disorder and crime' would, if read literally, only refer to future crimes.[97] However, Kempees observes that there is sufficient evidence that the ECtHR is willing to interpret the notion of 'prevention' as including the detection and the investigation of crimes,[98] which means that the focus rests not only on preventive, but also on reactive measures.

iii. Necessary in a Democratic Society

For an interference with Article 8(1) ECHR to be justified, the state measure has to be 'necessary in a democratic society', which requires the interference to be 'justified by a pressing social need' and proportionate to the legitimate aim pursued.[99] The notions of 'necessary in a democratic society' and 'pressing social need', however, are hardly definable in an objective manner.[100]

The *Moustaquim* judgment (1991)[101] is the first judgment where the Court describes an expulsion following criminal convictions as a violation of Article 8 ECHR.[102] Subsequently, criticism arose regarding the lack of precise criteria guiding the balancing process of Article 8 ECHR.[103] Harvey pointed out that the ECtHR's case law on expulsion is casuistic, lacks precision, clarity and consistency, and is therefore hardly predictable.[104] Both Harvey and Kroplin argued that this unpredictability promotes uncertainty.[105] Uncertainty in turn is problematic as it exacerbates, if not precludes, the attempts of national judges to bring their judgments into line with the ECtHR's judgments.[106] The ECtHR's inconsistent methodology leads, said Warbrick, to a situation where more cases are brought before the ECtHR,[107] which in turn increases the Court's workload. Harvey even

[95] *Udeh v Switzerland* App no 12020/09 (ECHR, 16 April 2013), para 42; *Boujlifa v France* App no 25404/94 (ECHR, 21 October 1997), para 38; *Beldjoudi v France* App no 12083/86 (ECHR, 26 March 1992), para 70.

[96] Roagna, *Protecting the Right to Respect for Private and Family Life under the European Convention on Human Rights* 43.

[97] Kempees, '"Legitimate Aims" in the Case Law of the European Court of Human Rights' 666.

[98] ibid.

[99] *Yildiz v Austria* App no 37295/97 (ECHR, 31 October 2002), para 41; *Berrehab v The Netherlands* App no 10730/84 (ECHR, 21 June 1988), para 28.

[100] A McHarg, 'Reconciling Human Rights and the Public Interest' (1999) 62 *Modern Law Review* 671, 686, 687; Farahat, 'Enhancing Constitutional Justice by Using External References' 310.

[101] *Moustaquim v Belgium*.

[102] In *Berrehab v The Netherlands*, the Court assessed for the first time a measure terminating residence, which was unrelated to a criminal conviction, against the background of Article 8 ECHR.

[103] *Beldjoudi v France*, dissenting opinion of Judge Pettiti.

[104] Harvey, 'Promoting Insecurity' 54, 55.

[105] E Koprolin, 'Introduction' in E Guild and P Minderhoud (eds), *Security of Residence and Expulsion* (The Hague, Kluwer Law International, 2001) 4; Harvey, 'Promoting Insecurity' 42.

[106] Harvey, 'Promoting Insecurity' 50.

[107] C Warbrick, 'The Structure of Article 8 ECHR' (1998) 1 *European Human Rights Law Review* 32, 36.

stated that the case-by-case approach adopted by the Court 'runs the risk of calling into question the legitimacy by the Court'.[108] ECtHR judges shared this criticism in their concurring and dissenting opinions and highlighted that the Court's casuistic approach undermines legal certainty.[109] Judge Martens even held that the 'case-by-case approach is a lottery … and a source of embarrassment for the Court'.[110] Other judges highlighted that the application of the proportionality test to second-generation migrants leads to different outcomes in cases in which the factors to be weighed would not seem to differ in any essential respect.[111] The introduction of the '*Boultif* criteria' 10 years after the *Moustaquim* judgment remedied this shortcoming to a certain extent as they provided guidance for the assessment of whether the expulsion is necessary in a democratic society.[112] Many of the criteria that were established in the *Boultif* judgment had already been applied by the Court in earlier case law[113] and are reflected in the above-mentioned non-binding instruments, in particular in Recommendation Rec(2002)4. Later, the *Boultif* criteria were refined by the Court in the *Üner* judgment.

a. The *Boultif* and *Üner* Criteria

In the *Boultif* judgment (2001),[114] the Court established the criteria for assessing whether an interference with Article 8 ECHR is necessary in a democratic society. While the *Boultif* criteria were initially applied in cases concerning the right to respect for family life, they were subsequently extended to cases concerning interference with the migrant's private life.

Mr Boultif, an Algerian national, entered Switzerland in 1992 when he was 25 and married a Swiss national in 1993. A year later, he committed several criminal offences, was convicted and was given a prison sentence of two years. He was released early from prison in August 1999 and the expulsion order prohibited him from entering Switzerland as of January 2000. The ECtHR assessed his case against the background of the notion of 'family life'.[115] The Court saw the main obstacle to expulsion in the difficulties Mr Boultif's wife would have to live in the applicant's country of origin and the difficulties the couple would face in staying together.

[108] Harvey, 'Promoting Insecurity' 44.

[109] *Beldjoudi v France*, concurring opinion of Judge Martens; *Boughanemi v France* App no 22070/93 (ECHR, 27 March 1996), dissenting opinion of Judge Martens, para 4; *Boujlifa v France*, joint dissenting opinion of Judges Baka and van Dijk.

[110] *Boughanemi v France*, dissenting opinion of Judge Martens, para 4.

[111] *Boujlifa v France*, joint dissenting opinion of Judges Baka and van Dijk.

[112] *Üner v The Netherlands*, para 58.

[113] *Beldjoudi v France*; *Nasri v France* App no 19465/92 (ECHR, 13 July 1995); *Boughanemi v France*; *El Boujaïdi v France* App no 25613/94 (ECHR, 26 September 1997); *Boujlifa v France*; *Baghli v France* App no 34374/97 (ECHR, 30 November 1999); *Moustaquim v Belgium*.

[114] *Boultif v Switzerland* App no 54273/00 (ECHR, 2 August 2001).

[115] ibid, para 39.

The Court established the relevant criteria for assessing whether an expulsion is necessary in a democratic society, which are the following:

> [T]he nature and seriousness of the offence committed by the applicant;
>
> the duration of the applicant's stay in the country from which he is going to be expelled;
>
> the time which has elapsed since the commission of the offence and the applicant's conduct during that period;
>
> the nationalities of the various persons concerned;
>
> the applicant's family situation, such as the length of the marriage;
>
> other factors revealing whether the couple lead a real and genuine family life;
>
> whether the spouse knew about the offence at the time when he or she entered into a family relationship;
>
> and whether there are children in the marriage and, if so, their age.[116]

Moreover, the Court pointed out that it

> will also consider the seriousness of the difficulties which the spouse would be likely to encounter in the applicant's country of origin, although the mere fact that a person might face certain difficulties in accompanying her or his spouse cannot in itself preclude expulsion.[117]

The Court applied these criteria to Mr Boultif's case and reached the conclusion that his expulsion amounted to a violation of Article 8 ECHR. The Court considered that his wife could not be expected to live in Algeria as she did not speak Arabic and had no ties with Algeria. In subsequent judgments concerning expulsion, the Court repeatedly referred to these criteria.[118]

In the *Üner* case, the ECtHR's Grand Chamber extended the *Boultif* criteria by two additional criteria, namely:

> [T]he best interest and well-being of the children, in particular the seriousness of the difficulties which any children of the applicant are likely to encounter in the country to which the applicant is to be expelled, and
>
> the solidity of social, cultural and family ties with the host country and with the country of destination.[119]

Moreover, the Court clarified that not all settled migrants who face expulsion or exclusion following a criminal conviction necessarily have a family life. Since the community in which a settled migrant lives forms part of the private life within the meaning of Article 8 ECHR, the Court held that the expulsion of a settled migrant

[116] ibid, para 48.

[117] ibid.

[118] See, eg, *Üner v The Netherlands*, para 57; *Chair and J.B. v Germany* App no 69735/01 (ECHR, 6 December 2007), para 58.

[119] *Üner v The Netherlands*, para 58.

always interferes with the right to private life, irrespective of whether the migrant has established a family.[120] This approach allows the Court to scrutinise a large number of expulsion cases against the background of Article 8 ECHR, as Farahat rightly points out.[121] Furthermore, the Court clarified in the *Üner* judgment that expulsions, which interfere with the right to respect for private life, must be assessed against the first three *Boultif* criteria, which are unrelated to the existence of family life.[122] Notwithstanding the Court's reference to the above-mentioned non-binding Council of Minister's Recommendations and the Parliamentary Assembly's Recommendation,[123] which recommend an enhanced protection against expulsion for long-term resident and settled migrants, even proposing a ban expulsion in certain cases,[124] the Court did not find a violation of Article 8 ECHR in the *Üner* case.

b. Application of the *Boultif* and *Üner* Criteria

The Court must strike a fair balance between the interests of the individual and the interests of the state that seeks to expel the individual.[125] The Court's balancing process is guided by the *Boultif* and *Üner* criteria, which provide a certain degree of legal certainty. Nevertheless, it remains unclear whether these criteria have the same value or whether some criteria are ascribed more weight in the balancing process than others.

In 2006 several ECtHR judges raised the question of how to assign relative weight to the various criteria developed by the Court as well as whether there is an 'implicit emergence of a method which gives priority to one criterion, relating to the offence, and treats the others as secondary or marginal?'[126] In the literature, several suggestions were made to determine the decisive criterion or, in the absence of one decisive criterion, to explore whether there exists a hierarchy of criteria.

Already in 1999, two years before the *Boultif* judgment, Alleweldt argued that the decisive criterion seems to be the age at which the migrant entered the host country and whether s/he was born there.[127] In 2007 Lambert pointed to the strength of family links as well as the seriousness of the offence as the decisive factors in the balancing process. She argued that it appeared the Court preferred a 'subjective appreciation of the degree of separation experienced' by the individual

[120] ibid, para 59.

[121] Farahat, 'Enhancing Constitutional Justice by Using External References' 311.

[122] *Üner v The Netherlands*, para 59.

[123] ibid, paras 37, 55.

[124] ibid.

[125] *C. v Belgium* App no 21794/93 (ECHR, 7 August 1996), para 36; *El Boujaïdi v France*, para 40; *Boujlifa v France*, para 43; *Boultif v Switzerland*, para 47.

[126] *Üner v The Netherlands*, joint dissenting opinions of Judges Costa, Zupančič and Türmen, para 16.

[127] R Alleweldt, 'Ausweisung und Abeschiebungsschutz' in K Barwig, G Brinkmann and K Hailbronner (eds), *Neue Regierung – Neue Ausländerpolitik?, Hohenheimer Tage zum Ausländerrecht* (Baden-Baden, Nomos, 1999) 280.

concerned over any specific criteria.[128] Moreover, she highlighted that in cases regarding integrated aliens, the Court seemed to shift its focus from elements such as the length of stay, schooling and social as well as economic links, to the existence of strong and effective family ties and the seriousness of the offence.[129] In 2008 Steinorth held that the different outcomes in the Court's judgments 'can neither be conclusively explained by the severity of the offences committed nor by the degree of the applicant's integration within the community'.[130] In 2009 Deibel pointed out that the Court takes the seriousness of the criminal offence into account and that it is particularly disadvantageous for the foreigner to be involved in drug-related offences.[131] In 2011 Kirkagac noted that the Court increasingly referred to the risk of reoffending[132] but also conceded that the Court was not consistent regarding this approach.[133]

Several scholars criticise the lack of explanation regarding the balancing or grading of criteria.[134] Farahat points out that the introduction of the *Boultif* and *Üner* criteria does not seem to have improved the structure or the foreseeability of the balancing process.[135] Steinorth holds that as long as the Court does not assign a primary weight to a criterion, 'the balancing process will continue to allow for diametrically opposed interferences'. The Court should, argues Steinorth, take a clear stance in order to give guidance to applicants and national authorities.[136] Stoyanova highlights that the 'Court does not follow a strict structure in its argumentation' and that 'it is unclear how much weight each factor has'.[137] She notes that this balancing style creates the impression 'that the Court can always reframe the factual substratum of a case to fit into a certain outcome'.[138]

Others acknowledge that a prioritisation of criteria is not always possible. Steinorth rightly points out that it 'is difficult to see how the "best interest and well-being of the children" involved can reasonably be balanced against the "nature and seriousness of the offence" committed by the applicant'.[139] Giving less importance

[128] Lambert, *The Position of Aliens in Relation to the European Convention on Human Rights* 70.

[129] ibid.

[130] C Steinorth, '*Üner v. The Netherlands*: Expulsion of Long-term Immigrants and the Right to Respect for Private and Family Life' (2008) 8 *Human Rights Law Review* 185, 186.

[131] K Deibel, 'Die Ausweisung von Ausländern unter Berücksichtigung der Rechtsprechung des Europäischen Gerichtshofes für Menschenrechte' (2009) 29 *Zeitschrift für Ausländerrecht und Ausländerpolitik* 121, 122.

[132] N Kirkagac, *Verdachtsausweisungen im deutschen Rechtsstaat* (Frankfurt, Peter Lang, 2011) 121.

[133] ibid, 123.

[134] Steinorth, '*Üner v. The Netherlands*' 194; V Stoyanova, 'Populism, Exceptionality and the Right of Migrants to Family Life Under the European Convention on Human Rights' (2018) 10 *European Journal of Legal Studies* 83, 118, 125.

[135] A Farahat, 'The Exclusiveness of Inclusion: On the Boundaries of Human Rights in Protecting Transnational and Second Generation Migrants' (2009) 11 *European Journal of Migration and Law* 253, 260.

[136] Steinorth, '*Üner v. The Netherlands*' 195, 196.

[137] Stoyanova, 'Populism, Exceptionality and the Right of Migrants to Family Life' 118.

[138] ibid.

[139] Steinorth, '*Üner v. The Netherlands*' 195.

to the right of the children because their father committed very serious crimes would reduce the fair balance approach *ad absurdum*.[140] Frowein acknowledges the difficulties resulting from the ECtHR's casuistic approach for domestic courts but concludes that this approach seems to be adequate.[141] Likewise, Thym points out that the *Boultif* criteria 'illustrate the willingness of the Court to build a coherent case law which facilitates the autonomous application of Article 8 ECHR by domestic courts'.[142] Alexy also refrains from sharing the concerns of the critics and highlights that computability and predictability are characteristics of a system of expulsion decisions which relies upon general prevention. He argues that the criteria developed by the Court render its decision-making process more transparent and structured.[143]

The criticism of the Court's case law must be seen in the context of the institutional setting in which the Court operates. The subsidiarity of the ECHR weakens the Court's position and the lack of enforcement mechanisms makes the Court dependent on the Contracting States' willingness to implement its judgments.[144] Moreover, immigration, residence and expulsion of foreigners are delicate policy areas, which are said to constitute, next to naturalisation, the core of state sovereignty.[145] When deciding on the compatibility of an expulsion decision with a Convention article, the Court has the difficult task of fulfilling its guardian function regarding the Convention right(s), on the one hand, and of respecting the Contracting Party's autonomy in matters of immigration law, on the other hand.[146] Given that the Contracting Parties refrained from addressing the issue of immigration in the Convention,[147] it is – despite all criticism – already remarkable that the Court established the *Boultif* criteria. A clarification of the weight that each of the *Boultif* criteria should be afforded in the balancing process would indeed enhance clarity and predictability. Yet, the ambiguity seems to be intended as the Court held that the weight attached to these criteria will 'inevitably vary according

[140] ibid.

[141] J Frowein and W Peukert, *Europäische Menschenrechtskonvention* (Kehl am Rhein, N. P. Engel Verlag, 1985) 306.

[142] Thym, 'Respect for Private and Family Life under Article 8 ECHR in Immigration Cases' 112.

[143] H Alexy, 'Subsumtion oder Abwägung – Was gilt im Ausweisungsrecht?' (2011) *Deutsches Verwaltungsblatt* 1185, 1189.

[144] Y Arai-Takahashi, *The Margin of Appreciation Doctrine and the Principle of Proportionality in the Jurisdiction of the ECHR* (Antwerp, Intersentia, 2001) 68.

[145] F Gatta, 'The Problematic Management of Migratory Flows in Europe and its Impact on Human Rights: The Prohibition of Collective Expulsion of Aliens in the Case-law of the European Court of Human Rights' in G Bruno, F Palombino and A Di Stefano (eds), *Migration Issues before International Courts and Tribunals* (Rome, CNR edizioni 2019) 121; W Kluth, 'Reichweite und Folgen der Europäisierung des Ausländer- und Asylrechts' (2006) 26 *Zeitschrift für Ausländerrecht und Ausländerpolitik* 1.

[146] Thym, 'Respect for Private and Family Life under Article 8 ECHR in Immigration Cases' 87; Farahat, 'The Exclusiveness of Inclusion' 257; S Morano-Foadi and S Andreadakis, 'The Convergence of the European Legal System in the Treatment of Third-country Nationals in Europe: The ECJ and ECtHR Jurisprudence' (2011) 22 *EJIL* 1071, 1080.

[147] Gatta, 'The Problematic Management of Migratory Flows in Europe' 124; Thym, 'Respect for Private and Family Life under Article 8 ECHR in Immigration Cases' 103, note 65.

to the specific circumstances of each case'[148] and that not all criteria will be relevant in every case.[149] Moreover, the Court allows domestic courts to decide on the weight ascribed to the criteria by stating that 'it is in the first instance for the domestic courts to decide, in the context of the case before them, which are the relevant factors and what weight is to accord to each factor'.[150] The subsidiarity of the Court's assessment is also illustrated by its emphasis on Contracting States' procedural obligations. In *Paposhvili* the Court held:

> [I]t is not for the Court to conduct an assessment, from the perspective of Article 8 of the Convention, of the impact of removal on the applicant's family life in the light of his state of health. In that connection the Court considers that this task not only falls to the domestic authorities, which are competent in the matter, but also constitutes a procedural obligation with which they must comply in order to ensure the effectiveness of the right to respect for family life. As the Court has observed above …, the machinery of complaint to the Court is subsidiary to national systems safeguarding human rights.[151]

At the same time the Court also ensures that it has the last word. In the *A.A.* judgment, the Court held that 'the State's margin of appreciation in this regard goes hand in hand with European supervision and the Court is therefore empowered to give the final ruling on whether an expulsion measure is reconcilable with Article 8'.[152]

While the ascription of a specific weight to each *Boultif* criterion or the creation of a hierarchy among them would simplify their application at the national level, it might result in a loss of flexibility to accommodate the particulars of the specific cases, potentially leading to situations where the facts of the individual case are not sufficiently considered due to a schematic application of these criteria.

c. The Margin of Appreciation

The ECtHR grants the Contracting Parties a margin of appreciation when determining whether an expulsion measure is necessary in a democratic society and proportionate to the legitimate aim pursued.[153] While the judge-made doctrine[154] of the margin of appreciation is criticised for being wide, blurred and creating legal uncertainty[155] it is also described as a 'doctrine' of judicial self-restraint,[156]

[148] *Maslov v Austria*, para 70; *A.A. v The United Kingdom*, para 57.

[149] *A.A. v The United Kingdom*, para 57.

[150] ibid.

[151] *Paposhvili v Belgium* App no 41738/10 (ECHR, 13 December 2016), para 224.

[152] *A.A. v The United Kingdom*, para 57.

[153] *Maslov v Austria*, para 76; *Boughanemi v France*, para 41.

[154] J Rubel, *Entscheidungsfreiräume in der Rechtsprechung des Europäischen Gerichtshofes für Menschenrechte und des Europäischen Gerichtshofes* 28.

[155] A Lester, 'The European Court of Human Rights After 50 Years' (2009) 4 *European Human Rights Law Review* 461, 474, 475; A Rupp-Swienty, *Die Doktrin von der margin of appreciation in der Rechtsprechung des Europäischen Gerichtshofs für Menschenrechte* (Munich, VVF, 1999) 260–64.

[156] T O'Donnell, 'The Margin of Appreciation Doctrine' (1982) 4 *Human Rights Quarterly* 474, 495; D Spielmann, 'Allowing the Right Margin: The European Court of Human Rights and the National

a natural product of the distribution of powers,[157] or a natural product of the principle of subsidiarity.[158]

The crucial question is how and according to which criteria the Court determines the width of the margin of appreciation. In general, criteria such as the provision invoked, the nature of the right protected, the nature of the activities being restricted, the aim pursued by the contested interference, the severity of the interference, specific national or regional characteristics, and specific situations are aspects that are taken into consideration by the Court when determining the margin of discretion.[159]

A narrow margin of appreciation for the Contracting State is generally said to result from a substantial consensus among the Contracting States.[160] If the existence or identity of an individual is at stake[161] or if the state measure concerns rights that are fundamental to democracy,[162] the margin of discretion will also be narrow. If, by contrast, procedural aspects are affected,[163] or if the measure concerns the Contracting States' social and economic policy,[164] the Court usually grants a wide margin of appreciation.

The application of these criteria to cases concerning expulsion results in a relatively wide margin of appreciation due to a lack of consensus among the Contracting Parties. While some Contracting Parties have adopted provisions that bar expulsions of migrants who were born in the state or arrived there at an early age, the Court also noted that the majority of states allow for the deportation of second-generation migrants.[165] Farahat observes that the Court did not find

Margin of Appreciation Doctrine: Waiver of Subsidiarity of European Review?' (2012) 14 *Cambridge Yearbook of European Legal Studies* 381, 383; P Mahony, 'Marvellous Richness of Diversity or Invidious Cultural Relativism?' (1998) 19 *Human Rights Law Journal* 1, 4.

[157] Mahony, 'Marvellous Richness of Diversity or Invidious Cultural Relativism?' 3.

[158] Arai-Takahashi, *The Margin of Appreciation Doctrine and the Principle of Proportionality in the Jurisdiction of the ECHR* 240; Rubel, *Entscheidungsfreiräume in der Rechtsprechung des Europäischen Gerichtshofes für Menschenrechte und des Europäischen Gerichtshofes* 50.

[159] Spielmann, 'Allowing the Right Margin' 394–409; Mahony, 'Marvellous Richness of Diversity or Invidious Cultural Relativism?' 5, 6; C Ovey, 'The Margin of Appreciation and Article 8 of the Convention' (1998) 19 *Human Rights Law Journal* 10, 11, 12; J Schokkenbroek, 'The Basis, Nature and Application of the Margin-of-Appreciation Doctrine in the Case-Law of the European Court of Human Rights' (1998) 19 *Human Rights Law Journal* 30, 35.

[160] S Greer, 'The Interpretation of the European Convention on Human Rights: Universal Principle or Margin of Appreciation' (2010) 3 *UCL Human Rights Review* 1, 4; I de la Rasilla del Moral, 'The Increasingly Marginal Appreciation of the Margin-of-Appreciation Doctrine' (2006) 6 *German Law Journal* 611, 617; O'Donnell, 'The Margin of Appreciation Doctrine' 495; Schokkenbroek, 'The Basis, Nature and Application of the Margin-of-Appreciation Doctrine in the Case-Law of the European Court of Human Rights' 34; M Tümay, 'The "Margin of Appreciation Doctrine" Developed by the European Court of Human Rights' (2008) 5 *Ankara Law Review* 201, 231; Roagna, *Protecting the Right to Respect for Private and Family Life under the European Convention on Human Rights* 45.

[161] F Fritzsch, *Der Schutz sozialer Bindungen von Ausländern* (Baden-Baden, Nomos, 2009) 78.

[162] O'Donnell, 'The Margin of Appreciation Doctrine' 495; Tümay, 'The "Margin of Appreciation Doctrine" Developed by the European Court of Human Rights' 219.

[163] Fritzsch, *Der Schutz sozialer Bindungen von Ausländern* 78.

[164] Rubel, *Entscheidungsfreiräume in der Rechtsprechung des Europäischen Gerichtshofes für Menschenrechte und des Europäischen Gerichtshofes* 38, 39.

[165] *Üner v The Netherlands*, paras 39, 55.

a common trend among the Contracting Parties of providing for an enhanced protection against expulsion of long-term and second-generation migrants.[166] Despite the relatively wide margin of discretion that is granted to the Contracting States, the final assessment as to whether the interference corresponds to a pressing social need, whether it is proportionate to the legitimate aim pursued,[167] and whether it is reconcilable with the Convention right, rests with the Court.

III. Interests of the Individual vs Interests of the State

In order to determine whether the state's interference with the individual's right to respect for private or family life can be justified pursuant to Article 8(2) ECHR, the Court has to conduct a balancing process between the competing interest of the foreigner and the interests of the state, which is guided by the above-addressed *Boultif* and *Üner* criteria. The outcome of this balancing process is influenced by a variety of factors, such as the starting point of the Court's assessment, the way in which the *Boultif* and *Üner* criteria are interpreted, the allocation of the burden of proof and the (ostensible) differences between positive and negative obligations.

The crucial question, as Andreadakis, Morano-Foadi and Steinorth put it, is whether the ECtHR gives primary importance to the interests of the state or to the rights of the (long-term resident) foreigner.[168] Even though no definite answer can be given to this question due to the Court's casuistic approach, the following sections address some of these aspects in order to provide insights into the question of whether the ECtHR gives primary importance to the interests of the state or the interests of the individual.

A. The Starting Point of the Court's Assessment

The starting point that the Court chooses for balancing the interests of the individual against the interests of the state sheds light on the rationale of its judgment. Moreover, it constitutes the foundation for the balancing process and can impact on its outcome. The Court has often stated that

> it is the Court's settled case law, that as a matter of well-established international law, and subject to their treaty obligations, including those arising from the Convention, Contracting States have the right to control the entry, residence and removal of aliens.[169]

[166] Farahat, 'Enhancing Constitutional Justice by Using External References' 317.

[167] *Berrehab v The Netherlands*, para 28.

[168] Steinorth, '*Üner v. The Netherlands*' 196; Morano-Foadi and Andreadakis, 'The Convergence of the European Legal System in the Treatment of Third-country Nationals in Europe' 1085.

[169] *N v The United Kingdom* App no 26565/05 (ECHR, 27 May 2008), para 30, see also *Üner v The Netherlands*, para 58.

In light of the scope of the Court's jurisdiction, which 'shall extend to all cases concerning the interpretation and application of the present Convention',[170] the Court could choose a Convention right as its starting point. By highlighting the Contracting Parties' right to determine the entry, residence and removal of foreigners, the Court seems to grant the interests of the state priority over the rights of the individual. This might indicate that the rights of the latter will only be considered within the framework of the rights and powers of the Contracting States and as subordinated to them.

Toner refers to the 'basic point of departure for Strasbourg' and stresses that it 'remains one of subjection and subordination of the individual and his or her choice of family residence to the interests of the State'.[171] Similarly, van Walsum argues that the interests of the state seem to prevail over those of settled migrants in the ECtHR's judgments.[172] However, it must also be noted that the starting point of the Court's balancing process is not always indicative of the outcome of the case, given that the Court emphasised the right of Contracting States to control the entry and residence of aliens also in cases where it found a violation of the Convention.[173]

B. The *Üner* Criterion of the Individual's Ties with the Host State

The criteria that are taken into consideration in the balancing process, which have been listed by the Court in the *Boultif* and *Üner* judgments, the weight that is ascribed to these criteria and the way in which they are interpreted have an impact on the outcome of the balancing process. The criteria, their interpretation and their weight in the balancing process differ, depending on the circumstances of the case, and shed light on the judgment's rationale.

A criterion that was established by the Court in the *Üner* judgment is the 'solidity of social, cultural and family ties with the host country and with the country of destination'.[174] Several aspects are considered when assessing the individual's ties with the 'host' state.[175] One aspect, which was evaluated by the Court even before the *Üner* judgment, is the wish of the foreigner to acquire the nationality of the host state and the application for naturalisation, respectively.[176] In several cases,

[170] Article 45 ECHR.

[171] Toner, 'Article 8 ECHR – Full Judicial Scrutiny?' 49.

[172] S van Walsum, 'Jurisprudentie over migratierecht en gezinsleven. Deel II: Artikel 8 EVRM' (2010) *Asiel & Migrantenrecht* 520, 527.

[173] *Mehemi v France* App no 25017/94 (ECHR, 26 September 1997), para 34; *Amrollahi v Denmark* App no 56811/00 (ECHR, 11 November 2002), para 33.

[174] *Üner v The Netherlands*, para 58.

[175] See *Beldjoudi v France*, para 77; *Moustaquim v Belgium*, para 45.

[176] *Beldjoudi v France*, para 77; *Boughanemi v France*, para 44; *El Boujaïdi v France*, para 40; *Boujlifa v France*, para 44; *Keles v Germany*, para 64.

the Court had emphasised the fact that the applicant had the possibility to acquire the nationality of the expelling state but chose not to acquire it, and used it to the detriment of the applicant.[177]

In *Boughanemi* the Court inferred from the lack of the foreigner's wish to acquire the nationality of the host state the existence of links with his country of nationality and ultimately ascribed a greater weight to the government's arguments. It held that the applicant

> kept his Tunisian nationality and, so it would seem, never manifested a wish to become French. It is probable, as the Government pointed out, that he retained links with Tunisia that went beyond the mere fact of his nationality. Before the Commission he did not claim that he could not speak Arabic, or that he had cut all his ties with his country of birth, or that he had not returned there after his deportation.[178]

Apart from the fact that the Court seems to be satisfied with a probability, the lack of the wish to acquire the nationality of the host state does not necessarily imply the existence of links with the home state and instead can have manifold causes. The Court's approach has been criticised as the protection offered by Article 8 ECHR depends neither on an application for naturalisation nor on loyalty towards the 'host' state.[179]

C. The Burden of Proof

Another aspect that might provide insight into the question of whether the interests of the state or the interests of the foreigner prevail is the allocation of the burden of proof. In principle, the individual has to demonstrate that the state measure interferes with his or her Convention rights,[180] whereas the state must provide an objective justification for the interference.[181] The obligation to justify the interference normally falls on the state[182] as it has to 'establish why in its assessment of the interests of the state and those of the person in question, it was necessary to let the interests of the State prevail'.[183] In some instances, however, the margin of

[177] *Boughanemi v France*, para 44; *El Boujaïdi v France*, para 40; *Boujlifa v France*, para 44: 'On the other hand, it seems that he did not show any desire to acquire French nationality at the time when he was entitled to do so'; *Kaya v Germany* App no 31753/02 (ECHR, 28 June 2007), para 64.

[178] *Boughanemi v France*, para 44.

[179] R Gutmann, 'Menschenrechtliche Fragen an das Ausländergesetz' (2000) 22 *Informationsbrief Ausländerrecht* 1, 5. For further criticism and analysis of this requirement see M-B Dembour, 'Human Rights Law and National Sovereignty in Collusion: The Plight of Quasi-Nationals at Strasbourg' (2003) 21 *Netherlands Quarterly of Human Rights* 86.

[180] Roagna, *Protecting the Right to Respect for Private and Family Life under the European Convention on Human Rights* 35.

[181] E Brems and J Gerards, *Shaping Rights in the ECHR: The Role of the European Court of Human Rights in Determining the Scope of Human Rights* (Cambridge, CUP, 2014) 2.

[182] Farahat, 'The Exclusiveness of Inclusion' 263.

[183] Lodders, 'Movement and Residence Rights of Third-Country Nationals' 151.

appreciation can lead to a factual shift of the burden of proof with the result that the individual has to prove not only the interference with his or her Convention right, but also that the interference is disproportionate.[184]

Normally, the foreigner has to prove the absence of ties with the country of origin.[185] In the *Amrollahi* case, however, the Court argued that 'nothing suggests that the applicant has maintained strong links, if any, with Iran'.[186] In light of the political situation in Iran in 1987 and the fact that the individual fled from Iran, this assumption is likely accurate. Nevertheless, it is remarkable that the Court imposed the burden of showing that the individual still had links with his country of origin on the respondent state, even though the individual spoke the language of his country of origin, had conducted all his schooling there and had only lived in the host state for eight years before he was charged with a crime.

The Court adopted a similar approach in the *Mehemi* case, where it did not require the individual to prove the existence of links with his country of origin, but rather imposed the burden of proof on the state. The Court was not satisfied with the proof submitted by the government and held that 'it has not been established that the applicant had links with Algeria other than his nationality'.[187] In contrast to the previous section, where the Court seemed to give priority to the interests of the state, the cases of *Amrollahi* and *Mehemi* suggest the opposite.

D. Positive and Negative Obligations

Finally, the distinction – or rather, the missing distinction – between states' positive and negative obligations could shed light on the question of whether the Court attaches primary importance to the interests of the individual or to the interests of the state. Positive obligations refer to the duty of the state to protect a right and can derive from the scope of the right itself. In order to determine whether or not a positive obligation has been breached, the Court assesses whether a fair balance between the general interest of the community and the interests of the individual has been struck.[188] An exception is the protection against ill-treatment, which is prohibited under Article 3 ECHR, as this protection is absolute and cannot be weighed against the interests of the community.[189] While an expulsion decision is usually not covered by the concept of positive obligations, the request of an expelled foreigner to be readmitted to the territory of the expelling state could fall under the scope of positive obligations.

[184] Farahat, 'The Exclusiveness of Inclusion' 263.
[185] Fritzsch, *Der Schutz sozialer Bindungen von Ausländern* 203.
[186] *Amrollahi v Denmark*, para 38.
[187] *Mehemi v France*, para 36.
[188] *Rees v United Kingdom* App no 9532/81 (ECHR, 17 October 1986), para 37.
[189] *Saadi v Italy* App no 37201/06 (ECHR, 28 February 2008), paras 138, 139; *Chahal v The United Kingdom* App no 22414/93 (ECHR, 15 November 1996), para 80.

Negative obligations, by contrast, refer to the duty of the state to refrain from interferences. Consequently, the Court first assesses whether the state action falls within the scope of the Convention right, secondly, whether it interferes with the Convention right and finally whether the interference can be justified.[190] Expulsion decisions are in principle covered by the notion of 'negative obligation' as they concern the duty of the state to refrain from an interference with the individual's right to respect to private and family life.

Several scholars have pointed out that the Court's case law reveals that states have a broader margin of appreciation in cases regarding positive obligations and that the ECtHR conducts a weaker scrutiny thereof, with the result that it is less likely to find a violation of the Convention right.[191] Van Dijk observes that, in cases concerning positive obligations, it seems 'appropriate that … the Court takes special account of the State's interests', whereas in cases in which the Contracting State has to refrain from interference 'the interests of the individual are at the foreground'.[192] Caroni also notes that, in the case of positive obligations, the position of the foreigner is 'weaker' compared to a situation in which a negative obligation is at stake.[193] It is therefore decisive whether a positive or a negative obligation is at issue; at the same time, it is problematic that the dividing line between the two sets of obligations is not clear. Furthermore, Van Dijk points out that the ECtHR used to apply a fair balance test in determining (the existence of) a positive obligation, whereas it applies a justification test in cases of negative obligations.[194]

The Court seems to have eliminated the difference between positive and negative obligations in the *Gül* judgment.[195] The *Gül* case revolved around the question whether parents who resided in Switzerland could be joined by their children who remained in Turkey. It was unclear whether the obligation resting upon the state was positive or negative. The Court held, with regard to the different obligations, that 'the applicable principles are nonetheless similar. In both contexts regard must be had to the fair balance that has to be struck between the competing interests of the individual and of the community as a whole'.[196] The ECtHR applied the fair balance test, which takes special account of the state's interests, and found that Switzerland had not interfered with the rights anchored in Article 8 ECHR.[197]

[190] Zeichen, 'Ausweisungsschutz für integrierte Fremde, Zeitschrift für öffentliches Recht' 447.

[191] Stoyanova, 'Populism, Exceptionality and the Right of Migrants to Family Life Under the European Convention on Human Rights' 103, 105; Ovey, 'The Margin of Appreciation and Article 8 of the Convention' 10; Rupp-Swienty, *Die Doktrin von der margin of appreciation in der Rechtsprechung des Europäischen Gerichtshofs für Menschenrechte* 66, 79.

[192] P van Dijk, 'Protection of "Integrated" Aliens Against Expulsion under the European Convention on Human Rights' in E Guild and P Minderhoud (eds), *Security of Residence and Expulsion* (The Hague, Kluwer Law International, 2001) 30.

[193] Caroni, *Privat- und Familienleben zwischen Menschenrecht und Migration* 433.

[194] van Dijk, 'Protection of "Integrated" Aliens Against expulsion under the European Convention on Human Rights' 27.

[195] ibid, 31; *Gül v Switzerland* App no 23218/94 (ECHR, 19 February 1996).

[196] *Gül v Switzerland*, para 38.

[197] ibid, para 43.

In later judgments the Court applied the fair balance test to cases concerning negative obligations or declared that, since the applicable criteria in cases of negative and positive obligations are similar, it was not necessary to determine in which of the two categories the impugned measure falls.[198] This reasoning is reflected in the *Paposhvili* case, where the Court held

> that in the context of both its positive and its negative obligations, the State must strike a fair balance between the competing interests of the individual and of society as a whole, and that the extent of the State's obligations will vary according to the particular circumstances of the persons involved and the general interest.[199]

Given that the legal position of the foreigner is weaker in cases assessed under the heading of a positive obligation or the 'fair balance test', the lack of a dividing line between positive and negative obligations is problematic. In principle, an expulsion decision falls under the heading of negative obligations according to which the state has a duty to refrain from an interference with the individual's right, which moves the interests of the individual to the foreground. However, given that the Court levelled the differences between positive and negative obligations, such a conclusion is called into question.

In sum, a definite answer to the question of whether the Court accords priority to the interests of the state or those of the Contracting State cannot be provided as the Court's case law is highly casuistic. In some cases, the Court is prepared to shift the burden of proof regarding a fact that in principle has to be demonstrated by the applicant to the respondent government, as evidenced in *Mehemi* and *Amrollahi*, which suggests that the Court gives primary importance to the interests of the individual. In other cases, by contrast, the non-acquisition of nationality of the 'host' Member State led the Court to conclude that the individual retained links with his country of nationality and used this fact to the detriment of the individual. Moreover, the starting point of the Court's assessment can, but does not necessarily have to, indicate the outcome of the balancing process.

IV. Summary and Conclusions

Expulsion measures often interfere with a migrant's right to respect for private and family life, which is protected by Article 8(1) ECHR. An interference can be justified according to Article 8(2) ECHR if the expulsion is in accordance with the law and necessary in a democratic society and if it pursues a legitimate aim. The question of whether the state measure is necessary in a democratic society requires a balancing between the interests of the foreigner and the interests of the state.

[198] *El Boujaïdi v France*, para 40; *Boujlifa v France*, para 43; *Boultif v Switzerland*, para 47; *Konstantinov v The Netherlands* App no 16351/03 (ECHR, 26 April 2006); *Jeunesse v The Netherlands* App no 12738/10 (ECHR, 3 October 2014), para 106.

[199] *Paposhvili v Belgium*, para 121.

The criteria that guide this balancing process have been established by the Court in the *Boultif* and *Üner* judgments.[200] Given that the Contracting Parties to the ECHR refrained from addressing the issue of migration in the Convention,[201] the development of the *Boultif* and *Üner* criteria by the ECtHR already constitutes a considerable achievement. The creation of this list of criteria not only offers guidance to domestic institutions, it simultaneously provides a protection scheme for the individual. Farahat argues that the *Boultif* and *Üner* judgments constitute a turning point as the Court 'has developed a meaningful new standard' for the protection of long-term and settled migrants by establishing these criteria.[202]

The Court did not ascribe an abstract value to the *Boultif* and *Üner* criteria and refrained from introducing a hierarchy among them. Even though the Court attaches a certain weight in its judgments to specific criteria, such as extended duration of residence or the fact that the foreigner committed a drug-related crime, this weight can differ from case to case. The ECtHR clarified that the weight attached to these criteria will 'inevitably vary according to the specific circumstances of each case'.[203] The Court's casuistic approach results in a greater flexibility and enhances the possibility to take the particulars of the individual case into account, but it also reduces predictability and legal certainty.

Despite this valid criticism, the Court's case law must be placed in context. The Court has to combine its guardian function towards the Convention's rights, on the one hand, and respect the autonomy of national immigration and expulsion decisions, on the other. The decision of who is entitled to reside on the national territory touches upon the core of state sovereignty. Therefore, the Court generally grants states a broader margin of appreciation in migration matters. This has an impact on the determination of what is necessary in a democratic society and thus on the legitimate justifications that can be invoked for an expulsion decision. Nevertheless, as Farahat rightly points out, the margin of discretion narrows in cases of long-term or second-generation migrants.[204] This is also underpinned by the protection scheme that is inherent in the *Boultif* and *Üner* criteria, which obliges states to consider the 'length of the applicant's stay in the country from which he is going to be expelled' and 'the solidity of social, cultural and family ties with the host country and with the country of destination'. These criteria emphasise the special position of settled migrants, even though the weight that is attached to these criteria can differ from case to case. Given that the ECHR and the ECtHR have a subsidiary function, the attachment of an abstract weight to a specific *Boultif* or *Üner* criterion would better be conducted at the national level. This does not imply that states are entirely free in this process, as the Contracting

[200] *Boultif v Switzerland*, para 48; *Üner v The Netherlands*, para 58.

[201] Thym, 'Respect for Private and Family Life under Article 8 ECHR in Immigration Cases' 103, note 65.

[202] Farahat, 'Enhancing Constitutional Justice by Using External References' 311, 312.

[203] *Maslov v Austria*, para 70; *A.A. v The United Kingdom*, para 57.

[204] Farahat, 'Enhancing Constitutional Justice by Using External References' 311.

Parties to the ECHR remain subject to the ECtHR's scrutiny. This was clarified by the Court when it stated that the state's 'margin of appreciation in this regard goes hand in hand with European supervision and the Court is therefore empowered to give the final ruling on whether an expulsion measure is reconcilable with Article 8'.[205] Apart from these institutional considerations, the Court's abstention from attaching an abstract weight to the *Boultif* and *Üner* criteria could have another advantage. An abstract weight might abet a schematic application of the criteria at the national level and result in insufficient consideration of the particulars of the individual case.

A brief comparison with the EU level might provide further explanations as to why the ECtHR refrained from attaching an abstract weight to the *Boultif* and *Üner* criteria. At the EU level, the public policy and public security exceptions serve as a justification for limiting fundamental freedoms. These limitations were already contained in Directive 64/221/EEC. They were subsequently refined by the CJEU's case law and further specified in the Citizenship Directive. First, the Citizenship Directive contains certain prohibitions, such as the prohibition on basing an expulsion decision on general preventive considerations[206] or on invoking economic grounds.[207] Comparable 'prohibitions' do not exist at the ECHR level. Article 8(2) ECHR even lists economic well-being as a legitimate interest for limiting the right to respect for private and family life. Second, Article 28(1) of the Citizenship Directive contains a non-exhaustive list of criteria that have to be considered in the balancing process and which resemble the *Boultif*/*Üner* criteria established by the ECtHR. The Convention, by contrast, refrains from establishing a list of criteria that have to be considered in the balancing process. Third, the Citizenship Directive even attaches a specific weight to the interests of the individual by requiring serious grounds of public policy or public security to justify an expulsion after five years of lawful residence.[208] After 10 years of lawful residence or if the Union citizen is a minor, only imperative grounds of public security can justify an expulsion.[209] While the relevant legal instrument at the EU level, the Citizenship Directive, already attaches a specific weight to the criteria that have to be considered in the balancing process, the ECHR does not even contain a list of criteria. Therefore, it is unsurprising that the ECtHR refrains from ascribing an abstract weight to the *Boultif* and *Üner* criteria.

Despite the fact that the statutory requirements for an expulsion decision against an EU citizen are stricter and more specific at the EU level compared to the Council of Europe, the CJEU does not always adopt a clear standpoint either.

[205] *A.A. v The United Kingdom*, para 57.

[206] Article 27(2) Citizenship Directive; admittedly, this requirement was not contained in the predecessor Directive 64/221/EEC. The predecessor contained the requirement of a 'personal conduct', which was interpreted by the CJEU as a bar to expulsions based upon general preventive grounds.

[207] Article 27(1) Citizenship Directive.

[208] Article 28(2) Citizenship Directive.

[209] Article 28(3) Citizenship Directive.

Even the CJEU, whose judgments have an *erga omnes* effect and which has a stronger institutional position compared to the ECtHR, sometimes leaves the final decision to the referring national court. In the context of expulsion, the CJEU stated in *Tsakouridis* that his conduct 'is capable of being covered by the concept of imperative grounds of public security'[210] and in *P.I.* that his crimes are 'capable of justifying an expulsion measure under Article 28(3)'.[211] Against the background of the approach that has sometimes been adopted by the CJEU, it is even more understandable that the ECtHR does not attach an abstract weight to the various criteria.

The fact that it is unsurprising or understandable, however, is not a valid argument against a further clarification of the applicable criteria. Judge Turković clearly emphasised the need for clarification in her dissenting opinion in the *Ndidi* case, when she stated that 'the inconsistences [*sic*] in application of the *Üner*, *Maslov* and *A.A.* principles, … may warrant their further clarification and/or elaboration'.[212] This applies all the more regarding settled migrants since there is an urgent need to acknowledge that they are de facto natives. Even though the majority of the Court refrains from postulating a prohibition of expulsion of settled migrants, the ECtHR grants this group a higher degree of protection against expulsion.[213] By stating that 'for a settled migrant … very serious reasons are required to justify expulsion',[214] the ECtHR attaches a greater weight to the interests of the individual in the balancing process. The definition or circumscription of serious reasons is, however, left to the state. A clearer stance of the Court would be desirable but it is also for the states to make a further commitment in order to strengthen the legal position of second-generation or even third-generation 'migrants'. Since the 1990s, several ECtHR judges have expressed the need to establish an absolute protection against expulsion for integrated foreigners.[215] Moreover, the legally non-binding recommendations that were adopted at the beginning of the millennium call for an enhanced security of residence of long-term residents. These developments sent clear signals to the states and urged them to acknowledge their responsibility and to enhance the protection of their de facto nationals.

[210] *Tsakouridis*, para 56.

[211] *P.I.*, para 33.

[212] *Ndidi v The United Kingdom* App no 41215/14 (ECHR, 14 September 2017), dissenting opinion of Judge Turković, para 7.

[213] Caroni, *Privat- und Familienleben zwischen Menschenrecht und Migration* 344, 408, 414.

[214] *Maslov v Austria*, para 75.

[215] *Beldjoudi v France*, concurring opinion of Judge Martens, para 2; *Beldjoudi v France*, separate opinion of Judge De Meyer; *Nasri v France*, partly dissenting opinion of Judge Morenilla, para 4.

3

The Charter of Fundamental Rights of the European Union

The threefold fundamental rights protection in the European Union comprises the rights codified in the Charter (Article 6(1) TEU),[1] the rights enshrined in the ECHR (Article 6(3) TEU) and, finally, fundamental rights that stem from general principles of Union law (Article 6(3) TEU). The Charter shall, according to Article 6(1) TEU, have the same legal status as the Treaties.

The Charter is important in the context of expulsion decisions and entry bans as it provides an additional layer of fundamental rights protection. According to Article 51(1) CFR, the Charter is binding for 'the institutions, bodies, offices and agencies of the Union' and for the Member States 'only when they are implementing Union law'. The Member States are implementing Union law not only when applying the Citizenship Directive or the Long-Term Residents Directive, but also when issuing SIS alerts or entry bans, as these measures are governed by the Return Directive (Directive 2008/115/EC) and the SIS Regulation (Regulation 2018/1861) respectively. The relevance of the Charter is underlined by the fact that the SIS Regulation refers to neither family nor private life, and the Return Directive, which contains a reference to family life,[2] omits to mention the right to respect for the foreigner's private life. Therefore, the right to respect for private and family life (Article 7 CFR) is addressed first, followed by the rights of the child (Article 24 CFR), which are closely connected to the former right. Moreover, protection in the event of removal, expulsion or extradition (Article 19 CFR) is discussed, before the right to an effective remedy and a fair trial (Article 47) is briefly examined, followed by concluding remarks.

I. Right to Respect for Private and Family Life and the Rights of the Child

The right to respect for private and family life, which is contained in Article 7 CFR, is of particular importance in the context of expulsion decisions, as evidenced by

[1] Regarding the different legal roles the ECHR takes in the EU legal order as reflected in Article 6 TEU, see W Weiß, 'Human Rights in the EU: Rethinking the Role of the ECHR After Lisbon' (2011) 7 *European Constitutional Law Review* 64, 65.

[2] Article 5(1)(b) Return Directive.

the previous chapter. Given that the right to respect for private and family life has a counterpart in Article 8 ECHR, the homogeneity clause of Article 52(3) CFR applies. As both provisions have an almost identical wording,[3] Article 7 CFR is to be interpreted in conformity with Article 8 ECHR. The last sentence of Article 52(3) CFR provides that 'This provision shall not prevent Union law providing more extensive protection', thereby suggesting that the ECHR constitutes a minimum standard.[4]

In contrast to the ECHR, which contains in Article 8(2) a list of legitimate aims that can serve as a justification for an interference with the right contained in Article 8(1) ECHR, such a list is not contained in Article 7 CFR nor in other provisions of the Charter. However, as Article 52(3) CFR stipulates that the meaning and scope of the Charter right shall be the same as the meaning and scope of the corresponding Convention right, the grounds listed in Article 8(2) ECHR also apply to Article 7 CFR. Grounds such as 'national security, public safety or the economic wellbeing of the country' can consequently serve as justifications for an interference with Article 7 CFR. Nevertheless, the expulsion of a beneficiary of the Citizenship Directive, which interferes with the right to respect for private and family life and which is motivated by the economic well-being of the country, would infringe Article 27(1) of the Citizenship Directive.

In *Tsakouridis*, which concerned the expulsion of an EU citizen after more than 10 years of lawful residence, the CJEU held that the national expulsion measure is liable to obstruct the right to respect for private and family life. The Court mentioned Article 7 CFR and Article 8 ECHR together,[5] but did not further elaborate on the scope and meaning of this right. Instead, the CJEU referred to the *McB* case, in which it held that 'Article 7 of the Charter must … be given the same meaning and the same scope as Article 8(1) of the ECHR, as interpreted by the case-law of the European Court of Human Rights'.[6] Furthermore, in *McB*, the CJEU referred to the relevant case law of the ECtHR.[7] In the *Khachab* case,[8] which did not concern an expulsion decision, but the interpretation of the Family Reunification Directive, the CJEU also had recourse to Article 7 CFR and stated that 'Article 7 of the Charter cannot be interpreted as depriving the Member States of the margin of appreciation available to them'.[9] Simultaneously the Court

[3] The only difference between these two provisions is the notion of correspondence used by Article 8 ECHR, whereas Article 7 employs the broader notion of communications.

[4] S Morano-Foadi and S Andreadakis, 'The Convergence of the European Legal System in the Treatment of Third-country Nationals in Europe: The ECJ and ECtHR Jurisprudence' (2011) 22 *EJIL* 1071, 1073; F Fritzsch, *Der Schutz sozialer Bindungen von Ausländern* (Baden-Baden, Nomos, 2009) 97; J Callewaert, 'The European Convention on Human Rights and European Union Law: A Long Way to Harmony' (2009) 6 *European Human Rights Law Review* 768, 777; Weiß, 'Human Rights in the EU' 67.

[5] Case C-145/09 *Tsakouridis* ECLI:EU:C:2010:322, [2010] ECR I-11979, para 52.

[6] Case C-400/10 PPU *McB*. ECLI:EU:C:2010:582, [2010] ECR I-08965, para 53.

[7] ibid, paras 54, 56.

[8] Case C-558/14 *Khachab* ECLI:EU:C:2016:285, [2016].

[9] ibid, para 28.

underlined that Member States have to 'examine applications for reunification with a view to promoting family life'.[10] In the same year, the Court decided the cases of *C.S.* and *Rendón Marín*, which concerned delinquent third-country national sole carers of minor EU citizens. The third-country nationals were subject to expulsion and the refusal of a residence permit, respectively, on grounds of public policy. In both cases, the CJEU referred to Article 7 CFR and to the *Tsakouridis* judgment and held that Article 7 of the Charter 'must be read in conjunction with the obligation to take into consideration the child's best interests, recognised in Article 24(2) thereof'.[11] While the Court incorporates Article 7 CFR in its judgments concerning expulsion decisions by stating that it is necessary to take account of the right to respect for private and family life, it has not (yet) found that Article 7 CFR has to be interpreted in such a way as to prevent Member States from adopting specific expulsion legislation or expulsion measures. The right to respect for private and family life has thus far served as a consideration in the balancing process and supported the Court's reasoning, but it seems that it has not fundamentally changed the outcome of the Court's judgments in expulsion cases.

The same finding applies with regard to Article 24 of the Charter, which is based on the United Nations Convention on the Rights of the Child. Article 24(2) CFR, which stipulates that the 'child's best interests must be a primary consideration' in all actions relating to children, was mentioned by the Court in both *Rendón Marín* and *C.S.*[12] Article 52(3) CFR, which is understood as an interpretational guideline in order to ensure that Charter rights are interpreted in accordance with the parallel provisions in the ECHR,[13] does not apply to Article 24 CFR as the latter provision has no counterpart in the Convention. Given the lack of an interpretational guideline and the fact that the Convention on the Rights of the Child has no enforcement mechanisms while the CJEU's judgments have *erga omnes* effect, the CJEU could use Article 24 CFR to enhance and strengthen the rights of the child at the EU level.

II. Protection in the Event of Removal, Expulsion or Extradition, Article 19 CFR

Article 19(1) CFR prohibits collective expulsion and has the same meaning and scope as Article 4 of Protocol No 4 to the ECHR. This provision prohibits the removal of foreigners without an examination of their personal circumstances

[10] ibid.

[11] Case C-165/14 *Rendón Marín* ECLI:EU:C:2016:675, [2016], paras 66, 81; Case C-304/14 *C.S.*, ECLI:EU:C:2016:674, [2016], paras 36, 48.

[12] *Rendón Marín*, paras 66, 81; *C.S.*, para 36.

[13] I Pernice, 'The Charter of Fundamental Rights in the Constitution of the European Union', WHI Paper 14/02, p 10.

and without giving them the possibility to put forward arguments against their expulsion.[14] Conversely, it requires that every expulsion decision must be based on an assessment of the facts and circumstances of the individual case.

Article 19(2) prohibits removal, expulsion or extradition 'to a State where there is a serious risk that he or she would be subjected to the death penalty, torture or other inhuman or degrading treatment or punishment'. This paragraph reflects the ECtHR's case law on Article 3 ECHR and has consequently been invoked before the CJEU in cases concerning applications for international protection.[15]

The prohibition of collective expulsion could have become relevant in the context of the dismantling of camps and the eviction of Roma from France. In September 2010 the European Commission decided to issue a letter of formal notice to France[16] demanding the full implementation of the Citizenship Directive. The letter was sent with a view to initiating infringement proceedings unless draft transposition measures and a detailed transposition schedule were provided by 15 October 2010.[17] An infringement proceeding was not started but, next to the incorrect transposition of the Citizenship Directive, an infringement of Article 19(1) CFR and other Charter provisions could have been addressed.[18]

III. The Right to an Effective Remedy and to a Fair Trial, Article 47 CFR

Article 47 CFR remedies the shortcomings that are inherent in Article 13 and Article 6 of the ECHR. While Article 13 ECHR grants the 'right to an effective remedy before a national authority', it does not refer to a tribunal. Article 6 ECHR grants the right to a fair trial and explicitly refers to an independent and impartial tribunal. However, Article 6 ECHR has a limited scope of application as it only applies to the determination of 'civil rights and obligations' and to any criminal charges. These notions were interpreted by the ECtHR as excluding 'decisions regarding the entry, stay and deportation of aliens'.[19] This shortcoming is remedied by Article 47 CFR, which grants the 'right to an effective remedy and to a fair trial' and which applies to all decisions, including decisions relating to immigration, asylum and expulsion. Article 47 CFR has implications not only for the procedure before a tribunal, but also for procedures before administrative authorities. The

[14] *Hirsi Jamaa and others v Italy* App no 27765/09 (ECHR, 23 February 2012), para 177.

[15] Case C-175/17 *X* ECLI:EU:C:2018:776, [2018], paras 32, 34, 37, 47; Case C-180/17 *X and Y* ECLI:EU:C:2018:775, [2018], paras 28, 30, 33, 43; Case C-353/16 *MP* ECLI:EU:C:2018:276, [2018], paras 41, 43.

[16] 'European Commission assesses recent developments in France, discusses overall situation of the Roma and EU law on free movement of EU citizens', 29 September 2010, IP/10/1207, point 5.

[17] ibid.

[18] For example, Articles 8, 21, 22, 24, 45 and 47 CFR.

[19] *Maaouia v France* App no 39652/98 (ECHR, 5 October 2000), para 40.

CJEU held that 'Effective judicial review, which must be able to cover the legality of the reasons for the contested decision, presupposes in general that the court to which the matter is referred may require the competent authority to notify its reasons'.[20]

The effectiveness of judicial review and the right to defence, moreover, require that the individual affected by a decision encroaching upon his or her right(s) granted by Union law is in a position to exercise the right to bring an action.[21] In order to enable the person affected by the decision to bring an action, (s)he must be informed by the authority regarding the grounds for its decision. The Court held that

> [i]t follows that any decision taken must be capable of being made the subject of judicial proceedings in which its legality under Community law can be reviewed and that the person concerned must be able to ascertain the reasons for the decision taken in his regard.[22]

This requires the decision maker, whose decision falls within the scope of EU law, to inform the foreigner of the grounds of his or her expulsion in order to enable the individual to challenge this decision.

IV. Concluding Remarks

In cases concerning expulsion, the Court has recourse to the right to respect for private and family life, which is protected by Article 7 CFR and which has a counterpart in Article 8 ECHR, and for the rights of the child, which is recognised by Article 24 CFR and which has no parallel provision in the ECHR. Given that the United Nations Convention on the Rights of the Child has no enforcement mechanism, Article 24 CFR could be used by the Court to advance the rights of children generally and to expand the protection against expulsion in cases where minors are subject to an expulsion decision or where children are affected by their parents' expulsion.

[20] Case C-222/86 *Unectef v Heylens* ECLI:EU:C:1987:442, [1987] ECR 04097, para 15.

[21] Joined Cases C-402/05 P and C-415/05 P *Kadi* and *Al Barakaat International Foundation* ECLI:EU:C:2008:461, [2008] ECR I-06351, para 336; Case T-318/01 *Omar Mohammed Othman* ECLI:EU:T:2009:187, [2009] ECR II-01627, para 85.

[22] Case C-340/89 *Vlassopoulou* ECLI:EU:C:1991:193, [1991] ECR I-02357, para 22.

4

Summary and Conclusions: Differences between the EU Level and the Council of Europe

The focus of this part rested on the European level and addressed the requirements that have been established by EU law and by the ECHR for expelling foreigners. EU law applies to several groups of foreigners, such as EU citizens, their (third-country national) family members, Turkish nationals covered by the EEC–Turkey Association Agreement, and long-term resident third-country nationals. While these groups can rely on both EU law and the ECHR, not all foreigners who can rely on the ECHR are also covered by EU law. Furthermore, a cross-fertilisation between the CJEU and the ECtHR can be observed, as the CJEU cites the ECHR and the ECtHR's case law,[1] and the ECtHR refers to EU law and the CJEU's case law.[2] The increasing linkages between these two systems might point to a convergence of standards but differences remain, as EU law grants a higher level of protection against expulsions than the ECHR.

First, EU law enjoys supremacy over national law, whereas the ECHR has a complementary[3] and subsidiary function[4] in relation to national systems, which is also expressed by the margin of appreciation granted by the ECtHR to the

[1] Case C-36/75 *Rutili* ECLI:EU:C:1975:137, [1975] ECR 01219, para 32, in which the CJEU referred to Articles 8–11 ECHR. Case C-60/00 *Carpenter* ECLI:EU:C:2002:434, [2002] ECR I-06279, paras 41 and 42 in which the CJEU referred to the ECHR and the ECtHR's judgment in *Boultif*. For further information see L Glas and J Krommendijk, 'From *Opinion 2/13* to *Avotiņš*: Recent Developments in the Relationship between the Luxembourg and Strasbourg Courts' (2017) 17 *Human Rights Law Review* 567, 568, 569.

[2] See *Maslov v Austria* App no 1638/03 (ECHR, 23 June 2008), paras 39–44; *Goodwin v The United Kingdom* App no 28957/95 (ECHR,11 July 2002), para 58.

[3] J Rubel, *Entscheidungsfreiräume in der Rechtsprechung des Europäischen Gerichtshofes für Menschenrechte und des Europäischen Gerichtshofes für Menschenrechte und des Europäischen Gerichtshofes* (Hamburg, Verlag Dr. Kovač, 2005) 24; Y Arai-Takahashi, *The Margin of Appreciation Doctrine and the Principle of Proportionality in the Jurisdiction of the ECHR* (Antwerp, Intersentia, 2001) 240; P Mahony, 'Marvellous Richness of Diversity or Invidious Cultural Relativism?' (1998) 19 *Human Rights Law Journal* 1, 3 ('under the Convention scheme of human rights protection there is an area of review conferred on the national authorities and an area of review conferred on the Strasbourg Commission and Court – in other words, a shared responsibility for enforcement …').

[4] Regarding the subsidiary function of the ECHR, see *Handyside v The United Kingdom* App no 5493/72 (ECHR, 7 December 1976), para 48: 'The Court points out that the machinery of protection established by the Convention is subsidiary to the national systems safeguarding human rights'.

Contracting Parties.[5] While judgments of the CJEU normally have an *erga omnes* effect,[6] judgments of the ECtHR are in principle only binding on the party to the proceeding, per Article 46 ECHR.

The different mechanisms to bring a case before the CJEU and the ECtHR respectively have implications not only for the affected individual, but also for the manner in which and the point in time when these two courts can provide guidance to national decision makers. At the EU level, domestic courts can refer a question to the CJEU by using the preliminary reference procedure (Article 267 TFEU). This allows the CJEU to give a binding interpretation of EU law at an early stage of the dispute and to guide the application of EU law at the national level. At the ECHR level, by contrast, local remedies have to be exhausted before the aggrieved individual can bring the case before the ECtHR.[7] This normally implies a considerable lapse of time before the infringement of a Convention right can be addressed by the ECtHR. Furthermore, it denies the ECtHR the possibility to provide its assessment at an early stage of the domestic dispute. On the other hand, the preliminary reference procedure before the CJEU, which seeks to ensure a uniform interpretation of EU law, builds on a 'direct cooperation between the Court of Justice and the national courts'.[8] The initiation of this procedure 'depends entirely on the national court's assessment as to whether a reference is appropriate and necessary',[9] with the consequence that it 'is completely independent of any initiative by the parties'.[10] Even though this procedure increases the CJEU's vulnerability to a refusal by national courts to cooperate and to refer a case to the CJEU, it simultaneously grants the latter a direct possibility – provided the Article 267 TFEU procedure is triggered – to exert influence. Another downside of this court-to-court procedure is its repercussions for the individual. The individual whose rights may be infringed is not only barred from triggering the preliminary reference procedure, as its initiation depends entirely on the national court, the individual is also not equipped with any mechanism to bring a claim relating to a violation of Charter rights before the CJEU. The absence of an individual complaint procedure underlines the nature of the CJEU's tasks and is reflected in a statement by the President of the CJEU, Lenearts, who, as Besselink notes, stated that 'The Court is not a human rights court: it is the Supreme Court of the Union'.[11] The different

[5] M Tümay, 'The "Margin of Appreciation Doctrine" Developed by the European Court of Human Rights' (2008) 5 *Ankara Law Review* 201, 205, 206, points out that the margin of appreciation doctrine stems directly from the principle of subsidiarity.

[6] For further information regarding the different categories of CJEU judgments and whether they have an *inter partes* or *erga omnes* effect, see M Ottaviano, *Der Anspruch auf rechtzeitigen Rechtsschutz im Gemeinschaftsprozessrecht* (Tübingen, Mohr Siebeck, 2009) 74, 75.

[7] Article 35(1) ECHR.

[8] Case C-210/06 *Cartesio* ECLI:EU:C:2008:723, [2008] ECR I-09641, para 90.

[9] Case C-2/06 *Kempter* ECLI:EU:C:2008:78, [2008] ECR I-00411, para 42.

[10] *Cartesio*, para 90.

[11] L Besselink, 'Acceding to the ECHR notwithstanding the Court of Justice Opinion 2/13' (*Verfassungsblog*, 23 December 2014) www.verfassungsblog.de/acceding-echr-notwithstanding-court-justice-opinion-213-2/.

tasks of the two courts are mirrored by the different benchmarks of assessment in the context of expulsion decisions. While the ECtHR assesses states' interferences with the right to respect for private and family life, the CJEU provides an interpretation of EU law, more specifically of the notions of public policy and public security, and of Charter rights.[12]

Despite these different benchmarks of assessment and the different mechanisms for bringing a case before the ECtHR and the CJEU, the CJEU is in a stronger institutional position to ensure a transposition of its judgments.

Turning from the procedural aspects to the substance of the provisions, the previous chapters have highlighted that the legislative instruments at the EU level grant a strong protection against expulsion to several groups of foreigners. EU citizens' protection against expulsion is governed by the Citizenship Directive. The Citizenship Directive lists the general principles that have to be observed when expelling EU citizens or their family members[13] and contains a non-exhaustive list of considerations that guide the balancing process between the competing interests of the individual and the interests of the state.[14] Moreover, the Citizenship Directive attaches a specific weight to the interests of the individual and the state respectively.[15] The protection granted by Article 8 ECHR, by contrast, is less detailed and does not contain a list of criteria that have to be considered in the balancing process. These criteria were only established by the ECtHR in the *Boultif* and *Üner* judgments, but the Court refrained from attaching a specific weight to these criteria.

Another group of foreigners that is granted a strong protection against expulsion is that of Turkish nationals covered by the EEC–Turkey Association Agreement. Article 14 of Association Council Decision 1/80 allows for interferences with Turkish nationals' rights on grounds of public policy, public security or public health. For a long time, the CJEU interpreted the notion of public policy by analogy to the interpretation given to this notion in the context of nationals of the EU Member States, which reinforced Turkish nationals' protection against expulsion. The CJEU's *Ziebell* judgment marked the end of a further application by analogy as the Court ruled that Turkish nationals cannot rely on the enhanced protection against expulsion provided for by Article 28(3)(a) of the Citizenship Directive. Nonetheless, the Court also clarified in the *Ziebell* judgment that Turkish nationals' protection against expulsion, which has been established by the Court in previous cases, continues to apply.[16]

A third group of foreigners that was discussed is that of long-term resident third-country nationals who are covered by the LTR Directive. Article 12 of the LTR Directive grants them an enhanced protection against expulsion. In the

[12] See *Tsakouridis*, para 52; *Rendón Marín*, paras 66, 81; *C.S.*, paras 36, 48.
[13] Article 27 Citizenship Directive.
[14] Article 28(1) Citizenship Directive.
[15] Article 28(2) and (3) Citizenship Directive.
[16] Case C-371/08 *Ziebell* ECLI:EU:C:2011:809, [2011] ECR I-12735, paras 81–84.

López Pastuzano judgment, the CJEU provided an interpretation of Article 12 by making reference to the *Ziebell* judgment and the principles and safeguards that govern Turkish nationals' protection against expulsion.[17] The Court synchronised Turkish nationals' and long-term resident third-country nationals' protection against expulsion and aligned it to the foundational principles of EU citizens' protection against expulsion. In particular, the Court stated that measures taken on grounds of public policy or public security may only be taken if 'the personal conduct of the individual concerned constitutes at present a genuine and sufficiently serious threat to a fundamental interest of society'.[18] This central feature of EU citizens' protection against expulsion is codified in Article 27(2) of the Citizenship Directive and had already been applied to Turkish citizens in earlier judgments.[19]

Finally, all foreigners who are covered by EU law can rely on the protection granted by the Charter. Article 52(3) of the Charter stipulates that Charter rights, which correspond to ECHR rights, shall be given the same scope and meaning as Convention rights but 'shall not prevent Union law from providing more extensive protection'. This provision suggests that the ECHR merely serves as a minimum standard of protection. Even though the right to respect for private and family life has been mentioned by the CJEU in cases concerning expulsion,[20] it has not been given an interpretation that differs from the interpretation given by the ECtHR in the context of Article 8 ECHR. At the same time, the safeguards against expulsion that have been afforded to the aforementioned groups of foreigners by EU law exceed the protection that is granted by Article 8 ECHR and the ECtHR's case law.

EU citizens' strong protection against expulsion is, at least in part, a result of the Court's own case law, which has been codified in the Citizenship Directive. In recent years, however, there has been shift in the Court's case law, which has led to an erosion of EU citizens' protection against expulsion, as demonstrated by the *Tsakouridis* case and the *P.I.* case. Both cases concerned EU citizens who were covered by Article 28(3) of the Citizenship Directive, which bars expulsions other than on imperative grounds of public security. The Court stated that the crimes committed by Tsakouridis and P.I., which undoubtedly fell within the scope of the notion of public policy, were capable of being covered by the narrower concept of public security. Apart from blurring the distinction between public policy and public security, the Court effectively undermined EU citizens' protection against expulsion and extended Member States' discretion by strengthening their capacity to expel EU citizens, even if the latter were covered by the most enhanced protection against expulsion that EU law can offer. Later, in the *M.G.* case, the Court further undermined EU citizens' protection against expulsion. It held that the

[17] Case C-636/16 *López Pastuzano*, ECLI:EU:C:2017:949, [2017] para 27; *Ziebell*, paras 82, 83.

[18] ibid.

[19] See, for example, Case C-340/97 *Nazli* ECLI:EU:C:2000:77, [2000] ECR I-00957, paras 56, 57; Case C-303/08 *Bozkurt* ECLI:EU:C:2010:800, [2010] ECR I-13445, para 60.

[20] *C.S.*, paras 36, 48; *Tsakouridis*, para 52.

protection against expulsion in the Citizenship Directive is 'based on the degree of integration of the persons concerned in the host Member State'.[21] Moreover, the CJEU stated that the 'degree of integration ... is a vital consideration underpinning both the right of permanent residence and the system of protection against expulsion measures'.[22] The same consideration was reiterated in the *Onuekwere* judgment,[23] which concerned the acquisition of the right of permanent residence by a delinquent third-country national family member of an EU citizen. Even though this case did not directly concern the protection against expulsion, it has an impact on the protection against expulsion granted by Article 28(2) of the Citizenship Directive, which presupposes the right of permanent residence. For third-country family members, Article 28(2) constitutes the most enhanced protection against expulsion as Article 28(3) of the Citizenship Directive applies exclusively to EU citizens. By linking the acquisition of the right of permanent residence to the umbrella concept of integration, the Court enabled Member States to deny the right of permanent residence by invoking a lack of integration. Simultaneously, it deprived delinquent third-country national family members of EU citizens and EU citizens who are denied the right of permanent residence due to a lack of integration of the possibility to rely on the protection against expulsion granted by Article 28(2) of the Citizenship Directive, irrespective of the length of their actual residence. In addition, the Court's approach even affects the most enhanced protection that is afforded to EU citizens after more than 10 years of residence. In the joined cases of *B* and *Franco Vomero*, the Court stipulated that the protection of Article 28(3)(a) of the Citizenship Directive is only available to EU citizens who satisfy the eligibility conditions of Article 28(2), which in turn requires the acquisition of the right of permanent residence.[24]

The Court adopted a different approach in the *Rendón Marín* and *C.S.* cases.[25] Both cases concerned delinquent third-country nationals who were sole carers of minor EU citizens. The Court established clear limits to Member States' capacity to refuse a residence permit (*Rendón Marín*) and expel the third-country national (*C.S.*) respectively. Even though the Court seemed to depart from the rationale that guided its *Tsakouridis*, *P.I.* and *M.G.* judgments, it must be noted that *Rendón Marín* and *C.S.* are highly fact specific and it would seem that they cover a relatively small group of individuals. Therefore, the principles that have been established in these cases do not necessarily lend themselves to application to cases with dissimilar facts and characteristics.

Compared to the case law concerning EU citizens and their third-country national family members, the Court's approach regarding Turkish citizens covered by the EEC–Turkey Association Agreement as well as long-term resident

[21] Case C-400/12 *M.G.*, ECLI:EU:C:2014:9, [2014], para 30.
[22] *M.G.*, para 32.
[23] Case C-378/12 *Onuekwere* ECLI:EU:C:2014:13, [2014], para 30.
[24] Joined Cases C-316/16 and C-424/16 *B* and *Franco Vomero* ECLI:EU:C:2018:256, [2018], para 49.
[25] *Rendón Marín*, para 15; *C.S.*, para 13.

third-country nationals follows a different rationale. Even though the *Ziebell* judgment marks the end of a further application by analogy of EU citizens' protection against expulsion to Turkish citizens, the judgment also clarifies that the safeguards against expulsion that had been established previously continue to apply. The Court consolidated the status quo of Turkish nationals' protection against expulsion and drew a link to the LTR Directive by stating that the latter Directive would henceforth constitute the relevant legal framework. In the *López Pastuzano* judgment, which concerned long-term resident third-country nationals, the Court synchronised Turkish nationals' and long-term resident third-country nationals' protection against expulsion by referring to the *Ziebell* judgment and the central elements of Turkish nationals' protection against expulsion.

The most enhanced protection against expulsion, Article 28(3) of the Citizenship Directive, remains reserved to EU citizens and thereby demonstrates their special status. While maintaining this distinction, the Court's case law points to a convergence of the standards that apply to the different groups of foreigners that are covered by EU law. This convergence entails a limitation of the protection against expulsion granted to EU citizens and their family members and a strengthening of the protection that is available to Turkish nationals and long-term resident third-country nationals, who can rely on the foundational principles of EU citizens' protection against expulsion.

PART II

The Effects of European Law on Expulsion Decisions Taken at the National Level

Part II assesses the impact of the European level on the national level. Part I outlined the European law requirements that have to be fulfilled for adopting a public policy or public security decision or a decision that interferes with the foreigner's private and family life, and thereby established the limitations of the states' margin of discretion when terminating foreigners' lawful residence after a criminal conviction. This part addresses the effects of the European level on the national level by assessing how the European requirements and the margin of discretion that is granted by the European level are implemented at the national level. It is divided into four chapters whereby Chapter 5 assesses the German system of expulsion decisions following a criminal conviction and briefly addresses the imposition of entry bans. Chapter 6 examines the Netherlands and outlines the Dutch system for the termination of lawful residence after a criminal conviction and the requirements for declaring a foreigner *persona non grata*. Chapter 7 analyses the deportation of foreign criminals from the United Kingdom. Chapter 8 compares the Dutch, British and German systems and outlines their differences and similarities. In particular, the differences between the German and Dutch systems are relevant for Part III, which addresses the effects that national expulsion decisions can have at the European level. Therefore, Chapter 8 focuses on the differences between these two Schengen states regarding criminal sentencing and the duration of the entry ban before expanding further on these differences in Part III.

5

Germany

This chapter explores the German law on expulsion by focusing on both the relevant legal provisions and their interpretation by the executive and the judiciary. It provides an overview of the scope of the legal provisions, their structure, legal consequences and rationale, and the criteria that are considered in the balancing process between the interests of the foreigner and the interests of the state.

Three aspects are central to this chapter. First, for an in-depth analysis and understanding of the current system of expulsion, some insight into the abolished system (1990–2015) and its deficiencies is indispensable. The main issue in the abolished system was the provision on mandatory expulsion, which prescribed an expulsion if the statutory requirements were fulfilled. This provision was characterised by the absence of a margin of discretion granted by the legislature to the executive and the judiciary. It barred the decision maker from taking the facts of the individual case into account and from conducting a balancing process, which rendered this provision incompatible with Article 8 ECHR (right to respect for private and family life).

Against the background of the deficiencies of the old system, the emergence of the new system of expulsion, as well as its structure and its rationale, constitute the second central aspect of this chapter. Emphasis rests on the duty of the decision maker to conduct a balancing process between the interests of the individual and the interests of the state before issuing an expulsion decision. At this point, the tensions between two elements of the *Rechtsstaat*, the principle of proportionality, which lies at the heart of the balancing process, and, second, the principle of legal certainty, become visible. The abolished provision on mandatory expulsion, which prescribed an expulsion decision if the statutory requirements were fulfilled, was conducive to the principle of legal certainty, despite being incompatible with the requirements of Article 8 ECHR. The new system of expulsion, by contrast, prescribes a balancing process and reduces the level of legal certainty. Therefore, the analysis addresses the question of whether the legislature struck an adequate balance between the principle of legal certainty and the principle of proportionality.

The third and final aspect of this chapter evaluates the current system of expulsion and assesses whether it ensures an open and unbiased balancing process, an aim that is deliberately stated in the explanatory memorandum.[1] Moreover, it

[1] Gesetzentwurf der Bundesregierung, 'Entwurf eines Gesetzes zur Neubestimmung des Bleiberechts und der Aufenthaltsbeendigung' (2015) Bundestagsdrucksache 18/4097, p 49.

assesses whether the new provisions on expulsion break with the old system, with its bias and its rationale, and whether the deficiencies of the old system have been remedied without creating new downsides.

This chapter is structured as follows. The first section explores the concept of expulsion decisions in German law. The second section focuses on the abolished provisions on expulsion. It introduces the different grounds that served as a basis for an expulsion decision (Subsection A) and explains the structural problems that were inherent in the abolished system (Subsection B) and the dilemma that was caused by the absence of a balancing process in the context of the provision on mandatory expulsion (Subsection C). Moreover, it addresses different suggestions that were advanced to incorporate a balancing process into the provision on mandatory expulsion and the problems that were precipitated by these approaches (Subsection D). Finally, it assesses the system's compatibility with the requirements of EU law (Subsection E). The third section provides an overview of the new provisions on expulsion, which entered into force in 2016. It outlines their structure, the legislature's objectives and the requirement of a balancing process, which takes centre stage in the new system. This section addresses the amendment and recalibration of the public interest in expelling the foreigner (Subsection A) and the system's compatibility with the requirements of EU law (Subsection B). In light of the strong emphasis on the requirement of a balancing process, it scrutinises the balance between the principle of legal certainty and the principle of proportionality (Subsection C). The remaining deficiencies of the new system are addressed by highlighting the lack of a necessity assessment, which is a foundational element of the principle of proportionality. Moreover, the new provisions' wording and structure are analysed to ascertain whether the new system departs from the rationale of the old system (Subsection D). The fourth section briefly addresses the entry ban that follows an expulsion decision. Finally, the findings of this chapter are summarised and evaluated in a conclusion.

I. Introduction to the Concept of Expulsion Decisions in German Law

An abstract legal definition of an expulsion decision does not exist in German law.[2] The Aufenthaltsgesetz[3] (Residence Act) determines and regulates the conditions and legal consequences of expulsion decisions. According to the Residence Act, an expulsion decision aims at preventing a foreigner's further stay in the national territory, results in the expiry of the residence title[4] or the exemption

[2] M Wollenschläger and A Schraml, 'Zum Recht der Ausweisung im neuen Ausländergesetz' (1992) 12 *Zeitschrift für Ausländerrecht und Ausländerpolitik* 66, 67.

[3] Gesetz über den Aufenthalt, die Erwerbstätigkeit und die Integration von Ausländern im Bundesgebiet of 25 February 2008, Federal Law Gazette Part I 162.

[4] Residence Act, s 51(1) no 5; s 51(9) no 2.

from the requirement of a residence title,[5] and imposes a duty on the foreigner to leave the territory.[6] Moreover, an entry ban is to be issued for an expelled foreigner[7] together with the expulsion decision.[8] The expelled foreigner cannot be issued with a new residence title[9] even if s/he would fulfil the requirements for the issuance of a residence permit. An expulsion decision declares the foreigner *persona non grata.*[10]

An expulsion decision is an administrative act,[11] which aims at averting a danger posed by the foreigner's presence or conduct. It serves the purpose of preventing future interference with public policy or public security[12] but is not limited to these grounds. A foreigner can also be subject to an expulsion if s/he endangers the free democratic basic order or other significant interests of the Federal Republic of Germany.[13] Since 2004, the rules governing the expulsion of EU and EEA citizens and their family members are set out in the Freedom of Movement Act/EU,[14] with the result that the provisions on expulsion in the Residence Act are inapplicable to this group of foreigners.

Even though an expulsion decision is said to be a preventive measure, the affected individual often perceives it as a measure which is more severe than,[15] or at least tantamount to,[16] a criminal penalty.

Due to its legal nature as a measure of administrative law, an expulsion decision issued after a criminal conviction is considered not to infringe the principle of *ne bis in idem.*[17] Doubts regarding this classification arise against the background of

[5] Residence Act, s 51(5).

[6] Residence Act, s 50(1) in conjunction with s 51(1).

[7] Residence Act, s 11(1).

[8] Residence Act, s 11(2).

[9] Residence Act, s 11(1).

[10] A Schmitt Glaeser, 'Individualgerechtigkeit im Ausländerrecht' (2003) 23 *Zeitschrift für Ausländerrecht und Ausländerpolitik* 176, 177.

[11] I Bauer, 'Vor §§ 53-56 AufenthG' in J Bergmann and K Dienelt (eds), *Ausländerrecht* 13th edn (Munich, C.H. Beck, 2020) para 21.

[12] K-G Mayer, 'Systemwechsel im Ausländerrecht – der Schutz "faktischer Inländer" mit und ohne familiäre Bindungen nach dem Grundgesetz und der Europäischen Menschenrechtskonvention (EMRK)' (2010) 101 *Verwaltungsarchiv* 482, 503; Federal Administrative Court, judgment of 31 March 1998, BVerwG 1 C 28.97, (1998) *Informationsbrief Ausländerrecht* 286.

[13] Residence Act, s 53(1).

[14] Gesetz über die allgemeine Freizügigkeit von Unionsbürgern (Freizügigkeitsgesetz/EU) of 30 July 2004, Federal Law Gazette Part I 1950 ('Freedom of Movement Act/EU').

[15] W Meyer, 'Die Ausweisung nach dem Ausländergesetz in der Rechtsprechung des Bundesverwaltungsgerichts' (1984) 3 *Neue Zeitschrift für Verwaltungsrecht* 13; Federal Administrative Court, judgment of 3 May 1973, Collection of Cases of the Federal Administrative Court, Volume 42, p 138; K Sieveking, 'Security of Residence and Expulsion: The German Experience' in E Guild and P Minderhoud (eds), *Security of Residence and Expulsion* (The Hague, Kluwer Law International, 2001) 109; C Mielitz, 'Die aufenthaltsrechtlichen Rechtsfolgen der Ausweisung' (2009) 29 *Zeitschrift für Ausländerrecht und Ausländerpolitik* 264.

[16] B Bowling and S Westenra, '"A Really Hostile Environment": Adiaphorization, Global Policing and the Crimmigration Control System' (2020) 24 *Theoretical Criminology* 167; J Wegner, 'Die Behandlung straffällig gewordender Einwanderer im neuen Ausweisungsrecht' (1993) 46 *Die Öffentliche Verwaltung* 1031, 1032.

[17] General Administrative Rules for the (Application of the) Residence Act ('*Allgemeine Verwaltungsvorschrift zum Aufenthaltsgesetz*'), Vor. 53.3.0.1.

the purpose of an expulsion decision. One purpose that is advanced is the isolation of the individual from the general public,[18] which follows the rationale of negative special prevention of crime. Another purpose is deterrence of other foreigners,[19] which is based on the rationale of negative general prevention of crime. Given that the criminal punishment (imprisonment) already serves the purpose of incapacitation and deterrence, the fact that the same considerations are advanced in the context of expulsion calls into question the purely administrative nature of an expulsion decision and thereby the statement that an expulsion following a criminal conviction is compatible with the prohibition of double jeopardy.

II. The Abolished System of Expulsion (1990–2015)

The 1990 Foreigner Act[20] opted for standardised grounds for expulsion and introduced an incremental system, which subsequently underwent a series of revisions and amendments.[21] This system provided for mandatory expulsion (section 53), expulsion as a rule (section 54), and expulsion following a balancing process (section 55).[22] While its predecessor, the 1965 Foreigner Act, granted a wide margin of discretion to the decision maker, the 1990 Foreigner Act curtailed the discretion of the executive and the judiciary. Even though the 1990 Foreigner Act guaranteed a higher degree of predictability,[23] thereby enhancing legal certainty,[24] it was criticised for its incompatibility with Article 8 ECHR and for resulting in a deterioration of the legal position of the affected foreigners.[25] The explanatory memorandum to the 1990 Foreigner Act did not provide a clear indication of the legislature's intention,[26] nor did it address the compatibility of the system of

[18] S Legomsky, 'Ausweisung und Abschiebung straffälliger Ausländer. The Expulsion of Criminal Aliens' in K Hailbronner and E Klein (eds), *Einwanderungskontrolle und Menschenrechte – Immigration Control and Human Rights, Beiträge anlässlich des Symposiums am 29–30 Juni 1998 in Potsdam* (Heidelberg, C.F. Müller Verlag, 1999) 164.

[19] ibid.

[20] Gesetz zur Neuregelung des Ausländerrechts (Ausländergesetz) of 9 July 1990, Federal Law Gazette Part I 1354.

[21] For example Gesetz zur Änderung des Strafgesetzbuches, der Strafprozeßordnung und anderer Gesetze (Verbrechensbekämpfungsgesetz) of 28 October 1994, Federal Law Gazette I 1386; Gesetz zur Steuerung und Begrenzung der Zuwanderung und zur Regelung des Aufenthalts und der Integration von Unionsbürgern und Ausländern (Zuwanderungsgesetz) of 30 July 2004, Federal Law Gazette Part I 1950; Gesetz über den Aufenthalt, die Erwerbstätigkeit und die Integration von Ausländern im Bundesgebiet (Aufenthaltsgesetz) of 25 February 2008, Federal Law Gazette Part I 163.

[22] S Beichel, *Ausweisungsschutz und Verfassung* (Berlin, Mensch & Buch, 2001) 17, 97.

[23] Mayer, 'Systemwechsel im Ausländerrecht' 487.

[24] Wollenschläger and Schraml, 'Zum Recht der Ausweisung im neuen Ausländergesetz' 74.

[25] F Franz, 'Der Gesetzesentwurf der Bundesregierung zur Neuregelung des Ausländerrechts' (1990) 10 *Zeitschrift für Ausländerrecht und Ausländerpolitik* 3, 8.

[26] C Sennekamp, 'Ist-Ausweisung menschenrechtswidrig?' (2002) 22 *Zeitschrift für Ausländerrecht und Ausländerpolitik* 136, 138.

expulsion with Article 8 ECHR.[27] In fact, the ECtHR only decided in 1991 that an expulsion following a criminal conviction constituted a violation of Article 8 ECHR.[28]

A. The Grounds for Expulsion

First, section 53 Residence Act stipulated that a foreigner was to be expelled where the statutory requirements were fulfilled. Section 53 listed three structurally different grounds for expulsion decisions. The first ground referred solely to the duration of the prison term or youth custody (three years), whereas the second ground required a combination of a specific offence and a specific duration of the prison sentence. The third ground required a specific offence and a prison sentence, where the duration of the prison sentence was irrelevant.

Secondly, section 54 Residence Act provided that an expulsion decision was the rule if one of the grounds listed in this provision were fulfilled, unless exceptional circumstances rebutted the assumption of the rule.

Finally, section 55 Residence Act granted discretion to the decision maker and required a balancing process between the interests of the foreigner and the interests of the state. Despite its compliance with the principle of proportionality, this provision exhibited other deficiencies.

Section 56 Residence Act, which did not constitute a legal basis for an expulsion decision, afforded some protection against expulsion, notably to those foreigners who had resided longer in the territory and held a specific type of residence permit. However, this provision did not grant an absolute protection against expulsion as the latter can only be achieved by way of naturalisation. The provision's personal scope was limited as it only applied to lawfully resident foreigners, without acknowledging that foreigners who are present in the territory irregularly can develop the same social, cultural and family links as foreigners who are lawfully resident. Section 56 Residence Act contained two safeguards. First, it clarified that foreigners covered by this provision shall only be expelled on serious grounds of public security and public policy. Second, it led to a 'reduction' of the respective category of expulsion. If the foreigner was subject to section 53 Residence Act, which mandatorily required an expulsion decision, the relevant framework of assessment was section 54 Residence Act, which stipulated expulsion as a rule. Where the foreigner was covered by section 54 Residence Act, the legal framework of section 55 Residence Act had to be applied, which required a balancing process.

[27] M Schmid-Drüner, *Der Begriff der öffentlichen Sicherheit und Ordnung im Einwanderungsrecht ausgewählter EU-Mitgliedstaaten* (Baden-Baden, Nomos, 2007) 349.

[28] *Moustaquim v Belgium* App no 12313/86 (ECHR, 18 February 1991).

B. The Structural Problems of the Abolished System of Expulsion

The system of expulsion in place between 1990 and 2015 was fraught with problems. The most obvious deficiencies were the lack of an individual assessment (i) and the rationale of the provisions and the resulting burden regarding the decision maker's duty to give reasons (ii).

i. The Absence of a Balancing Process

The incremental system of expulsion aimed at strengthening predictability and legal certainty but stood in contrast to the ECtHR's casuistic approach,[29] which requires a balancing process. The incremental system triggered the question of whether a balancing process conducted by the administrative authorities and courts is superfluous because the legislature had already taken the principle of proportionality into account when it drafted the provisions on expulsion.

The premise of this question disregards the ramifications of the principle of proportionality and the legal nature of a statutory provision. A separate balancing process conducted by administrative authorities is not superfluous as the *Rechtsstaatsprinzip* requires all three branches of the state to adhere to the principle of proportionality. As an Act of Parliament, the Residence Act must comply with the principle of proportionality. If an act of the legislature disproportionately limited fundamental rights, it could be declared unconstitutional and struck down by the Federal Constitutional Court.[30] However, the Federal Constitutional Court confirmed that the graduated system of mandatory expulsion (section 53), expulsion as a rule (section 54) and expulsion following a balancing process (section 55) was compatible with the requirements of the principle of proportionality.[31] Nevertheless, the provisions' compliance with the principle of proportionality does not imply that every decision taken on the basis of one of these provisions necessarily satisfies the requirements of the principle of proportionality. The provisions on expulsion are phrased in abstract and general terms to cover a variety of situations and a large group of foreigners. Given their abstract and general nature, they cannot simultaneously provide a concrete and individual answer to every case. Therefore, a separate balancing process between the interests of the individual and the interests of the state has to be conducted by the decision maker, who has to comply with the principle of proportionality. Expulsion decisions by administrative authorities can be subject to judicial scrutiny, whereby the judiciary also has to comply with the principle of proportionality.

[29] Mayer, 'Systemwechsel im Ausländerrecht' 487.
[30] Federal Constitutional Court Act, s 31(2).
[31] Federal Constitutional Court, decision of 10 August 2007, 2 BvR 535/06, para 18.

Contrary to the assumption that underlies the opening question, it is insufficient for only the provisions on expulsion to comply with the principle of proportionality. In order to ensure that the expulsion decision itself complies with the principle of proportionality, the decision maker must be able to take the facts of the individual case into account and balance the competing interests. However, an individual assessment was barred by section 53 Residence Act, which mandatorily prescribed an expulsion decision. Moreover, an open-ended balancing process was hampered by section 54, which required that the foreigner be issued with an expulsion decision, unless an exception applied.

ii. The Rationale of the Provisions on Expulsion: A Bias against the Foreigner

The provision on mandatory expulsion (section 53 Residence Act) contained the irrebuttable presumption that the foreigner remained a threat to society even after being released from prison; consequently, the foreigner had to be expelled. The state's interests always prevailed over the interests of the foreigner and the foreigner was barred from contesting the expulsion decision by arguing that it was unnecessary or disproportionate.

Section 54 Residence Act provided for a rebuttable presumption that the foreigner poses a threat to public policy or public security[32] and that s/he has to be expelled, unless the case exhibited exceptional features. If the case exhibited exceptional features, a balancing process between the interests of the foreigner and the interests of the state was required. However, this balancing process could still lead to the conclusion that the foreigner had to be expelled. The primary focus of this provision also rested on the interests of the state. The individual's interests would only be considered at a second stage, in order to determine whether the case exhibited exceptional features.

Only section 55 Residence Act provided for a more level playing field by requiring a balancing process and by listing the interests of the state (section 55(1) and (2)) and the interests of the individual (section 55(3)) that had to be considered in the balancing process. Nonetheless, the interests of the state were listed first, which underlined their importance.

According to Davy, the provisions on expulsion in the 1990 Foreigner Act exhibited a structural imbalance between the interests of the state and the interests of the foreigner at the expense of the latter.[33] Davy rightly pointed out that the interests of the individual were not perceived as weighing as much as the interests of the state.[34]

[32] R Gutmann, 'Assoziationsrechtliche Schranken gesetzgeberischer Gestaltungsbefugnis im Ausländerrecht' (2003) 23 *Zeitschrift für Ausländerrecht und Ausländerpolitik* 60, 64.

[33] U Davy, 'Aufenthaltssicherheit: Ein verlässliches Versprechen?' (2007) 27 *Zeitschrift für Ausländerrecht und Ausländerpolitik* 169, 173.

[34] ibid.

The wording and structure of the abolished provision on mandatory expulsion (section 53 Residence Act) and expulsion as a rule (section 54) not only had implications for the foreigner's security of residence, these provisions also affected the executive's and the judiciary's decision making and the duty to give reasons. The wording of the provision on mandatory expulsion (section 53) ruled out any discretion and thereby barred administrative authorities and courts at the outset from conducting a balancing process between the interests of the foreigner and the interests of the state. The legislature prescribed that an expulsion decision had to be taken; a balancing process, by contrast, might have led to the conclusion that the foreigner's expulsion was disproportionate. If the decision maker applied section 53 strictly, s/he would face a low burden regarding the duty to give reasons as the statutory provision clearly required the issuance of an expulsion decision. If, by contrast, the decision maker argued that the foreigner's expulsion was disproportionate and infringed Article 8 ECHR and therefore refrained from an expulsion decision, s/he would have acted *contra legem* as the legislature prescribed the issuance of an expulsion decision.

Section 54 Residence Act (expulsion as a rule) provided for a rebuttable presumption that the foreigner posed a threat to public policy or public security,[35] and thereby imposed the argumentative burden for refraining from an expulsion decision on the administrative authorities and courts.[36]

C. The Dilemma Caused by the Lack of a Balancing Process

The statutory provisions on mandatory expulsion and expulsion as a rule created a dilemma for the administrative authorities and courts. While the ECtHR requires a balancing process between the individual's and the state's interests where the state interferes with Article 8 ECHR,[37] the abolished provisions on expulsion, by contrast, limited or excluded the possibility to conduct such a balancing process. These limitations prompted the question of whether judges who review the expulsion decisions taken by administrative authorities can deliver fair judgments if they are 'tied' to the black letter law, which prescribes the content of their judgment. This conflict is linked to the role of the judiciary, the limits of its interpretative powers and the separation of powers. It concerns the question of whether the judge's role is strictly limited to the application of the black letter law, whether judges can be considered interpreters of the law,[38] or whether they can even assume the role of

[35] Gutmann, 'Assoziationsrechtliche Schranken gesetzgeberischer Gestaltungsbefugnis im Ausländerrecht' 64.

[36] Davy, 'Aufenthaltssicherheit' 173.

[37] *Boultif v Switzerland* App no 54273/00 (ECHR, 2 August 2001), para 58.

[38] G Hirsch, 'Zwischenruf: Der Richter wird's schon richten' (2006) 39 *Zeitschrift für Rechtspolitik* 161; G Hirsch, 'Auf dem Weg zum Richterstaat? Vom Verhältnis des Richters zum Gesetzgeber in unserer Zeit' (2007) 62 *Juristen Zeitung* 853, 858; cf B Rüthers, 'Zwischenruf aus der methodischen Wüste: "Der Richter wird's schon richten"(?)' (2006) 61 *Juristen Zeitung* 958, 958–60.

rule makers. The answer to this question affects the separation of power(s) and the principle of legal certainty.

If it were assumed that a judge is obliged to strictly apply the black letter law, s/he would have to issue an expulsion decision in cases covered by the provisions on mandatory expulsion (section 53 Residence Act) even if it led to a violation of Article 8 ECHR and Germany's obligations under the ECHR. At the same time, a strict application of section 53 would enhance legal certainty.

Alternatively, if it were assumed that a judge can interpret the law and integrate a balancing process into the provisions on expulsion, which is required by Article 8 ECHR, the question of the interpretative boundaries of the judge's powers arises. The prohibition of an interpretation *contra legem* clarifies that the wording of the provision demarcates the limits of its interpretation. The possibility to conduct a balancing process only arises if the wording of the relevant provision contemplates a balancing process or if it affords discretion to the decision maker.[39] The abolished provision on mandatory expulsion did not grant any discretion to the decision maker, thereby barring any interpretational possibilities at the outset.

Finally, it can be discussed whether a judge should be able to depart from the black letter law and assume the position of a rule maker if the strict application of a statutory provision to the individual case would result in an unfair judgment. While this approach is more likely to achieve balanced results, it disregards the will of the legislature, which imposed an obligation on the decision maker to issue an expulsion decision, as well as undermining the principle of legal certainty, as the administrative authorities and courts depart from the black letter law.

While some judges adhered to the first approach and strictly applied the provision on mandatory expulsion, others sought to incorporate a balancing process into this provision. Given the limitations imposed by the prohibition of an interpretation *contra legem*, several constructs were advanced, not only by the judiciary but also by scholars, to integrate a balancing process into the provision on mandatory expulsion.

D. Suggestions for Incorporating Article 8 ECHR into the System of Expulsion

The dilemma that was created in particular by the provision on mandatory expulsion was exacerbated by the ECHR's status in the German legal order. Pursuant to Article 59(2) German Basic Law, the ECHR has the ranking of an 'ordinary' federal law[40] and thus enjoys the same status as the Residence Act, which prevents the ECHR from prevailing over the provisions on expulsion.

[39] See also K Naumann, 'Die Prüfung der Verhältnismäßigkeit im Rahmen gebundener Entscheidungen' (2011) 64 *Die Öffentliche Verwaltung* 96, 98.

[40] See also Federal Constitutional Court, decision of 14 October 2004, 2 BvR 1481/04; F Fritzsch, *Der Schutz sozialer Bindungen von Ausländern* (Baden-Baden, Nomos, 2009) 27; H Landau, 'Die

i. The Different Approaches

Both the judiciary and various academics advanced suggestions on how to incorporate a balancing process between the interests of the foreigner and the interests of the state into the provisions on expulsion.

First, the judiciary referred to the obligation to interpret domestic law, if possible, in line with international obligations (*völkerrechtskonforme Auslegung*)[41] in order to avoid an infringement of Germany's public international law obligations. An obligation to interpret national law in light of the ECHR, however, only exists if such an interpretation is methodologically possible.[42] The prohibition of an interpretation *contra legem* limits the (interpretative) possibilities of administrative authorities and courts.[43] This prohibition also applies to an interpretation which aims at reading a provision of domestic law in light of the ECHR.[44] This approach could consequently not lead to a different interpretation of section 53 Residence Act, given that the wording of the provision was unequivocal and mandatorily required an expulsion decision to be taken.

A second approach suggested enhancing the status of the ECHR in the German legal order. The ECHR has the status of an 'ordinary' federal law, hence the same status as the provisions on expulsion in the Residence Act. Therefore, the concept of an *EMRK-inkorporierende Rechtsanwendung* was advanced; this would entail that the ECHR would be classed as a general part of the federal law to which the rule of *lex posterior* as well as the rule of *lex specialis* are inapplicable.[45] However, the Act of Parliament that implements the ECHR into German law does not provide a basis for such an approach.

Another approach suggested that the ECHR should have an intermediate ranking, between ordinary federal law and general rules of public international law. General rules of public international law constitute, according to Article 25 of the German Basic Law, an integral part of federal law, take precedence over the latter and directly create rights and obligations. However, Fritzsch rightly pointed out

Entwicklung der Menschenrechte in der Rechtsprechung des Bundesverfassungsgerichts und des Europäischen Gerichtshofs für Menschenrechte' (2008) *Deutsches Verwaltungsblatt* 1269, 1273; C Tomuschat, 'The Effects of Judgments of the European Court of Human Rights' (2010) 11 *German Law Journal* 513, 518.

[41] Federal Constitutional Court, decision of 26 March 1987, 2 BvR 589/79, 2 BvR 750/81, 2 BvR 284/85, Collection of the Cases of the Federal Constitutional Court Volume 74, p. 370; see also Tomuschat, 'The Effects of Judgments of the European Court of Human Rights' 518.

[42] Federal Constitutional Court, decision of 29 May 1990, BvL 20/84, 1 BvL 26/84, 1 BvL 4/86, Collection of the Cases of the Federal Constitutional Court, Volume 82, p 98.

[43] The prohibition of an interpretation *contra legem* was addressed by the CJEU among other judgments in Case C-212/04 *Adeneler and Others* ECLI:EU:C:2006:443, [2006] ECR I-06057, para 110; Case C-268/06 *Impact* ECLI:EU:C:2008:223, [2008] ECR I-02483, para 100; Case C-42/11 *Lopes Da Silva Jorge* ECLI:EU:C:2012:517, [2012], para 55. For critical assessment of the CJEU case law, see L Manthey and C Unseld, 'Der Mythos vom contra-legem Verbot: Vom Umgang des EuGH mit einem Verfassungsprinzip' (2011) 64 *Die Öffentliche Verwaltung* 921.

[44] Naumann, 'Die Prüfung der Verhältnismäßigkeit im Rahmen gebundener Entscheidungen' 98.

[45] K Grupp and U Stelkens, 'Zur Berücksichtigung der Europäischen Menschenrechtskonvention bei der Auslegung deutschen Rechts' (2005) 120 *Deutsches Verwaltungsblatt* 133, 141.

that not every ECHR right also constitutes a general rule of public international law.[46] Moreover, the German Basic Law does not even provide for such a category of norms (that is, norms ranked between general rules of international law and federal law).

These and other approaches sought to remedy the shortcomings and inadequacies that were inherent in the provisions on expulsion, in particular the provision on mandatory expulsion (section 53 Residence Act), but also in section 54, which required an expulsion decision as a rule.[47] While these approaches ensured compliance with the ECHR, they were also subject to criticism.

ii. Disadvantages of an Incorporation of Article 8 ECHR into the Provisions on Expulsion

Even though it was acknowledged that Article 8 ECHR necessitates the incorporation of a balancing process before an expulsion decision is taken, the approaches that facilitated such an integration were criticised. The main point of criticism related to legal certainty, which was said to be undermined by the divergence between statutory provisions on the one hand and judgments on the other.[48] It was pointed out that it is unforeseeable whether a case will be decided strictly in line with the statutory provision on expulsion or whether a balancing process, and thereby a proportionality assessment, will be conducted.[49]

Another point of criticism concerned the separation of powers.[50] According to Article 20(3) German Basic Law, administrative authorities and judges are bound by acts of Parliament. By not applying the law as it stands, the executive and judiciary were said to undermine the clear and well-defined will of Parliament.[51]

A third point of criticism referred to the Federal Constitutional Court's monopoly on declaring statutory provisions unconstitutional, which was said to be undermined by the courts' approaches.[52]

A further concern resulted from the so-called 'educational' argument,[53] which was developed in a slightly different context.[54] According to this argument, there

[46] Fritzsch, *Der Schutz sozialer Bindungen von Ausländern* 26; M Ruffert, 'Die Europäische Menschenrechtskonvention und innerstaatliches Recht' (2007) 35 *Europäische Grundrechte-Zeitschrift* 245, 246.

[47] For an overview see Ruffert, 'Die Europäische Menschenrechtskonvention und innerstaatliches Recht' 246, 247; Tomuschat, 'The Effects of Judgments of the European Court of Human Rights' 518, 519.

[48] Naumann, 'Die Prüfung der Verhältnismäßigkeit im Rahmen gebundener Entscheidungen' 99; Fritzsch, *Der Schutz sozialer Bindungen von Ausländern* 29.

[49] ibid.

[50] Naumann, 'Die Prüfung der Verhältnismäßigkeit im Rahmen gebundener Entscheidungen' 100.

[51] ibid.

[52] ibid.

[53] A Voßkuhle, 'Theorie und Praxis der verfassungskonformen Auslegung von Gesetzen durch Fachgerichte' (2000) 125 *Archiv des öffentlichen Rechts* 177, 189.

[54] The argument emerged in the context of judicial interpretation of ordinary law in line with constitutional law.

would be no need for the legislature to ensure compliance of draft legislation and statutes with European standards so long as judges interpreted these statutes in light of the ECHR and the ECtHR's case law. If the judiciary always rectified acts of the legislature, the latter could neglect international and European law obligations in the legislative process.

These concerns were well founded and underlined the need for a revision of the provision on expulsion, not least because the provisions undermined the credibility of judges. If they applied the statutory provision, they risked their judgments infringing the ECHR; if they took the ECHR into consideration, they were said to act against the clear will of the legislature.

iii. Judgments of the Federal Constitutional Court and the Federal Administrative Court

In 2007 both the Federal Constitutional Court and the Federal Administrative Court addressed the problems arising from the rigid system of expulsion. While the Federal Constitutional Court emphasised the importance of the ECHR and the ECtHR's case law for domestic expulsion decisions,[55] it sidelined the question of how to solve the tensions between the clear wording of the provisions on expulsion and the requirements of Article 8 ECHR.[56] In a decision issued in May 2007, the Federal Constitutional Court stressed the principle of proportionality, which guides the ECtHR's case law regarding Article 8 ECHR, and stated that this principle bars a standardisation of the types of criminal offences in the provisions on expulsion.[57] Three months later, the Court stipulated that the facts of the individual case have to be considered in expulsion decisions[58] and held that the standardised nature of the statutory provisions on expulsion was not designed for taking the facts of individual cases into account. Moreover, it emphasised that only by taking the facts of the individual case into consideration could justice be guaranteed.[59] The Court required that an expulsion decision motivated by reasons of general prevention has to observe the principle of proportionality and take case-specific circumstances into consideration.[60]

The Court's reference to the system of mandatory expulsion and expulsion as a rule (sections 53 and 54 Residence Act, respectively) and the remark that the facts of the individual case have to be taken into consideration were somewhat unclear, given that the clear wording of the provision on mandatory expulsion

[55] Federal Constitutional Court, decision of 10 May 2007, 2 BvR 304/07; Federal Constitutional Court, decision of 10 August 2007, 2 BvR 535/06.

[56] H Alexy, 'Subsumtion oder Abwägung – Was gilt im Ausweisungsrecht?' (2011) 126 *Deutsches Verwaltungsblatt* 1185, 1191.

[57] Federal Constitutional Court, decision of 10 May 2007, 2 BvR 304/07, para 42.

[58] Federal Constitutional Court, decision of 10 August 2007, 2 BvR 535/06, para 19.

[59] ibid.

[60] Federal Constitutional Court, decision of 10 August 2007, 2 BvR 535/06, paras 23, 24.

(section 53) did not provide any margin of discretion and barred the authorities and courts from taking the facts of the individual case into account. At the same time, the Federal Constitutional Court, which has the monopoly on striking down Acts of Parliament, considered the graduated system of mandatory expulsion (section 53), expulsion as a rule (section 54), and expulsion following a balancing process (section 55) to be compatible with the requirements of the principle of proportionality.[61]

The Federal Administrative Court emphasised the situation of the growing numbers of foreigners who were born and raised in the federal territory and, in light of this, it required expulsion decisions to be based on an individual assessment of the extent to which the foreigner is rooted in the federal territory.[62] Moreover, it held that it must be assessed whether the foreigner's rootedness bars, based on the grounds advanced for the expulsion as well as the particulars of the individual case, an expulsion decision.[63] Moreover, the Court stated that the schematic application of the system of mandatory expulsion and expulsion as a rule is of little assistance in taking the whole range of the individuals' affected interests into account. Therefore, the provision on expulsion following a balancing process (section 55 Residence Act), as the third form of expulsion provided for by the legislature, provides a higher guarantee that all aspects of the individual case will be considered and the relevant interests adequately balanced when deciding on an expulsion.

Even though the decisions of the Federal Administrative and the Federal Constitutional Court did not provide a solution to the discrepancy between the demands of the German law on expulsion and the balancing process that is required by Article 8 ECHR, they paved the way for a departure of the judiciary from the black letter law. After the Federal Administrative Court's decision, most domestic courts assessed the facts of the individual cases; they conducted a balancing process even in cases that were covered by the provision on mandatory expulsion (section 53 Residence Act)[64] and even if the special protection against expulsion (section 56 Residence Act) did not apply.[65] Returning to the different roles of judges,[66] the judiciary eventually adopted the third approach mentioned above and assumed the role of the law maker by taking the requirements of the ECHR and the principle of proportionality into account. Even though these developments were guided by the endeavour of the judiciary to ensure a fair outcome of its judgments and compliance with the ECHR, these approaches undermined legal

[61] Federal Constitutional Court, decision of 10 August 2007, 2 BvR 535/06, para 18.

[62] Federal Administrative Court, decision of 23 October 2007, 1 C 10.07, para 25.

[63] ibid.

[64] Higher Administrative Court Hamburg, judgment of 24 March 2009, 3 Bf 166/04 (juris), paras 92–115; Higher Administrative Court Nordrhein-Westfalen, decision of 26 May 2009, 18 E 1230/08 (juris); Higher Administrative Court Rheinland-Pfalz, judgment, 30 July 2010, 7 A 11230/09 (juris).

[65] Higher Administrative Court Baden-Württemberg, judgment of 20 October 2011, 11 S 1929/11 (juris); VG Oldenburg, judgment of 18 April 2012, 11 A 1369/11.

[66] See above, Section II.C.

certainty. Moreover, the judiciary overstepped the powers conferred on it by the Constitution as courts are confined to the interpretation of statutory provisions.[67]

E. The Abolished Provisions on Expulsion and their Compatibility with European Union Law

Apart from their incompatibility with the ECHR and the ECtHR's case law, the provisions on expulsion contained several features that were irreconcilable with EU law.

i. European Union Citizens

First, the provisions on expulsion did not comply with the standards for expelling EU citizens. Article 3(1) of Directive 64/221/EEC,[68] which required that 'Measures taken on grounds of public policy or of public security shall be based exclusively on the personal conduct of the individual concerned', had been codified at the national level by the 1969 Act on Residence of Nationals of the Member States of the European Economic Community.[69] However, this Act did not provide for a separate legal basis for the expulsion of nationals of the Member States (later EU citizens) and merely modified the provisions on expulsion in the Residence Act, which continued to apply to nationals of the Member States.[70] The joined cases of *Orfanopoulos and Olivieri* demonstrated that the German law on expulsion was incompatible with EU law.[71] The legal basis for the expulsion decision was the provision on mandatory expulsion and the CJEU clarified that EU law

> precludes legislation and national practices whereby a national of another Member State who has received a particular sentence for specific offences is ordered to be expelled … on the basis of a presumption that that person must be expelled, without proper account being taken of his personal conduct or of the danger which he represents for the requirements of public policy.[72]

On the day of the judgment the Citizenship Directive was adopted. It replaced Directive 64/221/EEC and it stipulates that the 'personal conduct of the individual

[67] Article 20(3) German Basic Law.

[68] Council Directive 64/221/EEC of 25 February 1964 on the co-ordination of special measures concerning the movement and residence of foreign nationals which are justified on grounds of public policy, public security or public health [1964] OJ 56/850.

[69] Gesetz über Einreise und Aufenthalt von Staatsangehörigen der Mitgliedstaaten der Europäischen Wirtschaftsgemeinschaft of 22 July 1969, Federal Law Gazette Part I 927. This law is the predecessor of the Freedom of Movement Act/EU.

[70] Higher Administrative Court Baden-Württemberg, judgment of 17 April 2002, 11 S 1823/01.

[71] Joined Cases C-482/01 and C-493/01 *Orfanopoulos/Olivieri* ECLI:EU:C:2004:262, [2004] ECR I-05257.

[72] ibid, para 100.

concerned must represent a genuine, present and sufficiently serious threat affecting one of the fundamental interests of society'. Moreover, it clarifies that 'justifications that are isolated from the particulars of the case or that rely on considerations of general prevention shall not be accepted'.[73] In August 2004 the Federal Administrative Court held the provisions in the Residence Act on mandatory expulsion (section 53) and expulsion as a rule (section 54) no longer applicable to EU citizens, explicitly declaring a change of its jurisprudence.[74] The legislature adopted the Freedom of Movement Act/EU,[75] which entered into force on 1 January 2005. This Act creates separate legal provisions for the expulsion of EU and EEA citizens and their (third-country national) family members.

ii. Turkish Nationals

Turkish nationals are covered by the EEC–Turkey Association Agreement and cannot directly rely on the provisions on expulsion and the safeguards against expulsion that are applicable to EU citizens. Nevertheless, the CJEU held that a public policy or public security decision pursuant to Article 14(1) of Association Council Decision 1/80 requires that the personal conduct of the individual concerned must pose a present, genuine and sufficiently serious threat to a fundamental interest of society.[76] In *Nazli* the CJEU clarified that an expulsion decision issued against a Turkish worker based on general preventive grounds is incompatible with Article 14(1) of Decision 1/80.[77]

Despite the fact that the provisions on expulsion in the Residence Act were *de jure* still applicable to Turkish nationals, the Federal Administrative Court implemented the requirements imposed by the CJEU's judgments by stipulating that an expulsion decision against a Turkish citizen must contain an assessment of the facts of the individual case.[78] Moreover, the Federal Administrative Court clarified that the provision in the Residence Act on mandatory expulsion (section 53) and expulsion as a rule (section 54) no longer applied to Turkish citizens covered by the Association Agreement, and that an expulsion decision against a Turkish national could only be based on section 55, which required a balancing process.[79]

[73] Article 27(2) of Directive 2004/38/EC of the European Parliament and of the Council of 29 April 2004 on the right of citizens of the Union and their family members to move and reside freely within the territory of the Member States amending Regulation (EEC) No 1612/68 and repealing Directives 64/221/EEC, 68/360/EEC, 72/194/EEC, 73/148/EEC, 75/34/EEC, 75/35/EEC, 90/364/EEC, 90/365/EEC and 93/96/EEC.

[74] Federal Administrative Court, judgment of 3 August 2004, 1 C 30.02.

[75] Freizügigkeitsgesetz/EU of 30 July 2004, Federal Law Gazette Part I 1950.

[76] Case C-303/08 *Bozkurt* ECLI:EU:C:2010:800, [2010] ECR I-13445, para 61; Case C-371/08 *Ziebell* ECLI:EU:C:2011:809, [2011] ECR I-12735, para 82.

[77] Case C-340/97 *Nazli* ECLI:EU:C:2000:77, [2000] ECR I-00957, para 63.

[78] Federal Administrative Court, judgment of 3 August 2004, 1 C 29.02.

[79] ibid.

iii. Long-term Resident Third-country Nationals

Regarding third-country nationals who are covered by the Long-Term Residents Directive (Directive 2003/109/EC), various academics have argued that an expulsion decision cannot be based on general preventive grounds.[80] This argument was confirmed retrospectively by the CJEU in *López Pastuzano*,[81] where the Court elaborated on the interpretation of Article 12 of the LTR Directive, which sets out the protection against expulsion. The Court emphasised, by reference to its *Ziebell* judgment, that an expulsion measure 'may not be ordered automatically following a criminal convention, but rather requires a case-by-case assessment'.[82]

The previous sections demonstrate that not only were the provisions on expulsion incompatible with ECHR standards, they also fell short of incorporating the requirements of EU law.

III. The New Provisions on Expulsion

A first effort to reform the old system of expulsion emerged in January 2013. The Green Party, an opposition party in the Federal Parliament (*Bundestag*), tabled a legislative proposal aimed at revising the legal position of Turkish nationals more generally.[83] On the matter of expulsion decisions,[84] the opposition's draft codified most of the CJEU's case law and drew parallels with the provision governing the termination of residence of EU citizens.[85]

A complete revision of the provisions on expulsion was initiated by the draft Act on the Redefinition of the Right of Residence and the Termination of Residence,[86] which was introduced by the federal government in February 2015. The Parliamentary Committee tabled its report on 1 July 2015,[87] and on 27 July 2015 the Act was approved in Parliament.[88] While all amendments became effective on 1 August 2015, the new provisions on expulsion only came into effect on

[80] R Marx, 'Aktuelle Entwicklungen im gemeinschaftsrechtlichen Ausweisungsschutz' (2007) 27 *Zeitschrift für Ausländerrecht und Ausländerpolitik* 142, 148.

[81] Case C-636/16 *López Pastuzano* ECLI:EU:C:2017:949, [2017].

[82] ibid, para 27.

[83] Gesetzentwurf der Abgeordneten Memet Kilic, Josef Philip Winkler, Dr. Konstantin von Notz, Volker Beck (Köln), Jerzy Montag, Claudia Roth (Augsburg), Wolfgang Wieland und der Fraktion BÜNDNIS 90/DIE GRÜNEN, 'Gesetzentwurf zur Klarstellung des assoziationsrechtlichen Rechtsstatus Staatsangehöriger der Türkei im Aufenthalts-, Beschäftigungserlaubnis- und Beamtenrecht' (2013) Bundestagsdrucksache 17/12193.

[84] ibid, p 12.

[85] Freedom of Movement Act/EU.

[86] Gesetzentwurf der Bundesregierung, 'Entwurf eines Gesetzes zur Neubestimmung des Bleiberechts und der Aufenthaltsbeendigung' (2015) Bundestagsdrucksache 18/4097.

[87] Gesetzentwurf der Bundesregierung, 'Entwurf eines Gesetzes zur Neubestimmung des Bleiberechts und der Aufenthaltsbeendigung' (2015) Bundestagsdrucksache 18/5420.

[88] Gesetz zur Neubestimmung des Bleiberechts und der Aufenthaltsbeendigung of 27 July 2015, Federal Law Gazette Part I 1386.

1 January 2016.[89] Pursuant to the explanatory memorandum, the new system aims at incorporating the case law of the Federal Administrative Court and the requirements of Article 8 ECHR.[90] The legislature sought to achieve these objectives by prescribing a balancing process between the interests of the foreigner and the interests of the state. The new system of expulsion begins with section 53(1) Residence Act, which provides:

> A foreigner whose presence threatens public policy, public security, the free democratic basic order or other significant interests of the Federal Republic of Germany, shall be expelled if the balancing process between the public interest in the foreigner's departure and the foreigner's interests in remaining in the federal territory, which must be based on the circumstances of the particular case, leads to the conclusion that the public interest prevails.

The balancing process between the interests of the foreigner and the interests of the state forms the leitmotiv of the new provisions on expulsion. Its prominent position at the beginning of the new provisions underpins the clear departure from the structure of the old system, which started with a provision on mandatory expulsion that barred any balancing process. The importance of the balancing process as an overarching principle is further underlined by the fact that all subsequent provisions are linked back to and depend on it as enshrined in section 53(1).

The next paragraph, section 53(2) Residence Act, contains a non-exhaustive[91] list of factors that have to be considered before an expulsion decision can be issued. This list is based on the criteria that were developed by the ECtHR in the context of Article 8 ECHR.[92] Section 53(2) provides that

> consideration shall in particular be given to the length of the foreigner's stay, his or her personal, economic and other ties in the federal territory and in the country of origin or in another state prepared to host him or her, the consequences of expulsion for his or her dependants and domestic partner, as well as whether the foreigner has abided with the law.[93]

A long residence will generally be beneficial to the foreigner's interest in remaining in the territory, whereas a short residence can be invoked by the state to justify the foreigner's termination of residence.[94] While the ECtHR repeatedly referred to 'the nature and seriousness of the offence committed by the applicant',[95] this criterion

[89] ibid, Article 9.

[90] See Bundesratsdrucksache 642/14, p 23; Gesetzentwurf der Bundesregierung, 'Entwurf eines Gesetzes zur Neubestimmung des Bleiberechts und der Aufenthaltsbeendigung' (2015) Bundestagsdrucksache 18/4097, pp 49–55 and pp 66, 67.

[91] See Gesetzentwurf der Bundesregierung, 'Entwurf eines Gesetzes zur Neubestimmung des Bleiberechts und der Aufenthaltsbeendigung' (2015) Bundestagsdrucksache 18/4097, p 50.

[92] See *El-Habach v Germany* App no 66837/11 (ECHR, 22 January 2013), para 29.

[93] Translation provided by the Language Service of the Federal Ministry of the Interior.

[94] Gesetzentwurf der Bundesregierung, 'Entwurf eines Gesetzes zur Neubestimmung des Bleiberechts und der Aufenthaltsbeendigung' (2015) Bundestagsdrucksache 18/4097, p 50.

[95] *Üner v The Netherlands* App no 46410/99 (ECHR, 18 October 2006), paras 57–59. For further information see Chapter 2.

has not been incorporated into section 53(2), but is specified in sections 54 and 55. Moreover, section 53(2) refers to the foreigner's 'law abidance', a criterion not established by the ECtHR and inserted retrospectively.

Section 53(3) Residence Act clarifies that refugees, Turkish citizens covered by the EEC–Turkey Association Agreement and long-term resident third-country nationals may only be expelled if their personal conduct constitutes a present and serious threat to public policy or public security and affects a fundamental interest of society and if expulsion is deemed necessary to protect this interest. This provision bars expulsion decisions that are based on grounds of general prevention. Other groups of foreigners, however, can be expelled on grounds of general prevention.[96] Finally, section 53(4) addresses expulsion decisions against failed asylum seekers.

The subsequent two provisions (sections 54 and 55 Residence Act) list the public's interest in expelling the foreigner and the foreigner's interest in remaining in Germany, respectively. Both provisions distinguish between particularly strong interests, which are of a very high importance and which are codified in the first paragraph, and important interests, which are set out in the second paragraph of each provision and which rank lower than the interests of a very high importance. Interestingly, the interests of the state are listed first (section 54), followed by section 55, which sets out the interests of the foreigner.

A. Recalibration of the Public Interest in Expelling the Foreigner

A comparison between the new and the old provisions on expulsion suggest that the revision has been used to lower the existing threshold for expulsion decisions (i) and to shift their focal point (ii).

i. The Lowering of the Threshold

The non-exhaustive[97] list of standardised public interests in expelling the foreigner is set out in section 54 Residence Act. The public interests in expelling the foreigner shall be accorded a particularly high importance in the balancing process if the foreigner has been sentenced to a prison term or a term of youth custody of at least two years and the sentence has become final.[98] This modification constitutes a reduction of the necessary duration of the prison term as the abolished provision

[96] Federal Administrative Court, BVerwG 1 C 21.18, DE:BVerwG:2019:090519U1C21.18.0, para 18; Federal Administrative Court, BVerwG 1 C 16.17, DE:BVerwG:2018:120718U1C16.17.0, paras 11, 16.

[97] Gesetzentwurf der Bundesregierung, 'Entwurf eines Gesetzes zur Neubestimmung des Bleiberechts und der Aufenthaltsbeendigung' (2015) Bundestagsdrucksache 18/4097, p 49.

[98] Residence Act, s 54(1) no 1.

on mandatory expulsion required a prison term of at least three years.[99] According to the abolished system, a prison term of at least two years would mandatorily have led to an expulsion decision only if the foreigner had committed specific offences (former section 53(2)).

Even though the new system does not mandatorily require the foreigner's expulsion and is therefore not directly comparable with the old system, its legal consequences can be the same, given that the public's interest in expelling the foreigner must be given a particularly high importance in the balancing process. Unless the public interest in expelling the foreigner is counterbalanced by an equally strong interest of the foreigner, the two-year prison sentence will lead to an expulsion decision as section 53(1) Residence Act provides that the foreigner 'shall be expelled' if the public interest takes precedence. If an equally strong interest of the foreigner cannot be invoked, the new system has exactly the same effects as the old provision of mandatory expulsion. The only difference between two provisions is the required duration of the prison term, which has been reduced from three to two years.

ii. The Grounds for Expulsion – A Reflection of the Zeitgeist

The new provisions reveal a shift of the public interest in expelling the foreigner. The abolished provision on mandatory expulsion (former section 53 Residence Act) focused on drug-related crimes (former section 53 no 2), breach of the peace (former section 53 no 2), and the smuggling of other foreigners (former section 53 no 3). These focal points were underpinned by the abolished provision on expulsion as a rule (former section 54), which referred to grounds of expulsion such as the smuggling of foreigners (former section 54 no 2) and the cultivation of drugs, their production, importation and trafficking (former section 54 no 3).

The new system of expulsion reflects the zeitgeist by shifting the focus on 'terrorism' and 'terrorism-related crimes', while the smuggling of foreigners is no longer explicitly mentioned. According to the new system of expulsion, the public interest in expelling the foreigner is particularly strong if the foreigner 'threatens the free democratic basic order or the security of the Federal Republic of Germany'.[100] Such a threat 'shall be assumed [to exist] where facts justify the conclusion that the foreigner is or has been a member of an organisation which supports terrorism or he or she supports or has supported such an organisation …'.[101] Moreover, the public interest in expelling the foreigner is particularly strong if the foreigner 'was one of the leaders of an organisation which was incontestably banned because its purposes or its activity contravenes criminal law or it is directed against the

[99] Residence Act, former s 53 no 1.
[100] See Residence Act, revised s 54(1) no 2.
[101] ibid. Translation provided by the Language Service of the Federal Ministry of the Interior.

constitutional order or the concept of international understanding'.[102] While the abolished provision on mandatory expulsion (former section 53 Residence Act) completely omitted any reference to terrorism-related crimes, 'terrorism' has been elevated to an interest of particular importance and takes centre stage in the new system of expulsion.

Nevertheless, the abolished provisions on expulsion contained references to terrorism(-related crimes), even though they would not mandatorily lead to an expulsion decision. The abolished provision that prescribed expulsion as a rule (former section 54 Residence Act) referred to the well-founded suspicion that the foreigner is a member of an organisation which supports terrorism (former section 54 no 5) or that s/he is preparing crimes that threaten the state (former section 54 no 5b). This ground has now been classed as a public interest of high importance in terms of section 54(1) no 2.

Another, even more remarkable, shift concerns a ground for expulsion that was previously codified in the provision on expulsion following a balancing process (former section 55 Residence Act). The abolished section 55(2) no 8 (a) and (b) provided that a foreigner can be expelled, if s/he publicly, in a meeting or by disseminating writings in a manner which is capable of disturbing public policy or public security, endorses or promotes crimes against peace, crimes against humanity, war crimes or acts of terrorism of comparable severity or incites hatred against parts of the population or against members of certain ethnic groups or religions.[103] This ground was codified alongside grounds such as prolonged homelessness (former section 55(2) no 5) or recourse to social assistance (former section 55(2) no 6), which underlined its reduced relevance. This ground for expulsion, which is directed at hatemongers,[104] has been slightly rephrased and has been upgraded to a public interest of particularly high importance (section 54(1) no 5).[105]

B. Compliance with the Standards of EU Law

The revised provisions on expulsion improved the protection against expulsion of both Turkish nationals covered by the EEC–Turkey Association Agreement and long-term resident third-country nationals.

[102] Residence Act, s 54(1) no 2. Translation provided by the Language Service of the Federal Ministry of the Interior.

[103] Note that sections of the provision have been omitted.

[104] Gesetzentwurf der Bundesregierung, 'Entwurf eines Gesetzes zur Neubestimmung des Bleiberechts und der Aufenthaltsbeendigung' (2015) Bundestagsdrucksache 18/4097, p 51.

[105] For comments see A Kießling, 'Fremdenpolizeirecht im Rechtsstaat (?) – Zu Herkunf und Zukunft des Ausweisungsrechts' (2016) 36 *Zeitschrift für Ausländerrecht und Ausländerpolitik* 45, 51, note 77.

i. The Protection of Turkish Nationals against Expulsion

Many of the changes that were proposed by the opposition party's draft in 2013 have been incorporated into the revised provisions on expulsion.[106] Section 56a(2) of the 2013 draft proposal[107] stipulated that Turkish nationals shall not be subject to expulsion decisions unless their personal conduct poses a present, genuine and sufficiently serious threat affecting a fundamental interest of society.[108] This requirement has been incorporated into section 53(3) of the revised Residence Act, which stipulates that a foreigner who is covered by the EEC–Turkey Association Agreement may only be expelled if the personal conduct constitutes a present and serious threat to public policy or public security, if it affects a fundamental interest of society, and if an expulsion is deemed indispensable to protect this interest. This provision reflects the CJEU's case law on the expulsion of Turkish citizens,[109] which bars expulsion decisions that are solely based on previous criminal convictions. According to the explanatory memorandum[110] this provision also bars expulsion decisions against Turkish nationals that are based on general preventive grounds which would contravene the CJEU's case law.[111] Section 56a(5) of the draft proposal, which prohibited termination of lawful residence of Turkish nationals on economic grounds,[112] has not been implemented.

ii. The Protection of Long-term Resident Third-country Nationals against Expulsion

Section 53(3) of the Residence Act stipulates that a foreigner who holds an EU long-term residence permit 'may be expelled only if the personal conduct constitutes a serious threat to public safety …'. This provision implements Article 12(1) of the LTR Directive, but while the LTR Directive refers to a 'sufficiently serious threat',[113] section 53(3) Residence Act only refers to a serious threat. However,

[106] Gesetzentwurf der Abgeordneten Memet Kilic, Josef Philip Winkler, Dr. Konstantin von Notz, Volker Beck (Köln), Jerzy Montag, Claudia Roth (Augsburg), Wolfgang Wieland und der Fraktion BÜNDNIS 90/DIE GRÜNEN, 'Gesetzentwurf zur Klarstellung des assoziationsrechtlichen Rechtsstatus Staatsangehöriger der Türkei im Aufenthalts-, Beschäftigungserlaubnis- und Beamtenrecht' (2013) Bundestagsdrucksache 17/12193.

[107] ibid, p 5.

[108] In parallel to the provisions guiding the expulsion of EU citizens and their family members, s 6(2) Freedom of Movement Act/EU, Article 27(2) of Directive 2004/38/EC.

[109] *Bozkurt*, para 61; *Ziebell*, para 82.

[110] Gesetzentwurf der Bundesregierung, 'Entwurf eines Gesetzes zur Neubestimmung des Bleiberechts und der Aufenthaltsbeendigung' (2015) Bundestagsdrucksache 18/4097, p 50.

[111] Case C-325/05 *Derin* ECLI:EU:C:2007:442, [2007] ECR I-06495, para 74; Case C-383/03 *Dogan* ECLI:EU:C:2005:436, [2005] ECR I-06237, para 24; *Nazli*, para 63.

[112] In parallel to the provisions guiding the expulsion of EU citizens and their family members, s 6(6) Freedom of Movement Act/EU, Article 27(1) of Directive 2004/38/EC.

[113] Article 12(1) of Directive 2003/109/EC.

Thym rightly points out that, according to settled CJEU case law, the notion of public policy refers to 'any "genuine and sufficiently serious threat … affecting one of the fundamental interests of society"'. The requirement of a 'sufficiently serious threat' is redundant as it is inherent in the concept of public policy.[114] Article 12(2) of Directive 2003/109/EC, by contrast, which requires that the 'decision referred to in paragraph 1 shall not be founded on economic considerations', has not been implemented.

Finally, Article 12(3) of Directive 2003/109 sets out a list of criteria that have to be considered before an expulsion decision can be issued against a long-term resident third-country national. These criteria correspond to those listed in section 53(2) Residence Act. Even though the foreigner's age is not explicitly mentioned in section 53(2), the wording 'in particular' clarifies that the list is not exhaustive and therefore enables the decision maker to consider other factors, including the foreigner's age.

C. Proportionality and Legal Certainty – In Search of an Adequate Balance

The principle of proportionality, which is a foundational element of the *Rechtsstaat*, requires a measure to be suitable, necessary and proportionate in the strict sense. The new provisions on expulsion integrate both the principle of proportionality and the principle of legal certainty. The foundational provision of the new system (section 53(1) Residence Act) requires the decision maker to conduct a balancing process between the interests of the foreigner and the interests of the state and thereby accommodates one of the elements of the principle of proportionality. The subsequent provisions (sections 54 and 55) pay tribute to the principle of legal certainty by providing for a non-exhaustive list of considerations that guide the decision maker in the balancing process.

A comparison with the ECtHR's case law demonstrates that a list of criteria that guide the balancing process is not always deemed to be sufficient to adequately safeguard the principle of legal certainty. In its *Boultif* judgment, the ECtHR listed the criteria that guide its assessment of deportation orders against the benchmark of Article 8 ECHR[115] but it refrained from ascribing an abstract weight to these criteria. In later judgments the ECtHR held that the weight attached to these factors will 'inevitably vary according to the specific circumstances of each case'[116] and that not all criteria will be relevant in every case.[117] This casuistic approach

[114] D Thym, 'Directive 2003/109/EC' in K Hailbronner and D Thym (eds), *EU Immigration and Asylum Law, A Commentary*, 2nd edn (Munich, C.H. Beck, 2016) Art. 12, para 4.

[115] *Boultif v Switzerland*, para 58.

[116] *Maslov v Austria* App no 1638/03 (ECHR, judgment of 23 June 2008), para 70; *A.A. v The United Kingdom* App no 8000/08 (ECHR, 20 September 2011), para 57.

[117] *A.A. v The United Kingdom*, para 57.

prompted criticism by both academics[118] and ECtHR judges[119] for undermining legal certainty.[120] Judge Martens even held that the 'case-by-case approach is a lottery ... and a source of embarrassment for the Court'.[121]

The new German provisions on expulsion strengthen the principle of proportionality as well as the principle of legal certainty by attaching a specific weight to the considerations that are relevant in the balancing process. Sections 54 and 55 Residence Act set out the interests of the public and the interests of the individual. Additionally, both provisions provide for a graduated differentiation between particularly important interests and important interests, thereby adding an additional layer of certainty to the balancing process and strengthening the principle of legal certainty. At the same time, these principles are not set in stone as the explanatory memorandum clarifies that the list of relevant considerations is not exhaustive,[122] and the weight that has been attached to them by the legislature can vary depending on the particular circumstances of the individual case.[123] This clarification grants the decision maker flexibility to respond to extraordinary or atypical cases, while ensuring that the decision maker is in principle bound by the weight that has been ascribed to these criteria by the legislature. In sum, the new provisions strike an adequate balance between the principle of proportionality and the principle of legal certainty by incorporating elements into the provisions of expulsion which are conducive to both principles.

D. Remaining Problems of the New System of Expulsion

Even though the new provisions on expulsion constitute a major improvement of the legal situation of both Turkish nationals and long-term resident third-country nationals and ensure compliance with Article 8 ECHR by providing for a balancing process, several shortcomings have not been tackled.

i. The Wording and Structure of the New Provisions

The declared aim of the new system of expulsion is to remedy the deficits of the old system and to provide for an open and unbiased balancing process.[124] This aim is

[118] S Zeichen, 'Ausweisungsschutz für integrierte Fremde' (2002) 57 *Zeitschrift für öffentliches Recht* 413, 452; N Kirkagac, *Verdachtsausweisungen im deutschen Rechtsstaat* (Frankfurt, Peter Lang, 2011) 121.

[119] *Beldjoudi v France* App no 12083/86 (ECHR, 26 March 1992), concurring opinion of Judge Martens; *Boughanemi v France* App no 22070/93 (ECHR, 27 March 1996), dissenting opinion of Judge Martens, para 4; *Boujlifa v France* App no 25404/94 (ECHR, 21 October 1997), joint dissenting opinion of Judges Baka and van Dijk.

[120] ibid.

[121] *Boughanemi v France*, dissenting opinion of Judge Martens, para 4.

[122] Gesetzentwurf der Bundesregierung, 'Entwurf eines Gesetzes zur Neubestimmung des Bleiberechts und der Aufenthaltsbeendigung' (2015) Bundestagsdrucksache 18/4097, pp 49, 53.

[123] ibid, p 50.

[124] Gesetzentwurf der Bundesregierung, 'Entwurf eines Gesetzes zur Neubestimmung des Bleiberechts und der Aufenthaltsbeendigung' (2015) Bundestagsdrucksache 18/4097, p 49.

called into question by the structure and wording of section 53(1) Residence Act, which is central to the new system. Even though section 53(1) requires the decision maker to conduct a balancing process, which constitutes a clear departure from the old system, an expulsion decision has to be taken ('shall be expelled') if the interests of the public in terminating the foreigner's residence take precedence over the interests of the foreigner. The provision does not grant discretion to the decision maker and thereby follows, to a certain extent, the rationale of the old system. A clear departure from the old system could have been achieved by providing that the foreigner 'can be expelled' instead of stipulating that the foreigner shall be expelled if the public interest prevails in the balancing process.

The lack of a margin of discretion regarding the issuance of an expulsion decision has implications for the decision maker's compliance with the principle of proportionality[125] as well as for the role of the executive and the judiciary. Even though the executive and courts independently conduct the balancing process, the legislature still prescribes the legal consequence of the result of this balancing process. Compared to the old provisions, the new system grants the decision maker a more autonomous role, but a complete renunciation of the old system would have required the legislature to grant the decision maker discretion regarding the issuance of an expulsion decision.

ii. Proportionality and the Necessity Assessment

The principle of proportionality requires a measure to be suitable, necessary and proportionate in the strict sense. While the new provisions on expulsion explicitly warrant a balancing process between the interests of the individual and the interests of the state, thus complying with the requirement of a proportionality assessment *stricto sensu*, they do not specifically refer to the expulsion decision's suitability and necessity. Even though the decision maker is assumed to assess the suitability and necessity of the measure before making an expulsion decision, an explicit mention of these criteria in the provisions on expulsion would have facilitated a more nuanced approach and would have broadened the spectrum of the decision maker's possible responses. Currently, once the balancing process has been conducted and the pendulum swings to the interests of the state, the foreigner has to be expelled.

The public's interest in excluding the foreigner could also be achieved by the withdrawal of the residence permit or its non-renewal,[126] which terminate the foreigner's right to remain[127] and oblige him or her to leave the federal territory.[128] These measures are less intrusive as they do not result in an entry ban, while an expulsion decision precipitates an entry ban.[129]

[125] See next point.
[126] See Residence Act, s 51(1).
[127] Residence Act, s 4(1).
[128] Residence Act, ss 50(1), 51(1).
[129] See Residence Act, s 11.

Even though it could be argued that these measures are not equally effective as an expulsion decision as they do not lead to an entry ban, a medium- to long-term exclusion of the foreigner by way of an entry ban is not always necessary. As a result, the question arises whether an expulsion decision is necessary.

Moreover, less intrusive alternatives to the termination of residence, such as mandatory rehabilitation measures, could have been mentioned in the statutory provisions. From a medium- and long-term perspective, rehabilitation measures could be more effective than an expulsion decision and a subsequent entry ban. A foreigner who has not been expelled and has engaged in reintegration measures could pose a lower risk compared to an expelled foreigner who is not rehabilitated and returns to the expelling state after the expiry of the entry ban. This calls into question the expulsion decision's suitability and necessity. Moreover, incorporating an assessment of a foreigner's best chance of rehabilitation would have been an acknowledgment of responsibility by the state; in particular with regard to delinquent foreigners who grew up or spent a considerable time in the expelling state, the latter state and its society arguably have some responsibility as it is in that context that the foreigner slipped into criminality. Shifting the burden of resocialisation to the state of nationality not only constitutes a negation of this responsibility, it also disregards the question of where rehabilitation can best be achieved.

The current wording of section 53(1) Residence Act, which prescribes that an expulsion decision has to be made once the public's interest in the foreigner's termination of residence takes precedence over the interests of the foreigner, does not account for these considerations. Therefore, the new system would benefit from imposing on the decision maker an obligation to incorporate an assessment of the expulsion decision's suitability and necessity.

iii. The Public's Interests and the Argumentative Burden

A problem that has not been tackled, and is possibly even exacerbated by the new provisions on expulsion, is the binary system, that is, the clear distinction between the public interest in terminating the foreigner's residence (section 54 Residence Act) and the interests of the foreigner in remaining in the federal territory (section 55). As early as in 2011, Bast rightly pointed out that the public's interests in the continued presence and residence of the foreigner on the federal territory should also be considered in the balancing process.[130] Indeed, the public's interests are not limited to the termination of residence as an interest in the foreigner's continued residence may exist, for example if the foreigner contributes to society despite having committed crimes. Bast's suggestion has not been taken up by the legislature and the binary system currently in place encourages the decision maker to disregard the public's interests in the foreigner's continued presence on

[130] J Bast, *Aufenthaltsrecht und Migrationssteuerung* (Tübingen, Mohr Siebeck, 2011) 81.

the territory. This omission undermines the new system's aim of achieving an open and unbiased balancing process.

Another aspect that might prevent an open balancing process is the risk of a 'box-ticking exercise'. While the enumeration of the conflicting interests and the prescription of the weight that has to be attached to these interests in the balancing process is conducive to legal certainty, it risks creating another downside, as pointed out by Kießling.[131] She argues that the balancing process might be reduced to a mere box-ticking exercise: the decision maker only has to identify the relevant interests by consulting the list of criteria that are set out in sections 54 and 55 Residence Act, including the weight that has to be attached to these interests. Subsequently, the decision maker sums up these interests and, in a final step, the interests of the public have to be set off against the interests of the foreigner.[132] If the interests of the public prevail over the interests of the foreigner, the decision maker is obliged to issue an expulsion decision pursuant to section 53(1).

Indeed, the well-structured list of sections 54 and 55 Residence Act might prevent the decision maker from considering the particulars of the individual case, especially if they are not reflected in the criteria listed in the statutory provisions. Even though the explanatory memorandum clarifies that the considerations listed in sections 54 and 55 are not exhaustive, that the weight attached to these criteria is mutable, and that the decision must be based on a comprehensive assessment of the circumstances of the individual case,[133] the decision maker is naturally inclined to apply the criteria that are listed in the statutory provisions. Moreover, any deviation from the statutory provisions implies an additional argumentative burden for the decision maker as s/he has to expound the reasons for considering additional criteria or altering the weight that has been ascribed to the criteria by the statutory provisions. The increased argumentative burden might foster 'box-ticking' on the part of the decision maker. Such an approach would be particularly harmful for atypical cases, which require consideration of criteria other than those listed in the statutory provisions.

iv. The Criterion of 'Law Abidance'

An open and unbiased balancing process might be undermined by the criterion of 'law abidance'. This criterion was inserted retrospectively into section 53(2) Residence Act, which contains a non-exhaustive[134] list of considerations that have to be considered before an expulsion decision can be taken. According to the explanatory memorandum,[135] this list is guided by the criteria that have been

[131] Kießling, 'Fremdenpolizeirecht im Rechtsstaat (?)' 52.
[132] ibid.
[133] Gesetzentwurf der Bundesregierung, 'Entwurf eines Gesetzes zur Neubestimmung des Bleiberechts und der Aufenthaltsbeendigung' (2015) Bundestagsdrucksache 18/4097, pp 49, 52.
[134] See ibid, p 50 and the wording of the provision 'in particular'.
[135] ibid.

developed by the ECtHR in the context of Article 8 ECHR. Indeed, the majority of criteria that are set out in section 53(2) match those developed by the ECtHR. However, the criterion of a foreigner's 'law abidance' has not been established by the ECtHR and has only been introduced by the Act on the Simplified Expulsion of Convicted Foreigners and Their Enhanced Exclusion from the Status of Asylum Seeker in March 2016,[136] hence some months after the new provisions on expulsion entered into force. Fuelled by crimes against women in Cologne during the night of New Year's Eve in 2015, public debate regarding the swift removal of foreign criminals accelerated as these crimes were said to have been mainly committed by foreigners.[137] The legislature reacted promptly and adopted the Act on the Simplified Expulsion of Convicted Foreigners and Their Enhanced Exclusion from the Status of Asylum Seeker, which contained, among other amendments, the criterion of 'law abidance'. The explanatory memorandum clarifies that the foreigner's law abidance will be considered in favour of the foreigner, while a law infringement, by contrast, will be used against the foreigner.[138] Given that the personal scope of the Act is limited to 'convicted foreigners', the criterion of law abidance will naturally not be fulfilled by the foreigner. The explanatory memorandum of the draft Act on the Redefinition of the Right of Residence and the Termination of Residence,[139] which introduced the new provisions on expulsion, stated that the criteria in section 53(2) are 'neutral' as they can be used in favour of and against the foreigner.[140] The criterion of 'law abidance', however, is not neutral when being applied to convicted foreigners. Therefore, Bergmann and Hörich argue that the criminal conviction that leads to the expulsion decision cannot be used a second time in the context of section 53(2) Residence Act.[141] The criterion of law abidance can therefore only refer to crimes other than those on which the expulsion decision has been based.

Another concern that arises in relation to the criterion of law abidance is its inherently unspecific and vague nature, which is capable of covering a variety of criminal offences ranging from minor offences to severe crimes. It carries the risk that petty crimes could be used to justify an expulsion decision, which would

[136] Gesetz zur erleichterten Ausweisung von straffälligen Ausländern und zum erweiterten Ausschluss der Flüchtlingsanerkennung bei straffälligen Asylbewerbern of 11 March 2016, Federal Law Gazette Part I 394.

[137] Report of the Ministry of the Interior of North-Rhine-Westphalia, 10 January 2016, p 12, www.mik.nrw.de/fileadmin/user_upload/Redakteure/Dokumente/Themen_und_Aufgaben/Schutz_und_Sicherheit/160111ssia/160111berppkoeln.pdf.

[138] Gesetzentwurf der Fraktionen der CDU/CSU und SPD, 'Entwurf eines Gesetzes zur erleichterten Ausweisung von straffälligen Ausländern und zum erweiterten Ausschluss der Flüchtlingsanerkennung bei straffälligen Asylbewerbern' (2016) Bundestagsdrucksache 18/7537, p 5.

[139] Gesetzentwurf der Bundesregierung, 'Entwurf eines Gesetzes zur Neubestimmung des Bleiberechts und der Aufenthaltsbeendigung' (2015) Bundestagsdrucksache 18/4097.

[140] ibid, p 50.

[141] M Bergmann and C Hörich, 'Besonders schwerwiegende Ausweisungsrechtsfehler – Kritische Anmerkungen zur jüngsten Reform des Ausweisungsrechts' (2016) 36 *Zeitschrift für Ausländerrecht und Ausländerpolitik* 269, 301; I Bauer and S Beichel-Benedetti, 'Das neue Ausweisungsrecht' (2016) *Neue Zeitschrift für Verwaltungsrecht* 416, 420.

substantially reduce the protection of the individual. However, it has already been clarified that this criterion shall not have an independent and autonomous meaning in the balancing process,[142] which suggests that the insertion of this criterion was primarily politically motivated.[143]

IV. Entry Ban

Section 11(1) of the Residence Act stipulates that an entry or residence ban for the national territory is to be issued for foreigners who have been expelled. If a foreigner is subject to a national entry and residence ban pursuant to section 11, an alert may be issued for the purpose of refusing entry.[144] The SIS alert is an entry ban with a Europe-wide dimension, and it is addressed in more detail below.[145]

Previously, a foreigner who was subject to an entry ban had to apply for limitation of the duration of the ban. However, in *Filev and Osmani* (2013)[146] the CJEU gave its interpretation of Article 11 of the Return Directive (Directive 2008/115/EC), which does not require an application for limitation of the duration of the entry ban. The CJEU held that the 'Member States are under an obligation to limit the effects in time of any entry ban in principle to a maximum of five years independently of an application made for that purpose by the relevant third-country national'.[147] Therefore, the entry ban has to be limited in time *ex officio*.[148] The duration of the entry ban shall not, in principle, exceed five years,[149] which corresponds to Article 11(2) Return Directive. Two exceptions are provided. First, if the foreigner has been expelled on grounds of a criminal conviction or if the foreigner poses a serious threat to public safety and order, the entry ban shall not to exceed 10 years.[150] According to the Federal Administrative Court, 10 years is usually the maximum period for which a prediction can realistically be conducted regarding the foreigner's expected future conduct.[151] The second exception concerns cases in which the foreigner was expelled on grounds of a crime against peace, a war crime or a crime against humanity, or to avert a terrorist threat or a threat to the security of the Federal Republic of Germany. In these circumstances, the duration of the entry ban shall generally be 20 years.[152]

[142] Higher Administrative Court Baden-Württemberg, decision of 11 April 2016, 11 S 393/16.
[143] Bergmann and Hörich, 'Besonders schwerwiegende Ausweisungsrechtsfehler' 302.
[144] Residence Act, s 50(6).
[145] See Part III.
[146] Case C-297/12 *Filev and Osmani* ECLI:EU:C:2013:569, [2013].
[147] ibid, para 27.
[148] Residence Act, s 11(2).
[149] Residence Act, s 11(3).
[150] Residence Act, s 11(5).
[151] Federal Administrative Court, DE:BVerwG:2012:131212U1C14.12.0, para 14.
[152] Residence Act, s 11(5a).

EU and EEA citizens are covered by the Freedom of Movement Act/EU, which provides that 'EU citizens or their dependants shall be required to leave the federal territory if the foreigners authority has established that no entitlement to entry and residence exists'.[153] Section 7(2) stipulates that 'EU citizens and their dependants who have lost their entitlement to freedom of movement … shall not be permitted to re-enter and stay in the federal territory'.

Previously, the entry ban was in principle unlimited in time and a limitation had to be requested by the EU citizen. The requirement of an application for the limitation of the entry ban was not only criticised by the European Commission,[154] it was also problematic in light of the CJEU's judgment in the case of *Filev and Osmani*. Therefore, section 7(2) Freedom of Movement Act/EU now stipulates that the entry ban shall be temporary *ex officio*.

V. Conclusions

The new provisions on expulsion remedy the most severe deficiency of the old system by providing for a balancing process between the interests of the individual and the interests of the state, which is also required by Article 8 ECHR. Moreover, the new system incorporates the standards of EU law regarding the expulsion of Turkish nationals covered by the EEC–Turkey Association Agreement and the expulsion of long-term resident third-country nationals covered by Directive 2003/109/EC. By introducing the requirement of a balancing process into the system of expulsion, the legislature enables the executive and courts to conduct an independent assessment and thereby strengthens their role. Finally, the new provisions strike an adequate balance between the principle of proportionality and the principle of legal certainty. By listing the criteria that have to be considered in the balancing process and by specifying the weight that should be attached to these criteria, the legislature makes the balancing process more transparent and predictable.

While the new provisions on expulsion respond to the most pressing needs for reform, they fall short of completely breaking with the rationale and biases of the old system. The central provision of the new system, section 53(1) Residence Act, still adheres to the logic of the abolished provision on mandatory expulsion (former section 53) as it prescribes that an expulsion decision has to be made ('shall be expelled') if the state's interest in expelling the foreigner prevails. The new provisions refrain from granting the decision maker a margin of discretion regarding the question of whether an expulsion decision has to be made, which has implications for both the principle of proportionality and the role of the decision

[153] Freedom of Movement Act/EU, s 7(1).

[154] See Press release by the EU Commission, 'Free movement: Commission asks Austria, Germany and Sweden to uphold EU citizens' rights', 21 June 2012, IP/12/646.

maker. Regarding the principle of proportionality, the absence of discretion and the obligation of the decision maker to make an expulsion decision if the interests of the state prevail make it difficult to apply less onerous but equally effective measures. This, however, is required by the proportionality principle's element of necessity.

With regard to the role of the decision maker, the new provisions have departed from the old provisions on expulsion by requiring a balancing process. The old provision on mandatory expulsion (former section 53 Residence Act), which barred the decision maker from conducting a balancing process and prescribed that an expulsion decision had to be issued, reduced the executive and the judiciary to mere executing bodies of the legislature's will. However, regarding the legal consequence, the new system still adheres to the rationale of the old system by requiring an expulsion decision ('shall be expelled', section 53(1)) if the interests of the state take precedence over the interests of the individual. Section 53(1) reveals that the role of the decision maker has not fundamentally been changed. In order to ensure an independent role of the executive and the judiciary in the process of an expulsion decision, the legislature has to grant discretion to the decision maker.

The sequence of the statutory provisions in the Residence Act, which list the interests of the state first (section 54) followed by the interests of the foreigner (section 55), underpins doubts as to whether the new provisions truly abandon the rationale of the old system.

Even though the new system prohibits expulsion decisions against Turkish nationals and long-term resident third-country nationals from being based on general preventive grounds and thereby complies with the requirements of EU law, it does not ban recourse to general preventive grounds in expulsion decisions against other groups of third-country nationals. General prevention, which serves the aim of deterring other foreigners from committing offences that are identical or similar to those committed by the expelled foreigner, is a concept of criminal law. Expulsion decisions, by contrast, are said to be measures of administrative law and are therefore considered compatible with the principle of *ne bis in idem*. Expulsion decisions which are, however, based on concepts of criminal law call this statement into question.

The new system of expulsion constitutes a further step in the reform process, which has not yet reached its final destination. The legislature still has to grant discretion to the decision maker to ensure full compliance with the principle of proportionality. Further reform processes will need to rethink the concept of expulsion decision more generally and address the question of whether the instruments of criminal law could constitute an adequate and sufficient response to the foreigner's criminal conduct and whether expulsion decisions can be abandoned or limited to very few cases.

6

The Netherlands

This chapter focuses on the Dutch provisions that regulate the termination of lawful residence following a criminal conviction and the requirements for imposing an entry ban (*ongewenstverklaring* or *inreisverbod*).

The chapter begins with a brief overview of the legal framework (Section I) and continues with the provisions regulating the termination of lawful residence following a criminal conviction (Section II). The decision to terminate lawful residence after a criminal conviction relies on the sliding scale (*glijdende schaal*). The sliding scale is an instrument which relates the duration of the foreigner's lawful stay in the Netherlands to the nature and seriousness of the committed offence, the maximum statutory prison term and the prison term that has been imposed on the foreigner.[1] Where residence is terminated, an entry ban can be imposed on the individual. The Dutch system provides for two different types of entry bans, the *inreisverbod* and the *ongewenstverklaring* (Section III). Both instruments declare the foreigner *persona non grata* but they have a different personal scope. While the *ongewenstverklaring* (Section IV) applies to EU, EEA and Swiss nationals and their family members and third-country nationals who are not covered by the Return Directive, the *inreisverbod* (Section V) can only be imposed on third-country nationals.

This chapter addresses two different margins of discretion, that is, the margin of discretion granted by the legislature to administrative authorities when terminating lawful residence and imposing an entry ban and the margin of discretion of administrative authorities vis-à-vis administrative courts (VI), which relates to the intensity of judicial scrutiny of administrative decisions.

Section VII addresses the sliding scale and its rationale, and is followed by a concluding section (Section VIII).

I. The Legal Framework

The Vreemdelingenwet 2000[2] (Dutch Law on Foreign Nationals – Vw 2000) came into effect in 2000 and replaced the Law on Foreign Nationals from 1965.

[1] Advies Raad van State, W 04.11.0396/I, 28 November 2011, Staatscourant 2012, no 14035, p 8; H Oosterom-Staples, 'Naar een Europese glijdende openbare ordeschaal voor het personenverkeer' (2012) 18 *Nederlands Tijdschrift voor Europees Recht* 265.

[2] Wet van 23 November 2000 tot algehele herziening van de Vreemdelingenwet ('Vreemdelingenwet 2000'), Official Gazette of the Kingdom of the Netherlands 2000, 495.

The Vw 2000 sets out the general rules, which are specified by the Vreemdelingenbesluit 2000 (Decree on Foreign Nationals – Vb 2000), the Voorschrift Vreemdelingen 2000 (Regulation on Foreign Nationals 2000) and the Vc 2000 (Circular on Foreign Nationals). 'Neither the *Vreemdelingenbesluit* 2000 nor the *Voorschrift Vreemdelingen* 2000 are acts of Parliament':[3] the Vb 2000 is an *Algemene Maatregel van Bestuur* (order in Council)[4] and the Voorschrift Vreemdelingen 2000 is a ministerial instruction. The Vw 2000 and the Vb 2000 authorise the minister to adopt legislative measures to specify the principles that are enshrined in the Vw and the Vb 2000.[5] The Vc 2000 is a ministerial instruction,[6] which contains policy rules that specify the discretion that is granted by the Vw and Vb 2000. These rules aim at enhancing predictability, legal certainty and consistency of the decision-making process.[7] The rules do not impose obligations upon the individual, but they are in principle binding for the administration.[8]

II. The Termination of Lawful Residence Following a Criminal Conviction

This section addresses the provisions regulating the termination of lawful residence following a criminal conviction in the same order in which they were discussed in the previous section and the previous chapter, that is, starting with EU citizens as the most privileged group followed by the other groups of foreigners. The focus rests on the regular residence permit (Articles 14–27 Vreemdlingenwet 2000), while the residence permit for asylum (Articles 28–45 Vw 2000) is not addressed as it is excluded from the scope of this book.

A. Termination of Residence Following a Criminal Conviction

The termination of residence of EU, EEA and Swiss citizens is regulated by Article 8.22 Vb 2000. Article 8.22 implements several of the safeguards and criteria that are contained in Articles 27 and 28 of the Citizenship Directive, for instance the requirement that lawful stay may only be terminated on grounds of public policy or public security if the personal conduct of the foreigner poses a genuine, present

[3] H Oosterom-Staples, 'Adjudicating the Schengen Agreement in the Netherlands' (2000) 2 *European Journal of Migration and Law* 53.

[4] ibid.

[5] ibid.

[6] *Arvelo Aponte v The Netherlands* App no 28770/05 (ECHR, 3 November 2011), para 27 refers to 'Aliens Act Implementation Guidelines'.

[7] Oosterom-Staples, 'Adjudicating the Schengen Agreement in the Netherlands' 54.

[8] Article 4:84 Algemene wet bestuursrecht (Awb).

and serious threat to a fundamental interest of society.[9] Regarding the interpretation of these requirements, a national court clarified that the different components of the criterion of a present, genuine and sufficiently serious threat to public policy or public security must be fulfilled cumulatively.[10] It held that they cannot be separated in a sense that the seriousness of the threat is demonstrated by a crime that has been committed nine years prior to the decision to terminate lawful residence or that the presence of the threat is proven by a minor offence committed two years prior to that decision.[11] Moreover, the Court stated the offence committed earlier can only be used to demonstrate the seriousness of the threat a foreigner poses if a risk of reoffending exists.[12] This interpretation has been upheld by the Raad van State.[13]

Interestingly, Article 8.22 Vb 2000 grants discretion regarding the termination of residence, while the Vreemdelingencirculaire 2000 (Vc 2000) provides that the IND (Immigration and Naturalisation Service) terminate EU citizen's residence.[14] Even though the Vb grants discretion, the policy rules in the Vc narrow this discretion and stipulate when residence is to be terminated.

The right of residence of permanently resident EU citizens and their family members[15] may only be terminated if serious reasons of public policy or national security require the termination,[16] which mirrors Article 28(2) of the Citizenship Directive. After 10 years of lawful residence or if a minor EU citizen is affected, lawful residence may only be terminated on imperative grounds of public security,[17] which mirrors Article 28(3) of the Citizenship Directive. After the refusal of a residence permit or the termination of regular residence, the EU citizen or his/her family members have to leave the Netherlands voluntarily within four weeks.[18] The four-week time limit for voluntary return can be reduced in urgent cases.[19] The threshold of four weeks is not in line with Article 30(3) of the Citizenship Directive, which provides for a one-month time period for voluntary return.

B. Residence Permits for Third-country Nationals Issued for a Limited or for an Unlimited Time

The Vw 2000 distinguishes between residence permits issued for a limited time[20] and residence permits issued for an unlimited time.[21] Irrespective of this

[9] Article 8.22(1) Vb 2000.
[10] Rechtbank 's-Gravenhage, AWB 10-23494, NL:RBSGR:2011:BP2584, para 25.
[11] ibid.
[12] ibid.
[13] ABRvS, 201102012/1/V2, NL:RVS:2011:BV3584.
[14] See B10/2.3 Vreemdelingencirculair 2000 ('Vc 2000').
[15] Article 8.17(1) Vb 2000.
[16] Article 8.18(2) Vb 2000.
[17] Article 8.22(3) Vb 2000.
[18] B10/2.3 Vc 2000.
[19] Article 8.24(3) Vb 2000.
[20] Articles 14–19 Vw 2000.
[21] Articles 20–22 Vw 2000.

differentiation, the sliding scale (Article 3.86 Vb 2000) is crucial for both categories as it determines whether a residence permit can be rejected or whether lawful residence can be terminated due to a criminal conviction.

A residence permit issued for a limited time can be withdrawn if the foreigner poses a threat to public policy or public security.[22] The threat to public policy is specified by the sliding scale. The residence permit issued for an unlimited time can be withdrawn or altered if, among other reasons, the foreigner has irrevocably been sentenced to a prison term for a crime which is punishable with imprisonment for up to three years or if the foreigner has been placed in a psychiatric hospital, per Article 22(2)(c) Vw 2000. The Vb 2000 specifies that a residence permit issued for an unlimited time can be withdrawn on the basis of Article 22(1)(c) Vw 2000 if the total amount of criminal punishment or measures is at least equal to the requirements set out in the sliding scale, more specifically in Article 3.86(2), (3) and (5) Vb 2000.[23]

The EU long-term residence permit can only be withdrawn if the foreigner poses an actual and serious threat to public policy or public security.[24] The Vb 2000 further clarifies that the EU long-term residence permit can be withdrawn if the total amount of criminal punishment or measures is at least equal to the requirements set out in the sliding scale, more specifically in Article 3.86(2), (3) and (5) Vb 2000.[25] The rules regarding the withdrawal of residence permits of UK citizens following the withdrawal of the United Kingdom from the European Union are further specified in Vc (B) 2000.[26]

As a consequence of a withdrawal of a residence permit, the foreigner's residence is no longer lawful[27] and the foreigner has to leave the Netherlands.[28] If the foreigner does not comply with this obligation, s/he can be removed.[29] The refusal of the prolongation of the duration of a residence permit or the withdrawal of a residence permit constitute a return decision.[30] These decisions can comprise an entry ban.[31]

C. Sliding Scale (*Glijdende Schaal*)

The decision to terminate lawful residence after a criminal conviction relies on the sliding scale.[32] It was introduced in 1990 to provide legal certainty and to enhance

[22] Article 19 in conjunction with Article 18(1)(e) Vw 2000.
[23] Article 3.98(1) Vb 2000.
[24] Article 45d(1)(b) Vw 2000.
[25] Article 3.127(3)Vb 2000.
[26] Article B13/2.4 and 3.5.
[27] Article 27(1)(a) Vw 2000.
[28] Article 27(1)(b) Vw 2000.
[29] Article 27(1)(b) Vw 2000, see also Article 27(1)(c) Vw 2000.
[30] Article 27(2)(c), in conjunction with Article 27(1) Vw 2000.
[31] Article 27(4) Vw 2000.
[32] Article 3.86 Vb 2000.

migrants' security of residence.[33] The sliding scale defines a threat to public policy by relating the duration of the foreigner's lawful stay in the Netherlands to the nature and seriousness of the offence committed, the maximum statutory prison term and the prison term that has been imposed.[34] The sliding scale already contains a balancing process *in abstracto* and requires a balancing process *in concreto* if residence can be terminated. The protection granted by the sliding scale increases the longer the foreigner lawfully resides in the Netherlands.

The sliding scale primarily applies to third-country nationals. For EU and EEA citizens and their family members it constitutes a minimum standard or safety net as EU law normally provides for a higher level of protection. Even though it was initially introduced to provide legal certainty and to strengthen the legal position and the security of residence of foreigners, Stronks points out that the sliding scale became an instrument of a more restrictive migration policy or at least a tool to enhance the appearance of a more restrictive migration policy.[35]

Both the 2010 and the 2012 coalition agreement aimed at tackling criminal offences committed by foreigners and stipulated that convicted foreigners shall be more quickly expellable.[36] The coalition agreements also provided that this ought to be achieved by a tightening of the sliding scale.[37] In 2012 the sliding scale was tightened by an amendment of the Vb 2000,[38] which precipitated several changes.

A significant change concerned the security of residence of long-term resident third-country nationals. Previously, two categories were exempted from expulsion, that is, third-country nationals who had resided for more than 20 years in the Netherlands, and third-country nationals who were born in the Netherlands or had lawfully resided there from before the age of 10 and had been resident for more than 15 years.[39] This protection was abolished in 2012 through an amendment of the Vb 2000.[40]

[33] Adviescommissie voor Vreemdelingenzaken (ACVZ), Advies 'Gewogen gevaar', uitgebracht aan de staatssecretaris van Justitie en Veiligheid, p 33.

[34] Oosterom-Staples, 'Naar een Europese glijdende openbare ordeschaal voor het personenverkeer' 265.

[35] M Stronks, 'Een bijna ongebreidelde beteugeling van de tijd, Een analyse van aanscherpingen van de glijdende schaal' (2013) 34 *Nederlands Juristenblad* 2306, 2307, 2314.

[36] Rijksoverheid, '"Bruggen slaan" Regeerakkoord VVD – PvdA', 29 October 2012, www.rijksoverheid.nl/documenten/rapporten/2012/10/29/regeerakkoord p 29; Rijksoverheid, 'Vrijheid en verantwoordelijkheid, Regeerakkoord VVD-CDA', 30 September 2010, www.rijksoverheid.nl/documenten/rapporten/2010/09/30/regeerakkoord-vvd-cda p 24.

[37] Rijksoverheid, 'Vrijheid en verantwoordelijkheid, Regeerakkoord VVD-CDA', 30 September 2010, p 24.

[38] By the 'Besluit van 26 maart 2012, houdende wijziging van het Vreemdelingenbesluit 2000 in verband met aanscherping van de glijdende schaal', Official Gazette of the Kingdom of the Netherlands 2012, 158.

[39] Article 3.86(7)(c) and Article 3.86(8)(b) Vb 2000 of the version that entered into force on 1 April 2001; Article 3.86(10)(b) and (11)(b) Vb 2000 of the version of the Vreemdelingenbesluit 2000 which was applicable on 18 April 2012. See K Groenendijk, 'Long-term Immigrants and the Council of Europe' in E Guild and P Minderhoud (eds), *Security of Residence and Expulsion* (The Hague, Kluwer Law International, 2001) 20; Stronks, 'Een bijna ongebreidelde beteugeling van de tijd' 2311, 2312.

[40] By the 'Besluit van 26 maart 2012, houdende wijziging van het Vreemdelingenbesluit 2000 in verband met aanscherping van de glijdende schaal', Official Gazette of the Kingdom of the Netherlands 2012, 158.

Moreover, the tightening of the sliding scale becomes clearly visible when comparing the 1990 sliding scale and its current form. The 1990 scale required a nine-month prison term for a termination of lawful residence of less than three years,[41] which was also the applicable threshold in 2001. The sliding scale in its current form only requires a prison term of one day to terminate lawful residence of less than three years.

i. Different Categories in the Sliding Scale/Different Sliding Scales

The sliding scale (Article 3.86 Vb 2000) specifies when a threat to public policy can lead to a termination of residence, and it distinguishes between different categories.

First, Article 3.86(1)(a) Vb 2000 covers situations in which the foreigner resides for less than three years in the Netherlands and is convicted of a criminal offence which is punishable with a term of imprisonment of two years or more. In situations covered by this category, a residence permit can be withdrawn if a prison term of one day (or more) has been imposed. Second, Article 3.86(1)(b) Vb 2000 addresses criminal offences which are punishable with a term of imprisonment of three years or more. Both Article 3.86(1)(a) and (b) Vb 2000 require that the judgment became final and that the total duration of the unconditionally imposed sentence must at least be equal to that in Article 3.86(2) and Article 3.86(3) respectively.

The applicable table or scale is determined by the statutory prison term that can be imposed for the crime that has been committed by the foreigner. The first table (Article 3.86(2) Vb) is applicable if the foreigner commits a criminal offence(s) punishable with a prison term of less than six years, while the second table (Article 3.86(3) Vb) is applicable if the committed crime is punishable with a prison term of more than six years. Within the respective scale, the duration of the foreigner's lawful residence is related to the prison term that has actually been imposed. The scales below indicate the lawful residence on the left-hand side, while on the right-hand side is the duration of the imposed prison term required to terminate the lawful residence.

Article 3.86(2) Vb 2000 applies to criminal offences punishable with a prison term of less than six years and provides:

Duration of the foreigner's regular stay[42]	**Duration of the prison term**
Less than 3 years:	1 day
At least 3 years, but less than 4 years:	5 months
At least 4 years, but less than 5 years:	7 months

[41] Stronks, 'Een bijna ongebreidelde beteugeling van de tijd' 2307.
[42] The duration is defined by Article 3.86(6) Vb 2000.

At least 5 years, but less than 6 years:	15 months
At least 6 years, but less than 7 years:	18 months
At least 7 years, but less than 8 years:	22 months
At least 8 years, but less than 9 years:	27 months
At least 9 years, but less than 10 years:	33 months
At least 10 years, but less than 15 years:	40 months
At least 15 years:	65 months

Article 3.86(3) Vb 2000 applies to criminal offences punishable with a prison term of more than six years and provides:

Duration of the foreigner's regular stay	**Duration of the prison term**
Less than three years	1 day
At least 3 years, but less than 4 years:	4 months and 2 weeks
At least 4 years, but less than 5 years:	6 months
At least 5 years, but less than 6 years:	12 months
At least 6 years, but less than 7 years:	15 months
At least 7 years, but less than 8 years:	18 months
At least 8 years, but less than 9 years:	22 months and 2 weeks
At least 9 years, but less than 10 years:	27 months
At least 10 years, but less than 15 years:	30 months
At least 15 years:	48 months

Finally, Article 3.86(4) Vb 2000 applies to repeat offenders, hence to individuals who have committed at least three offences. The relevant table is set out in Article 3.86(5) Vb 2000, which provides:

Duration of the foreigner's regular stay	**Duration of the prison term**
Less than 3 years:	1 day
At least 3 years, but less than 4 years:	4 months
At least 4 years, but less than 5 years:	5 months
At least 5 years, but less than 6 years:	6 months
At least 6 years, but less than 7 years:	7 months
At least 7 years, but less than 8 years:	8 months
At least 8 years, but less than 9 years:	9 months
At least 9 years, but less than 10 years:	10 months
At least 10 years, but less than 15 years:	12 months
At least 15 years:	14 months

Foreigners who have lawfully resided for more than 10 years in the Netherlands must either fulfil Article 22b(1) of the Dutch Criminal Code[43] or they must have committed an offence listed in the Narcotics Act which is punishable with a prison term of at least six years.[44]

Looking at the thresholds, it is striking that one day of imprisonment suffices to terminate lawful residence of less than three years. Moreover, the protection granted in the first 10 years of residence is not particularly strong. The thresholds contained in Article 3.86(2) and (3) Vb 2000 are of particular interest regarding those foreigners who have resided for more than 10 years in the Netherlands.[45] After more than 10 years of lawful residence, a prison term of (at least) 40 months (in case of Article 3.86(2) Vb 2000) or 30 months (in case of Article 3.86(3) Vb 2000) is required to terminate lawful residence. Moreover, Article 3.86(10) Vb 2000 establishes additional safeguards.

For repeat offenders (Article 3.86(5) Vb 2000) the thresholds are rather strict compared to the other two tables contained in Article 3.86(2) and (3) Vb 2000. After five years of regular residence, a prison term of six months suffices for the termination of lawful residence and after 15 years of regular residence even a prison term of 14 months suffices. However, Article 3.86(10) Vb 2000 establishes additional safeguards for residence exceeding 10 years.

ii. Scope Rationae Personae

The sliding scale does not mention EU citizens and is said not to be applicable to them[46] and their family members.[47] Nonetheless, the sliding scale provides a safety net which applies in the absence of more advantageous provisions. This is demonstrated by the Vc 2000, which stipulates that lawful residence is refused or terminated if the personal conduct of an EU citizen or a family member poses a present, genuine and serious threat to a fundamental interest of society unless the analogous application of Article 3.77 Vb 2000 and Article 3.86 Vb 2000 leads to the conclusion that residence shall not be terminated.[48]

The sliding scale mentions Turkish nationals covered by the EEC–Turkey Association Agreement but clarifies that it cannot be applied if its application

[43] An offence for which a prison term of six years or more can be imposed and which results in a serious interference with the bodily integrity of the victim or offences covered by Articles 181, 240b, 248a, 248b, 248c and 250 Criminal Code.

[44] Article 3.86(10) Vb 2000.

[45] See also Oosterom-Staples, 'Naar een Europese glijdende openbare ordeschaal voor het personen-verkeer 269, who points out that the sliding scale can be illustrated in a graph as a constant (increasing/decreasing) line which levels off after 10 years.

[46] Adviescommissie voor Vreemdelingenzaken (ACVZ), Advies 'Gewogen gevaar', uitgebracht aan de staatssecretaris van Justitie en Veiligheid, p 37.

[47] HG Egter van Wissekerke, *Regulier Verblijfsrecht* (The Hague, Boom Juridische Uitgevers, 2011) 155.

[48] B10/2.3 Vc 2000.

infringes the Association Agreement or Decision 1/80.[49] Moreover, it provides that a residence permit cannot be withdrawn unless the personal conduct poses a genuine, present and sufficiently serious threat to a fundamental interest of society.[50] In addition, the Vc 2000 specifies that the requirements that apply to EU citizens and that are laid down in Articles 8.22(1), 8.23 and 8.24 Vb 2000 shall also be applied to Turkish citizens.[51]

The EU long-term residence permit may be withdrawn if the third-country national poses an actual and serious threat to public policy or public security, per Article 45d(1)(b) Vw 2000. The Vb 2000 specifies this requirement and provides that the EU long-term residence permit may be withdrawn if the total amount of criminal punishment is at least equivalent to the respective thresholds in the sliding scale, more specifically in Article 3.86(2), (3) and (5) Vb 2000.[52] Moreover, the nature and seriousness of the threat posed to public policy or national security by the presence or conduct of the long-term resident or members of his family must be assessed.[53]

iii Obligation to Take Article 8 ECHR into Account

The sliding scale is the central part of the Dutch *ordre public* policy[54] and relates *in abstracto* the duration of the foreigner's lawful residence to the seriousness of the offence(s) committed.[55] If the duration of the foreigner's lawful residence does not outweigh the threat to public policy, the abstract balancing process of the sliding scale has to be supplemented by an assessment of the facts of the individual case. The sliding scale stipulates that the request for the prolongation of the validity of the residence permit will not be rejected if removal (*uitzetting*) of the foreigner conflicts with Article 8 ECHR and the foreigner's fundamental freedoms.[56] The work instructions of the IND prescribe a balancing process between the interests of the individual and the interests of the state; they refer to and elaborate on the *Üner* and *Boultif* criteria; they prescribe that the decision maker has to apply these criteria to the facts of the individual case and to identify and highlight those that have decisive weight in the balancing process.[57] However, an insufficient consideration of human rights could be facilitated and fostered by the obligation – incumbent on the IND – to terminate lawful stay if possible.[58]

[49] Article 3.86(16) Vb 2000.

[50] Article 3.86(15) Vb 2000.

[51] B10/4.4 Vc 2000.

[52] Article 3.127(3) Vb 2000.

[53] Article 3.86(13) Vb 2000.

[54] H Oosterom-Staples, 'Botsende openbare-ordebegrippen in het Europese Migratierecht' (2006) 8/9 *Nederlands Tijdschrift voor Europees Recht* 169, 180.

[55] Adviescommissie voor Vreemdelingenzaken (ACVZ), Advies 'Gewogen gevaar', uitgebracht aan de staatssecretaris van Justitie en Veiligheid, p 33.

[56] Article 3.86(17) Vb 2000.

[57] Immigratie- en Naturalisatiedienst, WI 2020/16 Richtlijnen voor de toepassing van artikel 8 EVRM, Werkinstructie 2020/16 (SUA), 18 November 2020, pp 13–39.

[58] B12/2.8 Vc 2000.

D. Termination of Lawful Residence after a Criminal Conviction and the *Inreisverbod* and *Ongewenstverklaring*

If residence can be terminated and the residence permit is withdrawn, the foreigner's residence is no longer lawful.[59] Moreover, the foreigner has to leave the Netherlands within the time limit referred to in Article 62 Vw 2000.[60] If the foreigner does not comply with this obligation s/he can be removed.[61]

The withdrawal of a residence permit is a return decision[62] and can comprise an *inreisverbod*,[63] the type of entry ban that can only be imposed upon third-country nationals covered by the Return Directive. Article 66a(1) Vw 2000 lists cases in which an *inreisverbod* must be issued, whereas Article 66a(2) Vw 2000 grants discretion as to its issuance. The other type of entry ban, the *ongewenstverklaring*, is regulated by Article 67 Vw 2000 and mainly covers EU citizens.

The legislature has granted discretion to the competent authority regarding the issuance of the *ongewenstverklaring*. Therefore, an *ongewenstverklaring* cannot be imposed as a standard measure; it can only be issued after the personal interests of the individual have been weighed against those of society/the state.[64] A foreigner who remains in the Netherlands despite an *inreisverbod* or an *ongewenstverklaring* shall be punished with a prison term of up to six months or a fine.[65]

III. Two Types of Entry Bans: *Inreisverbod* and *Ongewenstverklaring*

Before addressing both types of entry bans in more detail in the subsequent sections, it is useful to briefly outline the *inreisverbod* and *ongewenstverklaring*. Both instruments aim at excluding a foreigner (for a certain period of time) from the national territory and at declaring the foreigner *persona non grata*.[66] The *ongewenstverklaring*, in the strict sense, is a national measure that formally only bars a stay in the Netherlands.[67] The *inreisverbod* is an entry ban in terms of Article 3(6) of the Return Directive and leads to an SIS alert, which bars entry to all Schengen states.[68]

[59] Article 27(2)(c) in conjunction with (1)(a) Vw 2000.

[60] Article 62(1) Vw 2000 provides that the foreigner who is subject to a return decision has to leave the Netherlands within four weeks.

[61] Article 27(1)(b) Vw 2000.

[62] Article 27(2)(c) Vw 2000 in conjunction with Article 27(1) Vw 2000.

[63] Article 27(4) Vw 2000.

[64] S Roelofs, 'De maatregel tot ongewenstverklaring (deel 1)' (2002) *Migrantenrecht* 248, 252.

[65] Article 197 Wetboek van Strafrecht.

[66] M Bouma, 'Terugkeerrichtlijn: nationale en Europese uitspraken over inreisverbod en ongewenstverklaring' (2012) 16 *Journaal Vreemdelingenrecht* 172, 174.

[67] A Franken, *Detention and the Re-entry Ban in the Returns Directive – A Race to the Bottom?* (Masters Thesis, Tilburg University, 2010) 55.

[68] Article 66a(3) Vw 2000, Article 3.103b Vb 2000.

The grounds for imposing these measures are distinct. An *inreisverbod* requires irregular stay, whereas the reasons for imposing an *ongewenstverklaring* comprise, among other grounds, that the foreigner poses a threat to public policy or public security,[69] or has been convicted of a crime which is punishable with imprisonment of three years or more.[70] Even though the *inreisverbod* requires an irregular stay, it can be imposed together with the withdrawal of the residence permit or after the foreigner's residence permit was withdrawn due to a criminal conviction.

Another difference concerns the duration of these measures. The *ongewenstverklaring* is in principle unlimited in time and does not expire or end by operation of law,[71] meaning that the lifting of the *ongewenstverklaring* has to be requested.[72] The duration of the *inreisverbod*, by contrast, is prescribed by Article 11(2) of the Return Directive and, in principle, shall not exceed five years.[73]

A further difference concerns the personal scope. An *inreisverbod* can, according to the clear wording of Article 66a Vw 2000, only be issued against foreigners who are not EU citizens. The *ongewenstverklaring* may only be issued against EU citizens[74] and their family members, Swiss nationals and their family members, or third-country nationals who are not covered by the Return Directive. The *inreisverbod* and the *ongewenstverklaring* are mutually exclusive and an *ongewenstverklaring* can only be issued if an *inreisverbod* is not applicable.[75]

Finally, the *ongewenstverklaring* does not require a return decision, whereas the *inreisverbod* does.[76]

IV. The *Ongewenstverklaring*, Article 67 Vw 2000

Even though the Vw 2000 first addresses the *inreisverbod* followed by the *ongewenstverklaring*, these instruments will be addressed here in the reverse order. The latter is addressed first as it is the 'older' instrument and since the provisions regulating the application of the *inreisverbod* refer to those of the *ongewenstverklaring*.

[69] Article 67(1)(c) Vw 2000.

[70] Article 67(1)(b) Vw 2000; Article 6.6 Vb 2000.

[71] Bouma, 'Terugkeerrichtlijn: nationale en Europese uitspraken over inreisverbod en ongewenstverklaring' 175; S Roelofs, 'De maatregel tot ongewenstverklaring (deel 2)' (2002) *Migrantenrecht* 284, 289; R Imkamp, 'Terugkeerrichtlijn beschermt tegen dubbel inreisverbod' (2012) *Asiel & Migrantenrecht* 491.

[72] Article 68(1) Vw 2000.

[73] Implemented into Dutch law by Article 66a(4) Vw 2000 and specified by Article 6.5a Vb 2000.

[74] P Boeles, 'Criminalisering van illegaal verblijf' (2013) *Journaal Vreemdelingenrecht* 17; P Boeles, 'Wat betekent de Terugkeerrichtlijn voor ongewenstverklaring?' (2010) *Asiel & Migrantenrecht* 531; P Boeles, 'Is een oude ongewenstverklaring onder de Terugkeerrichtlijn nog geldig?' (2012) *Asiel & Migrantenrecht* 371.

[75] M van Riel, 'Nieuwe wetgeving ter implementatie van de Terugkeerrichtlijn' (2012) *Asiel & Migrantenrecht* 68, 74.

[76] Rechtbank 's-Gravenhage, 12/13307, 12/16616, 12/13306, 12/16607, NL:RBSGR:2012:BY4989, para 26.

A. The Criteria for Issuing an *Ongewenstverklaring*

The criteria for declaring the foreigner 'unwanted' are laid down in Article 67 Vw 2000 and comprise five alternative grounds. Among these grounds is the irrevocable conviction of a criminal offence punishable with a prison term of three years or more, or a measure provided for in Article 37a Dutch Criminal Code.[77] The discretion granted ('may be declared unwanted') to the competent authority by the Vw 2000 is specified by the Vc 2000. The Vc 2000 stipulates that a balancing process between the interests of the foreigner and the interests of the state has to be conducted when deciding on an *ongewenstverklaring*.[78] An *ongewenstverklaring* will not be issued if this would lead to an infringement of Article 8 ECHR,[79] whereby the balancing process is guided by the criteria developed by the ECtHR's case law.[80]

B. The *Ongewenstverklaring* Issued against EU and EEA Citizens

The EU Commission considered the system of issuing an *ongewenstverklaring* problematic after several EU citizens were imprisoned following criminal convictions and were declared undesirable on public policy grounds.[81] The Commission claimed that Dutch legislation facilitated 'a systematic and automatic connection between a criminal conviction and a measure ordering expulsion from the territory'.[82] Consequently, it brought an infringement procedure against the Netherlands for not complying with the requirements of Directive 64/221/EEC when expelling EU citizens. Even though the CJEU held in *Commission v The Netherlands* (2007) that it is not possible to ascertain whether Dutch law creates an absolutely automatic connection, it stated that it could not be ruled out that a decision to expel an EU citizen could be taken 'without regard either to their personal conduct or to whether there exists a genuine and sufficiently serious threat to the requirements of public policy'.[83] Therefore, the Court concluded that Dutch 'legislation relating to foreign nationals makes it possible to establish a systematic and automatic connection between a criminal conviction and a measure ordering expulsion in respect of citizens of the Union'.[84] Groenendijk pointed out that, prior to the judgment in *Commission v The Netherlands*, expulsion decisions against EU citizens were often based on the national sliding scale to the detriment of the

[77] Article 67(1)(b) Vw 2000.
[78] A4/3.1 Vc 2000.
[79] A4/3.1 Vc 2000.
[80] Rechtbank 's-Gravenhage, NL:RBSGR:2009:BJ2233, paras 4.4–4.11.
[81] Case C-50/06 *Commission v The Netherlands* ECLI:EU:C:2007:325, [2007] ECR I-04383, para 17.
[82] ibid, paras 17, 24.
[83] ibid, para 45.
[84] ibid, para 46.

stricter requirements established by Union law, which were frequently not taken into account.[85] He argued that the application of Dutch national public policy rules resulted, in effect, in the disregarding of the relevant criteria of EU law.[86]

After the CJEU's judgment, the requirements of Dutch law were amended. At the time of writing, an *ongewenstverklaring* against an EU, Swiss or EEA citizen and their family members must be adopted in compliance with Article 67 Vw 2000, Article 8.18(b) Vb 2000, and Article 8.22 Vb 2000,[87] which incorporate the requirements of EU law. The sliding scale cannot be applied to EU citizens, except in cases in which it functions as a safety net,[88] as its abstract balancing does not meet the stricter requirements of EU law. Groenendijk highlights that, in the aftermath of the CJEU's judgment, the number of Union citizens that were subject to an *ongewenstverklaring* decreased.[89]

On the other hand, Groenendijk emphasised that the effects of the judgment only lasted for a short period of time as another mechanism was used to declare EU citizens undesirable foreigners.[90] He pointed out that the policy shifted its focus initially onto EU citizens who repeatedly committed violent offences, to eventually comprise EU citizens who repeatedly committed minor criminal offences.[91] This policy was based on the European Commission's Communication establishing 'guidance for better transposition and application of Directive 2004/38/EC'. The latter provided that 'In certain circumstances, persistent petty criminality may represent a threat to public policy, despite the fact that any single crime/offence, taken individually, would be insufficient to represent a sufficiently serious threat'.[92] This sentence was incorporated into the Dutch policy rules in 2010,[93] and it served as a justification for terminating lawful residence of EU citizens who repeatedly committed (minor) offences and for issuing an *ongewenstverklaring*.[94]

The European Commission highlighted in its Communication that the conduct of the repeat offender must represent a threat to public policy; that the nature of the offences, their frequency, and the damage caused must be considered; and that the existence of multiple convictions is not enough in itself.[95] Even though these requirements are contained in the Vc 2000,[96] national authorities did not always assess these criteria thoroughly. Therefore, national courts had to reinforce these

[85] CA Groenendijk, 'Noot bij ABRvS (18 June 2013)' (2013) *Jurisprudentie Vreemdelingenrecht* 379.
[86] ibid.
[87] A4/3.8 Vc 2000.
[88] B10/2.3 Vc 2000.
[89] Groenendijk, 'Noot bij ABRvS' 379.
[90] ibid.
[91] ibid.
[92] COM(2009) 313 final, Communication from the Commission to the European Parliament and the Council on guidance for better transposition and application of Directive 2004/38/EC on the right of citizens of the Union and their family members to move and reside freely within the territory of the Member States, p 12.
[93] See B10/2.3 Vc 2000.
[94] B10/2.3 Vc 2000.
[95] COM(2009) 313 final, p 12.
[96] B10/2.3 Vc 2000.

criteria by stating that the fact that the individual was repeatedly convicted is as such not sufficient[97] and that an assessment which merely focuses on the number of criminal offences but not on the damage caused is likewise insufficient.[98]

Groenendijk highlighted that in 2010, 2011 and 2012 the number of EU citizens who were subject to an *ongewenstverklaring* increased. He argued that it is likely that the issuance of an *ongewenstverklaring* in these cases was based on the requirements of national public policy rules and not on the stricter conditions established by EU law.[99] In 2013 the Raad van State clarified that, in the context of *ongewenstverklaringen* against repeat offenders, it must be demonstrated that the foreigner poses a serious threat to a fundamental interest of society.[100]

C. Duration of the *Ongewenstverklaring*

The *ongewenstverklaring* does not automatically expire[101] but requires an application for annulment,[102] whereby the lifting of the *ongewenstverklaring* is subject to the discretion of the minister. However, if the foreigner has continuously lived outside the Netherlands for 10 years the *ongewenstverklaring* shall be lifted unless the foreigner's conduct during that time fulfils the conditions for issuing an *ongewenstverklaring*.[103] The Vb 2000 sets out further circumstances where shorter absences from the territory shall lead to a lifting of the *ongewenstverklaring*.[104]

Regarding EU citizens who were subject to a removal measure, EU law specifies that foreigners covered by the Citizenship Directive can submit a request for the annulment or lifting of the exclusion order. According to Article 32(1) of the Citizenship Directive, 'Persons excluded … may submit an application for lifting of the exclusion order after a reasonable period, depending on the circumstances, and in any event after three years from enforcement of the final exclusion order'. Similarly, according to Dutch law, the request for lifting the *ongewenstverklaring* can be filed after a reasonable time has elapsed or if at least three years have elapsed since removal.[105] The decision on the request has to be made within six months.[106] The documents that can serve as proof of residence outside the Netherlands are further specified in the Vc 2000 A.[107]

[97] Rechtbank Den Haag, AWB 12/31486, RBDHA:2013:CA1251, para 5.4.

[98] ibid, para 5.5.

[99] Groenendijk, 'Noot bij ABRvS' 379.

[100] ABRvS, 201207575/1/V1, NL:RVS:2013:62, para 3.7; ABRvS, 201205094/1/V1 NL:RVS:2013:1054, para 3.7.

[101] Bouma, 'Terugkeerrichtlijn' 174; Roelofs, 'De maatregel tot ongewenstverklaring' 289; Imkamp, 'Terugkeerrichtlijn beschermt tegen dubbel inreisverbod' 491.

[102] Article 68(1) Vw 2000.

[103] Article 68(2) Vw 2000.

[104] Article 6.6 Vb 2000.

[105] Article 8.22(4) Vb 2000.

[106] Article 8.22(5) Vb 2000, which implements Article 32(1) Directive 2004/38/EC.

[107] A/3.8 Vc 2000.

The unlimited duration of the *ongewenstverklaring* imposed on EU citizens and the requirement of an application for a lifting of the *ongewenstverklaring* are problematic against the background of EU law. A comparison with the Return Directive is instructive in this respect. The Return Directive, which is only applicable to third-country nationals, provides in Article 11(2) that 'The length of the entry ban shall be determined with due regard to all relevant circumstances of the individual case and shall not in principle exceed five years'. This demonstrates that the entry ban has to be limited in time, a notion underpinned by the CJEU's judgment in *Filev and Osmani*, wherein the Court held that Member States cannot require an application by the third-country national for limitation of the entry ban.[108] As an application cannot be required from third-country nationals, it follows that such a requirement cannot be imposed on EU citizens and their family members either, as this would entail that those subject to the Citizenship Directive would be put in a worse position than third-country nationals.

V. The *Inreisverbod*, Article 66a Vw 2000

The *inreisverbod* (Article 66a Vw 2000) is a national entry ban which leads to an SIS alert,[109] and which is addressed in more detail below.[110]

A. Personal Scope

The *inreisverbod* applies to third-country nationals and bars lawful stay.[111] EU citizens are excluded from its scope.[112] Third-country national family members of EU citizens who are covered by the Citizenship Directive can be entered into the SIS according to Regulation (EU) 2018/1861 ('SIS Regulation').[113] However, the Return Directive defines a third-country national as 'any person who … is not a person enjoying the Union right of free movement, as defined in Article 2 (5) of the Schengen Borders Code'.[114] According to Article 2(5) of the Schengen Borders Code,[115]

[108] Case C-297/12 *Filev and Osmani*, ECLI:EU:C:2013:569, [2013], para 34.

[109] Article 66a(3) Vw 2000, Article 3.103b Vb 2000.

[110] Chapter 10.

[111] Article 66a(6) Vw 2000.

[112] Article 66a(1) and (2) Vw 2000.

[113] Regulation (EU) 2018/1861 of the European Parliament and of the Council of 28 November 2018 on the establishment, operation and use of the Schengen Information System (SIS) in the field of border checks, and amending the Convention implementing the Schengen Agreement, and amending and repealing Regulation (EC) No 1987/2006 [2018] OJ L 312/14 ('SIS Regulation').

[114] Article 3(1) of Directive 2008/115/EC of the European Parliament and of the Council of 16 December 2008 on common standards and procedures in Member States for returning illegally staying third-country nationals [2008] OJ L 348/98 ('Return Directive').

[115] Regulation (EU) 2016/399 of the European Parliament and of the Council of 9 March 2016 on a Union Code on the rules governing the movement of persons across borders ('Schengen Borders Code') [2016] OJ L 77/1.

persons enjoying the Community right of free movement are 'Union citizens within the meaning of Article 20(1) TFEU, and third-country nationals who are members of the family of a Union citizen exercising his/her right to free movement to whom Directive 2004/38/EC … applies'. Consequently, family members of an EU citizen who are covered by the Citizenship Directive are excluded from the scope of the Return Directive. Since the *inreisverbod* was introduced by the Act implementing the Return Directive,[116] the personal scope of the *inreisverbod* (Article 66a Vw 2000) and the Return Directive must be identical. Therefore, third-country family members of EU citizens covered by the Citizenship Directive are excluded from the personal scope of the *inreisverbod*. Turkish nationals are covered by the Association Agreement and can only be subject to an *inreisverbod* if they pose a present, genuine and sufficiently serious threat to a fundamental interest of society.[117]

B. Grounds for Imposing an *Inreisverbod*

The Vw 2000 distinguishes between situations where an *inreisverbod shall* be issued[118] and situations where it *may* be issued.[119] The *inreisverbod* shall be issued if the foreigner must leave the territory immediately[120] or if the foreigner did not comply with the obligation to leave the territory within the specified time.[121]

Regarding the former category, Article 62(2) Vw 2000 lists grounds on which the four-week period for voluntary return can be reduced and grounds for determining that the foreigner has to leave the Netherlands immediately. Among these is the ground that a foreigner poses a threat to public policy, public security or national security, per Article 62(2)(c) Vw 2000.[122] Previously, the Vc 2000 provided that this ground covers situations in which the foreigner was suspected of having committed a crime or had been convicted of a criminal offence.[123] In the case of *Zh* and *O*,[124] the Dutch Raad van State sought an interpretation of Article 7(4) of the Return Directive, which is implemented into Dutch law by Article 62(2)(c) Vw 2000. Article 7(4) of the Return Directive provides that 'Member States may refrain from granting a period for voluntary departure, or may grant a period

[116] Wet van 15 december 2011 tot wijziging van de Vreemdelingenwet 2000 ter implementatie van de richtlijn nr. 2008/115/EG van het Europees Parlement en Raad van 16 december 2008 over gemeenschappelijke normen en procedures in de lidstaten voor de terugkeer van onderdanen van derde landen die illegaal op hun grongebied verblijven, Official Gazette of the Kingdom of the Netherlands 2012, 663.

[117] Rechtbank Den Haag, NL20.19837, NL:RBDHA:2021:3942, paras 10.2, 12.

[118] Article 661(1) Vw 2000.

[119] Article 66a(2) Vw 2000.

[120] Article 66a(1)(a) in conjunction with Article 62(2) Vw 2000.

[121] Article 66(1)(b) Vw 2000.

[122] Article 62(2)(c) Vw 2000; see also Article 7(4) Return Directive.

[123] A3/3 Vc 2000.

[124] Case C-554/13 *Zh* and *O* ECLI:EU:C:2015:377, [2015].

shorter than seven days', among others 'if the person concerned poses a risk to public policy, public security or national security'. The CJEU was asked whether an illegally staying third-country national poses a risk to public policy 'merely because he is suspected of having committed a criminal offence under national law', or whether it is 'necessary that he should have been convicted in a criminal court for the commission of that offence and, in the latter case, must that conviction have become final and absolute?'[125] Importantly, the Court held that

> a Member State is required to assess the concept of 'risk to public policy', within the meaning of Article 7(4) … on a case-by-case basis, in order to ascertain whether the personal conduct of the third-country national concerned poses a genuine and present risk to public policy.[126]

It clarified that Article 7(4)

> must be interpreted as precluding a national practice whereby a third-country national … is deemed to pose a risk to public policy within the meaning of that provision on the sole ground that he is suspected, or has been criminally convicted, of an act punishable as a criminal offence under national law.[127]

Moreover, the Court noted that if the illegally staying third-country national

> is suspected, or has been criminally convicted, of an act punishable as a criminal offence under national law, other factors, such as the nature and seriousness of that act, the time which has elapsed since it was committed and the fact that that national was in the process of leaving the territory … may be relevant in the assessment of whether he poses a risk to public policy within the meaning of that provision.[128]

The CJEU added that 'any matter which relates to the credibility of the suspicion that the third-country national concerned committed the alleged criminal offence is also relevant to that assessment'.[129] Even though the mere suspicion that a third-country national has committed an act punishable as a criminal offence cannot serve as the sole ground, the Court held that this suspicion, 'together with other factors relating to the case in question' may be 'used as a basis for a finding that he poses a risk to public policy within the meaning of Article 7(4)'.[130] Hence, under certain conditions, the suspicion that the illegally staying third-country national has committed a crime can constitute, together with other factors, a ground for finding that the person poses a risk to public policy.

Importantly, Article 66a(8) Vw 2000 provides for the possibility to abstain from an *inreisverbod* for humanitarian or other reasons. Moreover, an *inreisverbod* shall, among other grounds, not be issued if it would result in a violation

[125] ibid, para 38.
[126] ibid, para 54.
[127] ibid.
[128] ibid, para 65.
[129] ibid.
[130] ibid, para 52.

of Article 8 ECHR or if the person holds a residence permit issued by another EU/EEA Member State.[131]

The Vw 2000 distinguishes between a light (*licht*) *inreisverbod*, which has a maximum duration of five years, and a serious (*zwaar*) *inreisverbod*,[132] though in practice both entry bans bar a regular stay.[133] This distinction is based on the Return Directive, which provides that the duration of the *inreisverbod* shall not exceed five years, unless the foreigner poses a serious threat to public policy, public security or national security.[134] The Dutch Raad van State held that it follows from the CJEU's judgment in *Zh* and *O.* that an *inreisverbod* of more than five years requires an actual, present and sufficiently serious threat to a fundamental interest of society.[135]

VI. Intensity of Judicial Scrutiny: In-depth or Marginal Assessment?

Judicial scrutiny in administrative law has traditionally been marginal.[136] The doctrine of marginal scrutiny was established in 1949 by the Hoge Raad in *Doetinchemse Woonruimtevordering*[137] and served the aim of protecting citizens against the unelected judiciary.[138] The doctrine is based on the separation of powers and entails that the judiciary, which enjoys the least democratic legitimation, exercise self-restraint if the executive has been granted a margin of discretion by the legislature.[139] Marginal scrutiny limits judicial intervention to situations where no reasonable person would have reached the decision that was reached by the executive,[140] or, in other words, if there is an obvious disproportionality between the interests of the state and the interests of the individual.[141]

[131] A4/2.2 Vc 2000.

[132] See Article 66a(7) Vw 2000; A2/12.2 Vc 2000.

[133] Boeles, 'Criminalisering van illegaal verblijf'; P Boeles, 'Strafbaarstelling van illegaal verblijf en het Unierecht' (2013) *Asiel & Migrantenrecht* 66.

[134] Article 11(2) Return Directive, Article 66a(4) Vw 2000.

[135] ABRvS, 201600798/1/V1, ECLI:NL:RVS:2016:2063, para 1.2; ABRvS, 201506288/1/V1, ECLI:NL:RVS:2016:1550, para 7.1.

[136] Roelofs, 'De maatregel tot ongewenstverklaring' 252; N Verschaeren and M Peeters, 'Vreemdelingenrechtelijke verweren in een strafzaak' (2013) *Journaal Vreemdelingenrecht* 165, 169.

[137] Hoge Raad, 8127, NL:HR:1949:AG1963.

[138] R Ortleb and W Zorg, 'Marginale rechterlijke toetsing onder druk: een voortgaande trend vooruit?' in R Ortleb, F Groothuijse, J Kiewiet, R Nehmelman (eds), *De rechter onder vuur* (Oisterwijk, Wolf Legal Publishers, 2016) 4.

[139] T Barkhuysen, 'Een revolutie in het bestuursrecht?' (2015) 24 *Nederlands Juristenblad* 1583.

[140] ibid.

[141] E Hirsch Ballin, 'Dynamiek in de bestuursrechtspraak' in E Hirsch Ballin, R Ortlep and A Tollenaar, *Rechtsontwikkeling door de bestuursrechter* (Den Haag, Boom Juridische uitgevers, 2015) 22, with reference to H van Wijk, W Konijnenbelt and R van Male, *Hoofdstukken van bestuursrecht* (Deventer, Kluwer, 2014) 330.

Marginal scrutiny in the context of the termination of residence implies that administrative courts normally assess whether the competent authority conducted a balancing process,[142] whether its decision was sufficiently reasoned, and whether it took all relevant aspects into consideration.[143] While it is for the judge to examine in depth whether all relevant criteria have been considered by the competent authority, the question of whether a fair balance has been struck was said to fall within the competence of the administration and remains outside the court's scrutiny.[144]

Academics have discussed the question of whether the doctrine of marginal scrutiny is a consequence of, or required by, the ECtHR's case law, which affords Contracting Parties a margin of appreciation.[145] Spijkerboer points out that a margin of appreciation is granted to the legislature, the judiciary and the executive, and that the ECtHR's case law does not specify how this discretion is divided across these three powers.[146] It is for the Contracting State to ensure that its measures are compatible with the ECHR.

Boeles criticises the limitation of judicial scrutiny[147] and points out that the ECtHR conducts a full scrutiny of the facts of the individual case. He states that there is no room for limiting the assessment conducted by national courts,[148] and argues that Article 8(2) ECHR requires national judges to assess all relevant interests independently and then examine the decision of the administration.[149]

The ECtHR's case law neither explicitly requires nor bars a full judicial scrutiny of administrative decisions. The ECtHR encourages judges to make a careful assessment, as demonstrated by the Court's judgment in *Da Silva and Hoogkamer*.[150] The competent Dutch authorities held that the applicant was irregularly present when giving birth to her daughter and attached a considerable weight to this factor in the balancing process. The ECtHR found that, by attaching paramount importance to the element of irregular presence, 'the authorities may be considered to have indulged in excessive formalism'.[151] This remark could be understood as a reminder to courts 'that an approach which fails to scrutinize decisions properly, and attaches, or permits administrative authorities to attach, excessive weight to a

[142] ABRvS, 200901216/1/V1, NL:RVS:2009:BK6145; ABRvS, 201208909/1/V4, NL:RVS:2012:BY4042.

[143] ABRvS, 200808634/1/V3, NL:RVS:2009:BJ7520, para 2.5.3: the Court held that the administration did not or did not sufficiently consider the *Boultif* and *Üner* criteria in the balancing process.

[144] K Geertsema, 'Noot bij ABRvS (1 April 2010)' (2010) *Jurisprudentie Vreemdelingenrecht* 195; F Schüller, 'Wakker worden! Verblijf na opheffing ongewenstverklaring' (2010) *Asiel & Migrantenrecht* 185, 186.

[145] For further information see P Boeles, 'Noot bij ABRvS (17 December 2004)' (2005) *Jurisprudentie Vreemdelingenrecht* 65; TP Spijkerboer, 'Noot bij ABRvS (18 October 2004)' (2004) *Jurisprudentie Vreemdelingenrecht* 468; Geertsema, 'Noot bij ABRvS (1 April 2010)' 195.

[146] Spijkerboer, 'Noot bij ABRvS (18 October 2004)' 468.

[147] P Boeles, 'Het gezin als de hoeksteen van de wereld' (2007) *Migrantenrecht* 4, 6.

[148] P Boeles, 'De aanval op de gezinshereniging en de rol van het international recht' (2005) *Migrantenrecht* 116, 121; Boeles, 'Noot bij ABRvS' (17 December 2004)' 65.

[149] Boeles, 'De aanval op de gezinshereniging en de rol van het international recht' 120.

[150] *Rodrigues da Silva and Hoogkamer v The Netherlands* App no 50435/99 (ECHR, 31 January 2006).

[151] ibid, para 44.

single particular factor, may result in findings of violations of Article 8 ECHR'.[152] The judgment could be seen as an invitation to reconsider the doctrine of marginal judicial scrutiny.

Indeed, the doctrine of marginal judicial scrutiny has not been strictly followed[153] and is developing in light of the principle of effective judicial protection (Article 47 CFR, Article 6 ECHR). While the doctrine rests on the separation of powers and requires judicial self-restraint in favour of the executive, the principle of judicial protection of the individual against executive action limits the doctrine by allowing for more judicial scrutiny in order to avoid a legal vacuum. Even though the principle of effective judicial protection will normally require a more comprehensive scrutiny,[154] the exact intensity of scrutiny will be determined by the facts of the case,[155] in particular by the rights that are affected, the interests that are at stake, and the relationship between the various persons that are involved. The Hoge Raad noted in 2018 that the doctrine of marginal scrutiny currently points towards a full judicial scrutiny of decisions in light of the principle of proportionality and the duty to give reasons.[156] This applies in particular in the context of EU law.

Indeed, a return decision or an *inreisverbod* pursuant to Article 66a Vw 2000, which implements Article 11 of the Return Directive, must be assessed against the benchmark of EU law, in particular against the CFR.[157] The right to an effective remedy and to a fair trial (Article 47 CFR), combined with the obligation of Member States to give full effect to EU law and thereby also to Charter rights, is difficult to reconcile with a limited judicial scrutiny.

Additionally, the courts operate the balancing process required in the context of Article 8 ECHR and assess the question of whether a fair balance has been struck between the interests of the foreigner and the interests of the state, even though the scrutiny by the court should be cautious, if possible.[158]

VII. The Rationale of the Sliding Scale

The termination of lawful residence after a criminal conviction relies on the sliding scale.[159] The protection it grants increases the longer the foreigner lawfully resides in the Netherlands. The sliding scale relates *in abstracto* the interests of the state

[152] H Toner, 'Article 8 ECHR – Full Judicial Scrutiny?' (2007) *Migrantenrecht* 48, 49.
[153] Rechtbank Den Haag, AWB 12/24574, NL:RBDHA:2013:BZ6766, para 5.6.2.
[154] Barkhuysen, 'Een revolutie in het bestuursrecht?' 1583.
[155] Ortleb and Zorg, 'Marginale rechterlijke toetsing onder druk' 18.
[156] Hoge Raad, 17/01954, NL:PHR:2018:177, para 4.18
[157] See Article 51(1) Charter of Fundamental Rights.
[158] Rechtbank Den Haag, AWB 19/1849, AWB 20/3966 and AWB 20/3968, NL:RBDHA:2021:2676, para 8.3.
[159] Article 3.86 Vb 2000.

to those of the individual and addresses them at the same stage of assessment, thereby creating a level playing field. The interests taken into consideration in the sliding scale are the duration of lawful residence (on the part of the individual) and the seriousness of the committed offence (on the part of the state). The different tables of the sliding scale disregard, on the part of the foreigner, considerations such as the existence of private and/or family life, cultural and economic integration, the age of the foreigner, and the links with the country of nationality; these considerations have to be addressed in the concrete balancing process.[160] On the part of the state, the different tables of the sliding scale consider the maximum prison sentence that could be imposed, the prison sentence that has actually been imposed, and whether the crime has been committed repeatedly. This abstract balancing does not account for the specific circumstances of the crime and does not allow accommodation of considerations that reflect a particular interest of the state in terminating the foreigner's residence. However, this abstract balancing process is only sufficient if the duration of a foreigner's lawful residence outweighs the interests of the state so that residence cannot be terminated. If the duration of the foreigner's lawful residence does not outweigh the imposed prison term, it is necessary to conduct a balancing *in concreto*, which takes the facts of the specific case into account.

Two situations must be distinguished when assessing the rationale of the sliding scale. The first concerns cases in which the abstract balancing of the competing interests by the sliding scale leads to the result that the duration of the foreigner's lawful residence outweighs the imposed prison term. In these cases, the interests of the foreigner, even though solely determined by the duration of lawful residence, take precedence over the interests of the state. Interestingly, the reverse situation does not apply. The sliding scale omits any reference to cases in which the interests of the state per se take precedence over the interests of the foreigner, irrespective of the facts of the individual case. Viewed from this angle, the sliding scale seems to afford a higher protection to the foreigner. At the same time, it must be noted that a relatively long residence is required to outweigh the prison term, with the consequence that a strong protection is usually only acquired after 10 years of lawful residence.

The second situation concerns cases in which the duration of the foreigner's lawful residence does not outweigh the imposed prison term. In these cases, discretion is granted as to whether the foreigner's residence may be terminated. As the sliding scale only contains a balancing of the competing interests *in abstracto*, a balancing of interests *in concreto* is required and it has to take Article 8 ECHR into account.[161] Even though the work instructions of the IND prescribe a balancing process in line with the *Üner* and *Boultif* criteria,[162] the IND's obligation to

[160] Article 3.86(17) Vb 2000.
[161] See also Article 3.86(17) Vb 2000.
[162] Immigratie- en Naturalisatiedienst, WI 2020/16 Richtlijnen voor de toepassing van artikel 8 EVRM, Werkinstructie 2020/16 (SUA), 18 November 2020, pp 13–39.

terminate lawful stay where possible[163] might have an impact on the balancing process. Previously it had been noted that administrative authorities did not always assess the facts of the individual case sufficiently and did not always conduct an adequate balancing process.[164] The risk that the foreigner's residence is terminated without a proper balancing process might be exacerbated by the fact that two important factors in the balancing process, the duration of the foreigner's lawful residence and the seriousness of the criminal offence as expressed by the prison term, are already considered by the abstract balancing contained in the sliding scale. Hence, the application of the sliding scale might foster a reduction of the balancing process *in concreto*.

The protection offered by the sliding scale, which was in force from 1990 to 2002, was rather beneficial for the foreigner. It provided that lawful residence of less than three years might only be terminated if a prison term of at least nine months were imposed on the foreigner. As the protection against the termination of residence was very strong, the circumstances of the individual case were not assessed.[165] The rationale of the sliding scale underwent changes over time. Stronks points out that the initial concept focused not only on the systematisation of the policy regarding the termination of residence, but also on the protection and the strengthening of the legal position of foreigners.[166] This ambition was reflected in the high thresholds set by the sliding scale for terminating a foreigner's residence. Moreover, it was reflected in the absolute protection against expulsion granted to long-term resident foreigners after 20 years of residence and to foreigners who lawfully resided in the Netherlands before the age of 10 and were resident for more than 15 years. Regarding this absolute protection, Stronks stresses that after 20 years of residence a foreigner was considered to be rooted.[167] Rootedness was equated with integration, but the parallelism of rootedness and integration no longer exists.[168] Currently, the foreigner can be rooted but it does not necessarily follow that s/he is considered integrated.[169] The sliding scale became, according to Stronks, an instrument to give the appearance of a more restrictive migration policy and to deport foreigners more easily.[170] Compared to the sliding scale that was applicable in 2000–01, the one currently applicable considerably reduced the protection granted to foreigners. At the moment, a one-day prison term is sufficient to terminate lawful residence of less than three years. However, contrary to the previous situation, the currently applicable sliding scale requires an assessment of the facts of the individual case. Since the balancing *in abstracto* is no longer so beneficial for

[163] B12/2.8 Vc 2000.
[164] Advies Raad van State, W 04.11.0396/I, 28 November 2011, Staatscourant 2012, no 14035, p 20.
[165] Stronks, 'Een bijna ongebreidelde beteugeling van de tijd' 2309.
[166] ibid, 2307.
[167] ibid, 2313.
[168] ibid.
[169] ibid.
[170] ibid, 2306, 2307, 2309.

the individual, a balancing *in concreto* must be conducted in those cases in which the interests of the foreigner do not outweigh the interests of the state.

In the last two decades, the required prison term for the termination of lawful residence of less than three years was reduced from nine months to one day. Not only were the thresholds for a residence of less than three years reduced, but the entire system became stricter, which points to an increasingly strong emphasis on the interests of the state.

VIII. Summary and Recommendations

The Vw 2000 leaves discretion to the executive regarding the termination of lawful residence.[171] This discretion is further specified in the Vreemdelingenbesluit 2000 (Decree on Foreign Nationals). The decision to terminate lawful residence after a criminal conviction relies on the sliding scale codified in Article 3.86 Vb 2000, which relates the duration of lawful residence to the prison term. If the crime (both with regard to the maximum prison term that could be imposed and the prison term that has been imposed) is not serious enough to outweigh the duration of residence, the foreigner's lawful residence cannot be terminated. The sliding scale thereby enhances predictability and clarity.

Clear downsides of the sliding scale are the low thresholds for the termination of a foreigner's lawful stay in the first years of residence as a prison term of one day suffices to terminate lawful residence of less than three years.[172] Even residence of four to five years does not create a considerably high threshold as a prison term of seven months (for crimes punishable with imprisonment of up to six years),[173] six months (for crimes punishable with imprisonment of more than six years),[174] and five months (regarding repeat offenders)[175] suffices to terminate the foreigner's stay. Even a lawful residence of 15 years or more may be terminated if the imposed prison term exceeds 65 months, provided the foreigner committed a crime that is punishable with imprisonment for up to six years, or 48 months, provided the foreigner committed a crime that is punishable with imprisonment of more than six years.[176] The legal situation is particularly harsh for repeat offenders: a lawful residence of more than 15 years may be terminated where the repeat offender was sentenced to a prison term of 14 months,[177] provided that the requirements of Article 3.86(10) Vb 2000 are fulfilled.

[171] Articles 19 and 22 Vw 2000.
[172] Article 3.86(2), (3) and (5) Vb 2000.
[173] See Article 3.86(2) Vb 2000.
[174] See Article 3.86(3) Vb 2000.
[175] Article 3.86(5) Vb 2000.
[176] Article 3.86(2), Article 3.86(3) Vb 2000.
[177] Article 3.86(5) Vb 2000.

If residence may be terminated according to the sliding scale, the competent authority has to conduct a balancing process and has to take Article 8 ECHR into account.[178] Moreover, the CFR has to be observed if the termination of residence falls within the scope of EU law.

Whether the competent authority conducted a balancing process,[179] whether it sufficiently motivated its decision, and whether it took all relevant aspects into consideration[180] is subject to judicial scrutiny. The weight attached by the competent authority to the respective criteria and the question of whether it struck a fair balance between the competing interests was initially not subject to judicial scrutiny, which was said to be marginal. However, in recent years judicial scrutiny has become more comprehensive. In fact, cases involving foreigners who are covered by EU law require full judicial scrutiny.

If lawful residence is terminated an entry ban (*inreisverbod/ongewenstverklaring*) may be issued. Even though the termination of lawful residence after a criminal conviction and the issuance of an *inreisverbod/ongewenstverklaring* have their own framework of assessment, it has been noted that a criminal conviction often leads to an *ongewenstverklaring* or an *inreisverbod*.[181] It will depend on the facts of the individual case, however, whether a criminal conviction actually leads to an *onge wenstverklaring/inreisverbod*.

The *ongewenstverklaring*, hence the entry ban that primarily applies to EU citizens, is regulated by the Vw 2000 and the Vb 2000, which leave discretion to the competent authorities. Therefore, a balancing process must be conducted that takes the facts of the individual case into account. An *ongewenstverklaring* cannot be issued if this would lead to a violation of Union law or Article 8 ECHR.

The issuance of an *inreisverbod*, hence the entry ban, which can only be imposed upon third-country nationals, is mandatory in cases covered by Article 66a(1) Vw 2000. Despite its mandatory nature, it will not be imposed if it would result in an infringement of Article 8 ECHR.[182] Moreover, EU law can require the competent authority to abstain from an *inreisverbod* if it would infringe EU law, in particular the CFR. In cases where the *inreisverbod* is considered mandatory because the individual is not granted a period for voluntary return, since s/he is considered a risk to public policy, the *Zh* and *O* judgment is relevant. Here the Court clarified that Member States must 'assess the concept of "risk to public policy"

[178] Article 3.86(17) Vb 2000.

[179] ABRvS, 200901216/1/V1, NL:RVS:2009:BK6145; ABRvS, 201208909/1/V4, NL:RVS:2012:BY4042, para 2.4. The Court points out that a balancing process was not conducted despite an interference with Article 8 ECHR.

[180] ABRvS, 200808634/1/V3, NL:RVS:2009:BJ7520 (2009) *Journaal Vreemdelingenrecht*, 353.

[181] See R Heringa, 'Ongewenstverklaring en verblijfsbeëindiging: een gemiste kans' (2001) *Migrantenrecht* 144, 145; N Verschaeren and M Peeters, 'Vreemdelingenrechtelijke verweren in een strafzaak' (2013) *Journaal Vreemdelingenrecht* 165, 176; Roelofs, 'De maatregel tot ongewenstverklaring (deel 1)' 248; S van Walsum, 'Jurisprudentie over migratierecht en gezinsleven. Deel II: Artikel 8 EVRM' (2010) *Asiel & Migrantenrecht* 520, 529.

[182] A4/3.1 Vc 2000 and A4/2.2 Vc 2000.

… on a case-by-case basis, in order to ascertain whether the personal conduct of the third-country national concerned poses a genuine and present risk to public policy'.[183] This implies that neither the denial of a period for voluntary return nor the imposition of an *inreisverbod* can be the automatic consequence of a criminal conviction. Article 66a(2) Vw 2000 grants discretion regarding the issuance of an *inreisverbod*. The competent authority has to conduct a balancing process and has to refrain from issuing an *inreisverbod* if this would result in an infringement of Article 8 ECHR.[184] Moreover, the Vc 2000 lists cases in which an alert shall be entered into the SIS.[185]

The discretion granted by the Vw 2000 regarding the termination of lawful residence and the issuance of an entry ban (*ongewenstverklaring* and *inreisverbod*) is not further specified by the Vw 2000, which is an Act of Parliament, but by the Vb 2000, which is a decision of the executive, and the Vc 2000, which is a ministerial instruction. The discretion granted by the legislature to the executive in combination with the doctrine of marginal scrutiny granted a considerable power to the executive. Against this background, the shift from a marginal to a more comprehensive judicial scrutiny is to be welcomed.

Regarding EU citizens and their family members, the requirements of the Citizenship Directive and the CJEU's case law are mainly incorporated into the Vb 2000[186] and the Vc 2000.[187] However, Article 30(3) of the Citizenship Directive is not implemented correctly. The Directive provides for a period of one month to leave the territory voluntarily, whereas national legislation only grants four weeks.

The unlimited duration of an *ongewenstverklaring* issued against EU citizens or family members and the requirement of an application for lifting the *ongenwenstverklarig* cannot be maintained as they are not compatible with EU law. Even an entry ban issued against third-country nationals covered by the Return Directive[188] has to be limited in time. The CJEU clarified in *Filev and Osmani* that Member States cannot require an application by a third-country national for limitation of the entry ban.[189] As the application requirement cannot even be maintained regarding third-country nationals, it cannot be required for Union citizens. Hence, the entry ban must be limited in time. On application of the affected individual, it must be assessed whether the duration of the entry ban must further be limited, and whether it must be lifted.

[183] *Zh* and *O*, para 50.
[184] A4/3.1 Vc 2000 and A4/2.2 Vc 2000.
[185] A2/12.2 Vc 2000.
[186] For example, Articles 8.7 and 8.22 Vb 2000.
[187] For example, B10/2.3 Vc 2000.
[188] Article 11 Return Directive.
[189] *Filev and Osmani*, para 34.

7

The United Kingdom

This chapter focuses on the deportation of convicted foreigners from the United Kingdom. The starting point of the analysis is the concept of automatic deportation (section 32 Borders Act 2007 (BA 2007)), which displays a certain similarity to the abolished German provision on mandatory expulsion. Inextricably linked to the concept of automatic deportation is the margin of discretion that is granted by the legislature to the executive. A system that requires an automatic deportation once the statutory requirements are fulfilled normally excludes any margin of discretion of the executive. However, an interference with the deportee's human right(s) requires a balancing process between the interests of the foreigner and the interests of the state, which normally presupposes a margin of discretion. This chapter examines how the balancing process between the interests of the foreigner and the interests of the state in the context of Article 8 ECHR is integrated into the system of automatic deportation. It addresses the question of whether, and to what extent, the considerations that are relevant in the balancing process are prescribed by the legislature, and to what extent the executive enjoys a margin of discretion when deciding on the convicted foreigner's deportation. The analysis focuses on the right to respect for private and family life and examines the factors that have to be considered in the balancing process, the weight that is ascribed to these factors, and whether the factors and their weight are determined by the executive or the legislature. The analysis simultaneously addresses the relationship between the principle of proportionality and the principle of legal certainty. The former requires an open-ended case-by-case analysis, while the latter is fostered by a balancing process that is guided by clear criteria and by a specific weight that is ascribed to each criterion beforehand. Next to the margin of discretion, the analysis focuses on the rationale of the system and whether it creates a level playing field for the balancing of the interests of the foreigner and the interests of the state.

The United Kingdom has not been a Schengen state and, even though it took part in certain aspects of the Schengen Agreement, it has never participated in the Regulation on the establishment, operation and use of the second generation Schengen Information System ('SIS II Regulation'). Consequently, the findings of this chapter are of no immediate relevance for the third part of this book, which addresses the effects of national expulsion decisions and entry bans on the European level. As a result, the UK system of deportation is addressed with the necessary brevity. It is nonetheless interesting to explore how a country that operates a system of automatic deportation, which exhibits parallels to the abolished

German system of mandatory expulsion, complies with its obligations under the ECHR.

This chapter is structured as follows: section I introduces the legal provisions that govern the deportation of convicted foreigners, followed by a section on convicted foreigners and their right to respect for private and family life under Article 8 ECHR (Section II), which is subdivided into a subsection on the Immigration Rules (A) and another subsection on Part 5A of the Nationality, Immigration and Asylum Act 2002 (B). Section III addresses the balance between the principle of proportionality and the principle of legal certainty against the background of the provisions on deportation. Section IV explores the rationale of the provisions governing the deportation of convicted foreigners, followed by concluding remarks (Section V).

I. The Provisions Governing the Deportation of Convicted Foreigners

The Immigration Act 1971 (IA 1971) grants the Secretary of State for the Home Department (SSHD or Home Secretary) and the Home Office a wide discretionary power to order the deportation of foreign nationals.[1] Section 3(5)(a) IA 1971 stipulates that a person who is not a British citizen may be subject to deportation from the United Kingdom if the Secretary of State deems his/her deportation to be conducive to the public good. The policy of the Home Office was to consider deportation when the offender was sentenced to at least 12 months in prison.[2] In late April 2006 it 'emerged that, in 1,013 cases, the Home Office had not considered whether to deport foreign national prisoners … before releasing them at the end of their custodial terms'.[3] In order to ensure that foreign criminals were considered for deportation, the Borders Act 2007 (BA 2007) was passed, 'which replaced the SSHD's discretion with "automatic deportation" for most cases concerning foreign national offenders'.[4] The BA 2007 created a statutory presumption by stipulating that 'the deportation of a foreign criminal is conducive to the public good', per section 32(4).[5] Since the deportation of a foreign criminal is conducive to the public good, the Home Secretary is in principle under an obligation to deport delinquent foreigners,[6] unless an exemption applies.[7]

[1] KE Otto, 'The Foreign National Prisoner's Dilemma in the United Kingdom: The Human Rights Implications of Restricting Article 8 Claims' (2015) 24 *Transnational Law & Contemporary Problems* 431, 434.

[2] L Dubinsky, *Foreign National Prisoners: Law and Practice* (Legal Action Group, 2012) 35, 36.

[3] ibid, 69.

[4] Otto, 'The Foreign National Prisoner's Dilemma in the United Kingdom' 434.

[5] J Collinson, 'Suspended Deportation Orders: A Proposed Law Reform' (2020) 40 *Oxford Journal of Legal Studies* 291, 294.

[6] Borders Act 2007, s 32(5).

[7] Borders Act 2007, s 33.

Even though the foreigner must be 'convicted in the United Kingdom of an offence',[8] not every conviction leads to the foreigner's deportation. The provision on automatic deportation (section 32 BA 2007) requires either that the foreigner is 'sentenced to a period of imprisonment of at least 12 months'[9] or that s/he is a serious criminal, that is, if the offence 'is specified by order of the Secretary of State under section 72(4)(a) of the Nationality, Immigration and Asylum Act 2002', and if s/he 'is sentenced to a period of imprisonment'.[10] The concept of automatic deportation is difficult to reconcile with the ECHR and, previously, with the requirements of EU law. Therefore, section 33 BA 2007 provides for several exceptions which accommodate, among others, the United Kingdom's international obligations. In this regard, an important exception, which is discussed in more detail below, is established by section 33(2)(a) BA 2007 and concerns cases in which a deportation would breach the ECHR. Another exception relates to EU law. Even though the United Kingdom is no longer a Member State of the European Union, it must honour its obligations under the Withdrawal Agreement. Article 20(1) of the Withdrawal Agreement provides that 'the conduct of Union citizens … their family members, and other persons, who exercise rights under this Title, where that conduct occurred before the end of the transition period, shall be considered in accordance with Chapter VI of Directive 2004/38/EC'.[11] Therefore, section 3(5A) IA 1971 stipulates that

> the Secretary of State may not deem a relevant person's deportation to be conducive to the public good … if the person's deportation would be in breach of the obligations of the United Kingdom under Article 20 of the EU withdrawal agreement.

For criminal conduct that occurred after the transition period, Article 20(2) Withdrawal Agreement provides that it 'may constitute grounds for restricting the right of residence by the host State or the right of entry in the State of work in accordance with national legislation'.

II. Convicted Foreigners and Article 8 ECHR

Initially, UK legislation did not specify how deportations had to be evaluated in the context of Article 8 ECHR. This gap was filled by the judiciary by the establishment of a five-stage test in *R (Razgar) v Secretary of State for the Home Department*.[12] The case concerned an asylum seeker whom the United Kingdom sought to transfer to Germany according to the Dublin Convention. Lord Bingham held that, in

[8] Borders Act 2007, s 32(1)(b).
[9] Borders Act 2007, s 32(2).
[10] ibid.
[11] Agreement on the withdrawal of the United Kingdom of Great Britain and Northern Ireland from the European Union and the European Atomic Energy Community [2019] OJ C 384 I/14.
[12] *R (Razgar) v Secretary of State for the Home Department* [2004] UKHL 27, para 17.

cases where the individual relies on Article 8 ECHR, it has to be assessed whether (1) removal will be an interference with the exercise of the applicant's right to respect for his private or family life; (2) such interference will have consequences of such gravity as potentially to engage the operation of Article 8 ECHR; (3) such interference is in accordance with the law; (4) it is necessary in a democratic society and pursues one of the legitimate aims; and (5) it is proportionate to the legitimate public end sought to be achieved.[13]

A. The Immigration Rules

As stated above, the IA 1971 granted the executive wide discretion concerning the deportation of foreigners. The exercise of this discretion was governed by the Immigration Rules which took effect in March 1990 (HC 251). The Immigration Rules are not law[14] but a statement of administrative practice, which gives effect to the policy of the Secretary of State.[15] Prior to 2012 the Immigration Rules 'did not specifically address the requirements of article 8'.[16] In order to structure the assessment in cases where a deportee's Article 8 ECHR rights are affected, paragraphs 398 et seq (HC 194) were inserted into the Immigration Rules in June 2012. These rules 'were intended to promote consistency, predictability and transparency in decision-making … and to clarify the policy framework'.[17] Paragraph 398 distinguishes between three different categories. The first category covers foreigners who were sentenced to a period of imprisonment of more than four years (paragraph 398(a)); those within this group will normally be deported, unless exceptional circumstances apply. The second category covers foreigners who were sentenced to a period of imprisonment between 12 months and four years (paragraph 398(b)), and the third category covers foreigners whose offending has caused serious harm or who are persistent offenders and show a particular disregard for the law (paragraph 398(c)). The latter two categories of foreign offenders will be deported unless they can rely on the family life or the private life exception (paragraphs 399 and 399A of the Immigration Rules). The family life exception covers 'a genuine and subsisting parental relationship with a child' or 'a genuine and subsisting relationship with a partner', whereby these persons must fulfil certain requirements.[18] The private life exception applies where 'the person has been lawfully resident in the UK for most of his life' and 'is socially and culturally integrated in the UK' and

[13] ibid, para 17.

[14] *Hesham Ali* [2016] UKSC 60, Lord Reed, paras 17, 53.

[15] *Binaku* [2021] UKUT 00034 (IAC), para 78; *Odelola v SSHD* [2009] UKHL 25, Lord Hoffmann, para 6; *Hesham Ali*, Lord Reed, para 17 with further references.

[16] Otto, 'The Foreign National Prisoner's Dilemma in the United Kingdom' 436; *Hesham Ali*, Lord Reed, para 19.

[17] *Hesham Ali*, Lord Reed, para 21.

[18] Para 399 Immigration Rules.

'there would be very significant obstacles to his integration into the country to which it is proposed he is deported'.[19]

Even where the family life or the private life exceptions do not apply, the foreigner's Article 8 ECHR claim will not be rejected.[20] Instead, the claim will be dealt with, as Lord Reed elaborated, 'on the basis that great weight should generally be given to the public interest in the deportation of such offenders, but that it can be outweighed, applying a proportionality test, by very compelling circumstances'.[21] However, Lord Reed also added that these cases 'are likely to be a very small minority'.[22]

According to the Home Office's Statement of Intent, the Immigration Rules set out the Secretary of State's position on proportionality by providing 'how the balance should be struck between the public interest and individual rights, taking into account relevant case law'.[23] In *Hesham Ali*, Lord Reed stated that even though the rules are not law, they 'are nevertheless a relevant and important consideration for tribunals determining appeals …, because they reflect the assessment of the general public interest made by the responsible minister and endorsed by Parliament'.[24]

Regarding the question of whether the rules are binding on the judiciary, the Court of Appeal held in *MF (Nigeria)* that 'the new rules are a complete code' for Article 8 ECHR claims.[25] In *AJ (Angola)* the Court of Appeal stated that

> the fact that the new rules are intended to operate as a comprehensive code is significant, because it means that an official or a tribunal should seek to take account of any Convention rights of an appellant through the lens of the new rules themselves, rather than looking to apply Convention rights for themselves in a free-standing way outside the new rules[26]

In *Izuazu*[27] the Upper Tribunal (UT) took a more nuanced approach by stating that it endorses the observation that

> judges called on to make decisions about the application of Article 8 in cases to which the new rules apply, should proceed by first considering whether a claimant is able to benefit under the applicable provisions of the Immigration Rules designed to address Article 8 claims. If he or she does, there will be no need to go on to consider Article 8 generally.[28]

[19] Para 399A Immigration Rules.
[20] *Hesham Ali*, Lord Reed, para 36.
[21] ibid, para 38.
[22] ibid.
[23] Home Office, *Statement of Intent: Family Migration*, June 2012, para 38.
[24] *Hesham Ali*, Lord Reed, para 53.
[25] *MF (Nigeria)* [2013] EWCA Civ 1192, para 44.
[26] *AJ (Angola) v SSHD* [2014] EWCA Civ 1636, para 39.
[27] *Izuazu* [2013] UKUT 45 (IAC).
[28] ibid, para 40.

If this is not the case 'it will be necessary for the judge to go on to make an assessment of Article 8 applying the criteria established by law'.[29] Interestingly, the UT held that it does 'not accept that all the criteria set out in HC 194 accord with the criteria for an Article 8 assessment established by the existing case law'.[30] It explained that 'The more the new rules restrict otherwise relevant and weighty considerations from being taken into account, the less regard will be had to them in the assessment of proportionality'.[31] Finally, the UT concluded that 'there can be no presumption that the Rules will normally be conclusive of the Article 8 assessment or that a fact sensitive inquiry is not normally needed' and that 'the conclusion under the Rules may often have little bearing on the judge's own assessment of proportionality'.[32]

Later, in *Hesham Ali* (2016) Lord Reed clarified that 'the idea that the new rules comprise a complete code appears to have been mistakenly interpreted in some later cases as meaning that the Rules, and the Rules alone, govern appellate decision-making'.[33] He highlighted that the Rules are not law and 'therefore do not govern the determination of appeals, other than appeals brought on the ground that the decision is not in accordance with the Rules'.[34] Similarly, Lord Kerr held in the same case that the rules must necessarily contain a series of checks or filters in order to make the administrative decision-making process workable, but 'that failure to qualify under the rules should not inhibit the open-minded examination of whether article 8 mandates … to refuse to make a deportation order'.[35] The same approach had already been taken by Lord Bingham nine years earlier when he stated in *Huang* that 'an applicant's failure to qualify under the Rules is … the point at which to begin, not end, consideration of the claim under article 8. The terms of the Rules are relevant to that consideration, but they are not determinative'.[36]

B. Part 5A of the Nationality, Immigration and Asylum Act 2002

Two years after the new Immigration Rules were adopted, statutory guidance for the Article 8 balancing process was provided by the Immigration Act 2014. The Immigration Act inserted Part 5A (sections 117A–117D) into the Nationality, Immigration and Asylum Act 2002 (NIAA), which 'applies where a court or tribunal is required to determine whether a decision made under the Immigration Acts

[29] ibid, para 41.
[30] ibid, para 52.
[31] ibid.
[32] ibid, para 67.
[33] *Hesham Ali*, Lord Reed, para 52.
[34] ibid, para 53.
[35] ibid, Lord Kerr, para 154.
[36] *Huang* [2007] UKHL 11, Lord Bingham, para 6.

breaches a person's right to respect for private and family life under Article 8'.[37] Part 5A NIAA not only lists the considerations that have to be considered, it also expresses 'the intended balance of relevant factors in direct statutory form'.[38] The new provisions are said to diminish the weight placed on Article 8 ECHR rights and have thus made it easier to deport foreign offenders.[39]

Part 5A NIAA stipulates that, in cases concerning the deportation of foreign criminals, the court or tribunal must have particular regard to the considerations listed in section 117C when weighing the public interest.[40] Section 117C begins with the general rule that 'deportation of foreign criminals is in the public interest'[41] and continues by clarifying that the more serious the offence, the greater that interest.[42] Lord Carnwath aptly noted in *KO (Nigeria)* that there is 'no express indication as to how or at what stage of the process those general rules are to be given effect'.[43] Moreover, he highlights that the 'remainder of the section enacts specific rules for two categories of foreign criminals, defined by reference to whether or not their sentences were of four years or more, and two precisely defined exceptions'.[44]

Indeed, the first scenario is set out in section 117C(3) NIAA and covers 'the case of a foreign criminal ("C") who has not been sentenced to a period of imprisonment of four years or more'. This scenario in principle applies to foreigners who have been sentenced to a period of imprisonment of at least 12 months and no more than four years. In these cases, the 'public interest requires C's deportation unless Exception 1 or Exception 2 applies'.[45]

Exception 1 concerns the person's private life and 'applies where C has been lawfully resident in the United Kingdom for most of C's life, is socially and culturally integrated …, and there would be very significant obstacles to C's integration into the country to which C is proposed to be deported'.[46] Exception 2 concerns the person's family life and 'applies where C has a genuine and subsisting relationship with a qualifying partner, or a genuine and subsisting parental relationship with a qualifying child, and the effect of C's deportation on the partner or child would be unduly harsh'.[47] For a sentence of less than four years, these criteria 'are enough, if they are met, to remove the public interest in deportation'.[48] They create a hard rule, and a protection for those who fall within the scope of the exception.

[37] Nationality, Immigration and Asylum Act 2002, s 117A(1)(a) (NIAA).
[38] *KO (Nigeria) v SSHD* [2018] UKSC 53, Lord Carnwath, para 21.
[39] Otto, 'The Foreign National Prisoner's Dilemma in the United Kingdom' 432; M Griffiths, 'Foreign, Criminal: A Doubly Damned Modern British Folk-devil' (2017) 21 *Citizenship Studies* 527, 534.
[40] NIAA, s 117A(2).
[41] NIAA, s 117C(1).
[42] NIAA, s 117C(2).
[43] *KO (Nigeria)*, Lord Carnwath, para 20.
[44] ibid, para 20.
[45] NIAA, s 117C(3).
[46] NIAA, s 117C(4).
[47] NIAA, s 177C(5).
[48] *KO (Nigeria)*, Lord Carnwath, para 21.

Interestingly, the initial 'C' for criminal is used and not the initial 'F' for foreigner, even though it is a person's status as a foreigner that makes him or her liable to deportation, as nationals are in principle non-deportable. Given that the distinguishing factor is the nationality and not the criminal behaviour, the initial 'C' might be somewhat misleading. At the same time both terms reinforce each other, as noted by Griffiths, who states that '"Foreign" has become an adjective to entrench the wickedness of the Criminal, and "Criminal" is increasingly a term utilised to delegitimise mobility'.[49]

Section 117C(6) NIAA outlines the second scenario, which concerns foreigners who have been sentenced to a prison term of four years and more. In this case 'the public interest requires deportation unless there are very compelling circumstances, over and above those described in Exceptions 1 and 2'.

While courts and tribunals are obliged to adhere to Part 5A NIAA, the question of whether they are under an obligation to take the Immigration Rules into account seemed to be unclear for some time. In 2019 Leggatt LJ stated in *CI (Nigeria)* that

> it is generally unnecessary for a tribunal or court in a case in which a decision to deport a 'foreign criminal' is challenged on article 8 grounds to refer to paragraphs 398–399A of the Immigration Rules, as they have no additional part to play in the analysis.[50]

This approach was endorsed in *Binaku* in 2021: the UT stated that 'the structured approach set out in section 117C of the 2002 Act … governs the task to be undertaken by a tribunal, not the provisions of the Rules'[51] and that 'considering an Article 8 appeal in the context of deportation begins and ends with Part 5A of the 2002 Act'.[52] Even though Part 5A exhibits clear parallels to the Immigration Rules, these judgments demonstrate that there are differences and that the NIAA, an Act of Parliament, is the relevant guide for the judiciary.

III. The Balance between the Principle of Proportionality and the Principle of Legal Certainty

An interference with the right to respect for private and family life by way of deportation requires a balancing process between the interests of the foreigner and the interests of the state in order to establish if the interference is proportionate or whether it is disproportionate and therefore amounts to a violation of that right. A balancing process which lacks criteria is likely to vitiated by inconsistency and arbitrary results, thereby undermining legal certainty and fairness. If, on the

[49] Griffiths, 'Foreign, Criminal' 540.
[50] *CI (Nigeria)* [2019] EWCA Civ 2027, para 21.
[51] *Binaku* [2021] UKUT 00034 (IAC), para 79.
[52] ibid, para 91.

other hand, the criteria that have to be considered in the balancing process as well as their weight are prescribed in such a way that they bar the decision maker from considering the facts of the individual case, they curtail the balancing process and thereby undermine the principle of proportionality, which requires that the balancing process be open ended.

Section 32(5) BA 2007 obliges the Secretary of State to make a deportation order in respect of a foreign criminal unless an exception applies. Sedley LJ noted in this regard that

> it can safely be said that there is no longer any requirement for the Home Secretary to form her own view of where the public interest lies when deciding on the need to deport a foreign criminal (as she) is now bound by the legislative policy spelt out in ss.32 and 33 of the 2007 Act.

Moreover, he adds,

> even if the Home Secretary were to take the view that deportation would be unjust in relation to a statutory foreign criminal in whose favour there were no sufficient contra-indications under s.33(2), her hands would be tied: she would be bound to make a deportation order. So, too, in the absence of a statutory exception, the tribunal must uphold a deportation order against a foreign criminal, not because the Home Secretary considers that the public interest requires deportation but because Parliament does.[53]

Fripp et al argue that if a foreigner is covered by the section 32 scheme and no exception applies, the 'Secretary of State's view of the individual case becomes in essence irrelevant'.[54] The obligation that is imposed on the Secretary of State by section 32(5) BA 2007 to make a deportation order is also criticised by Lord Kerr, who argues that this

> transformed the open-ended discretion that the Secretary of State had under section 5(1) of the 1971 Act into a circumscribed judgment as to whether the person to be deported came within any of the exceptions in section 33 of the 2007 Act.[55]

If an exception applies, in particular Article 8 ECHR,[56] the consideration of this exception is further specified by Part 5A NIAA. Interestingly, the title of Part 5A, 'Article 8 of the ECHR: public interest considerations' refers neither to a balancing process nor to the foreigner's interests. Part 5A NIAA not only establishes the criteria that have to be considered when determining whether a deportation would violate Article 8 ECHR, it also attaches an abstract weight to these criteria, whereby a term of imprisonment of four years, in section 117C(3) and (6) NIAA, is a key distinguishing factor. While such an approach enhances legal certainty, as the outcome of the decision-making process is more predictable, it limits an

[53] *Gurung v SSHD* [2012] EWCA Civ 62, para 9.

[54] s.n., 'Part C: Deportation, Removal, Exclusion' in E Fripp (ed), *The Law and Practice of Expulsion and Exclusion from the United Kingdom* (Oxford, Hart Publishing, 2015) 283.

[55] *Hesham Ali*, Lord Kerr, para 127.

[56] Borders Act 2007, s 33(2)(a).

open-ended balancing process. The question is how much discretion section 117C NIAA grants to the decision maker.

Section 117C(2) seems to grant some discretion to the decision maker in determining the public interest in deportation as it stipulates that 'the more serious the offence committed by a foreign criminal, the greater is the public interest in deportation of the criminal'. At the same time, this section contains detailed rules as to when a foreigner who is convicted and sentenced to a term of imprisonment of less or more than four years can successfully invoke the Article 8 ECHR exception. Lord Carnwath noted in *KO (Nigeria)* that exception 1 (the private life exception), 'seems to leave no room for further balancing' as it 'is precisely defined by reference to three factual issues', none of which 'turns on the seriousness of the offence'.[57] With regard to exception 2 (the family life exception) Lord Carnwath noted that given 'that exception 1 is self-contained, it would be surprising to find exception 2 structured in a different way'.[58] Even though exception 2 is perhaps less clearly worded than exception 1, he noted that the word 'unduly harsh' does not seem to be 'intended as a reference back to the issue of relative seriousness introduced in subsection (2)'.[59] Indeed, it seems that section 117C does not leave room for an assessment of the seriousness of the offence that goes beyond the weight that has been ascribed to the duration of the prison term by the statutory provision.

In light of the statement that a balancing process 'frequently requires judges to balance incomparable considerations' which cannot be quantified,[60] the clear criteria in Part 5A NIAA, and in particular the specific weight that has been attached to them by the legislature, could be seen as an improvement as these clear rules absolve the decision makers to some extent from this difficult task. On the other hand, the limitations of the decision-making process that are precipitated by the criteria in Part 5A NIAA, in particular by section 117C, have raised several concerns. Otto warns that a limitation of judicial discretion can 'dangerously enlarge the power of the legislature and the executive branch, especially in the United Kingdom where the judiciary already lacks the ability to overturn Parliamentary Acts'.[61] In Lord Kerr's view, the balancing process in the context of Article 8 ECHR 'must be open-textured so that sufficient emphasis is given to each of the factors as they arise in particular cases'.[62] He argues that the factors or criteria that are considered in the balancing process 'cannot be given a pre-ordained

[57] *KO (Nigeria)*, Lord Carnwath, para 21.
[58] ibid, para 22.
[59] ibid, para 22.
[60] JN Drobak and DC North, 'Understanding Judicial Decision-Making: The Importance of Constraints on Non-Rational Deliberations' (2008) 26 *Washington University Journal of Law & Policy* 131, 139.
[61] Otto, 'The Foreign National Prisoner's Dilemma in the United Kingdom' 445.
[62] *Hesham Ali*, Lord Kerr, para 115.

weight' and that 'Any attempt to do that would run counter to the essential purpose of the exercise'.[63] He adds that 'giving pre-emptive, indicative weight to particular factors on a generic basis is impermissible if it distorts the proper assessment of these in their peculiar and individual setting'.[64] Moreover, he holds that if the *Boultif* criteria 'are relevant to a potential deportee's situation, they *must* be taken into account and they *must* be given the weight that they deserve, following an open-ended and rounded evaluation of the case'.[65] Similarly Justice Green warns of a 'tick box approach' and states that

> it is important that officials … should be vigilant to avoid a tick box mentality and should bear the policy guidance in mind seeking to stand back after working through the analysis required so as to formulate in an overall manner a view as to whether there might be a good arguable case of disproportionality if leave to remain was not granted.[66]

Even though his warning concerns the Immigration Rules, the risk of a tick box approach can also emerge in the context of Part 5A NIAA.

Collinson criticises that the application of Part 5A of the NIAA creates 'hard cases' that seem to be arbitrary. He provides the example of the family life exception (section 177C(5) NIAA), according to which a delinquent foreigner who has been sentenced to imprisonment for a period ranging from 12 months up to four years can invoke the exception to automatic deportation if s/he can rely on family life by having 'genuine and subsisting parental relationship with a qualifying child, and the effect of the foreigner's deportation on the … child would be unduly harsh'.[67] A 'qualifying child' is a minor who is either a British citizen or 'has lived in the United Kingdom for a continuous period of seven years or more'.[68] Collinson rightly points out that a child who has continuously lived in the United Kingdom for 2,550 days is likely to experience his/her parent's deportation no less harshly than a child who has been resident in the United Kingdom for 2,555 days (that is, seven years).[69] Yet, only in the second case would the child, if s/he was a non-British citizen, be a qualifying child, because s/he has reached the 'arbitrary'[70] threshold of seven years. Part 5A NIAA improves the consistency of the decision-making process of the executive by establishing clear requirements and thresholds. While these rules enhance predictability and thereby foster legal certainty, they bar both the decision maker and courts from conducting a holistic assessment in which potential shortcomings (that is, missing a threshold by a couple of days or months) can be outweighed by other considerations.

[63] ibid.
[64] ibid.
[65] ibid, para 120.
[66] *Ahmed* [2014] EWHC Admin 300, para 33.
[67] NIAA, s 177C(5).
[68] NIAA, s 177D(1).
[69] Collinson, 'Suspended Deportation Orders' 298, 304.
[70] ibid, 304.

For Collinson the problem lies in the binary nature of the system of deportation (that is, deportation or abstention from deportation), which precludes the possibility of providing the nuanced outcomes required by the principle of proportionality.[71] He argues 'that there simply is no less restrictive means available to promote the legitimate aim of preventing crime and disorder under article 8(2) ECHR'.[72] Indeed, it has been argued elsewhere in this book that expulsion or deportation of a convicted foreigner is not only problematic in light of the requirement of necessity (the least intrusive means test), but that it is even possible to call into question the suitability of the measure.[73] In light of the shortcomings of the current system, Collinson suggests supplementing the binary system with a third option, the so-called 'suspended deportation order'.[74] He argues that the concept of suspended deportation orders addresses the problem of 'hard cases' in deportation orders on both side of the 'divide' and is therefore politically neutral.[75] His suggestion has clear advantages and could constitute a useful instrument not only for the British system of deportation, but also for the German system of expulsion,[76] which prescribes an expulsion decision once the public's interest in the foreigner's termination of residence takes precedence over the interests of the foreigner,[77] and leaves no discretion to refrain from an expulsion.

However, the 'hard' cases which the system creates are a consequence of its rigid rules. As has been argued elsewhere in this book,[78] statutory provisions are phrased in abstract and general terms to cover a variety of situations and a large group of persons. As Drobak and North put it, 'The world is too complex and dynamic to enable even a comprehensive statutory regime to provide answers for all the problems that are sure to arise'.[79] Given the abstract and general nature of statutory provisions, they cannot replace a balancing process that takes the situation of the individual into account. Therefore, a separate balancing process between the interests of the individual and the interests of the state has to be conducted in each case by those who apply the statutory provisions. While a balancing process is regularly guided by a list of criteria and possibly by a specific weight that has been attached to these criteria in order to enhance consistency and avoid arbitrariness, the statutory provisions cannot replace a balancing process and should not bar the decision maker from taking the facts of the individual case into account. While section 3(5) IA 1971 grants the executive considerable discretion, the provisions of the BA 2007 and Part 5A NIAA significantly circumscribe the discretion of the decision maker and undermine an open-ended balancing process.

[71] ibid, 301.
[72] ibid.
[73] See Chapter 5.
[74] Collinson, 'Suspended Deportation Orders' 301.
[75] ibid.
[76] See Chapter 5.
[77] German Residence Act, s 53(1).
[78] See Chapter 5.
[79] Drobak and North, 'Understanding Judicial Decision-Making' 133.

IV. Rationale of the Provisions Governing the Deportation of Convicted Foreigners

The IA 1971, which provides in section 3(5)(a) that a person who is not a British citizen is subject to deportation from the United Kingdom if the Secretary of State deems it conducive to the public good, grants the Secretary of State a wide discretion and places the state's interests above those of the individual. Section 32(4) BA 2007 narrows this discretion to some extent by providing that 'the deportation of a foreign criminal is conducive to the public good', but it does not affect the rationale that transpires from section 3(5)(a) IA 1971. Both provisions refrain from referring to the foreigner's interests, as their focus rests solely on the interests of the state in removing certain foreigners from its territory. Lord Kerr rightly points out the terms of section 32(4) BA 2007 'that the deportation of a foreign criminal is conducive to the public good, purport to foreclose any legal debate as to whether the deportation of anyone who comes within that category can be other than conducive to the public good'.[80]

The rationale of section 3(5)(a) IA 1971 and section 32(4) BA 2007 is reinforced by section 33(5) BA 2007, which even imposes an obligation on the Secretary of State to make a deportation order in respect of a foreign criminal. In brackets, section 32(5) provides that this obligation is 'subject to section 33'. Section 33 BA 2007 lists, among other exceptions, foreigners' rights that arise from the United Kingdom's international obligations. These rights can bar a deportation but they are not on an equal footing with the interests of the state: they are the exception to the rule of deportation, which demonstrates their subordinate position. The subordinate position of the foreigner's interests is underpinned by Part 5A NIAA, which is entitled 'Article 8 of the ECHR: public interest considerations'. The public interest seems to be the only relevant consideration, as highlighted by an absence of a reference to the foreigner's interests. This is reflected by section 117C NIAA, titled 'Article 8: additional considerations in cases involving foreign criminals', which reiterates the default position that 'The deportation of foreign criminals is in the public interest'.[81] The focus rests on the state's or the public's interests, which take precedence over the interests of the foreigner. This position is corroborated by the structure of section 117C, which provides that if the foreigner has been sentenced to a specific period of imprisonment, the 'public interest requires' the foreigner's deportation, unless an exception applies (section 117C(3) NIAA 2002) or unless there are 'very compelling circumstances over and above' those exceptions (section 117C(6) NIAA 2002).

A strong presumption that deportation is necessary has been created by section 32(4) BA 2007 and is maintained by section 117C NIAA 2002. The

[80] *Hesham Ali*, Lord Kerr, para 126.
[81] NIAA, s 117C(1).

foreigner's interests are only considered within the framework of exceptions. Their exceptional nature weakens the foreigner's standpoint and supports the view that

> the deportation of a person convicted of a criminal offence and sentenced to more than 12 months' imprisonment is to be considered as immutably in the public good, irrespective of, for instance, any philanthropy or other worthy endeavours in which he may have engaged since his incarceration.[82]

At the same time, it must be noted that if an exception applies, the public interest in deportation is removed.

V. Conclusions

The IA 1971 granted the executive considerable discretion regarding the deportation of (delinquent) foreigners. This discretion was limited by the BA 2007, which established a system of automatic deportation supplemented by a list of exceptions. This chapter focused specifically on the ECHR exception and the extent to which statutory provisions afford the decision maker a margin of discretion when deciding on whether a deportation constitutes a proportionate interference with the right to respect for private and family life guaranteed by Article 8 ECHR. A balancing process without any guidelines abets inconsistency and can precipitate arbitrary decisions. On the other hand, a detailed prescription of the criteria, which forecloses an open-ended balancing process and bars the decision maker from taking the particulars of the individual case into account, is equally problematic. While the latter approach fosters predictability and legal certainty, it considerably circumscribes the balancing process. Part 5A NIAA, which is titled 'Article 8 of the ECHR: public interest considerations', not only establishes the criteria that have to be considered and their weight, it also establishes thresholds to rely on Article 8 ECHR, which have been said to be arbitrary. These rigid rules, while enhancing predictability and legal certainty, restrict the decision maker's margin of discretion and limit him or her in conducting a holistic assessment which takes the particular facts of the individual case into account.

Finally, the wording and structure of the provision on automatic deportation (section 32 BA 2007) and section 117C NIAA subordinate the foreigner's interests to the interests of the state by placing a strong emphasis on the latter.

[82] *Hesham Ali*, Lord Kerr, para 126.

8

Comparison of Germany, the Netherlands and the United Kingdom

After having outlined the German system of expulsion (Chapter 5), the requirements applicable in the Netherlands for terminating lawful residence after a criminal conviction and declaring the foreigner *persona non grata* (Chapter 6), and the deportation of convicted foreigners from the United Kingdom (Chapter 7), this chapter aims at exploring the similarities, but in particular the differences, between these systems. The differences between the German and the Dutch systems are relevant for the third part of this book, which addresses the effects that national expulsion decisions can have at the European level. Where national decisions are given a European dimension by entering an alert into the SIS for the purpose of refusing entry to the third-country national, other states are, in principle, bound by this national decision. Against the background of these consequences, possible differences between the national systems concerning the requirements for expulsion decisions following a criminal conviction and the entry of alerts into the SIS are relevant. They are relevant as diverging criteria for entering an alert into the SIS undermine the coherence of the European approach. Importantly, such divergences could mean that a foreigner with regard to whom an alert has been entered into the SIS by one Member State following his/her criminal conviction must be refused entry to the Schengen area by another Member State, even if this Member States would not have entered an alert into the SIS if the same situation had occurred on its territory.

Section I draws a comparison between the general features of the Dutch, German and British systems. Subsequently, the differences in sentencing and the duration of the entry ban in Germany and the Netherlands are outlined (Section II) (these are recalled and further expanded upon in the next part),[1] followed by a brief conclusion (Section III).

I. General Observations

In comparing the systems in the Netherlands, Germany and the United Kingdom several observations can be made.

[1] Chapter 10.

First, focusing on the margin of discretion granted by the legislature to the executive, the three states under scrutiny take different approaches. The Dutch statutory provisions grant the executive a considerable margin of discretion in the Vw 2000. A residence permit issued for a limited time can be withdrawn if the foreigner poses a threat to public policy or public security.[2] A residence permit issued for an unlimited time can be withdrawn or altered if, among other reasons, the foreigner has irrevocably been sentenced to a prison term for a crime which is punishable with imprisonment for up to three years.[3] The wide discretion that is granted by the legislature is then specified by the Vb 2000.

In Germany, section 53 Residence Act is the central statutory provision regulating the expulsion of delinquent foreigners. It requires the decision maker to conduct a balancing process between the interests of the foreigner and the interests of the state, but stipulates that if the interests of the public in terminating the foreigner's residence take precedence over the interests of the foreigner, the latter must be expelled. Sections 53–55 contain non-exhaustive lists of considerations that guide the balancing process and sections 54 and 55 attach a specific weight to the criteria contained therein.

The UK Borders Act 2007 provides for automatic deportation[4] and imposes an obligation on the Secretary of State to 'make a deportation order in respect of a foreign criminal'.[5] This obligation is not absolute as it is supplemented by a list of exceptions[6] to ensure that, among others, the United Kingdom's obligations under the ECHR are met. If a case engages Article 8 ECHR, a balance must be struck between, on the one hand, the foreigner's right to respect for private and family life and, on the other hand, the public interest in deporting the foreigner. The balancing process that is required by Article 8 ECHR is, in the context of deportation, circumscribed by the legislature. Part 5A NIAA 2002 determines in great detail when the public interest in deportation prevails, leaving little discretion to the decision maker.

Second, none of the three systems provides for an absolute protection against expulsion or deportation irrespective of the foreigner's criminal conduct. The Dutch system previously protected certain groups of long-term resident foreigners from the termination of lawful residence on grounds of a criminal conviction, but it abolished this protection in 2012. However, both the Dutch and the British system grant a certain protection based on long lawful residence, depending on the duration of the term of imprisonment.

In the Netherlands, the 'sliding scale' (Article 3.86 Vb 2000) relates the duration of the foreigner's lawful residence to the duration of the term of imprisonment

[2] Article 19 in conjunction with Article 18(1)(e) Vw 2000.
[3] Article 22(2)(c) Vw 2000.
[4] Borders Act 2007, s 32.
[5] Borders Act 2007, s 32(5).
[6] Borders Act 2007, s 33.

and the seriousness of the crime. If the criminal offence is not serious enough in light of the foreigner's lawful residence, residence cannot be terminated.

In the United Kingdom, the Home Secretary is obliged to order the deportation of a criminal foreigner unless an exception applies. Part 5A NIAA 2002, in particular section 117C, stipulates in great detail the requirements for relying on the Article 8 ECHR exception. A foreigner who has been sentenced to a term of imprisonment of less than four years can rely, for example, on the private life exemption if s/he has been lawfully resident in the United Kingdom for most of their life, is socially and culturally integrated in the United Kingdom, and there would be very significant obstacles to their integration into the country to which s/he is proposed to be deported.[7] If an exception applies, the obligation of the Secretary of State to order the deportation does not apply,[8] and the public interest in deportation is removed.

According to the German system, the question of whether a foreigner will be expelled depends on the outcome of the balancing process, which takes the facts of the individual case into account. The German provisions on expulsion do not contain exceptions to expulsions or a system that provides that a long lawful residence per se can outweigh a prison term.

Third, the systems take different approaches in addressing the interests of the foreigner and the interests of the state. The Dutch sliding scale directly relates the duration of the foreigner's lawful stay to the imposed prison term and thereby addresses the foreigner's interest and the state's interest at the same stage of assessment. Equally, the German system, which requires a balancing process between the interests of the individual and the interests of the state,[9] creates a level playing field, even though the state's interests are listed first,[10] followed by the interests of the foreigner.[11] The British system refrains from creating a level playing field. The deportation of a foreign criminal is the rule (as it is considered conducive to the public good),[12] therefore the Secretary of State must make a deportation order[13] unless an exception applies.[14] The foreigner's interests are only addressed in a second step, as possible exceptions to the rule of deportation. However, even within the scope of application of exceptions, the state's interests take precedence over the interests of the individual. This becomes evident when focusing on the Article 8 ECHR exception, which is particularly relevant in the context of deportation. If Article 8 ECHR is engaged in the context of deportation, Part 5A NIAA 2002 provides further guidance. The title of Part 5A, 'Article 8 of the ECHR: public

[7] NIAA, s 117C(4).
[8] Borders Act 2007, s 33(1).
[9] Residence Act, s 53(1).
[10] Residence Act, s 54.
[11] Residence Act, s 55.
[12] Borders Act 2007, s 32(4).
[13] Borders Act 2007, s 32(5).
[14] Borders Act 2007, s 32(5) in conjunction with Borders Act 2007, s 33.

interest considerations', mentions neither a balancing process nor the foreigner's interests. Section 117C, which specifically addresses Article 8 ECHR in the context of convicted foreigners, reiterates the rule that the deportation of foreign criminals is in the public interest.[15] Again, the interests of the state prevail unless the individual can rely on the narrowly defined exceptions.[16]

Fourth, the level of legal certainty that is offered by these three systems differs and is to some extent determined by the margin of discretion that is granted by the legislature to the executive.

In the Netherlands, two situations must be distinguished. First, in constellations where the criminal offence is not serious enough in light of the duration of the foreigner's lawful residence according to the requirements in the sliding scale, the interests of the individual prevail and the foreigner's residence cannot be terminated on grounds of his/her criminal conviction. In these situations, a high level of certainty is afforded as both the duration of residence and the prison term are objective and measurable parameters, making it possible to determine whether the foreigner can benefit from this protection. Notably, the sliding scale does not address the reverse situation, that is, cases in which the interests of the state per se trump the interests of the foreigner and take priority over the latter.[17] Second, if the criminal offence is serious enough in light of the duration of the foreigner's lawful residence, a balancing process between the interests of the foreigner and the interests of the state has to be conducted as the relevant provisions in the Vw 2000 and the Vb 2000 both grant discretion (*kan*). This process shall be guided, in case Article 8 ECHR applies, by the *Üner* and *Boultif* criteria.[18] However, as previously highlighted, there is a risk that the obligation incumbent on the IND to terminate lawful stay if possible[19] leads to an insufficient consideration of human rights. This risk might be exacerbated by the fact that the sliding scale already incorporates core aspects of the balancing process, such as the duration of the foreigner's residence and the seriousness of the crime committed, and could consequently create the presumption that the termination of residence is justified. However, in principle this balancing process must be open ended and take all the facts of the individual case into account, which, however, provides for a lower level of legal certainty.

Germany provides an increased level of legal certainty by establishing a non-exhaustive list of criteria[20] that must be considered in the balancing process and

[15] NIAA, s 117C(1).

[16] NIAA, s 117C (4), (5).

[17] However, it must be noted that Article 3.86(11) Vb 2000 contains a derogation from the thresholds established by the sliding scale and provides that the residence permit can be rejected on grounds of Article 18(1)(e) Vw 2000 if there are serious reasons for believing that the foreigner has committed an offence referred to in Article 1 F Geneva Refugee Convention. This ground does not require a criminal conviction.

[18] Immigration and Naturalisation Service ('Immigratie- en Naturalisatiedienst'), 'Richtlijnen voor de toepassing van artikel 8 EVRM', Werkinstructie 2020/16 (SUA), 18 November 2020, pp 13–39.

[19] B12/2.8 Vc 2000.

[20] Residence Act, s 53(2).

by attaching a specific weight to certain balancing factors.[21] The outcome of this balancing process is open ended, which supports the principle of proportionality.

The UK statutory provisions provide for a high level of legal certainty by limiting the discretion of the executive and by prescribing the deportation of a criminal foreigner unless an exception applies.[22] Even if a foreigner can have recourse to the Article 8 ECHR exception, the relevant statutory provisions stipulate in a very detailed manner when the Article 8 exception can successfully be invoked where the foreigner has been sentenced to a term of imprisonment of less than four years[23] or a term of imprisonment of more than four years.[24]

These clear requirements enhance legal certainty for both foreigners, who are covered by the Article 8 ECHR exception, and those who fall outside of these clearly specified requirements. At the same time, these clear provisions bar the decision maker from conducting a holistic assessment which takes the facts of the individual case into account, thereby weakening the principle of proportionality.

Fifth, the margin of discretion granted by the legislature to the executive sheds light on the allocation of powers. The Dutch legislature grants discretion regarding the termination of lawful residence and the issuance of an *ongewenstverklaring* and *inreisverbod*,[25] which is, in general, to be welcomed as it enables the authorities and courts to conduct a balancing process. Nevertheless, this system can have its downsides. Given that only the Vw 2000 is an Act of Parliament, while the Vb 2000 and the Vc 2000, which specify the discretion granted by the Vw 2000, are not,[26] the executive has a considerable discretion vis-à-vis the Parliament. Moreover, the Vc 2000 prescribes cases in which residence has to be terminated.[27]

In the United Kingdom the situation is almost the reverse. The Borders Act 2002 prescribes that the Secretary of State has to make a deportation order in respect of a criminal foreigner, unless an exception applies.[28] Part 5A NIAA 2002 specifies in detail the requirements that have to be fulfilled in order for the foreigner to successfully invoke Article 8 ECHR,[29] which precludes an open-ended balancing process. The limited discretion granted by the legislature is problematic against the background of the already strong position of Parliament. The doctrine of parliamentary sovereignty entails that Parliament is supreme, that it can make and unmake any law it wishes and that nobody, including the courts, has the power to strike down an Act of Parliament. Even though a declaration of incompatibility

[21] See Residence Act, ss 54–55.

[22] Borders Act 2007, s 32(5).

[23] NIAA, s 117C(3); the exceptions are listed in NIAA, s 117C (4) and (5).

[24] NIAA, s 117C(6).

[25] With the exception of Article 66a(1) Vw 2000, which requires the issuance of an *inreisverbod*.

[26] The Vb 2000 is an *Algemene Maatregel van Bestuur* (order in Council) and not a law in the formal sense. The Vc 2000 is a ministerial instruction.

[27] See for example B10/2.3 Vc 2000.

[28] Borders Act 2002, s 32(5).

[29] NIAA, s 117C (3)–(6).

may be made if a court is satisfied that a statutory provision is incompatible with a Convention right,[30] this declaration does not affect the validity of the statutory provision.[31] If the executive enjoyed a greater discretion in applying Article 8 ECHR in the context of deportation, the courts would be able to review the exercise of this discretion. However, Parliament stipulates in detail if and under which circumstances a convicted foreigner can rely on Article 8 ECHR to challenge his/her deportation, thereby securing itself an unfettered power to determine when the state's interests prevail.

In Germany the legislature leaves discretion to the executive as it is the latter that conducts the balancing process between the interests of the state and the interests of the individual. This balancing process is, however, guided to a certain extent by statutory provisions that establish a non-exhaustive list of criteria and attach weight to certain criteria.

Sixth, the three systems differ with regard to the protection that is linked to a specific type of residence title. The Dutch sliding scale refers to the duration of the foreigner's residence, which in essence means lawful residence in terms of Article 8 (a)–(e) Vw 2000,[32] and creates a link between the duration of the foreigner's lawful residence and the imposed prison term. The longer the foreigner's lawful residence, the higher the threshold for a criminal conviction before residence may be terminated.

The German system creates a link between the type of residence permit held by the foreigner and the weight that is attached to the foreigner's interest in remaining in Germany. If the foreigner holds a permanent settlement permit and has lawfully resided in the federal territory for at least five years, the foreigner's interests shall be accorded a particularly high importance in the balancing process.[33] If, by contrast, the foreigner holds a temporary residence permit and has resided in the federal territory for at least five years, the foreigner's interests in remaining shall be accorded a high importance,[34] but not a particularly high importance.

The UK system, like the Dutch system, refers to lawful residence but does not attach a particular weight to a specific type of residence title.

II. Differences between Germany and the Netherlands in Sentencing and the Duration of the Entry Ban

Even though Germany and the Netherlands assess the threat posed by the individual to public policy or public security with reference to, among other criteria, the

[30] Human Rights Act 1998, s 4(2).
[31] Human Rights Act 1998, s 4(6)(a).
[32] See Article 3.86(6) Vb 2000.
[33] Residence Act, s 55(1) no 1.
[34] Residence Act, s 55(2) no 2.

crimes committed and the prison term that has been imposed, the prison terms imposed for identical offences are not necessarily identical in Germany and the Netherlands respectively. A Dutch court ruled with regard to a foreigner who was sentenced in Germany to a prison term of eight years for acting as a member of a criminal organisation and repeatedly dealing drugs that he probably would have been punished with a prison term of five or six years in the Netherlands.[35]

In *Arvelo Aponte* the individual was sentenced by a German court to two years and six months' (30 months') imprisonment for the importation of cocaine. The prosecution department at the Amsterdam Regional Court was requested to assess whether the sentence imposed was comparable to the sentence that would have been imposed in the Netherlands if the offence had been committed there.[36] It held that if the foreigner had been convicted in the Netherlands s/he would probably have been sentenced to 15 to 24 months' imprisonment.[37] Hence, an individual might not only face differences regarding the administrative procedure concerning the withdrawal of a residence permit and the imposition of an entry ban following a criminal conviction, differences may already arise at the stage of determination of the term of imprisonment.

Next to the differences in sentencing, and the termination of lawful residence following a criminal conviction, set out in the previous section, the maximum duration of an entry ban can differ between the Netherlands and Germany. EU law requires that an entry ban be limited in time but does not prescribe a maximum time limit for the duration of an entry ban. Article 11(2) of the Return Directive stipulates that the length of the entry ban shall not in principle exceed five years, but that it may exceed five years 'if the third-country national represents a serious threat to public policy, public security or national security'.

Article 6.5a(6) of the Dutch Vb 2000 provides for a maximum duration of 20 years for an *inreisverbod* if the foreigner poses a serious threat to national security or if serious reasons require a duration of more than 10 years. In Germany, section 11(5) Residence Act provides that the duration of the entry ban shall not exceed 10 years if the foreigner was expelled on grounds of a criminal conviction or if the foreigner poses a serious threat to public safety and order. The Federal Administrative Court stated in 2012 that 10 years is usually the maximum period for which a prediction can realistically be conducted on expected future conduct.[38] Only if the foreigner were expelled on grounds of a crime against peace, a war crime or a crime against humanity, or to avert a terrorist threat or a threat to the security of the Federal Republic of Germany, the duration of the entry ban would generally be 20 years.[39]

[35] Rechtbank's-Gravenhage, 14 September 2012, AWB 11/33681.

[36] *Arvelo Aponte v The Netherlands* App no 28770/05 (ECHR, 3 November 2011), para 13.

[37] ibid.

[38] Federal Administrative Court, DE:BVerwG:2012:131212U1C14.12.0, para 14.

[39] Residence Act, s 11(5a).

III. Conclusions

This part addressed the termination of residence following a criminal conviction and the imposition of entry bans in Germany and the Netherlands, as well as the deportation of criminal foreigners from the United Kingdom. It highlighted the differences and commonalities between these three systems, whereby the focus rested on Germany and the Netherlands, as both countries can give a European effect to their national decision by way of an alert into the SIS.

In the United Kingdom, the Borders Act 2007 provides for the automatic deportation of criminal foreigners, which considerably limits the margin of discretion of the decision maker. Even though the system of automatic deportation is augmented with exceptions,[40] to honour the United Kingdom's international obligations, for example under the ECHR, these exceptions do not grant a wide margin of discretion to the decision maker. The balancing process that is required by Article 8 ECHR in situations where a deportation interferes with the foreigner's right to respect for private and family life is prescribed in a detailed manner by the legislature.[41] While these clear guidelines enhance legal certainty, they impair an open-ended balancing process.

The Dutch Vw 2000 grants discretion to the decision maker regarding the termination of lawful residence after a criminal conviction. The exercise of this discretion is further specified by the sliding scale (Article 3.86 Vb 2000), which relates the duration of the foreigner's lawful residence to the imposed prison term and establishes an increasing protection the longer the foreigner lawfully resides in the Netherlands. If the duration of lawful residence outweighs the term of imprisonment, residence cannot be terminated. If the foreigner's residence does not outweigh the prison term and residence may be terminated, a balancing process must be conducted, which shall be guided, where Article 8 ECHR applies, by the *Üner* and *Boultif* criteria.[42] The termination of lawful residence after a criminal conviction counts among the measures that can lead to an entry ban (*inreisverbod* or *ongewenstverklaring*). The *inreisverbod*, which applies only to third-country nationals, has to be limited in time, with the maximum duration of the entry ban being 20 years.

The German system requires a balancing process between the interests of the state and the interests of the foreigner,[43] and provides for a non-exhaustive list of criteria that have to be considered in the balancing process.[44] Moreover, it attaches a specific weight to interests of the foreigner[45] and those of the state.[46] However,

[40] Borders Act 2007, s 33.

[41] NIAA, s 117C.

[42] Immigration and Naturalisation Service ('Immigratie- en Naturalisatiedienst'), 'Richtlijnen voor de toepassing van artikel 8 EVRM', Werkinstructie 2020/16 (SUA), 18 November 2020, pp 13–39.

[43] Residence Act, s 53(1).

[44] Residence Act, s 53(2).

[45] Residence Act, s 55.

[46] Residence Act, s 54.

in contrast to the Dutch system, the German system does not provide for a sliding scale that bars the termination of residence if the duration of the foreigner's lawful stay outweighs the imposed prison term. The German system stipulates that the foreigner's residence has to be terminated if the state's interests in terminating the foreigner's residence outweigh the interests of the foreigner. While both states provide that an entry ban shall normally not exceed five years, the duration of the entry ban in the Netherlands can be up to 20 years if the foreigner poses a serious threat to national security or if serious reasons require an entry ban that exceeds 10 years. In Germany, the duration of the entry ban shall not exceed 10 years[47] if the foreigner was expelled on grounds of a criminal conviction or if the foreigner poses a serious threat to public safety and order. The grounds on which a 20-year entry ban shall be imposed are limited to a crime against peace, a war crime or a crime against humanity, the need to avert a threat to the security of the Federal Republic of Germany, or a terrorist threat. The differences between Germany and the Netherlands that are set out in this part will be recalled and further expanded upon in the next part.[48]

[47] Residence Act, s 11(5).

[48] Chapter 10.

PART III

Transnational Administrative Acts: The Effects of National Expulsion Decisions and Entry Bans on the European Level

This part of the book focuses on transnational administrative acts by highlighting the effects of national expulsion decisions and entry bans on the European level. The first part outlined the European standards that have to be observed when expelling delinquent foreigners, while the second part focused on the implementation and observance of these requirements at the national level. The third part zooms out of the national level and explores the effects of national expulsion decisions and entry bans on the European level and thereby on other Member States.

Three features are central for this third part. First, national provisions regulating the termination of residence after a criminal conviction and declaring a foreigner *persona non grata* share several common characteristics. Despite these commonalities, they also display differences as they use different thresholds and grant different margins of discretion to national decision makers. The decisions that are adopted on the basis of these national provisions can consequently also differ.

Second, despite these differences, national expulsion decisions can be given a European dimension by an entry of an alert into the SIS. The requirements for entering an alert into the SIS were previously broadly framed, with the consequence that Member States enjoyed a considerable margin of discretion to pursue their national priorities by entering alerts for a variety of reasons. The disparities in Member States' practice were particularly obvious under the 1990 Convention Implementing the Schengen Agreement (CISA),[1] where alerts were entered with regard to truck drivers who failed to pay traffic fines or with regard to rejected

[1] Convention implementing the Schengen Agreement of 14 June 1985 between the Governments of the States of the Benelux Economic Union, the Federal Republic of Germany and the French Republic on the gradual abolition of checks at their common borders [2000] OJ L 239/19.

asylum seekers.[2] CISA's successor, the SIS II Regulation,[3] imposed stricter requirements but still afforded Member States rather broad discretion.[4] The two legal instruments that are currently in use to give European effect to national expulsion decisions and entry bans are the SIS Regulation[5] and the Return Directive.[6] Even though both the 2018 SIS Regulation and the Court's case law have further specified the grounds for entering SIS alerts, which precipitated a limitation of Member States' discretion, they refrain from providing strict criteria, such as an exhaustive list of criminal offences that can justify a Europe-wide entry ban. Interestingly, the 2018 SIS Regulation refers to terrorist offences, while its predecessor, the 2006 SIS II Regulation still omitted such a reference. This underscores the heightened importance of the so-called 'fight against terrorism' and the link between security and migration that has been created by the Member States. The SIS Regulation establishes a very low threshold for entering a terrorism-related alert into the SIS, by providing that 'serious grounds for believing that a third-country national has committed a serious criminal offence, including a terrorist offence' or 'clear indications of his or her intention to commit such an offence'[7] suffice to enter an alert, provided that the requirements of Article 24(1)(a) are met. This requirement not only affords Member States a considerable discretion to ban third-country nationals from the entire Schengen area, it is also problematic in that it allows them to adopt such a severe measure without any criminal conviction.

Third, national expulsion decisions and entry bans that have been given a European dimension by the entry of an alert into the SIS constitute transnational administrative acts as they yield effects beyond the national territory. An SIS alert that has been issued by one of the states must in principle be recognised by all other participating states, despite the different criteria for adopting expulsion decisions and entry bans.[8] Thus, a state has to recognise an alert that has been entered by another state for a reason that would not necessarily have led to the entry of an alert by the state that has to refuse entry to the third-country national. Mutual recognition of decisions that were adopted on the basis of different criteria can

[2] Statewatch, 'Three quarters of a million "illegal aliens" banned from Schengen area' (2005), www.statewatch.org/news/2005/april/statewatch-news-online-three-quarters-of-a-million-quot-illegal-aliens-quot-now-banned-from-schengen-area/.

[3] Regulation (EC) No 1987/2006 of the European Parliament and of the Council of 20 December 2006 on the establishment, operation and use of the second generation Schengen Information System (SIS II) [2006] OJ L 381/4 ('SIS II Regulation').

[4] See Article 24 SIS II Regulation.

[5] Regulation (EU) 2018/1861 of the European Parliament and of the Council of 28 November 2018 on the establishment, operation and use of the Schengen Information System (SIS) in the field of border checks, and amending the Convention implementing the Schengen Agreement, and amending and repealing Regulation (EC) No 1987/2006 [2018] OJ L 312/14.

[6] Directive 2008/115/EC of the European Parliament and of the Council of 16 December 2008 on common standards and procedures in Member States for returning illegally staying third-country nationals [2008] OJ L 348/98.

[7] Article 24(2)(b) SIS Regulation.

[8] Subject to limitations: the SIS Regulation and the Return Directive provide for certain exceptions to the obligation to recognise the entry ban/SIS alert.

have drawbacks. It can negatively impact the person who is subject to an entry ban as it might encroach on third-country nationals' fundamental rights, in particular on their right to respect for private and family life.[9] Even though the state entering the ban assesses its compatibility with the person's human rights, the assessment normally only covers the expelling state's territory.[10] However, the third-country national might have a family life in a second state, a factor that is not necessarily accounted for by the assessment of the first state. Moreover, the lack of approximated requirements for either adopting national expulsion decisions and entry bans or entering an alert into the SIS can have negative repercussions on the European Union's endeavour to build a coherent approach to migration. Mutual recognition of national decisions without a certain degree of harmonisation of the substantive requirements for adopting these decisions or giving them a European dimension runs the risk of undermining the coherence of the European Union's approach to migration, and it impinges on legal certainty.

The differences between national expulsion decisions and entry bans might be surprising in light of the requirements of European law that have been outlined in the first part. European law, in particular EU law, limits Member States' discretion to expel foreigners. However, the strictest or most developed safeguards limiting Member States' discretion concern the expulsion of EU, EEA and Swiss citizens and their family members. This group of foreigners cannot be entered into the SIS (with the exception of their third-country national family members). The other groups of foreigners, that is, Turkish citizens and long-term resident third-country nationals, enjoy a lower level of protection by EU law in the sense that the requirements of EU law are less specific, leaving Member States increased discretion. Finally, third-country nationals whose expulsion is not regulated by EU law can 'only' invoke the protection granted by the ECHR. The margin of discretion of states regarding their power to terminate residence hence gradually increases in parallel with the progressive decline of protections granted by EU law to the respective categories of foreigners. Therefore, decisions that are subject to fewer restrictions and where states thereby enjoy a greater margin of discretion can lead to SIS alerts that must in principle be recognised by other states. By contrast, decisions taken in the area most regulated by EU law and which leave Member States little discretion are not mutually recognised as EU citizens cannot be subject to SIS alerts. Complete or partial harmonisation of the criteria for adopting expulsion decisions and entry bans or entering an SIS alert could remedy or reduce the currently existing problems. At the same time a complete harmonisation would entail a departure from the current system of mutual recognition as complete harmonisation makes reliance on the mechanism of mutual recognition superfluous.

[9] Article 7 Charter of Fundamental Rights of the European Union; Article 8 European Convention on Human Rights.

[10] Higher Administrative Court Bremen, decision of 14.08.2019 – 2 B 159/19.

This part is structured as follows. Chapter 9 introduces the concept of transnational administrative acts and the two EU legal instruments, the SIS Regulation and the Return Directive, which can give a European dimension to national expulsion decisions and entry bans. National decisions that have been given a European effect constitute transnational administrative acts as they generate effects beyond the confines of the national territory. Chapter 10 focuses on the national provisions governing the termination of lawful residence after a criminal conviction, the national requirements for imposing an entry ban and entering an alert into the SIS, and the duration of an entry ban. In light of the discrepancies both at the national and the European level, Chapter 11 addresses different options to remedy the remaining problems, as well as the likelihood that these options will be implemented.

9

Transnational Administrative Acts: The European Effect of National Expulsion Decisions and Entry Bans

This chapter focuses on transnational administrative acts and explores the two legal instruments, the SIS Regulation and the Return Directive, which can give a European effect to national decisions by the entry of an alert into the SIS. The different modes of administrative decision making and the concept of transnational administrative acts will be introduced in a first step. Subsequently, the relevant EU instruments are addressed, whereby the overview begins with the 1990 Convention Implementing the Schengen Agreement (CISA), followed by its successor, the 2006 SIS II Regulation, before the most recent instrument, the 2018 SIS Regulation, is explored. Finally, the 2008 Return Directive, the second legal instrument capable of giving a European effect to a national expulsion decision and entry ban, is addressed. The focus of this chapter rests on the entry of alerts into the SIS for the purpose of refusing entry or stay in terms of Article 24 of the SIS Regulation.

I. Transnational Administrative Acts

A transnational administrative act is defined as a public decision that aims to have effects outside the territory of the state whose administration issued the act.[11] Essential for the so-called transnational administrative act[12] is the principle of mutual recognition[13] as it constitutes the underlying mechanism attaching a transnational effect to a national administrative decision. Administrative decision

[11] A Gerontas, *Europäisierung und Internationalisierung des Verwaltungshandelns* (Baden-Baden, Nomos, 2011) 41, 42.

[12] E Schmidt-Aßmann, 'Verwaltungskooperation und Verwaltungskooperationsrecht in der Europäischen Gemeinschaft' (1996) 31 *Europarecht* 270, 300.

[13] For a comprehensive overview, see C Janssens, *The Principle of Mutual Recognition in EU Law* (Oxford, OUP, 2013).

making and cooperation between national and European authorities can take different forms,[14] among them the transnational model and the so-called reference model, whereby the latter leaves more autonomy to the participating states than the transnational model. According to the reference model, a reference decision is adopted by one Member State;[15] on the basis of the latter decision, other states then conduct their own recognition procedures. An example of this type of decision is the marketing authorisation procedure for medicinal products in the European Union. After a first Member State (the Member State of reference) adopts a marketing authorisation for a specific medicinal product, other Member States conduct an approval procedure, which does not comprise a full assessment but a limited one, since the authorisation has already been issued by the Member State of reference. Approval can only be rejected based on the argument that the medicine is harmful to health. Upon rejection, the authorities in the Member States that have reached different conclusions regarding that medicine must reach a common position. If they are unable to reach a common position, the European Medicines Agency provides expertise on the basis of which the European Commission adopts a position which is binding for the Member States.[16] Advantages of this type of cooperation comprise the respect for the decision-making authority of every Member State, and thereby the principle of subsidiarity, while reducing divergent implementation measures by the Member States.[17] A downside of this model, however, is the high administrative costs and efforts incurred if other Member States refuse an approval.[18]

The so-called transnational administrative act[19] functions differently in that one Member State issues a decision which is in principle binding upon the other Member States. Examples of transnational administrative acts comprise admission decisions relating to the freedom of establishment or the freedom to provide services,[20] or the deliberate release into the environment of genetically

[14] For further information see Schmidt-Aßmann, 'Verwaltungskooperation und Verwaltungskooperationsrecht in der Europäischen Gemeinschaft' 270–301; G Sydow, 'Vollzug des europäischen Unionsrechts im Wege der Kooperation nationaler und europäischer Behörden' (2006) 59 *Die Öffentliche Verwaltung* 66; M Ruffert, 'Der transnationale Verwaltungsakt' (2001) 34 *Die Verwaltung* 453.

[15] Sydow, 'Vollzug des europäischen Unionsrechts' 67.

[16] See Title III, Chapter 4 (Mutual recognition and decentralised procedure) of Directive 2001/83/EC of the European Parliament and of the Council of 6 November 2001 on the Community code relating to medicinal products for human use [2001] OJ L 311/67 (last amended by Regulation (EU) 2019/5).

[17] Sydow, 'Vollzug des europäischen Unionsrechts' 67; M Laas, *Die Entstehung eines europäischen Migrationsverwaltungsraumes* (Baden-Baden, Nomos, 2008) 67–69.

[18] Sydow, 'Vollzug des europäischen Unionsrechts' 69.

[19] Schmidt-Aßmann, 'Verwaltungskooperation und Verwaltungskooperationsrecht in der Europäischen Gemeinschaft' 300. Moreover, he introduced the concepts of 'vermittelete Transnationalität', if the effect of the decision of the authority of one Member State depends upon an explicit confirmation of that act by another Member State, and 'Transnationalität unter Prüfungsvorbehalt' where the national authorities consider that act as their own administrative act and they only conduct their own assessment regarding particular aspects; see ibid, 301. For further differentiations see Gerontas, *Europäisierung und Internationalisierung des Verwaltungshandelns* 222.

[20] For further examples see Ruffert, 'Der transnationale Verwaltungsakt' 459, 460.

modified organisms.[21] In the context of migration law, examples of transnational administrative acts are Schengen visas[22] and entry bans according to the Return Directive.[23]

Further examples of legal regimes that can give transnational legal effects to national decisions are the Dublin Regulation, the LTR Directive,[24] Directive 2001/40/EC on mutual recognition of decisions on the expulsion of third-country nationals, the Return Directive and the SIS.[25] However, decisions that are adopted on the basis of the Dublin Regulation and the LTR Directive do not have a transnational legal effect in the strict sense.[26] The long-term resident status provided for by the LTR Directive grants its beneficiary a set of rights in the awarding state, but the exact same rights are not available to the beneficiary in the second Member State unless this state also grants the long-term resident status. Decisions adopted on the basis of the LTR Directive are said to function as a point of reference for decisions that are adopted in the second Member State,[27] which seems to move them closer to the above-mentioned model of reference decisions. According to Laas, both the reference and the transnational model can be utilised for migration law.[28]

Transnational administrative acts can yield several positive effects, such as a reduction of divergent implementations of decisions at the Member State level due to the establishment of some common minimum standards. Moreover, they can lead to a lowering of administrative costs. However, transnational administrative acts also engender several downsides. Sydow highlights the loss of decision-making power of the executing states, who have to recognise and implement the issuing state's decision without having any influence on the decision-making process.[29] Secondly, he argues that the transnational model cannot ensure a sufficient proximity between the decision maker and the citizen, and that the decision maker is not necessarily familiar with the needs of the citizens.[30] Finally, several scholars point out that the horizontal shift of competences is more problematic than a vertical shift of competences from the Member States to the European Commission.[31]

[21] Sydow, 'Vollzug des europäischen Unionsrechts' 69.

[22] Gerontas, *Europäisierung und Internationalisierung des Verwaltungshandelns* 230.

[23] ibid, 185.

[24] Directive 2003/109/EC of 25 November 2003 concerning the status of third-country nationals who are long-term residents [2003] OJ L 16/44 amended by Directive 2011/51/EU of 11 May 2011 amending Council Directive 2003/109/EC to extend its scope to beneficiaries of international protection [2011] OJ L 132.

[25] J Bast, 'Transnationale Verwaltung des europäischen Migrationsraums' (2007) 46 *Der Staat* 1, 16; Gerontas, *Europäisierung und Internationalisierung des Verwaltungshandelns* 132, 185; Laas, *Die Entstehung eines europäischen Migrationsverwaltungsraumes* 106, 107, 222.

[26] Bast, 'Transnationale Verwaltung des europäischen Migrationsraums' 19, 31.

[27] ibid; for further differentiation see Laas, *Die Entstehung eines europäischen Migrationsverwaltungsraumes* 229, 230 ('bedingt transnationale Entscheidungen mit Berücksichtigungspflicht').

[28] Laas, *Die Entstehung eines europäischen Migrationsverwaltungsraumes* 266.

[29] Sydow, 'Vollzug des europäischen Unionsrechts' 69.

[30] ibid.

[31] ibid; Laas, *Die Entstehung eines europäischen Migrationsverwaltungsraumes* 41.

The European Commission is acting in the interests of all EU Member States and has a higher degree of pan-European legitimacy.[32] Sydow therefore argues that far-reaching decisions with a Europe-wide dimension cannot be taken by one Member State alone.[33]

In order to reduce at least some of its detrimental effects, the transnational model can be supplemented by two options. The first option is an *ex ante* mechanism that compensates Member States for the loss of their decision-making authority by granting them some influence in the decision-making process. The Directive on the deliberate release into the environment of genetically modified organisms provides for this option by affording Member States the possibility to raise objections. Where Member States cannot reach a common approach, the European Commission ultimately decides.[34] The second option compensates Member States for the loss of their decision-making power by way of retroactive involvement, hence by granting them the possibility to temporarily suspend the effects of the decision adopted by the first Member State. In that case, the European Commission can either oblige the state that issued the original decision to withdraw it, or it can oblige the second state to lift the suspension and to give full effect to the decision issued by the first state.[35] While both variants lessen the negative effects of transnational administrative acts on the executing Member State(s), they also yield negative effects as they entail higher administrative costs.

Focusing on the negative effects of transnational administrative acts on the individual in the context of SIS alerts, the absence of substantive harmonisation of the applicable rules needs further attention. In this regard Directive 2001/40/EC on the mutual recognition of decisions on the expulsion of third-country nationals[36] is instructive as it relies on the mechanism of mutual recognition in order to facilitate the enforcement of expulsion decisions issued by one Member State against a third-country national who is present in another Member State. Even though the focus of this research does not rest on the enforcement of expulsion decisions issued by other states, the criticism regarding the system of mutual recognition voiced in the context of Directive 2001/40/EC is relevant for the SIS Regulation and the Return Directive, more so given that mutual recognition under Directive 2001/40/EC is voluntary, whereas it is in principle binding under the SIS Regulation and the Return Directive.

[32] ibid.

[33] Sydow, 'Vollzug des europäischen Unionsrechts' 69.

[34] Article 18 of Directive 2001/18/EC of the European Parliament and of the Council of 12 March 2001 on the deliberate release into the environment of genetically modified organisms and repealing Council Directive 90/220/EEC – Commission Declaration [2001] OJ L 106/1, amended by Directive (EU) 2015/412 of the European Parliament and of the Council of 11 March 2015 amending Directive 2001/18/EC as regards the possibility for the Member States to restrict or prohibit the cultivation of genetically modified organisms (GMOs) in their territory [2015] OJ L 68/1.

[35] Sydow, 'Vollzug des europäischen Unionsrechts' 70.

[36] Council Directive 2001/40/EC of 28 May 2001 on the mutual recognition of decisions on the expulsion of third-country nationals [2001] OJ L 149/34.

A major point of criticism that was voiced against Directive 2001/40/EC is that it encourages mutual recognition without establishing common rules and procedures. Shortly after its entry into force it was already criticised that it was premature to apply this Directive and the measures established therein without unifying the standards on expulsion.[37] Groenendijk argued that 'mutual recognition is not a substitute for harmonisation or for common rules'.[38] He drew a comparison with CISA and emphasised that the parties to CISA agreed to mutually recognise their decisions, but that they simultaneously harmonised their rules and procedures (for example visa rules, Article 9 CISA; surveillance procedures, Article 6(3) CISA; common rules for the examination of visa applications, Article 17 CISA). He criticised that the only common standards that are 'available' with regard to mutual recognition of expulsion decisions in the context of Directive 2001/40/EC are the few minimum rules that can be inferred from the jurisprudence of the ECtHR.[39] Likewise, Cholewinski considered the concept of mutual recognition 'highly inappropriate and suspect in those areas of immigration law where Member States' legal rules are not harmonised to a significant degree and where the consequences of poor decision-making may result in serious human rights implications for the individual concerned'.[40] Regarding expulsion decisions, Cholewinski noted that there are considerable differences among Member States as to the manner in which expulsion decisions are adopted, the grounds on which they are taken and the way in which they are executed.[41]

Despite differences between national expulsion decisions and entry bans, they have to be mutually recognised once they have been given a European effect by an SIS alert. Mutual recognition is based on mutual trust and mutual trust has been 'interpreted as if factual trust actually existed',[42] without, however, providing for a mechanism to cultivate trust among the Member States. Laas rightly argues that the creation of mutual trust among the Member States is crucial for the legitimacy of transnational decisions.[43] Therefore, he suggests fostering mutual trust by way of procedural coordination and substantive harmonisation.[44] A form of

[37] COM(2002) 564 final, Opinion of the European Economic and Social Committee on the Communication from the Commission to the Council and the European Parliament on a Community return policy on illegal residents, p 54, para 3.2.

[38] K Groenendijk, 'The Directive on Mutual Recognition of Expulsion Decisions: Symbolic or Unbalanced Politics' in P De Bruycker (ed), *The Emergence of a European Immigration Policy* (Brussels, Bruylant, 2003) 461.

[39] ibid.

[40] R Cholewinski, 'The Criminalisation of Migration Policy in EU Law and Policy' in A Baldaccini, E Guild and H Toner (eds), *Whose Freedom, Security, and Justice?* (Oxford, Hart Publishing, 2007) 309.

[41] R Cholewinski, 'Mutual Recognition of Expulsion Decisions' in S Peers and N Rogers (eds), *EU Immigration and Asylum Law, Text and Commentary* (Leiden, Martinus Nijhoff, 2006) 792.

[42] T Wischmeyer, 'Generating Trust Through Law? Judicial Cooperation in the European Union and the "Principle of Mutual Trust"' (2016) 17 *German Law Journal* 339, 359.

[43] Laas, *Die Entstehung eines europäischen Migrationsverwaltungsraumes* 39.

[44] ibid, 39, 40.

procedural coordination that could enhance mutual trust among Member States and thereby the legitimacy of transnational administrative acts, he argues, is the participation of Member States in the decision-making process of the state that issues the transnational administrative act.[45] However, Laas also acknowledges that the extent to which other Member States participate in the decision-making process of the state that issues the transnational administrative act is relatively minor. Therefore, he argues that procedural coordination can only supplement, but not replace, substantive harmonisation.[46]

The crucial question is to what extent Member States' provisions can and should be approximated. A high level of substantive harmonisation of Member States' rules, which affords them little or no discretion, renders mutual recognition redundant as the rules for adopting decisions are congruent across all participating states, with the consequence that the decisions that are adopted on the basis of these rules are largely similar. In this context it should be recalled that the concept of mutual recognition flanked by some (minimum) harmonisation has the advantage of affording more discretion to the Member States than full harmonisation. This discretion is crucial for enhancing cooperation and thereby promoting European integration in sensitive policy areas, where Member States seek to retain their sovereignty, and which are therefore not susceptible to full substantive harmonisation.[47] Given that decisions on the admission and presence of foreigners on the state's territory are an attribute of its sovereignty,[48] a comprehensive substantive harmonisation of the provisions governing expulsion will be difficult to achieve. In the absence of substantive harmonisation of national provisions, the principle of mutual recognition is a vital prerequisite for the functioning of a border-free Area of Freedom, Security and Justice (AFSJ). Mutual recognition in the AFSJ affords extraterritorial effects to national decisions[49] and 'enables the arm of the law to become longer by acquiring a transnational reach'.[50]

[45] ibid, 40.

[46] ibid, 268.

[47] V Mitsilegas, 'The Symbiotic Relationship Between Mutual Trust and Fundamental Rights in Europe's Area of Criminal Justice' (2015) 6 *New Journal of European Criminal Law* 457, 466; D Düsterhaus, 'Judicial Coherence in the Area of Freedom, Security and Justice – Squaring Mutual Trust with Effective Judicial Protection' (2015) 8 *Review of European Administrative Law* 151, 154.

[48] W Kälin, 'Aliens, Expulsion and Deportation' in R Wolfrum (ed), *The Max Planck Encyclopedia on Public International Law* (2008–) § 2, www.opil.ouplaw.com/view/10.1093/law:epil/9780199231690/law-9780199231690-e 745.

[49] K Nicolaïdis, 'Trusting the Poles? Constructing Europe Through Mutual Recognition' (2007) 14 *Journal of European Public Policy* 682, 689; Mitsilegas, 'The Symbiotic Relationship Between Mutual Trust and Fundamental Rights in Europe's Area of Criminal Justice' 466; F Maiani and S Migliorini, 'One Principle to Rule Them All? Anatomy of Mutual Trust in the Law of the Area of Freedom, Security and Justice' (2020) 57 *CML Rev* 7, 12.

[50] K Lenaerts, 'La vie après l'avis: Exploring the Principle of Mutual (Yet Not Blind) Trust' (2017) 54 *CML Rev* 805, 809.

II. The Schengen Information System

The SIS provides the framework for the registration of national alerts with regard to third-country nationals who are to be refused entry to the Schengen area.[51] An individual with regard to whom an alert is entered can in principle not obtain a visa (Article 32(1)(a)(v) of the Visa Code)[52] and has to be refused entry (Article 6(1)(d) and Article 14(1) of the Schengen Borders Code).[53] The Commission Implementing Decision 2017/1528 sets out the specific steps to be taken concerning individuals with regard to whom an alert is to be entered in the SIS.[54]

The SIS constitutes a cornerstone of the rapidly evolving network of EU surveillance systems relating to border and crime control. The European Union's external borders are reinforced by the extensive control systems Eurosur (European Border Surveillance System) and Frontex (the border policing agency), and by the collection and sharing of data (for example by using the Eurodac database that contains the fingerprints of asylum seekers). The common Visa Information System (VIS) and SIS are part of the transnational border control and police cooperation architecture, and, together with the external border control systems, are crucial components of the AFSJ.[55]

The SIS has its origins in the Schengen Agreement of 1985,[56] which resulted in the relaxation and ultimately the abolition of internal border controls, precipitating the need for compensatory measures. The Convention Implementing the Schengen Agreement (CISA) of 1990 provided the intergovernmental framework and the legal bases (Articles 92–119 CISA) for the establishment of the SIS, which was integrated into the EU framework by the Treaty of Amsterdam. The Schengen

[51] For a comprehensive overview and analysis of the SIS, see E Brouwer, *Digital Borders and Real Rights* (Leiden, Brill Martinus Nijhoff, 2008); for further information on the technical structure and functioning of the SIS, see S Kabera Karanja, *Transparency and Proportionality in the Schengen Information System and Border Control Co-operation* 183 (regarding the first generation of the SIS).

[52] Regulation (EC) No 810/2009 of the European Parliament and of the Council of 13 July 2009 establishing a Community Code on Visas [2009] OJ L 243/1.

[53] Regulation (EU) 2016/399 of the European Parliament and of the Council of 9 March 2016 on a Union Code on the rules governing the movement of persons across borders (Schengen Borders Code) [2016] OJ L 77/1.

[54] Commission Implementing Decision (EU) 2017/1528 of 31 August 2017 replacing the Annex to Implementing Decision 2013/115/EU on the SIRENE Manual and other implementing measures for the second generation Schengen Information System (SIS II) (notified under document C(2017) 5893), C/2017/5893.

[55] L Zedner, 'Citizenship Deprivation, Security and Human Rights' (2016) 18 *European Journal of Migration and Law* 222, 224; KF Aas, '"Crimmigrant" Bodies and Bona Fide Travelers: Surveillance, Citizenship and Global Governance' (2011) 15 *Theoretical Criminology* 331, 332.

[56] Agreement between the Governments of the States of the Benelux Economic Union, the Federal Republic of Germany and the French Republic on the gradual abolition of checks at their common borders [2000] OJ L 239/13. For further information on the history of border controls prior to Schengen, the Schengen Agreement, the abolition of border controls and their reinstatement, see K Groenendijk, 'Reinstatement of Controls at the Internal Borders of Europe: Why and Against Whom?' (2004) 10 *European Law Journal* 150.

Agreement and the transnational surveillance system that was developed and refined by the different generations of the SIS provide for cooperative policing arrangements to offset the abolition of internal controls by an 'increased use of profiling, surveillance, and checks of those deemed to pose a risk'.[57] The SIS has been continuously updated, with the first generation of the SIS being replaced by the SIS II Regulation of 2006, which became operational in 2013.[58] The second generation SIS enhanced surveillance measures, for instance by providing for the possibility to use biometrics[59] or to link alerts.[60] The second generation SIS already acknowledged the need, and was guided by the aim, 'to further consider harmonising the provisions on the grounds for issuing alerts concerning third-country nationals for the purpose of refusing entry or stay'.[61] The SIS II Regulation was replaced by the updated SIS Regulation in 2018.[62]

The SIS builds upon the national systems and is composed of a central system (Central SIS)[63] for the operational management of which eu-LISA is responsible,[64] and a national system (N.SIS).[65] In contrast to the first generation of the SIS, which had an intergovernmental structure, the currently operational SIS is a centralised system with a centralised administration.[66] Each Member State has to set up, operate and maintain its N.SIS[67] and to designate an authority (the N.SIS Office) which shall have central responsibility for its N.SIS.[68] Moreover, each Member State 'shall designate the authority which shall ensure the exchange of all supplementary information (the SIRENE[69] Bureau)'.[70]

The maximum duration of an SIS alert is not specifically stipulated. Article 39(1) provides that 'Alerts shall be kept only for the time required to achieve the purposes for which they were entered'. However, Article 39(2) states that the 'issuing Member State shall, within three years of the entry of an alert into SIS, review the need to retain it'. If the national decision that forms the basis of the SIS alert

[57] Zedner, 'Citizenship Deprivation, Security and Human Rights' 224; Aas, '"Crimmigrant" Bodies and Bona Fide Travelers' 337, 338.

[58] Article 1 of Council Decision of 7 March 2013 fixing the date of application of Regulation (EC) No 1987/2006 of the European Parliament and of the Council on the establishment, operation and use of the second generation Schengen Information System (SIS II) [2013] OJ L 87/10.

[59] See Recital 12 of the Preamble and Article 22(c) SIS II Regulation.

[60] See Article 37 SIS II Regulation.

[61] See Recital 10 of the Preamble to the SIS II Regulation.

[62] Regulation (EU) 2018/1861 of the European Parliament and of the Council of 28 November 2018 on the establishment, operation and use of the Schengen Information System (SIS) in the field of border checks, and amending the Convention implementing the Schengen Agreement, and amending and repealing Regulation (EC) No 1987/2006 [2018] OJ L 312/14.

[63] Article 4(1)(a) of Regulation (EU) 2018/1861.

[64] Article 15(1) of Regulation (EU) 2018/1861.

[65] Article 4(1)(b) of Regulation (EU) 2018/1861.

[66] Laas, *Die Entstehung eines europäischen Migrationsverwaltungsraumes* 112.

[67] Article 6 of Regulation (EU) 2018/1861.

[68] Article 7(1) of Regulation (EU) 2018/1861.

[69] Supplementary Information Request at the National Entry.

[70] Article 7(2) of Regulation (EU) 2018/1861.

'provides for a longer period of validity than three years, the alert shall be reviewed within five years'.[71]

A. Aim and Purpose

The SIS[72] is a database of undesirable or unwanted persons,[73] which contains data not only on persons, but also on objects. The declared aim of the SIS is to secure a high level of security within the AFSJ.[74] At the end of 2020, 93 million alerts were stored in the SIS. This meant 2.3 million additional alerts in 2020 compared to 2019, which amounted to a 3 per cent increase in alerts.[75] However, it was also noted that 'this is lower than the trend of annual increases between 8% and 12% in previous years'.[76] The reason for this decrease was said to be the 'COVID-19 crisis and the related reduction in activities'.[77] Generally, there has been a 'sharp drop in the use' of the SIS in 2020 due to COVID-19.[78]

The list of Member States providing the majority of alerts was headed by Italy 'with over 23% of the total, followed by France with 17%, Germany with 13% and Spain with 8%'.[79] The list of Member States performing the majority of searches was headed by France 'with 21% of the total in 2020, followed by Spain with 12%, Germany with 8%, and Italy with 7%'.[80] In 2020 'there was a 44% reduction in searches compared to the previous year. 28 Member States reported a substantial reduction in searches due to restrictions of activities' precipitated by the COVID-19 pandemic.[81]

B. The Personal Scope of the SIS Regulation

The SIS Regulation 'establishes the conditions and procedures for the entry and processing of alerts in SIS on third-country nationals for the purpose of refusing

[71] Article 39(2) of Regulation (EU) 2018/1861.

[72] The SIS I as well as its successor the SIS II.

[73] G Papagianni, *Institutional and Policy Dynamics of EU Migration Law* (Leiden/Boston, Martinus Nijhoff, 2006) 118; E Brouwer, 'Legal Boundaries and the Use of Migration Technology' in H Dijstelbloem and A Meijer (eds), *Migration and the New Technological Borders of Europe* (London, Palgrave Macmillan, 2011) 150; Kabera Karanja, *Transparency and Proportionality in the Schengen Information System and Border Control Co-operation* 216.

[74] Article 1 of Regulation (EU) 2018/1861.

[75] European Union Agency for the Operational Management of Large-Scale IT Systems in the Area of Freedom, Security and Justice, SIS II – 2020 statistics, March 2021, p 11.

[76] ibid.

[77] ibid.

[78] ibid, p 8.

[79] ibid, p 11.

[80] ibid, p 7.

[81] ibid, p 7.

entry into and stay on the territory of the Member States'.[82] The notion of third-country national is defined in negative terms as 'any person who is not a citizen of the Union within the meaning of Article 20(1) TFEU'.[83] However, third-country nationals 'who are beneficiaries of rights of free movement equivalent to those of citizens of the Union under agreements between the Union and third countries' are also excluded from the personal scope.[84] Finally, Article 40(3) of the SIS Regulation excludes from the personal scope of the Regulation individuals who acquire the citizenship of a State whose nationals are beneficiaries of the right to free movement.

Third-country national family members of EU (and EEA and Swiss) citizens who exercise their right of free movement can still be entered into the SIS; in contrast to the Return Directive,[85] they are not excluded from the scope of the SIS Regulation. As early as 2006, however, the CJEU provided for additional safeguards in *Commission v Spain*,[86] where it ruled that Spain's refusal of entry to a third-country family member of a Union citizen solely based upon an entry of an alert into the SIS, without any further assessment as to whether the individual concerned posed a genuine, present and sufficiently serious threat affecting one of the fundamental interests of society, infringes EU law.[87] The Court imposed the obligation to conduct this additional assessment not only on the state to which the individual seeks access, but also on the state which enters the alert. In fact, it held that the assessment of whether 'the presence of that person constitutes a genuine, present and sufficiently serious threat affecting one of the fundamental interests of society' must be conducted by the issuing Member State.[88] Hence, both states, the issuing state and the state to which the individual seeks access, have to conduct the assessment.

The Court's case law is reflected in the SIS Regulation, which obliges the state that enters an alert regarding a third-country national 'who is a beneficiary of the right of free movement in accordance with Directive 2004/38/EC' to ensure that the alert is 'in conformity with the rules adopted in implementation of that Directive'.[89] The state to which the third-country seeks access 'shall immediately consult the issuing Member State, through the exchange of supplementary information, in order to decide without delay on the action to be taken'.[90]

The legal position of Turkish nationals covered by the Association Agreement is not specifically addressed by the SIS Regulation. Given that, according to the

[82] Article 2 of Regulation (EU) 2018/1861.
[83] Article 3(4) of Regulation (EU) 2018/1861.
[84] ibid.
[85] Article 3(1) of the Return Directive in conjunction with Article 2(5) of the Schengen Borders Code excludes third-country family members of Union citizens from its scope.
[86] Case C-503/03 *Commission v Spain* ECLI:EU:C:2006:74, [2006] ECR I-01097.
[87] ibid, paras 55, 59.
[88] ibid, para 52.
[89] Article 26(1) of Regulation (EU) 2018/1861.
[90] Article 26(2) of Regulation (EU) 2018/1861.

Court's interpretation of Article 14(1) of Decision 1/80, a Turkish national cannot be subject to an expulsion decision unless their conduct constitutes a genuine and serious threat to public policy, public security or public health,[91] these requirements must at least be fulfilled before a Turkish national can be entered into the SIS.

Even though long-term resident third-country nationals enjoy a privileged status according to the LTR Directive, they fall within the scope of the SIS Regulation. Regarding the predecessor of the current SIS Regulation, the former SIS II Regulation, Brouwer pointed out that their registration in the SIS could conflict with the LTR Directive, which imposes stricter public policy and public security requirements than the SIS II Regulation.[92] Groenendijk argued that long-term resident third-country nationals should be excluded from the scope of the SIS II Regulation.[93] The draft SIS II Regulation contained a reference to the LTR Directive and provided that 'Member States shall issue the alerts without prejudice to any provision which may be more favourable for the third-country national laid down in Directive 2003/109/EC'.[94] This provision was deleted from the final version of the SIS II Regulation and is also absent from the current SIS Regulation. Nonetheless, an alert regarding a beneficiary of the LTR Directive can only be entered into the SIS if the public policy criteria of Article 12 of the LTR Directive are met.

Finally, the question of the legal position of foreigners whose protection against expulsion is governed by Article 8 ECHR arises. Back in 2000, requests for a reform of the SIS were voiced 'to balance public security with individual rights'.[95] Concerns were expressed that the SIS did not fulfil the requirements of Article 8(2) ECHR.[96] Eicke pointed out that it is noticeable that the relevant Schengen provisions make no reference to Member States' obligation under the ECHR[97] and provided a possible explanation. He stated that the infringement of Article 3 or Article 8 ECHR does not result from the SIS alert itself but from the refusal of entry of the individual by the immigration officer in another Member State based on the SIS alert. He argued that the liability for any breach in terms of the ECHR rests with the State which refuses entry and not with the state whose official made the entry.[98]

[91] Case C-325/05 *Derin* ECLI:EU:C:2007:442, [2007] ECR I-06495, para 54; *Ergat* ECLI:EU:C:2000:133, [2000] ECR I-01487, paras 45, 46; Case C-373/03 *Aydinli* ECLI:EU:C:2005:434, [2005] ECR I-06181, para 27.

[92] Brouwer, *Digital Borders and Real Rights* 65, 529.

[93] House of Lords, Schengen Information System II (SIS II): Report with Evidence, 9th Report of Session 2006–2007, Minutes of Evidence by K Groenendijk, 11 October 2006, p 26.

[94] COM(2005) 236 final, Proposal for a Regulation of the European Parliament and of the Council on the establishment, operation and use of the second generation Schengen information system (SIS II), Article 15(2)(b).

[95] Migration Policy Group, 'ILPA/MPG Amsterdam Proposals' (London/Brussels, 2000) 161.

[96] ibid, 162.

[97] T Eicke, 'Paradise Lost? Exclusion and Expulsion from the EU' in K Groenendijk, E Guild and P Minderhoud (eds), *In Search of Europe's Borders* (The Hague, Kluwer Law International, 2003) 162.

[98] ibid, 163.

However, the duty to strike a fair balance between the conflicting interests rests with both the state which enters the alert and the executing state. Therefore, Article 8 ECHR can be violated by the state that refuses entry on the basis of an alert but also by the state that enters the alert since the existence of the alert hinders the individual from returning to the Schengen area where s/he has family or social links protected by Article 8 ECHR. Given that the entry of an alert constitutes an implementation of EU law in terms of Article 51(1) CFR, not only must Article 8 ECHR be observed, but also the corresponding Article 7 CFR.

C. The Requirements for Entering an Alert into the SIS

Article 24 of the SIS Regulation sets out the conditions for entering an alert into the SIS for refusal of entry and stay. Article 24 provides:

1. Member States shall enter an alert for refusal of entry and stay when one of the following conditions is met:
   (a) the Member State has concluded, based on an individual assessment which includes an assessment of the personal circumstances of the third-country national concerned and the consequences of refusing him or her entry and stay, that the presence of that third-country national on its territory poses a threat to public policy, to public security or to national security, and the Member State has consequently adopted a judicial or administrative decision in accordance with its national law to refuse entry and stay and issued a national alert for refusal of entry and stay; or
   (b) the Member State has issued an entry ban in accordance with procedures respecting Directive 2008/115/EC in respect of a third-country national.
2. The situations covered by point (a) of paragraph 1 shall arise where:
   (a) a third-country national has been convicted in a Member State of an offence carrying a penalty involving the deprivation of liberty of at least one year;
   (b) there are serious grounds for believing that a third-country national has committed a serious criminal offence, including a terrorist offence, or there are clear indications of his or her intention to commit such an offence in the territory of a Member State; or
   (c) a third-country national has circumvented or attempted to circumvent Union or national law on entry into and stay on the territory of the Member States.

By the end of December 2020, 93,419,371 alerts were stored in the SIS.[99] The alerts on persons amounted to 964,720,[100] which account for about 1 per cent of all alerts.[101] The majority of alerts (76 per cent) were on issued documents.[102] The alerts

[99] European Union Agency for the Operational Management of Large-Scale IT Systems in the Area of Freedom, Security and Justice, SIS II – 2020 statistics, March 2021, p 10.
[100] ibid, p 13.
[101] ibid, p 11.
[102] ibid.

on persons comprise a number of different categories. Article 24 alerts amounted to a total of 519,530,[103] whereas hits on Article 24 alerts reported in 2020 amounted to 38,927.[104] The 2015 European Migration Network Ad-Hoc Query on entry bans entered into the SIS disclosed that several Member States, such as Germany, did not keep the statistics on 'how many entry bans are entered into SIS due to the non-compliance with national migration laws and as a sanction of a criminal offence'.[105]

i. *Comparison of Article 24 of the SIS Regulation with its Predecessors*

Comparing the old Article 96 CISA and the new Article 24 of the SIS Regulation, the threshold for the issuing of an alert on grounds of a perceived threat to public policy or public security has been reduced to some extent. While Article 96(2)(b) CISA still required the existence of 'clear evidence of the intention to commit offences', Article 24(2)(b) of the SIS Regulation refers to 'clear indications of his or her intention to commit such an offence' and dropped the evidence requirement.

Even though the vagueness of the notion 'serious grounds for believing that he has committed serious criminal offences' contained in Article 96(2)(b) CISA was already subject to criticism,[106] it is still present in Article 24(2)(b) of the SIS Regulation. Moreover, the requirement for an SIS alert was further reduced by only requiring 'a serious offence' instead of 'serious offences'. While Article 96(2) CISA provided that decisions 'may' be based on a threat to public policy, Article 24(1)(a) of the SIS Regulation provides that an alert shall be entered by a Member State where 'the presence of that third-country national on its territory poses a threat to public policy'.

However, in contrast to Article 96 CISA, which did not contain the individual assessment requirement, Article 24(1) of the SIS Regulation requires an assessment of the personal circumstances of the third-country national. Consequently, the registration of a third-country national in the SIS cannot be conducted as a matter of routine.

Article 96 CISA was not only considered to be vague, it was also criticised for containing non-exhaustive grounds for listing an individual in the SIS and for leaving a considerable margin of discretion to the Contracting Parties with their diverging systems.[107] Cholewinski argued that the 'application of different rules in

[103] ibid, p 13.

[104] ibid, p 14.

[105] European Migration Network Ad-Hoc Query on Entry Bans Entered into the SIS and Consultation Procedures in Member States, requested by COM on 13th February 2015, Query No 2015.662, pp 2, 9.

[106] The criticism was voiced by the Economic and Social Committee in its Opinion on the Green Paper on a Community return policy on illegal residents (COM(2002) 175 final), p 64, paras 4.3.7. and 4.3.8. with regard to the identical phrase contained in Article 3(1)(a) of Directive 2001/40/EC.

[107] H Oosterom-Staples, 'Botsende openbare-ordebegrippen in het Europese Migratierecht' (2006) 8/9 *Nederlands Tijdschrift voor Europees Recht* 169, 173, 174; J Parkin, *The Difficult Road to the Schengen Information System II* (CEPS, 2011) 6; H Oosterom-Staples, 'Adjudicating the External Schengen Border'

different Member States was likely to lead to inequality of migrants in an irregular situation and to have a disproportionate impact on certain individuals'.[108] The successor to Article 96 CISA, Article 24 of the SIS II Regulation, still granted a considerable margin of discretion to the Member States. It distinguished between situations where an SIS alert shall be entered (Article 24(2)), and situations where an alert may be entered (Article 24(3) of the SIS II Regulation). The list of situations where an alert shall be entered was not exhaustive. Instead, two particular examples were provided of where such a situation shall arise.

The Commission Staff Working Document on the evaluation of the second generation Schengen Information System (SIS II)[109] from December 2016 pointed out that the wording of Article 24(3) of the SIS II Regulation 'is unhelpful in that it proposes that an alert "may" be entered'.[110] It was noted that 'Different national interpretations of this text have resulted in some Member States entering alerts whilst others do not, even though this negates the EU-wide effect'.[111] This problem has been remedied by the current SIS Regulation insofar as the optional issuance of an alert ('may') has been removed from the text of the Regulation.

Moreover, Article 24 of the current SIS Regulation partially remedies the problems of Article 24(2) of the old SIS II Regulation. Article 24(2) of the present SIS Regulation contains an exhaustive list of situations in which an alert shall be entered. However, the exhaustive list in Article 24(2) still allows considerable discretion. The first situation excludes some criminal offences as it concerns a third-country national's conviction of an offence carrying a penalty involving the deprivation of liberty of at least one year.[112] However, it still leaves discretion to national decision makers, which could have been reduced to some extent by providing for a catalogue of crimes that warrant an SIS alert.

The second situation that is provided for in Article 24(2) of the currently applicable SIS Regulation refers to 'serious grounds for believing that a third-country national has committed a serious criminal offence, including a terrorist offence, or there are clear indications of his or her intention to commit such an offence in

in K Groenendijk, E Guild and P Minderhoud (eds), *In Search of Europe's Borders* (The Hague, Kluwer Law International, 2002) 222; J Steenbergen, 'All the King's Horses …: Probabilities and Possibilities for the Implementation of the New Title IV EC Treaty' (1999) 1 *European Journal of Migration and Law* 29, 50; Migration Policy Group, 'ILPA/MPG Amsterdam Proposals' 170; R Cholewinski, 'The EU *Acquis* on Irregular Migration Ten Years On: Still Reinforcing Security at the Expense of Rights?' in E Guild and P Minderhoud (eds), *The First Decade of EU Migration and Asylum Law* (Leiden/Boston, Martinus Nijhoff, 2012) 144; K Alfenaar, 'De toegang tot het grondgebied van de Europese Unie en de toegang tot Nederland' in E Brouwer and K Groenendijk (eds), *Derdelanders in de Europese Unie* (Utrecht, Forum, 2001) 27; Cholewinski, 'The Criminalisation of Migration Policy in EU Law and Policy' 308.

[108] Cholewinski, 'The EU *Acquis* on Irregular Migration Ten Years On' 144.

[109] SWD(2016) 450 final, Commission Staff Working Document accompanying the document report from the Commission to the European Parliament and the Council on the evaluation of the second generation Schengen Information System (SIS II).

[110] SWD(2016) 450 final, 7.4.

[111] SWD(2016) 450 final, 7.4.

[112] Article 24(2)(a) of Regulation (EU) 2018/1861.

the territory of a Member State'.[113] This provision does not even require a criminal conviction, thereby leaving considerable discretion to the Member States.

With regard to the predecessor version, Article 24(2) of the SIS II Regulation, which was similarly worded, Brouwer noted that the notions 'serious grounds', 'serious criminal offences' and 'clear indications' left the Member States a wide margin of discretion, which can be used to 'extend the categories of serious offences every time this is considered politically necessary'.[114]

The third situation that is listed in Article 24(2) of the present SIS Regulation refers to cases where 'a third-country national has circumvented or attempted to circumvent Union or national law on entry into and stay on the territory of the Member States'.[115] The predecessor version, Article 24(3) of the SIS II Regulation, provided that an alert may be issued with regard to a third-country national who is subject to a prohibition on residence, which is 'based on a failure to comply with national regulations on the entry or residence of third-country nationals'.

This provision was considered problematic as it allowed for the registration of third-country nationals 'if they violated a relatively unimportant rule' of (national) immigration law.[116] Brouwer stated that even foreigners who apply too late (by a day or a week) for a renewal of their residence permit or who fail to submit the complete information on time can be subject to an alert in the SIS. She argued that 'these reasons for reporting someone in the SIS seem disproportionate, considering that this measure results in a ban on entry to the entire EU territory'.[117] Even though the current version requires a circumvention of, instead of a failure to comply with, national regulations on entry and stay, thereby putting emphasis on the third-country national's intention as opposed to mere negligence, it also broadens the scope of the provision. It broadens the scope by referring first to an attempt as opposed to an outright infringement of these rules. Second, the number of provisions that can be infringed is greater. While the old SIS II Regulation referred to national regulations, the SIS Regulation refers to 'Union or national law on entry into and stay on the territory of the Member States'.[118] Finally, while Article 24(3) of the SIS II Regulation stipulated that this conduct may trigger an SIS alert, Article 24(2) of the SIS Regulation lists situations that shall lead to an SIS alert, provided that the requirements of Article 24(1)(a) of the SIS Regulation are met.

ii. *The Principle of Proportionality*

Like its predecessor, the SIS Regulation explicitly addresses the principle of proportionality. Article 21 provides that Member States are bound by the principle

[113] Article 24(2)(b) of Regulation (EU) 2018/1861.
[114] Brouwer, *Digital Borders and Real Rights* 527.
[115] Article 24(2)(c) of Regulation (EU) 2018/1861.
[116] Brouwer, *Digital Borders and Real Rights* 527.
[117] ibid.
[118] Article 24(1)(c) of Regulation (EU) 2018/1861.

of proportionality and have to assess, before they issue an alert, 'whether the case is adequate, relevant and important enough to warrant an alert in SIS'.[119]

The predecessor of the SIS Regulation, the SIS II Regulation, contained a similarly worded reference to the principle of proportionality in Article 21, while simultaneously providing for mandatory SIS alerts, which barred a balancing process. Peers rightly pointed out that it is not clear 'how the issue of a mandatory alert is compatible with the proportionality rule in Article 21'.[120] Moreover, it must be noted that even if the principle of proportionality were not explicitly mentioned, Member States would still be under an obligation to respect the CFR as they implement Union law in line with Article 51(1) CFR. This entails Member States would still have to respect the CFR when they apply the SIS Regulation and enter an alert into the SIS. Hence, if an alert affected the right(s) guaranteed by the CFR, for example the right to private and family life enshrined in Article 7, a balancing process between the interests of the state and those of the individual would have to be conducted. Even if an alert according to Article 24 of the SIS Regulation were mandatory, the Member State would have to refrain from entering it if it resulted in a violation of Charter right(s).

D. Lessons Learned? The Transition from SIS, to SIS II, to the Current SIS Regulation

The need to harmonise the criteria for entering an alert into the SIS was acknowledged by the former Schengen Joint Supervisory Authority,[121] as well as by the European Commission.[122] As early as in 2008, Brouwer argued that the 'need for a common interpretation of the reasons for excluding an individual from the territory of the EU derives both from the principle of equal treatment and the duty of the Member States to respect the rights of third-country nationals'.[123] With regard to the SIS II Regulation, Peers argued that it is 'unfortunate that, contrary to the Commission's proposals, there has been no attempt to harmonise the substantive rules for listing persons to be denied entry'[124] and that the already rather vague grounds for issuing an alert are not even exhaustive.[125] This shortcoming has been

[119] Article 21(1) of Regulation (EU) 2018/1861.

[120] S Peers, 'Key Legislative Developments on Migration in the European Union: SIS II' (2008) 10 *European Journal of Migration and Law* 89; S Peers, 'Schengen Information System' in S Peers, E Guild and J Tomkins (eds), *EU Immigration and Asylum Law (Text and Commentary), Volume 1: Visas and Border Controls* (Leiden, Martinus Nijhoff, 2012) 106.

[121] The Schengen Information System II Supervision Coordination Group replaced the Schengen Joint Supervisory Authority after the SIS II entered into force; Opinion of the Joint Supervisory Authority on the proposed legal basis for SIS II, 27 September 2005, p 22.

[122] COM(2005) 236 final, pp 3, 9 (Recital 10 of the Preamble to the draft Regulation).

[123] Brouwer, *Digital Borders and Real Rights* 528.

[124] Peers, 'Key Legislative Developments on Migration in the European Union' 102; House of Lords, Schengen Information System II (SIS II): Report with Evidence, 9th Report of Session 2006–2007, p 24.

[125] Peers, 'Key Legislative Developments on Migration in the European Union' 102.

remedied by the SIS Regulation to some extent as it contains an exhaustive list of three situations set out in Article 24(2) specifying the grounds on which an alert can be entered.

Interestingly, the draft SIS II Regulation made an attempt to harmonise the criteria for the entry of an alert in the SIS. Article 15(1)(a)(i) of the draft SIS II Regulation,[126] which contained the conditions for issuing an alert, referred to the offences listed in Article 2(2) of Council Framework Decision 2002/584/JHA on the European arrest warrant and thereby made the requirements for an alert more specific.[127] However, this clarification was removed from the final version of the Regulation. In light of the rejection of the list contained in Article 2(2) of the Framework Decision, the question arises why Member States refrained from agreeing on these common criteria. The Council noted that the lack of understanding between the Member States regarding the criteria for entering an alert into the SIS 'is in part due to diverging national legislations on this issue'.[128] Moreover, the lack of agreement among the Member States to establish clear criteria for SIS alerts seems to be connected to the fact that the entry and residence of foreigners on the territory is closely interlinked with state sovereignty.[129] An interesting comment is made by Oosterom-Staples, who considers that the lack of common definitions for key concepts such as the notion of public policy 'have put the Contracting Parties above the individual'.[130] This supports the argument that a lack of harmonisation and thereby a greater discretion enables the Member States to pursue their own objectives and to retain as much sovereignty and as many competences as possible in relation to the question of who can, or rather cannot, enter their territory.

A shortcoming of the old SIS II Regulation was the lack of an alignment between an entry ban according to the Return Directive and an SIS alert. Recital 18 of the Preamble to the Return Directive explicitly states that Member States should have rapid access to information on entry bans and that this information sharing should take place in accordance with the SIS II Regulation. However, the SIS II Regulation did not provide for such an option. The Commission's report on the evaluation of SIS II found 'links but also inconsistencies between the provisions on entry bans as set out in the Return Directive and alerts for refusal of entry or stay as set out in Regulation (EC) No 1987/2006'.[131] This shortcoming was remedied

[126] COM(2005) 236 final.

[127] S Peers, 'The Schengen Information System and EC Immigration and Asylum Law' in J de Zwaan and F Goudappel (eds), *Freedom, Security and Justice in the European Union* (The Hague, T.C.M. Asser Press, 2006) 183.

[128] Council of the European Union, Note from the Presidency, 'Selected issues concerning the legal basis for SIS II' 20 April 2006, doc. 8537/06, p 5.

[129] See Article 79(5) TFEU, which is an expression of this sovereignty.

[130] Oosterom-Staples, 'Adjudicating the External Schengen Border' 235.

[131] COM(2016) 880 final, Report from the Commission to the European Parliament and the Council on the evaluation of the second generation Schengen Information System (SIS II) in accordance with artt 24 (5), 43 (3) and 50 (5) of Regulation (EC) No 1987/2006 and artt 59 (3) and 66 (5) of Decision 2007/533/JHA, p 14, point 4.4.2.

by Article 24(1)(b) of the SIS Regulation, which provides that Member States shall enter an alert in the SIS if the 'Member State has issued an entry ban in accordance with procedures respecting Directive 2008/115/EC in respect of a third-country national'.

E. Summary: New Design, Same Concept?

Article 24 of the SIS Regulation, which establishes the criteria for entering alerts regarding third-country nationals into the SIS, replaced Article 24 of the SIS II Regulation, which in turn replaced Article 96 CISA. Through these transitions and reforms, the requirements for entering an alert into the SIS have become clearer and have been narrowed down, but they still leave Member States a margin of discretion. It is to be welcomed that the CJEU has established safeguards for third-country family members of Union citizens exercising their right to free movement that are partially codified in Article 26 of the SIS Regulation. The legal position of Turkish nationals covered by the Association Agreement is not specifically addressed in the SIS Regulation, but an alert cannot be entered unless the presence or the conduct of the person poses a genuine and serious threat to public policy, public security or public health.[132]

Whereas the draft SIS II Regulation contained a reference to the LTR Directive, the current version of the Regulation does not contain any reference to the LTR Directive. An alert should, however, only be entered if the requirements of Article 12 LTR Directive are met. Given that Member States implement Union law in terms of Article 51(1) CFR, when they enter an alert into the SIS, Charter rights such as the right to private and family life guaranteed by Article 7 have to be observed.

III. Return Directive

The Proposal for the Directive on common standards and procedures in Member States for returning illegally staying third-country nationals was tabled by the Commission in September 2005.[133] It ultimately culminated in the adoption of the Return Directive, which entered into force in 2008.

The Return Directive aims at giving a European dimension to the effects of (national) return measures 'by establishing an entry ban prohibiting entry into and stay on the territory of all the Member States'.[134] In the Netherlands,

[132] *Derin*, para 54; *Ergat*, paras 45, 46; *Aydinli*, para 27.

[133] COM(2005) 391 final, Proposal for a Directive of the European Parliament and of the Council on common standards and procedures in Member States for returning illegally staying third-country nationals.

[134] Recital 14 of the Preamble to the Return Directive.

the withdrawal of a residence permit (for instance after a criminal conviction) is a return decision[135] and can comprise an entry ban[136] in terms of the Return Directive. In Germany, the expulsion decision (sections 53–55 Residence Act) as such is said not to be covered by the notion of return decision in terms of Article 3(4) of the Return Directive,[137] while the national entry and residence ban (section 11(1) Residence Act), which is precipitated by an expulsion decision, is covered by the scope of the Return Directive.[138]

A European effect of national decisions terminating lawful stay after a criminal conviction and obliging the foreigner to leave the territory can be achieved by an entry ban pursuant to Article 11 of the Return Directive, which in turn shall result in an SIS alert.[139] Gerontas highlights that the entry ban illustrates the transnational character of national decisions adopted according to the Return Directive.[140]

A. Aim and Scope

The Directive's purpose is to lay down EU-wide rules on the return of irregular third-country nationals, as an effective return policy is considered a necessary element of a well-managed migration policy.[141] The Return Directive addresses the duration of pre-removal detention and the imposition of re-entry bans, and provides legal safeguards. Many safeguards that were likely to prevent or delay the process of removal were rejected by the Member States in the drafting process, with the result that the Directive triggered fierce criticism from NGOs and mainly from Latin American states.[142]

[135] Article 27(2)(c) Vw 2000 in conjunction with Article 27(1) Vw 2000.

[136] Article 27(4) Vw 2000. The entry ban (*inreisverbod*) is addressed by Article 66a Vw and was further discussed in Chapter 6.

[137] Higher Administrative Court Baden-Württemberg, decision of 15.10.2013 – 11 S 2114/13, para 8 with further references; F Dollinger, '§ 11 AufenthG' in J Bergmann and K Dienelt (eds), *Ausländerrecht*, 13th edn (Munich, C.H. Beck, 2020) paras 23, 24.

[138] Dollinger, '§ 11 AufenthG', para 28.

[139] Article 24(1)(b) of Regulation (EU) 2018/1861.

[140] Gerontas, *Europäisierung und Internationalisierung des Verwaltungshandelns* 185, 215.

[141] P de Morree, 'Mutual Trust in Migration Law: The Returns Directive and Mutual Recognition of Entry Bans' in H Battjes, E Brouwer, P de Morree and J Ouwerkerk (eds), *The Principle of Mutual Trust in European Asylum, Migration and Criminal Law* (Utrecht, Forum, 2011) 30.

[142] A Baldaccini, 'The Return and Removal of Irregular Migrants under EU Law: An Analysis of the Returns Directive' (2009) 11 *European Journal of Migration and Law* 1, 2; D Acosta Arcarazo, *Latin American Reactions to the Adoption of the Returns Directive* (CEPS, 2009) 2, 3; D Acosta Arcarazo, 'The Good, the Bad and the Ugly in EU Migration Law: Is the European Parliament Becoming Bad and Ugly? (The Adoption of Directive 2008/15: The Returns Directive)' (2009) 11 *European Journal of Migration and Law* 19, 22; E Fornalé, 'The European Returns Policy and the Re-Shaping of the National: Reflections on the Role of Domestic Courts' (2012) 31 *Refugee Survey Quarterly* 134, 139; B Franßen-de la Cerda, 'Die Vergemeinschaftung der Rückführungspolitik – das Inkrafttreten der EU-Rückführungsrichtlinie' (2008) *Zeitschrift für Ausländerrecht und Ausländerpolitik* 377, 378; A Bombeke and K Franssen, 'De Terugkeerrichtlijn: over de normen voor de terugkeer van illegaal verblijvende derdelanders' (2010) *Asiel & Migrantenrecht* 257, 260.

Regarding its scope, the Directive applies to illegally staying third-country nationals. Third-country national family members of EU citizens who exercise their free movement rights are excluded from its scope,[143] whereas Turkish nationals covered by the Association Agreement fall under the Directive's scope.[144] Third-country nationals who are covered by the LTR or Family Reunification Directive are also covered by the scope of the Return Directive.

Illegal stay is defined as

> the presence on the territory of a Member State, of a third-country national who does not fulfil, or no longer fulfils the conditions of entry as set out in Article 5 of the Schengen Borders Code or other conditions for entry, stay or residence in that Member State.[145]

Pollet argues that the Directive seems to lag behind the initial objective of harmonisation, its declared aim to set common standards[146] and its objective to give a European dimension to the effects of return decisions[147] due to the numerous exceptions and the discretion left to Member States.[148]

B. Entry Ban

The entry ban provided for by Article 11 of the Return Directive, which, according to Article 24(1)(b) of the SIS Regulation, shall result in an SIS alert, prohibits the foreigner who is subject to such a ban from re-entering the territory of the participating states[149] and is considered a major deterrent to irregular stay.[150]

i. The Entry Ban and its Exceptions

Article 11 determines when an entry ban shall or may be issued and specifies its length, withdrawal and exceptions. There exist two cases in which Member States shall impose an entry ban, namely if no period for voluntary return has been

[143] Article 2(3) Return Directive in conjunction with Article 2(5)(a) of Regulation (EU) 2016/399.

[144] Franßen-de la Cerda, 'Die Vergemeinschaftung der Rückführungspolitik' 381.

[145] Article 3(2) Return Directive.

[146] Recital 11 of the Preamble to the Return Directive, Article 1 Return Directive.

[147] Recital 14 of the Preamble to the Return Directive.

[148] K Pollet, 'The Negotiations on the Return Directive: Challenges, Outcomes and Lessons Learned from an NGO Perspective' in K Zwaan (ed), *The Returns Directive: Central Themes, Problem Issues, and Implementation in Selected Member States* (Nijmegen, Wolf Legal Publishers, 2011) 32, 38.

[149] For further information regarding the states that apply the Directive see Recitals 25–30 of the Preamble to the Return Directive.

[150] K Eisele (ed), European Parliamentary Research Service, 'The Return Directive 2008/115/EC, European Implementation Assessment' 77; Baldaccini, 'The Return and Removal of Irregular Migrants under EU Law' 9. Nevertheless, Baldaccini questions the deterrent effect of the entry ban and points out that it might even foster the circle of irregular migration of those individuals for whom illegal entry remains the only option available.

granted to the individual or if the individual does not comply with the obligation to leave the territory.[151] The former situation is covered by Article 7(4), which provides that Member States may refrain from granting a period for voluntary departure if there 'is a risk of absconding, … or if the person concerned poses a risk to public policy, public security or national security'. In the *Zh* and *O* case[152] the Court provided an interpretation of the notion of public policy, which is addressed in more detail in the next section. In all other cases of Article 11(1), 'return decisions may be accompanied by an entry ban',[153] which leaves discretion to the Member States. The Directive establishes several cases in which a Member State must or may refrain from issuing an entry ban, or withdraw or suspend it.

First, an entry ban shall not be issued if the individual has been granted a residence permit pursuant to Directive 2004/81/EC as a victim of trafficking in humans or if the foreigner has been the subject of an action to facilitate illegal immigration and cooperates with the authorities, subject to the condition that this individual neither fulfils the requirements of Article 11(1)(b) of the Return Directive nor poses a threat to public policy or public security.[154]

Second, the Member State 'shall consider withdrawing or suspending the entry ban when a third-country national' who is the subject of a discretionary entry ban 'can demonstrate that he or she has left the territory of a Member State in full compliance with a return decision'.[155]

In two other cases, Member States have discretion to refrain from issuing an entry ban or they can withdraw or suspend an already issued entry ban. They can do so for humanitarian reasons[156] or for other reasons.[157] Hence, Member States are given broad discretion to refrain from issuing an entry ban, to withdraw or to suspend it.

Another provision relevant in this context is Article 11(4) Return Directive. It refers to cases in which a Member State considers issuing a residence permit or another authorisation to 'a third-country national who is the subject of an entry ban issued by another Member State'. Article 11(4) Return Directive, which has clear parallels with Article 27 of the SIS Regulation, provides that the former Member State 'shall first consult the Member State having issued the entry ban and shall take account of its interests in accordance with Article 25 of the Convention implementing the Schengen Agreement'.[158] Hence, a Member State that considers issuing a residence permit is not unconditionally bound to accept the entry ban issued by another Member State, but it is also not free to completely override the first Member State's decision.

[151] Article 11(1) of Directive 2008/115/EC.
[152] Case C-554/13 *Zh* and *O* ECLI:EU:C:2015:377, [2015].
[153] Article 11(1) second subparagraph of Directive 2008/115/EC.
[154] Article 11(3), second subparagraph of Directive 2008/115/EC.
[155] Article 11(3) of Directive 2008/115/EC.
[156] Article 11(3) third subparagraph of Directive 2008/115/EC.
[157] Article 11(3) fourth subparagraph of Directive 2008/115/EC.
[158] Concerning the interpretation of Article 25 CISA see Case C-240/17 *E*. ECLI:EU:C:2018:8, [2018].

ii. Interpretation of the Notion of 'Risk to Public Policy'

The CJEU's case law concerning the interpretation of the notion of public policy in the context of the Return Directive resulted in a limitation of Member States' discretion. In the case of *Zh* and *O*, the Court stated that the 'risk to public policy' in terms of Article 7(4) of the Return Directive must be assessed 'on a case-by-case basis'[159] in order to ascertain whether there is 'a genuine, present and sufficiently serious threat affecting one of the fundamental interests of society'.[160] Moreover, the Court highlighted that Member States must have 'regard to the requirements relating to an individual examination of the case concerned and to the principle of proportionality'.[161] Finally, the Court emphasised that the fact that the third-country national 'has been criminally convicted, cannot, in itself, justify a finding that that national poses a risk to public policy'.[162] By establishing these requirements the CJEU narrowed the interpretation of the notion 'public policy' in the context of the Return Directive and aligned it to the definition provided by Article 27(2) of the Citizenship Directive, which sets out the general principles of EU citizens' protection against expulsion. These general principles have been transferred by the Court's case law to Turkish nationals' and long-term resident third-country nationals' protection against expulsion. By providing the same interpretation of the notion of public policy in the Return Directive and in the context of Turkish nationals' and long-term resident third-country nationals' protection against expulsion, the Court's case law helps ensure consistency between the requirements for expulsion decisions and entry bans. Remarkably, the interpretation of the notion of public policy applies to all groups of third-country nationals who are covered by the Return Directive.

In the *H.T.* case,[163] which concerned the interpretation of the national security or public order notion in the Qualification Directive,[164] the Court reiterated the interpretation of the notion of public policy in the context of Article 27(2) of the Citizenship Directive.[165] While acknowledging that the Citizenship Directive pursues different objectives to those pursued by the Qualification Directive, the Court emphasised that the extent of the protection a society intends to afford to its fundamental interests cannot vary depending on the legal status of the person that undermines those interests.[166]

[159] *Zh* and *O*, para 50.
[160] ibid, para 60.
[161] ibid, para 50.
[162] *Zh* and *O*, para 50.
[163] Case C-373/13 *H. T.* ECLI:EU:C:2015:413, [2015].
[164] Council Directive 2004/83/EC on minimum standards for the qualification and status of third country nationals or stateless persons as refugees or as persons who otherwise need international protection and the content of the protection granted [2004] OJ L 304/12.
[165] *H. T.*, para 79.
[166] ibid, para 77.

This line of case law was continued in the *J.N.* case,[167] which concerned the Reception Conditions Directive.[168] In *J.N.* the Court stated that the 'interpretation which the case-law of the Court of Justice gives to the concepts of "national security" and "public order" found in other directives also applies in the case of Directive 2013/33'.[169] Moreover, the CJEU held that the

> concept of 'public order' entails, in any event, the existence in addition to the disturbance of the social order which any infringement of the law involves of a genuine, present and sufficiently serious threat affecting one of the fundamental interests of society.[170]

The *H.T.* case and the *J.N.* case point towards a parallel interpretation given to the notion of public policy in the context of the Citizenship Directive and in the context of Directives concerning third-country nationals.

The principles that were established in the *Zh* and *O* case were subsequently reiterated in the *E.* case,[171] which concerned the interpretation of Article 25 CISA in the context of a return decision accompanied by an entry ban according to the Return Directive against a third-country national who held a residence permit issued by another Schengen State.[172]

However, the subsequent *E.P.* judgment,[173] which concerned the interpretation of the notion of public policy contained in Article 6(1)(e) of the Schengen Borders Code, constitutes a turning point. The Court held that

> any reference by the EU legislature to the concept of 'threat to public policy' does not necessarily have to be understood as referring exclusively to individual conduct representing a genuine, present and sufficiently serious threat affecting one of the fundamental interests of the society of the Member State concerned.[174]

The same approach was adopted by the Court in the joined cases of *G.S.* and *V.G.*, which concerned the question of whether the notion of public policy in the Family Reunification Directive[175] has the same meaning as the notion of public policy in Article 27(2) of the Citizenship Directive.[176]

Nonetheless, in the subsequent *WM* case,[177] which related to the interpretation of Article 16 of the Return Directive on the conditions of detention, the Court referred again to the *Zh* and *O* judgment[178] and held that 'the requirement of a

[167] Case C-601/15 PPU *J. N.* ECLI:EU:C:2016:84, [2016].

[168] Directive 2013/33/EU laying down standards for the reception of applicants for international protection (recast) [2013] OJ L 180/96.

[169] *J. N.*, para 64.

[170] ibid, para 65.

[171] *E.*, para 49.

[172] ibid, paras 22–29.

[173] Case C-380/18 *E.P.* ECLI:EU:C:2019:1071, [2019].

[174] *E.P.*, para 31.

[175] Council Directive 2003/86/EC of 22 September 2003 on the right to family reunification [2003] OJ L 251/12.

[176] Joined Cases C-381/18 and C-382/18 *G.S.* ECLI:EU:C:2019:1072, para 54.

[177] Case C-18/19 *WM* ECLI:EU:C:2020:511, [2020].

[178] *WM*, paras 42 and 43 refer to *Zh* and *O*.

genuine, present and sufficiently serious threat affecting one of the fundamental interests of society' applies a fortiori to justify detention in prison accommodation under the second sentence of Article 16(1) of Directive 2008/115'.[179]

The *Zh* and *O* case, the *E.* case and the *WM* case confirm a parallel interpretation of the notion of public policy in the context of the Citizenship Directive and in the context of the Return Directive. The *E.* case, which concerned the interpretation of Article 25 of the Convention Implementing the Schengen Agreement against the background of an entry ban according to the Return Directive, suggests that the interpretation of the notion of public policy that applies in the context of the Return Directive also applies in the context of the SIS Regulation. On the other hand, and against such an interpretation, the *E.P.* case can be advanced, where the Court rejected such a parallel interpretation of the notion of public policy in the context of the Schengen Borders Code.[180] This judgment corresponds to the Court's judgment in *Commission v Spain*, admittedly a judgment from 2006, where the Court held that 'it is clear that the concept of public policy within the meaning of Article 2 of Directive 64/221 does not correspond to that in Article 96 CISA'.[181]

However, given that an entry ban according to the Return Directive shall lead to an SIS alert according to the SIS Regulation,[182] the interpretation given to the notion of public policy in the context of the Return Directive must also apply to the SIS Regulation, as two different interpretations of the notion of public policy in the Return Directive and in the SIS Regulation do not seem to be workable. Nonetheless, these different considerations underpin the need for clarification. In order to enhance clarity and legal certainty, the strict interpretation that has been given to the notion of public policy in the *Zh* and *O* judgment and subsequent judgments should therefore be reflected in the text of both the Return Directive and the SIS Regulation.

iii. The Principle of Proportionality

One of the key findings of the 2020 Implementation Assessment of the Return Directive is that

> Member States tend to implement Article 11(1) of the Return Directive by automatically imposing entry bans if the voluntary departure is not granted … The 'shall' provision in Article 11(1) may rule out an individual assessment, disregarding the principle of proportionality.[183]

[179] *WM*, para 45.
[180] *E.P.*, para 31.
[181] *Commission v Spain*, para 48.
[182] Article 24(1)(b) of Regulation (EU) 2018/1861.
[183] Eisele (ed), European Parliamentary Research Service, 'The Return Directive 2008/115/EC, European Implementation Assessment' 18.

Admittedly, the Directive addresses the principle of proportionality mainly in the context of coercive measures[184] or detention,[185] but refrains from mentioning it in the context of the issuance of an entry ban or its duration. However, van Riel points out that the principle of proportionality is enshrined (even though not explicitly mentioned) in Article 4(3) of the Directive (more favourable provisions) and Article 11(2) of the Directive (length of the entry ban).[186]

Moreover, the principle of proportionality is a general principle of EU law and must be taken into account in all decisions, including those on entry bans. The relationship between general principles and secondary legislation was addressed by the CJEU's *Siples* judgment, where the Court clarified that a provision of secondary EU law cannot limit a general principle.[187] In addition, Recital 6 of the Preamble to the Return Directive provides that decisions taken under this Directive should be adopted on a case-by-case basis. The need for a case-by-case assessment was also highlighted by the Court in the *Zh* and *O* judgment.[188] In particular, the Court reiterated that 'the principle of proportionality must be observed throughout all the stages of the return procedure established by that directive'.[189] Even though the Directive does not further specify how the obligatory entry ban provided for in Article 11(1) can be reconciled with the principle of proportionality and the requirement of a case-by-case assessment, Member States must refrain from imposing an entry ban if it is disproportionate and thereby infringes the principle of proportionality. Finally, as pointed out in the context of the SIS Regulation, Member States have to respect the CFR when they implement Union law in terms of Article 51(1) CFR. If an entry ban interfered with the foreigner's right(s) guaranteed by the Charter, for example the right to respect for private and family life (Article 7 of the Charter), a balancing process between the interests of the foreigner and the interests of the state would have to be conducted. If an entry ban resulted in a violation of a Charter right, Member States would have to refrain from imposing such a ban, despite it being obligatory according to Article 11(1).

iv. The Duration of the Entry Ban

Originally, the European Council suggested that 'Member States may impose an indefinite re-entry and residence ban'.[190] However, the Return Directive stipulates in Article 11(2) that 'the length of the entry ban shall be determined with due

[184] Recital 13 of the Preamble to the Directive and Article 8 Directive.

[185] Recital 16 of the Preamble to the Directive.

[186] M van Riel, 'Nieuwe wetgeving ter implementatie van de Terugkeerrichtlijn' (2012) 2 *Asiel & Migrantenrecht* 68, 74.

[187] Case C-226/99 *Siples* ECLI:EU:C:2001:14, [2001] ECR I-00277, paras 16–19.

[188] *Zh* and *O*, para 50.

[189] ibid, para 49.

[190] Council Document 6624/07 of 28 February 2007, p 4.

regard to all relevant circumstances of the individual case and shall not in principle exceed five years'. In *Filev and Osmani* the CJEU clarified that it follows from the phrase '"[t]he length of the entry ban shall be determined" that Member States are under an obligation to limit the effects in time of any entry ban in principle to a maximum of five years'.[191] The Court underlined this finding by reference to Recital 14 of the Preamble to the Return Directive and by invoking the definition of 'entry ban' provided for by Article 3(6) of the Directive, according to which it is a ban 'for a specified period'.[192] Moreover, the Court had recourse to Article 7(1), which addresses the period for voluntary departure and that 'Member States may provide in their national legislation that such a period shall be granted only following an application by the third-country national concerned'. The Court ruled that if 'the European Union legislature had intended to provide Member States with a discretionary power in relation to determining a limit to the length of an entry ban, it would have done so expressly in Article 11(2) of that directive'.[193]

Regarding those entry ban decisions that were taken before the Return Directive became applicable, the Court held that

> Article 11(2) of Directive 2008/115 precludes a continuation of the effects of entry bans of unlimited length made before the date on which Directive 2008/115 became applicable beyond the maximum length of entry ban laid down by that provision, except where those entry bans were made against third-country nationals constituting a serious threat to public order, public security or national security.[194]

Entry bans exceeding the five-year limit are only permissible if the foreigner poses a serious threat to public order, public security or national security. If a Member State considers it necessary to impose an entry ban exceeding five years it has to determine a time limit as entry bans of an unlimited duration are not in line with the Directive. The starting point of the period of application of an entry ban must be calculated from the date on which the person actually left the territory of the Member State,[195] not from the date on which the decision to impose that entry ban was imposed.

v. Discretion Granted to the Member States

Several provisions of the Directive leave discretion to the Member States, which can result in diverging practices. First, for the Return Directive to apply, the individual must, according to Article 2(1), be illegally present on the Member State's territory. Illegal stay,[196] despite the conditions on entry listed in the Schengen

[191] Case C-297/12 *Filev and Osmani* ECLI:EU:C:2013:569, [2013], para 27.
[192] ibid, paras 28, 29.
[193] ibid, para 30.
[194] ibid, para 44.
[195] Case C-225/16 *Ouhrami* ECLI:EU:C:2017:590, para 58.
[196] Defined in Article 3(2) of Directive 2008/115/EC.

Borders Code, is mainly a question of national law.[197] Therefore, the stay of an individual can be considered illegal by one Member State according to its national laws, whereas another Member State would not necessarily classify it as such. Second, even though the first sentence of Article 11(1) Return Directive is phrased imperatively and obliges the Member States to impose an entry ban, the following sentence, which provides that 'In other cases return decisions may be accompanied by an entry ban', grants discretion to the Member States. This might result in situations where some Member States generally link a return decision with an entry ban whereas others refrain from making such a link. Third, Article 2(2) grants Member States the possibility to exclude certain categories of foreigners from the scope of the Directive, including third-country nationals who 'are subject to return as a criminal law sanction or as a consequence of a criminal law sanction, according to national law, or who are the subject of extradition procedures', Article 2(2)(b). However, as Acosta Arcarazo argues, this provision must be interpreted narrowly as it constitutes an exception from the general rule.[198] The margin of discretion granted by these provisions can result in differences between Member States regarding the application of the Directive, the imposition of entry bans and the process of return. Despite these differences, an entry ban in principle has to be mutually recognised by the Member States.

vi. Conclusions on Entry Bans and a Comparison with the SIS Regulation

The withdrawal of a residence permit following a criminal conviction and a national entry ban are covered by the scope of the Return Directive. The application of the Return Directive depends to a certain extent on national law insofar as the latter defines whether the stay of the foreigner is irregular. In addition, Member States are granted the possibility to exclude certain foreigners from the scope of the Directive, and the Directive leaves Member States discretion in certain circumstances regarding the imposition of an entry ban. Despite these margins of discretion and the possibility of resulting divergences between national decisions, all decisions taken by a Member State must (with a few exceptions, for example Article 11(4) Return Directive) in principle be recognised by the other Member States.

According to the Return Directive, an entry ban shall lead to an SIS alert,[199] even though several differences exist between entry bans according to the Return Directive and SIS alerts under the SIS Regulation. First, an entry ban issued

[197] de Morree, 'Mutual Trust in Migration Law' 36.
[198] D Acosta Arcarazo, 'The Returns Directive' in S Peers, E Guild, D Acosta Arcarazo, K Groenendijk and V Moreno-Lax (eds), *EU Immigration and Asylum Law (Text and Commentary), Volume 2: EU Immigration Law* (Leiden, Martinus Nijhoff Publishers, 2012) 491–93.
[199] See Article 24(1)(b) Regulation (EU) 2018/1861.

according to the Return Directive requires a return decision, which is not envisaged by the SIS Regulation. Second, an SIS alert can only be issued if the presence of the third-country national 'poses a threat to public policy, public security or to national security',[200] a condition which is not required for an entry ban according to the Return Directive. The Return Directive stipulates that an entry ban shall be imposed if 'no period for voluntary departure has been granted'[201] or 'if the obligation to return has not been complied with'.[202] In the remaining cases, 'return decisions may be accompanied by an entry ban'.[203] Even though Article 7(4) of the Return Directive stipulates that Member States can refuse a period for voluntary departure if 'the person concerned poses a risk to public policy, public security or national security', the Return Directive does not mandatorily require a risk to public policy or public security for the imposition of an entry ban. Another difference between the SIS Regulation and the Return Directive is that the Return Directive lists the grounds on which an entry ban may be suspended or withdrawn, whereas the same grounds are not foreseen by the SIS Regulation. Finally, the duration of an entry ban according to the Return Directive shall in principle not exceed five years,[204] whereas the retention of SIS alerts shall in principle be reviewed after three years.[205]

IV. Summary and Conclusions Regarding Mutual Recognition, Modes of Administrative Decision Making, SIS Alerts and Entry Bans

The previous sections introduced the system of mutual recognition and different modes of administrative decision making, and discussed two instruments that can give a European effect to national expulsion decisions and entry bans. In a first step, the system of mutual trust and mutual recognition employed by both the Return Directive and the SIS Regulation was addressed. This system was already subject to criticism in the context of Directive 2001/40/EC on the mutual recognition of decisions on the expulsion of third-country nationals. A major point of criticism regarding Directive 2001/40/EC concerned the fact that mutual recognition is established without providing for common rules and procedures. Mutual recognition is mainly employed in sensitive policy areas where full harmonisation is impossible. Decisions on entry, residence and expulsion of foreigners are

[200] Article 24(1)(a) Regulation (EU) 2018/1861.
[201] Article 11(1)(a) Directive 2008/115/EC.
[202] Article 11(1)(b) Directive 2008/115/EC.
[203] Article 11(1) Directive 2008/115/EC.
[204] Article 11(2) Directive 2008/115/EC.
[205] Article 39(2) Regulation (EU) 2018/1861.

at the core of state sovereignty, which is why harmonisation is difficult to achieve. Even though mutual recognition and full harmonisation are mutually exclusive, as mutual recognition would be superfluous if a policy area is fully harmonised, some common standards and a minimum level of harmonisation should be established to achieve some degree of consistency across the decisions that are mutually recognised.

Despite the advantages of mutual recognition, which allows states to attach a transnational effect to their national administrative decisions that frees them from the confines of the national territory and grants them an extraterritorial effect, transnational administrative acts also display disadvantages. These were discussed above, together with options to mitigate them. The 2018 SIS Regulation has already remedied several shortcomings of its predecessor, by, inter alia, specifying the requirements for entering an alert into the SIS, which in turn limits the discretion of Member States, thereby ensuring greater consistency among Member States' decisions.

Despite these improvements, it is worth examining whether the two options that were discussed in the context of decisions concerning the deliberate release into the environment of genetically modified organisms could also be of use in the context of SIS alerts. The first option grants Member States involvement in the decision-making process and the second option gives them the possibility to suspend the decision after it was adopted.

The 'prior involvement' option is probably not the most suitable and practical instrument for every decision on an entry ban or an SIS alert. As rightly pointed out by Bast, the number of transnational decisions taken in the area of migration law renders it impossible to consult all Member States involved.[206] Moreover, and in contrast to the deliberate release into the environment of genetically modified organisms, the interests at stake in the context of SIS alerts are unlikely to trigger the involvement by other Member States in the decision-making process. The second option, the temporary suspension of the decision of the first Member State, exhibits parallels to the possibility granted by the Return Directive and the SIS Regulation to issue a residence permit to a third-country national despite an alert or entry ban having been issued with regard to this person.[207] However, in the context of the deliberate release into the environment of genetically modified organisms, this option envisages a final decision by the European Commission, which can either oblige the first Member State to lift its original decision or oblige the second Member State to give full effect to the decision issued by the first Member State. It is unlikely that the Commission will get involved in the decision as to whether an entry ban or SIS alert should be upheld.

Regarding the margin of discretion and thereby the potential for diverging decisions, the Return Directive, which presupposes illegal stay, grants Member

[206] J Bast, 'Transnationale Verwaltung des europäischen Migrationsraums' 29.
[207] See Article 11(4) of Directive 2008/115/EC and Article 27 Regulation (EU) 2018/1861.

States the possibility to exclude certain foreigners from its scope.[208] Moreover, unless an entry ban is obligatory, Member States have discretion to impose an entry ban when adopting a return decision.[209] As a consequence, some Member States might issue an entry ban whereas others, in the same situation, would not do so. Despite these differences, an entry ban issued by one Member State has to be recognised, in principle, by all other Member States.

The SIS Regulation aimed to achieve 'a greater level of effectiveness, harmonisation and consistency … by making it mandatory to enter into SIS all entry bans' adopted in accordance with the Return Directive and 'by setting common rules for entering alerts for refusal of entry and stay upon the return of an illegally staying third-country national'.[210]

The SIS Regulation has not only made the grounds for entering an alert into the SIS more specific, it also established a legal basis for entry bans under the Return Directive to be mandatorily recorded in the SIS.[211] However, the requirements for SIS alerts according to the SIS Regulation and the requirements for imposing entry bans according to the Return Directive, which shall then lead to SIS alerts, differ. First, in contrast to an SIS alert, the entry ban according to the Return Directive requires a return decision. Second, an SIS alert can only be issued if a threat to public policy or public security or to national security exists, a condition which is not required by the Return Directive. Third, the Return Directive lists the grounds on which an entry ban may be suspended or withdrawn, which are not provided by the SIS Regulation. Moreover, the duration of an entry ban according to the Return Directive (in principle a maximum of five years) and the duration of an alert according to the SIS II Regulation (in principle three years) is also not entirely clear.

On a positive note, it must be highlighted that Member States' margin of discretion under the Return Directive has been limited by the Court's interpretation of the notion of public policy in *Zh* and *O*[212] and subsequent cases.[213]

[208] Article 2(2) of Directive 2008/115/EC.
[209] Article 11(1) Return Directive.
[210] Recital 26 of the Preamble to Regulation (EU) 2018/1861.
[211] Article 24(1)(b) Regulation (EU) 2018/1861.
[212] *Zh* and *O*, para 50.
[213] *H. T.*, para 79; *J. N.*, paras 65, 65; *E.*, para 49; *WM*, para 45.

10

National Expulsion Decisions and Entry Bans and their European Dimension

The previous chapter addressed the system of mutual recognition and the developments, aims, functioning and deficiencies of the SIS Regulation and the Return Directive. Both instruments can give national expulsion decisions and entry bans following a criminal conviction a European dimension by way of a Europe-wide entry ban, which attaches a transnational effect to these decisions. This chapter focuses on the implementation of the SIS Regulation and the Return Directive at the national level and explores how Member States use the margin of discretion granted by these instruments. It recalls the differences between Germany and the Netherlands regarding expulsion decisions and the termination of lawful stay after a criminal conviction respectively.[1] Moreover, it addresses in greater detail the question of whether decisions taken on the basis of these criteria can or even have to lead to a national entry ban and an SIS alert, and further expands on the differences regarding the duration of entry bans in these two countries.

Differences between national decisions are relevant as an alert entered by one state must be recognised by the other states unless an exception applies. Mutual recognition of possibly diverging decisions is problematic in light of the negative repercussions on the individual and on the common European approach to migration; this underlines the need for further approximation of the criteria for adopting these decisions or of the criteria for entering an alert into the SIS.

Differences can occur at three points. First, the provisions on expulsions and entry bans can differ. The differences between the German and Dutch systems have already been highlighted in the second part of the book but they will be briefly recalled as these decisions can lead to an SIS alert. Second, the national requirements for entering an alert into the SIS are relevant. Differences can occur on the question of whether an alert can or shall to be entered into the SIS. Third, differences between these two countries can occur concerning the determination of the duration of the entry ban/SIS alert.

[1] For a detailed overview of these differences see Chapters 5, 6 and 8.

I. Differences between Germany and the Netherlands Regarding Expulsion Decisions and the Termination of Lawful Residence after a Criminal Conviction

The German Residence Act requires a balancing process between the interests of the foreigner and the interests of the state before an expulsion decision can be issued.[2] The legislature established a non-exhaustive list of balancing criteria and attached a specific weight to (some of the) interests of the foreigner and (some of the) interests of the state, respectively.[3] An expulsion decision has to be issued if the interests of the state in terminating the foreigner's residence outweigh the interests of the foreigner to remain in the country.[4] An expulsion decision results in the expiry of the residence title[5] or the exemption from the requirement to have a residence title,[6] establishes the duty to leave the territory,[7] and shall lead to an entry and residence ban for the federal territory.[8]

In the Netherlands the termination of lawful residence after a criminal conviction requires the prison term to outweigh the duration of the foreigner's lawful residence as specified by the sliding scale. If the crime is not serious enough in light of the duration of the foreigner's lawful residence, residence cannot be terminated, at least not as a result of a criminal conviction.[9] If the duration of the foreigner's residence does not outweigh the prison term, a balancing process between the interests of the foreigner and those of the state has to be conducted. As addressed above,[10] protection afforded by the sliding scale increases the longer the foreigner lawfully resides in the Netherlands. In particular, residence exceeding 10 years affords the foreigner a higher degree of protection and could lead to situations in which a foreigner's lawful residence can no longer be terminated if the crime is not serious enough. Germany, by contrast, does not provide a sliding scale. Hence, even though both states provide for the termination of lawful residence after a criminal conviction, the two systems differ particularly in regard to the consequences resulting from the duration of the foreigner's lawful residence. This difference can have implications for the termination of lawful residence and ultimately for the question of whether an alert can be entered into the SIS.

[2] Residence Act, s 53(1).
[3] Residence Act, s 55; Residence Act, s 54.
[4] Residence Act, s 53(1).
[5] Residence Act, s 51(1) no 5; s 51(9) no 2.
[6] Residence Act, s 51(5).
[7] Residence Act, s 50(1) in conjunction with s 51(1).
[8] Residence Act, s 11(1).
[9] Further grounds for terminating lawful residence are listed in Article 19 Vw 2000 in conjunction with Article 18 Vw 2000 as well as in Article 22 Vw 2000.
[10] Chapter 6.

II. Requirements at the National Level for Entry Bans and SIS Alerts

A. Germany

An expulsion decision leads to an entry and residence ban for the federal territory,[11] hence a national entry ban. The entry of an alert into the SIS can be initiated by the foreigner authority, based on section 50(6) Residence Act. Section 50(6) provides that as regards a foreigner, who is subject to a ban on entry and residence pursuant to section 11, an alert may be issued for the purpose of refusing entry. Section 50(6) grants discretion and requires the authority to conduct an assessment based on the facts of the individual case to determine whether, and if so for how long, an alert shall be issued.[12] For the federal police the legal basis for entering an alert is section 30(5) of the Federal Police Act (*Bundespolizeigesetz*). In Germany, the Federal Criminal Police Office (*Bundeskriminalamt*) is the responsible SIRENE office and is in charge of entering alerts into the national SIS (N-SIS).[13]

i. Previous System of SIS Alerts and its Reform

Previously, there was no statutory basis for initiating the entry of an alert into the SIS, which led Brouwer to note that the legal situation regarding the entry of an alert lacked transparency.[14] The Residence Act stipulated that a national expulsion decision results in the expiry of the residence title[15] and a national entry ban for the federal territory (*Bundesgebiet*),[16] and that it obliges the foreigner to leave the federal territory.[17] The General Administrative Rules for the Residence Act, which provide guidance to the administration and which are still in place, provide that the competent authority has to initiate, without delay, the entry of an alert into the SIS according to Article 96(3) CISA (now Article 24 SIS Regulation) if the foreigner is subject to an expulsion decision.[18] National courts confirmed that the expulsion decision not only leads to a national entry ban, but also precipitates an SIS alert.[19]

[11] Residence Act, s 11(1).
[12] Administrative Court Koblenz, 24 July 2007, 3 L 1035/07.KO.
[13] Federal Criminal Police Office Act (*Bundeskriminalamtgesetz*), s 3(2); F Dollinger, '§ 50 AufenthG' in J Bergmann and K Dienelt (eds), *Ausländerrecht*, 13th edn (Munich, C.H. Beck, 2020) para 33.
[14] Brouwer, *Digital Borders and Real Rights* (Leiden, Brill Martinus Nijhoff, 2008) 440.
[15] Residence Act, s 51(1) no 5; s 51(9) no 2.
[16] Residence Act, s 11(1).
[17] Residence Act, s 50(1).
[18] General Administrative Rule for the Residence Act (*Allgemeine Verwaltungsvorschrift zum Aufenthaltsgesetz*) 5.5.4.1.1.
[19] Administrative Court Munich, decision of 5 March 2012, M 10 E 12.561; Administrative Court Augsburg, judgment of 30 April 2013, Au 1 K 13.316, para 22.

A synchronisation between a national entry ban and the SIS alert enhances the effectiveness of the national entry ban as only the SIS alert can effectively prevent the re-entry of the expelled foreigner into Germany, given the abolition of internal border controls in the Schengen area. Another argument for the entry of an alert into the SIS in case of an expulsion decision following a criminal conviction results from Article 24(1)(a) in conjunction with Article 24(2)(a) of the SIS Regulation. Article 24(2)(a) stipulates that an alert shall be entered, provided that the conditions of Article 24(1)(a) are met, if a third-country national has been convicted in a Member State of an offence carrying a penalty involving the deprivation of liberty of at least one year. Article 24(2)(a) of the SIS Regulation provides for a relatively low threshold by referring to crimes that carry a penalty involving the deprivation of liberty of at least one year. This provision would cover a considerable number of criminal convictions and necessitate an SIS alert.

However, against a synchronisation of national entry bans and SIS alerts, several arguments can be invoked. First, section 50(6) Residence Act grants discretion to the competent authority, which necessitates a proportionality assessment, so that the initiation of an SIS alert cannot be the automatic consequence of an expulsion decision. Second, even though the wording of section 11 Residence Act stipulates that an entry and residence ban shall be imposed on a foreigner who is subject to expulsion, it explicitly refers to the federal territory (*Bundesgebiet*) and thus requires a national entry and residence ban. Third, an automatic SIS alert upon expulsion is problematic against the background of Article 24(1)(a) of the SIS Regulation, which requires an assessment of the facts of the individual case before entering an alert into the SIS. Moreover, any automatism would be difficult to reconcile with the principle of proportionality laid down in Article 21 of the SIS Regulation. Finally, the CFR is applicable as the entry of an SIS alert constitutes an implementation of Union law in terms of Article 51(1) CFR. An automatic entry of an alert into the SIS does not guarantee that the rights enshrined in the Charter are considered. Therefore, a balancing process between the interests of the state and those of the individual has to be conducted before an alert is entered into the SIS.

ii. Developments Triggered by the Return Directive

Regarding its territorial scope, the national entry ban is not identical with the EU-wide entry ban referred to in the Return Directive, which is to be achieved by an entry of an alert into the SIS. The national entry ban constitutes a component of the EU-wide entry ban as it bars the foreigner's stay in the federal territory. Therefore, the duration of the national entry ban had to be aligned to the requirements of the Return Directive. To that end legislation was adopted in 2011[20] that

[20] Gesetz zur Umsetzung aufenthaltsrechtlicher Richtlinien der Europäischen Union und zur Anpassung nationaler Rechtsvorschriften an den EU-Visakodex of 22 November 2011, Federal Law Gazette Part I 2258.

led to the insertion of an additional sentence into section 11(1) Residence Act,[21] which provides that the (national) entry ban may exceed five years if the foreigner was expelled on grounds of a criminal conviction or poses a serious threat to public policy or public security.

In *Filev and Osmani* the parallel between the national and the European entry ban became apparent. Mr Filev was subject to removal from Germany[22] and Mr Osmani was subject to a German expulsion decision.[23] Both decisions triggered a national entry ban according to section 11(1) Residence Act, which was, back then, unlimited in time. The national court asked the CJEU whether 'national legislation which provides that the effects of expulsion or removal orders are not in principle limited in time, unless the interested party lodges an application for a time-limit, comply with European Union law, in particular Article 11(2)'.[24] The CJEU held that Article 11(2) of the Return Directive

> must be interpreted as precluding a provision of national law, such as Article 11(1) of the Law on the residence …, which makes the limitation of the length of an entry ban subject to the making by the third-country national concerned of an application seeking to obtain the benefit of such a limit.

In sum, while the national entry ban has to fulfil the requirements of the Return Directive, the parallel between the requirements of the European entry ban and the national entry ban does not imply that both are the same and that the national entry and residence ban also has to lead to a European entry ban.

Even though the entry of an alert in the SIS was previously often the automatic consequence of a national entry ban,[25] both the national legal basis for initiating an entry of an alert into the SIS, as well as Article 21 and Article 24(1)(a) of the SIS Regulation, require an assessment of the facts of the individual case, which bars any automatism between a national entry ban and an SIS alert. The question whether Germany has made use of the possibility provided for by Article 2(2)(b) of the Return Directive to exclude from the scope of application of the Directive third-country nationals who are subject to return as a consequence of a criminal law sanction has been answered negatively by the Federal Administrative Court.[26]

B. The Netherlands

In the Netherlands a criminal conviction can lead to the termination of lawful residence (withdrawal of the residence permit) as specified by the sliding scale.[27]

[21] Residence Act, s 11(1) fourth sentence.

[22] Case C-297/12 *Filev and Osmani* ECLI:EU:C:2013:569, [2013], para 12.

[23] ibid, para 15.

[24] ibid, para 23.

[25] R Gutmann, 'Ausländerrecht: Die Befristung der Ausweisung' (2009) 62 *Neue Juristische Wochenschrift* 2657; Administrative Court Munich, decision of 5 March 2012, M 10 E 12.561.

[26] Federal Administrative Court, decision of 6 May 2020, 1 C 14.19.

[27] Article 3.86 Vb 2000.

The withdrawal of a residence permit constitutes a return decision[28] and can comprise an entry ban (*inreisverbod*).[29] The consequences of the return decision vary. The Dutch provision on the entry ban, Article 66a Vw 2000, corresponds to Article 11(1) of the Return Directive. Article 66a(1) Vw 2000 stipulates that an entry ban shall be imposed, if, among other grounds, the foreigner has been ordered to leave the Netherlands immediately according to Article 62(2) Vw 2000. This can be the case if the foreigner poses a threat to public policy, public security or national security.[30] Hence, if the foreigner, following his or her criminal conviction and the termination of residence, has been ordered to leave the territory of the Netherlands immediately, Article 66a(1)(a) Vw 2000 stipulates that an *inreisverbod* shall be imposed, which then automatically triggers an SIS alert.[31] However, in *Zh* and *O* the CJEU clarified the need for an assessment on a case-by-case basis, which bars any automatism. Moreover, the Court stipulated that the 'principle of proportionality must be observed throughout all the stages of the return procedure',[32] which obliges national authorities to refrain from imposing an *inreisverbod* if it would be disproportionate.

Article 66a(2) Vw 2000 provides that an entry ban *may* be imposed, and hence leaves discretion to the competent authority. The exercise of this discretion is specified by the Vc 2000 and was addressed in more detail above.[33] The competent authority must refrain from imposing an entry ban if it would result in a violation of Article 8 ECHR.[34]

The civil servants responsible for border control or for the surveillance of foreigners send a request for an *inreisverbod* to the IND if they are of the opinion that there are reasons for imposing an *inreisverbod*. The IND is the competent authority to decide on whether an *inreisverbod* will be imposed.[35] An *inreisverbod* in terms of Article 66a Vw 2000 automatically triggers an SIS alert.[36] This automatism and the lack of a separate balancing process have been criticised.[37]

III. Duration of the Entry Ban

Differences between Germany and the Netherlands can occur regarding the question of whether an entry ban will be imposed and regarding the duration of the entry ban.

[28] Article 27(2)(c) Vw 2000.
[29] Article 27(4) Vw 2000.
[30] Article 62(2)(c) Vw 2000.
[31] Article 66a(3) Vw 2000.
[32] Case C-554/13 *Zh* and *O* ECLI:EU:C:2015:377, [2015], para 49.
[33] Chapter 6.
[34] ARBvS, 19 November 2012, 201208909/1/V4.
[35] A4/2.4.1. in conjunction with A4/3.2 Vc 2000.
[36] Article 66a(3) Vw 2000, Article 3.103 b (1) Vb 2000.
[37] Commissie Meijers, 'Wijziging van de Vreemdelingenwet 2000 ter implementatie van de Terugkeerrichtlijn' (TK 32 420), reference: CM 1013, of 3 September 2010, p 3; Commissie Meijers, 'Strafbaarstelling overtreding inreisverbod' (TK 2010-2011, 32 420, nr. 9), reference: CM 1018, 24 December 2010.

A. Germany

Previously, the duration of the entry ban entered into the SIS was not necessarily identical with the duration of the domestic entry and residence ban. The General Administrative Rules for the Residence Act differentiated between the duration of a national entry ban and an SIS alert. The duration of the national entry ban was determined in accordance with the classification of the abolished system of expulsion, which distinguished between mandatory expulsion (section 53), expulsion as a rule (section 54) and expulsion following a balancing process (section 55). The General Administrative Rules stipulate that the duration of the national entry ban shall be: three years for expulsion decisions based upon section 55 Residence Act; seven years for expulsion decisions based upon section 54 Residence Act; and 10 years for expulsion decisions based upon section 53 Residence Act.[38]

Regarding the duration of the SIS alert, the General Administrative Rule provided: three years for an expulsion decision based upon section 55 Residence Act; six years for an expulsion decision based upon section 54 Residence Act; and six years for an expulsion decision based upon section 53 Residence Act.[39]

This system was incompatible with the Return Directive, which provides that 'the length of the entry ban shall be determined with due regard to all relevant circumstances of the individual case …',[40] which is why the Residence Act was amended. The current version of section 11 Residence Act stipulates that the duration of the entry ban has to be determined according to the facts of the individual case and may not exceed five years unless the requirements of paragraph 5 to 5b are met.[41] The upper limit of five years aims at implementing the Return Directive.[42] It can be exceeded if the foreigner was expelled on grounds of a criminal conviction or if the foreigner poses a serious threat to public policy or public security, in which case the length of the entry ban shall not exceed 10 years.[43] In 2012 the Federal Administrative Court clarified that the threshold of 10 years is generally a maximum period for which a prediction can realistically be made.[44] Hence, an entry ban shall normally not exceed the 10-year limit. For these entry bans the duration may be reduced if there are particular protection needs.[45] Finally, the duration of the entry ban shall be 20 years if the foreigner was expelled on grounds

[38] General Administrative Rule for the Residence Act (*Allgemeine Verwaltungsvorschrift zum Aufenthaltsgesetz*) 11.1.4.6.1.

[39] General Administrative Rule for the Residence Act (*Allgemeine Verwaltungsvorschrift zum Aufenthaltsgesetz*) 5.5.4.2.1.

[40] Article 11(2) Directive 2008/115/EC.

[41] Residence Act, s 11(3).

[42] Gesetzentwurf der Fraktionen der CDU/CSU und FDP, 'Entwurf eines Gesetzes zur Umsetzung aufenthaltsrechtlicher Richtlinien der Europäischen Union und zur Anpassung nationaler Rechtsvorschriften an den EU-Visakodex' (2011) Bundestagsdrucksache 17/5470, p 17.

[43] Residence Act, s 11(5).

[44] Federal Administrative Court, judgment of 13 December 2012, 1 C 14.12; Higher Administrative Court Lüneburg, judgment of 14 February 2013, 8 LC 129/12.

[45] Residence Act, s 11(4).

of a crime against peace, a war crime or a crime against humanity, or to avert a threat to the security of the Federal Republic of Germany or a terrorist threat.[46] While five years and 10 years respectively are upper limits, which allow the decision maker to determine the duration of the entry ban by recourse to the facts of the individual case and to stay below this limit, the 20-year entry ban shall in principle be imposed, unless it is an atypical case.[47]

These provisions allow for a greater differentiation, for taking the circumstances of the individual case into account when determining the length of the entry ban, and they ensure consistency with Article 11(2) Return Directive. Even though the current system refrains from establishing a schematic determination of the duration of the entry ban that was still inherent in the system of the General Administrative Rules, the present system allows the imposition of entry bans of a considerably higher duration compared to the old maximum limits of entry bans.

B. The Netherlands

An entry ban (*inreisverbod*) issued against the third-country national automatically triggers an SIS alert.[48] The *inreisverbod* must be limited in time as an indefinite *inreisverbod* infringes Article 11(2) of the Return Directive.[49] Article 66a(4) Vw 2000, which corresponds to Article 11(2) of the Return Directive, provides that the *inreisverbod* shall not exceed five years unless the foreigner poses a serious threat to public policy, public security or national security.[50] A serious threat to public policy, public security or national security can, for example, result from a drug-related crime or from a violent crime.[51]

Article 66a Vw 2000 is further specified by Article 6.5a Vb 2000. Article 6.5a(1) Vb 2000 provides for a maximum period of two years for the entry ban. By way of derogation Article 6.5a(2) provides for a maximum period of one year if the foreigner has exceeded the time by which the foreigner is allowed to stay in the Netherlands for more than three and less than 90 days. By way of derogation from the first and second paragraphs, the maximum duration of the entry ban is three years if the foreigner has been sentenced to a period of imprisonment of less than six months.[52] If the foreigner has been sentenced to a prison term of six months or more, used false or falsified travel or identity papers, has already been subject

[46] Residence Act, s 11(5a).

[47] Dollinger, '§ 11 AufenthG', para 69.

[48] Article 66a (3) Vw 2000, Article 3.103 b (1) Vb 2000.

[49] ARBvS, 19 February 2013, 201112529/1/V4.

[50] Article 11(2) Return Directive states that the entry ban 'shall not in principle exceed five years. It may however exceed five years if the third-country national represents a serious threat to public policy, public security or national security'.

[51] Further examples are listed in Article 6.5a(5) Vb 2000.

[52] Article 6.5a(3) Vb 2000.

to one or more return decisions[53] or entered the Netherlands while he was subject to an entry ban, the maximum duration of the entry ban is five years.[54] If the foreigner poses a serious threat to public policy or public security, the maximum duration of the entry ban is 10 years.[55] Such a threat can result, in particular, from a conviction for a violent crime or a drug-related crime, from a conviction for a crime which can be punished with imprisonment of more than six years, grounds listed in Article 1 F Geneva Refugee Convention or the imposition of a measure as referred to in Article 37a Dutch Criminal Code. Finally, the maximum duration of the entry ban is 20 years if the foreigner poses a serious threat to national security or if serious reasons require a duration of more than 10 years.[56]

A general determination of the duration of an entry ban without considering the individual circumstances of the case is precluded by Article 6.5a(1) Vb 2000 and Article 11(2) of the Return Directive.[57] Moreover, an entry ban can be lifted or temporarily lifted *ex officio* or due to a change of circumstances or upon request by the foreigner.[58] This discretion is further specified in Article 6.5b Vb 2000.

C. Comparison between Germany and the Netherlands Concerning the Duration of the Entry Ban

The Dutch Vb 2000 provides for maximum limits of entry bans, thereby allowing the competent authority to set the entry ban's duration below these limits. This enables the decision maker to take the facts of the individual case into account as required by Article 11(2) of the Return Directive and to determine the duration of the entry ban in accordance with the individual circumstances. The maximum duration provided for by the Dutch system is relatively high compared to the system which was previously provided for by the German General Administrative Rules. However, compared to the current German system, it exhibits several similarities. Both countries provide for a maximum duration of the entry ban of 20 years. However, in the Netherlands 20 years is the upper limit for an *inreisverbod*,[59] which means that the competent authority can impose an entry ban that falls below this limit. In Germany, by contrast, the entry ban shall be 20 years if the foreigner was expelled on grounds of a crime against peace, a war crime or a crime

[53] The IND or the civil servant responsible for border control or control of foreigners issues an *inreisverbod* in application of Article 6.5a (4)(c) Vb 2000 when issuing the third return decision, A4/2.3 Vc 2000.

[54] Article 6.5a(4) Vb 2000.

[55] Article 6.5a(5) Vb 2000.

[56] Article 6.5a(6) Vb 2000.

[57] Rechtbank 's-Gravenhage, 3 December 2012, AWB 12/22644.

[58] Article 66b(1) Vw 2000.

[59] Article 6.5a(6) Vb 2000.

against humanity, or to avert a threat to the security of the Federal Republic of Germany or a terrorist threat.[60]

In contrast to the German Residence Act, the Dutch Vb provides for a more nuanced system. First, it establishes a more fine-grained system of time limits for the entry bans by providing for entry bans of one, two, three, five, 10 and 20 years. The German system, by contrast, differentiates between entry bans of five, 10 and 20 years.

Second, the provisions in the Netherlands are more specific than the German provisions as they link the maximum duration of the entry ban to the duration of a conviction. The maximum duration of the entry ban in the Netherlands is three years if the foreigner has been sentenced to a period of imprisonment of less than six months.[61] If the prison term is six months or longer, the maximum duration of the entry ban is five years.[62] An entry ban with a maximum duration of 10 years can, among other reasons, be imposed if the foreigner has been sentenced to a prison term for a violent or drug-related crime.[63]

The German provision, by contrast, merely stipulates that the entry ban shall not exceed 10 years if the foreigner was expelled on grounds of a criminal conviction or if the foreigner poses a serious threat to public policy or public security,[64] thereby allowing a greater discretion to the decision maker than the Dutch provisions. Interestingly, the crimes listed in Article 1 F Geneva Refugee Convention, which comprise crimes against peace, war crimes, and crimes against humanity, shall trigger a 20-year entry ban in Germany,[65] whereas they can lead to an entry ban of a maximum duration of 10 years in the Netherlands.[66]

IV. Summary and Conclusions

This chapter recalled the differences between the German and Dutch systems regarding the termination of lawful residence after a criminal conviction.[67] Moreover, it addressed the imposition of national entry bans and their duration as well as the question of whether an alert can be entered into the SIS.

The first area where differences can occur relates to the termination of lawful residence after a criminal conviction.[68] The Dutch sliding scale[69] bars the termination of lawful residence following a criminal conviction if the criminal offence is

[60] Residence Act, s 11(5a).
[61] Article 6.5a(3) Vb 2000.
[62] Article 6.5a(4)(a) Vb 2000.
[63] Article 6.5(5) Vb 2000.
[64] Residence Act, s 11(5).
[65] Residence Act, s 11(5a).
[66] Article 6.5a (5)(c) Vb 2000.
[67] See Chapters 5, 6 and 8.
[68] See Chapter 5 and 6.
[69] Article 3.86 Vb 2000.

not serious enough in light of the duration of the foreigner's lawful residence. If, conversely, lawful residence does not outweigh the criminal conviction and residence can be terminated, a balancing process between the interests of the foreigner and the interests of the state must be conducted, which has to take Article 8 ECHR into account.[70] The termination of lawful residence is a return decision[71] and can comprise an entry ban.[72]

The German statutory system always requires a balancing process between the interests of the foreigner and the interests of the state,[73] whereby the statutory provisions attach a specific weight to certain interests of the state[74] and interests of the foreigner[75] respectively. The German system does not provide for a sliding scale and consequently does not bar the termination of residence in certain cases. Hence, the termination of residence could be barred by the Dutch sliding scale where the duration of lawful residence outweighs the seriousness of the crime, whereas the same case, if decided by German authorities, might lead to the conclusion that the state's interest in expelling the foreigner outweighs the foreigner's interest, in which case the foreigner has to be expelled.[76]

Second, the rules on national entry bans and SIS alerts differ. In Germany an expulsion decision triggers a national entry ban,[77] which has to be limited in time. As regards the entry of an SIS alert, the Residence Act (section 50(6) second sentence) grants discretion to the competent authority and thereby requires a balancing process, which precludes any automatism between the national entry ban and the SIS alert. In the Netherlands the termination of lawful residence after a criminal conviction and the issuance of an entry ban (*inreisverbod*) both have their own framework of assessment. In contrast to the German system, which bars any automatism, the national entry ban for the Netherlands automatically leads to an SIS alert. The issuance of a national entry ban (*inreisverbod*) is obligatory in situations covered by Article 66a(1) Vw 2000 but despite its obligatory nature the competent authority must refrain from imposing an entry ban if EU law, in particular the principle of proportionality[78] and fundamental rights, would be violated. In the remaining cases the competent authority has discretion regarding the imposition of the entry ban, which is further specified by the Vc 2000.

Third, the rules for the determination of the duration of the entry ban differ in certain points. The German system previously linked the duration of the national

[70] Article 3.86(17) Vb 2000.
[71] Article 27(2)(c) Vw 2000.
[72] Article 27(4) Vw 2000.
[73] Residence Act, s 53.
[74] Residence Act, s 54.
[75] Residence Act, s 55.
[76] Residence Act, s 53(1).
[77] Residence Act, s 11(1).
[78] *Zh* and *O*, paras 49, 50.

entry ban and the SIS alert to the different grounds for an expulsion decision, whereby the duration of the national entry ban and the SIS alert were not necessarily identical. The new German system sets maximum thresholds (apart from the 20-year duration of the entry ban) and requires the decision maker to establish the duration of the entry ban with due regard to the facts of the individual case.[79] In contrast to the old system, the new maximum limits for national entry bans are relatively high. The new system provides for three different time limits – five, 10 and 20 years – leaving a broad margin of discretion to the national decision maker. In particular in situations concerning entry bans triggered by an expulsion decision following a criminal conviction, the decision maker enjoys a considerable margin of discretion as section 11(5) Residence Act only stipulates that the entry ban shall not exceed 10 years.[80] The Dutch system also establishes maximum thresholds for the national entry ban (*inreisverbod*), which provide legal certainty as the duration of the entry ban cannot exceed the limit. At the same time, these provisions leave discretion to the competent authority to take the particulars of the individual case into account and to establish the duration of the entry ban in light of these circumstances. In contrast to the German system, the Dutch system circumscribes the decision maker's discretion to a greater extent by establishing more maximum limits for the duration of the entry ban and by linking the entry ban's maximum duration to the maximum duration of the imposed prison term.

The previous sections demonstrated that national decisions terminating lawful residence after a criminal conviction can differ, depending on the facts of the case, as Germany and the Netherlands use different mechanisms and thresholds for determining whether residence has to be terminated or not. Therefore, situations can arise in which residence could no longer be terminated in the Netherlands, as the duration of the foreigner's lawful residence outweighs the imposed prison term, whereas, in a comparable situation, the balancing process between the interests of the foreigner and the interests of the state that has to be conducted by the German authorities could lead to the conclusion that the interests of the state have more weight than the foreigner's interests, in which case an expulsion decision has to be issued.

While an entry ban and thereby an SIS alert would not be issued in the Netherlands, a national entry ban for the German territory would be issued. Moreover, an SIS alert could be issued, thereby giving a European dimension to the national (German) entry ban. The Netherlands would in principle have to recognise the German SIS alert, even if it would not have issued an entry ban (*inreisverbod*) which leads to an SIS alert. These disparities have effects on the common European approach to migration as the re-entry of the third-country

[79] Residence Act, s 11(3).
[80] Residence Act, s 11(5).

national to the Schengen area would in principle be barred due to the German SIS alert, even though s/he would not be barred in a comparable situation had the case been decided in the Netherlands.

Even if both Member States issued SIS alerts, the duration of the alerts entered by the Member States could differ. Despite these possible differences, in principle alerts are mutually recognised. In light of these discrepancies the next chapter discusses options to remedy remaining problems.

11

Options to Remedy Remaining Divergences

The previous two chapters demonstrated that the present system still exhibits some divergences both at the national and the European level, even though major improvements have already been made.

At the EU level, the 2018 SIS Regulation improved the coordination between the SIS Regulation and the Return Directive, which can both attach a European effect to a national expulsion decision and entry ban. In contrast to the old SIS II Regulation, the SIS Regulation now stipulates that an entry ban according to the Return Directive shall lead to an SIS alert. Moreover, the SIS Regulation has specified the requirements for entering alerts for the purpose of refusing entry to third-country nationals, which in turn limits the margin of discretion of states and thereby reduces divergences between the reasons for entering an alert. Member States' discretion in the context of the Return Directive has been limited by the CJEU's interpretation of the notion of public policy in the *Zh* and *O* case and subsequent cases.[1] However, both the Return Directive and the SIS Regulation still afford discretion to the Member States, which allows entry bans and SIS alerts to be imposed for different reasons.

At the national level, the reform of the German system on expulsion as well as the alignment of the provisions on entry bans to the requirements of the Return Directive have reduced differences between the German and Dutch systems. Despite these major improvements, differences still exist between the German and Dutch approaches regarding termination of residence following a criminal conviction, the requirements for entering an alert into the SIS, and the duration of an SIS alert. Therefore, this chapter discusses different options to remedy the remaining problems and the likelihood of the implementation of these options. It starts with a brief overview of the deficiencies of the current system (Section I), followed by a discussion of the options to remedy these deficiencies (Section II). The proposed options are EU-wide rules for expulsion decisions, two types of entry ban, a reorganisation of the current system that draws on historic examples, and a

[1] Case C-554/13 *Zh* and *O* ECLI:EU:C:2015:377, [2015], paras 50, 60; Case C-373/13 *H. T.* ECLI:EU:C:2015:413, [2015], para 79; Case C-601/15 PPU *J. N.* ECLI:EU:C:2016:84, [2016], paras 65, 65; Case C-240/17 *E.* ECLI:EU:C:2018:8, [2018], para 49; *WM* ECLI:EU:C:2020:511, [2020], para 45.

further clarification of the notion of public policy. Subsequently, the likelihood of a harmonisation of the criteria for national expulsion decisions (Section III) and a further specification of the criteria for entering alerts into the SIS are examined (Section IV). The chapter closes with final remarks and an outlook (Section V).

I. Deficiencies of the Current System

Article 24 of the SIS Regulation sets out the 'conditions for issuing alerts on refusal of entry or stay' in respect of third-country nationals. It is based on national decisions that have been taken in accordance with national law and which have culminated in a 'national alert for refusal of entry and stay'.[2] The existing system 'borrows' from the different national systems, which affords Member States autonomy to accommodate their national policy decisions. It relies on mutual recognition of national decisions taken on the basis of criteria established by the different Schengen states rather than fully harmonising the criteria that have to be applied by all participating states. The criteria that are contained in Article 24 of the SIS Regulation are already more specific than the criteria of the predecessor regulation[3] but they are still sufficiently vague to accommodate a range of different national provisions and thereby a variety of individual conducts leading to an SIS alert. Article 24(2)(a) stipulates that, following a proportionality assessment, an alert shall be entered if the 'presence of that third-country national on its territory poses a threat to public policy, to public security or to national security'. One of the three exhaustive examples where such a situation shall arise is if the third-country national 'has been convicted in a Member State of an offence carrying a penalty involving the deprivation of liberty of at least one year'.[4] This provision grants states a considerable discretion as it establishes a relatively low threshold by referring to an offence carrying a penalty involving the deprivation of liberty of at least one year.

The development of a list of crimes which can lead to an SIS alert could reduce Member States' diverging approaches to some extent. The reference contained in Article 15(1)(b) of the draft SIS II Regulation to the offences listed in the instrument regarding the European arrest warrant would have been a first step to limit the number of criminal offences that can lead to an SIS alert. However, even if the required prison term were specified, differences could still occur among the states because the penal framework of the Member States differs. Moreover, Member States attach a different weight to the lawful residence of the foreigner when relating it to the imposed prison term, as demonstrated by the comparison between Germany and the Netherlands. Consequently, it would also be necessary to adjust the weight that is attached to the respective criteria in the balancing process.

[2] Article 24(1) Regulation (EU) 2018/1861.
[3] Regulation (EC) 2006/1987.
[4] Article 24(2)(a) Regulation (EU) 2018/1861.

However, a criminal conviction is not even required for an SIS alert. The second situation where an SIS alert shall be entered, provided that the requirements of Article 24(1)(a) are met, concerns 'serious grounds for believing that a third-country national has committed a serious criminal offence, including a terrorist offence, or there are clear indications of his or her intention to commit such an offence in the territory of a Member State'.[5] Divergences between Member States can be even greater regarding those alerts. These differences have an impact on the question of whether a national entry ban will be issued, which in turn affects the applicability of Article 24(1)(a) of the SIS Regulation as it presupposes a national alert for refusal of entry and stay.

Article 11(1) of the Return Directive establishes two cases in which an entry ban is mandatory and states that in other cases a return decision may be accompanied by an entry ban. A return decision is defined by Article 3(4) of the Return Directive as 'an administrative or judicial decision or act, stating or declaring the stay of a third-country national to be illegal and imposing or stating an obligation to return'. The illegality of the stay is primarily determined by national law, despite the conditions on entry listed in the Schengen Borders Code. A return decision is taken on the basis of national criteria and can be linked to an entry ban which is in principle binding for other Member States.

Moreover, there is a lack of coordination between the SIS Regulation and the Return Directive concerning the discretion granted to Member States. The SIS Regulation prescribes the entry of an alert, provided that the criteria of Article 24(1)(a) are met, in three cases that are exhaustively listed in Article 24(2). The discretion that had been granted by the SIS II Regulation,[6] which provided in Article 24(3) that Member States 'may' enter an alert, has been abolished by the SIS Regulation. Even though the Return Directive prescribes the imposition of an entry ban in two situations,[7] it also provides that 'In other cases return decisions may be accompanied by an entry ban'.[8] This provision grants a considerable discretion to the Member States to impose entry bans, which shall then lead to an SIS alert.[9]

Another problem relates to the duration of the SIS alert and entry ban, respectively. The Return Directive stipulates that the entry ban shall, in principle, not exceed five years unless 'the third-country national represents a serious threat to public policy, public security or national security'.[10] It refrains, however, from imposing an upper limit. Even though the Netherlands and Germany both establish an upper limit of a 20-year entry ban for specific crimes, these crimes differ in the Netherlands and Germany, respectively. Moreover, the Netherlands provides

[5] See Article 24(2)(b) of Regulation (EU) 2018/1841.
[6] Regulation (EC) 1987/2006.
[7] Article 11(1)(a) and (b) of Directive 2008/115/EC.
[8] Article 11(1) of Directive 2008/115/EC.
[9] Article 24(1)(b) of Regulation (EU) 2018/1861.
[10] Article 11(2) of Directive 2008/115/EC.

for a more specific and nuanced system with a greater number of limits for the determination of the duration of the entry ban in comparison to the German system. Taking a brief look at other countries, the 2020 study on the Return Directive conducted by the European Parliamentary Research Service points out that 'While some countries do not clarify the length of an entry ban related to public order (BG), others do (EL) and have sometimes various thresholds (DE and IT)'.[11] Moreover, the study points out that 'the most common length of an entry ban is one year in SE, three years in ES, and five years in BG'.[12] Given that differences between the Member States regarding the duration of the entry ban result in differences in the third-country national's possibilities to return to the Schengen area and thereby negatively impact the common European approach to migration, the rules on the duration of entry bans should be specified. Moreover, the duration of the entry ban according to the Return Directive, which shall in principle not exceed five years,[13] and the SIS Regulation, which stipulates that alerts shall in principle be reviewed after three years,[14] should be aligned.

Finally, the legal position of third-country nationals who are covered by EU law needs to be addressed. Third-country family members of EU citizens can still be subject to an SIS alert but not to an entry ban according to the Return Directive. Even though the CJEU already clarified in *Commission v Spain* the criteria that have to be observed when entering a third-country family member, who is covered by the Citizenship Directive,[15] into the SIS, and even though these criteria are to some extent reflected in Article 26 of the SIS Regulation, a synchronisation between the personal scope of the SIS Regulation and the Return Directive would be welcome.

II. Options for Improvement

The above-mentioned deficiencies can be addressed from different angles or starting points. The proposals to address these deficiencies are inextricably linked but are nevertheless introduced separately in order to provide a better overview.

A. EU-wide Rules for Expulsion Decisions

A greater coherence might be achieved by a harmonisation of the grounds for adopting expulsion decisions which then lead to an SIS alert. If national requirements

[11] K Eisele (ed), European Parliamentary Research Service, 'The Return Directive 2008/115/EC, European Implementation Assessment' 80.

[12] ibid.

[13] Article 11(2) return Directive.

[14] Article 39(2) Regulation (EU) 2018/1861.

[15] The Citizenship Directive was not applicable to the case but rather Directive 64/221/EEC, which was replaced by the Citizenship Directive.

for expulsion decisions were the same in all Member States and if the decisions based on these requirements triggered an SIS alert, differences regarding the entry of an SIS alert could, at least to a certain extent, be reduced. The 2002 Green Paper on a Community Return Policy underpins that the Commission sought to achieve a greater level of harmonisation regarding expulsion decisions. It stated that Directive 2001/40/EC on the mutual recognition of decisions on the expulsion of third-country nationals sets 'initial standards for expulsion'.[16] The Commission suggested that 'on the basis of these general definitions more detailed, specific statutory grounds for an expulsion decision could be developed'.[17] Interestingly, the paper proposed that a distinction could be drawn 'between mandatory reasons for expulsion decisions on the grounds of extraordinary danger and other legitimate reasons, which would normally lead to an expulsion decision'.[18] The Green Paper proposed that mandatory expulsion decisions could be established in two cases: first, when a third-country national is sentenced to a prison term for a period of time that has to be mutually agreed by the Member States; and second, if the third-country national has been sentenced to a term of imprisonment for specific intentional criminal acts, such as the 'production, transport and sale of drugs, the smuggling or trafficking of human beings, terrorism and other offences against national security'.[19] Moreover, the Green Paper stated that 'it could be assessed whether other compelling reasons, such as the threat to national or public security' should lead to a mandatory SIS alert.[20] Subsequently, the Green Paper emphasised that an expulsion decision 'cannot be taken regardless of the character of the residence status' and listed certain groups of individuals that require special protection and 'may only be removed for grave reasons of public security and public order'.[21] Importantly, the Green Paper stipulated that 'Special protection might also be envisaged for third-country nationals, who are born in a Member State and have never lived in their country of nationality'.[22]

Later in 2002 the Commission tabled a Communication stipulating that 'minimum standards on expulsion decisions should be set at the EU level, defining mandatory and other grounds for expulsion, identifying groups with specific protection needs …'.[23] On a positive note, it stands out that the Green Paper explicitly refers to the residence status of the individual concerned and acknowledges the need for special protection of de facto natives.

The Commission's proposal to establish mandatory expulsions could indeed enhance coherence and reduce diverging approaches as it would be mandatory

[16] COM(2002) 175 final, p 12.
[17] ibid, p 13.
[18] ibid.
[19] ibid.
[20] ibid.
[21] ibid.
[22] ibid.
[23] COM(2002) 564 final.

for expulsion decisions to be taken in certain situations. At the same time, such an approach is difficult to reconcile with the principle of proportionality. Given that the abolished German system employed the concept of mandatory expulsion, which could not be maintained due to its incompatibility with Article 8 ECHR, it should not be introduced at the European level.

Even in the absence of mandatory expulsions, an EU-wide system that specifies the grounds for an expulsion decision, ie by providing for specific crimes combined with a specific minimum prison term, could still lead to diverging expulsion decisions. First, and as argued above, the penal frameworks of the Member States differ. Second, in the absence of mandatory expulsion decisions, a balancing process between the interests of the individual and the interests of the state has to be conducted. This balancing process could lead to diverging outcomes as different states attach a different weight to the factors in the balancing process. Moreover, such a system would have to clarify whether lawful residence can be terminated on grounds other than a criminal conviction. All three instruments – CISA, the 2006 SIS II Regulation and the 2018 SIS Regulation – provide for the possibility to enter an SIS alert if 'serious grounds for believing that the third-country national has committed serious criminal offences' exist or if there is clear evidence/indication of an intention to commit such an offence,[24] with the 2018 SIS Regulation explicitly referring to terrorist offences. In contrast to CISA, the 2006 and the 2018 SIS Regulations even provide that such a situation shall lead to an SIS alert. The vagueness of these provisions is difficult to reconcile with the principle of legal certainty but underpins states' strong interest in keeping this ground for an SIS alert. Even if the grounds leading to expulsion were harmonised, the retention of such a vague provision, which grants states considerable discretion, could undermine the purpose of a harmonisation, provided that such a provision was kept.

Importantly, the proposed system seems to imply an internal–external parallel. A national expulsion decision could only be adopted on the basis of a European provision which then triggers an EU-wide entry ban. It would require a harmonisation of the national rules regarding expulsion, which does not seem realistic. The comparison between Germany and the Netherlands already demonstrated that the rules applicable in those two states differ and a harmonisation of all different systems is currently not conceivable. Moreover, it would affect the competence of the Member States to decide on their internal public policy rules. The European Union is, as clarified by Article 72 TFEU, barred from exhaustively regulating the content and consequences of the internal public policy of the Member States in areas covered by Title V TFEU.

Finally, there is a risk that Member States with the strictest rules will refuse to commit to such system unless their rules are reflected at EU level, which might in the end lead to a deterioration of the legal position of third-country nationals.

[24] Article 96(2)(b) CISA, Article 24(2)(b) Regulation (EC) 2006/1987, Article 24(2)(b) Regulation (EU) 2018/1861.

This speaks in favour of specifying the requirements for entering an alert into the SIS rather than harmonising the grounds for an expulsion decision. Only the entry of an alert into the SIS can give a European dimension to domestic expulsion decisions. Hence, if the requirements for entering an alert into the SIS were specified and if it were provided that only certain expulsion decisions could lead to an SIS alert, the concretisation of the criteria for an SIS alert could produce the same results as a harmonisation of the reasons for an expulsion decision following a criminal conviction which could then lead to an SIS alert. Moreover, the concretisation of the criteria for entering an SIS alert would have the advantage of addressing entry bans that are unrelated to expulsion decisions. It thereby has a broader scope and is more likely to remedy the differences regarding possible SIS alerts that are not based upon a criminal conviction.

B. Two Types of Entry Ban Entered into the SIS

A higher threshold or more specific requirements for entering an alert into the SIS would limit Member States' discretion and would reduce the divergences between alerts. A first step in this direction was already made by Article 15 of the draft SIS II Regulation, which referred to the offences listed in Article 2(2) of Framework decision 2002/584/JHA on the European arrest warrant. The fact that this reference was not kept in the final version of the Regulation provides evidence that Member States are not very likely to agree on the specification of offences that can lead to an alert. Moreover, a list of offences that can lead to an SIS alert would reduce but not solve the problem of diverging entries given that Member States can attach a different weight to the particulars of the individual case, such as the duration of the foreigner's lawful residence. Therefore, as a variant of this system, it might be considered to provide for two types of entry bans which are both entered into the SIS: a binding and a non-binding entry ban.

A state could enter an SIS alert which is absolutely binding for other Member States or an alert which grants other Member States discretion to depart from it. This would grant Member States sufficient discretion to enter SIS alerts for other reasons or offences than those mutually agreed upon by all states, which affords them the possibility to express their national priorities. Other states, in turn, would not be obliged to recognise this alert and they would not be bound by it. Compared to the present system, this variant would imply an extension of the exceptions allowing a state to depart from an SIS alert.

However, it is debatable whether this approach would reform the currently existing practice. Member States might be inclined to refuse a third-country national access to their territory if the person were subject to an SIS alert issued by another Member State, even if this alert were not binding. In the end, this approach could have the same effects for the individual as the system that is currently in place. Moreover, Member States implement EU law when entering alerts and are bound by the CFR,[25] in particular by Article 47 and Article 7. Article 47 (right to an effective remedy and to a fair trial) comprises the obligation of the administration to give reasons for a decision that encroaches upon the right of the affected person in order to enable him or her to bring an action against this decision. Consequently, Member States are obliged to give reasons for their decisions, both for the entry of an alert and the rejection of the foreigner's application for entry. Insofar as respect for private and family life (Article 7 CFR) is affected by the decision to refuse entry, the competent authority has to balance the rights of the third-country national against the interests of the state and substantiate its decision. The requirement to assess the application for entry and residence of a third-country national who is subject to a non-binding entry ban causes an additional administrative burden, which might increase opposition by the Member States to such an approach.

C. Inspirations Drawn from Historic Examples

A brief look at the structure of expulsion decisions in the German *Reich*[26] might be instructive for the structure of a possible European provision. The German *Reich*, established in 1871, was a federal state which consisted of several entities called *Bundesstaaten* (federal states). The legislative competence regarding criminal law and foreigner law rested with the *Reich*.[27] The *Reich* used its power to regulate expulsion decisions only very scarcely.[28] Moreover, it had no power to execute an expulsion decision. Provisions in the Criminal Code provided for expulsion decisions against foreigners who committed serious crimes but also crimes such as gambling (section 284(2) Reichsstrafgesetzbuch – RStGB), unwillingness to work and begging (sections 361 and 362 RStGB). Moreover, Jesuits could be expelled.[29] On the basis of their territorial sovereignty, *Bundesstaaten* were able to expel a foreigner on grounds of mere disutility.[30] Expulsion decisions from a *Bundesstaat* did not entail the termination of residence in the *Reich*, even though in practice most *Bundesstaaten* were not willing to accept a foreigner who was subject to an expulsion decision by another *Bundesstaat*.[31] Nevertheless, under certain conditions, a *Bundesstaat* was obliged to take back a foreigner.[32] Expulsion decisions

[25] Article 51(1) CFR.

[26] For a brief overview see G Renner, 'Staatliche Souveränität und die Verweigerung des weiteren Aufenthalts, Zur Geschichte des deutschen Ausweisungsrechts' in K Barwig, G Brinkmann, B Huber, K Lörcher and C Schumacher (eds), *Ausweisung im demokratischen Rechtsstaat, Hohenheimer Tage zum Ausländerrecht 1995* (Baden-Baden, Nomos, 1996) 23–28.

[27] Article 4(13) Reichsverfassung of 16 April 1871.

[28] M Schuback, *Die Ausweisung nach dem Ausländergesetz in der Rechtsprechungskonzeption der Gerichte* (Frankfurt, Peter Lang, 2003) 33.

[29] G Renner, *Ausländerrecht in Deutschland* (Munich, C.H. Beck, 1998) 10.

[30] ibid, 11; Renner, 'Staatliche Souveränität und die Verweigerung des weiteren Aufenthalts' 29.

[31] Renner, 'Staatliche Souveränität und die Verweigerung des weiteren Aufenthalts' 29.

[32] ibid: namely when the foreigner was dependent on assistance in that *Bundesstaat*.

against nationals of one *Bundesstaat* by another *Bundesstaat* were barred by Article 3 of the 1871 Constitution. In addition to expelling foreigners from their territory, *Bundesstaaten* were also entitled to expel foreigners from the territory of the *Reich* if these foreigners committed crimes listed in the Criminal Code or criminal provisions of the *Reich*.[33]

A distinction between an expulsion from a part of the territory and the whole territory could also be established at the EU level. Where the third-country national has committed (a) very severe crime(s), which are to be defined by the Member States, they should be able to expel this foreigner from the territory of the European Union – a power Member States currently do not possess – combined with an EU-wide entry ban/SIS alert. This system exhibits certain parallels with the current system.

In the remaining cases, Member States could issue an expulsion decision against a third-country national, which obliges the foreigner to leave the territory of the respective Member State but not the territory of the European Union, which mirrors the currently existing national entry ban. Since the foreigner is not obliged to leave the territory of the European Union, an alert could not be entered into the SIS. The Member State could, however, issue a national entry ban. If the foreigner previously resided in another Member State an obligation of this other Member State to take back the foreigner could be considered.[34]

Such a system would entail a partial departure from the system of mutual recognition regarding those cases that are not serious enough to trigger an expulsion decision from the territory of the European Union. Regarding those cases in which an expulsion from the European Union can be ordered, the decisions are mutually recognised but they would be taken on the basis of uniform criteria mutually agreed on by the states. The differentiation provided for by this system would limit interference with the legislative sovereignty of the Member States. Member States would still be able to define, independently from the coordination with the other participating states, the criteria to determine whether there is a threat to their national public policy or public security. A threat to their national public policy or public security could then trigger a national expulsion decision leading to a national entry ban which is not entered into the SIS.

A clear downside of this system is the lack of compatibility or alignment with the SIS, which is a compensatory measure for the abolition of internal borders. In a Europe without borders there is no possibility to prevent the re-entry of an individual with regard to whom only a national entry ban was issued. It could only be prevented by reinstating border checks, which in turn undermines the purpose of Schengen.

[33] The competence to issue an expulsion decision from the *Reich* rested with the higher police authority, section 39(2) Criminal Code 1871.

[34] A similar procedure is provided for in Article 22(2) and (3) LTR Directive.

D. Further Clarification of the Notion of Public Policy in the SIS Regulation and the Return Directive

The concept of public policy is central to the SIS as its declared purpose is 'the maintenance of public security and public policy and the safeguarding of security in the territories of the Member States'.[35] An alert shall be entered into the SIS if an entry ban in terms of the Return Directive has been imposed[36] or if the 'presence of that third-country national on the (Member State's) territory poses a threat to public policy, to public security or to national security'.[37] The SIS Regulation determines which national public policy decisions can be entered into the SIS by providing for an exhaustive list in Article 24(2).

Taking a brief look at the early 2000s, the need for narrowing and clarifying the notion of public policy and the criteria for entering alerts into the SIS, respectively, had already been discussed. In 2000, ILPA[38] and MPG[39] tabled a proposal for 'Directive 2000/04 on border controls ensuring the absence of any controls on persons when crossing internal borders and establishing measures concerning the crossing of the external borders of the Member States, including the issue of long-term visas'.[40] The proposed Article 28(2)–(4), which aimed at replacing Article 96 CISA (now Article 24 of the SIS Regulation), read as follows:

> (2) A third-country national's name may only be reported for the purposes of being refused entry if he or she represents a fundamental present threat to the public policy or public security of a Member State, in accordance with Articles 2(2), 3(1) and 3(2) of Directive 64/221, by reason of conduct having an effect that would be subject to repressive measures throughout the European Community and that can be demonstrated to the satisfaction of a court of competent jurisdiction in accordance with Article 32. The conduct in question must be such that it has led to a substantial sentence of imprisonment, or would have led to such a substantial sentence had it been the subject of criminal proceedings.
>
> (3) A person cannot be reported for the purposes of being refused entry pursuant to paragraph 2 if there has been a substantial lapse of time since that person's criminal convictions and there has been no further criminal conviction.
>
> (4) A citizen of the European Union and members of his or her family, as defined by Community law, cannot be reported as persons not to be permitted entry. If a third-country national acquires the citizenship of the Union or the status of a family member of a citizen of the Union, Member States shall ensure that his or her name shall be immediately removed from the list of persons not to be permitted entry.[41]

[35] Article 1 Regulation (EU) 2018/1861.
[36] Article 24(1)(b) Regulation (EU) 2018/1861.
[37] Article 24(1)(a) Regulation (EU) 2018/1861.
[38] Immigration Law Practitioners' Association.
[39] Migration Policy Group.
[40] Migration Policy Group, 'ILPA/MPG Amsterdam Proposals' (London/Brussels, 2000) p 175.
[41] ibid, pp 187, 188.

According to the explanation provided by ILPA/MPG, given the drastic nature of the SIS alert, which leads to an exclusion from the territory of the Union, it would be unfair to have diverging national systems for excluding an individual.[42] Article 28(2) is designed to replace Article 96(2) and (3) CISA (now Article 24 of the SIS Regulation) and specifies the requirements for entering an alert into the SIS, which were considered 'vague and non-exhaustive'.[43] Article 28(3) aims at taking the rehabilitation of ex-offenders into account. Article 28(4) excludes EU citizens and members of their families from the scope of the draft Directive. The draft Article 28(4) is also designed to apply to all family members of Union citizens, not just those who exercised their right of free movement.[44]

Article 28(4) of the draft Directive would have avoided the case of *Commission v Spain*, in which a third-country national family member of an EU citizen was listed in the SIS and was consequently refused entry. Importantly, Article 28(2) of the proposal would have introduced a parallel between the notion of public policy used in the context of EU citizens (at that time Directive 64/221/EEC) and the notion of public policy used in the context of Schengen. The need to improve the coordination of the interpretation of public policy was also acknowledged by the European Parliament in 2000, when it pointed out that it 'Deplores, in a "European area of freedom", the abusive use by Member States of public policy as grounds for expulsions'.[45] Moreover, it considered 'it essential, therefore, for Member States to endeavour to ensure that they improve their coordination of the interpretation of the concept of public policy, particularly in the context of the Schengen agreements'.[46] In 2007 Schmid-Drüner noted that the lack of harmonisation of the notion of public policy carries the risk of an inconsistent application of EU law, which could hamper European integration.[47] The CJEU ultimately limited Member States' discretion in the *Zh* and *O* case[48] when it specified the notion of public policy in the context of the Return Directive, by aligning it to the definition provided by Article 27(2) of the Citizenship Directive. In order to enhance clarity and legal certainty, the requirements that have been established by the CJEU should be codified in the Return Directive and the SIS Regulation, as already mentioned above.

[42] ibid, p 170.

[43] ibid.

[44] ibid, p 171.

[45] European Parliament resolution on the report from the Commission to the Council and the European Parliament on the implementation of Directives 90/364, 90/365 and 93/96 (right of residence) and on the communication from the Commission on the special measures concerning the movement and residence of citizens of the Union which are justified on grounds of public policy, public security or public health (COM(1999)127, COM(99)372–C5-0177/1999, C5-0178/1999–1999/2157(COS)), www.europarl.europa.eu/sides/getDoc.do?reference=P5-TA-2000-0368&type=TA&language=EN&redirect point 6.

[46] ibid.

[47] M Schmid-Drüner, *Der Begriff der öffentlichen Sicherheit und Ordnung im Einwanderungsrecht ausgewählter EU-Mitgliedstaaten* (Baden-Baden, Nomos, 2007) 461.

[48] *Zh* and O, paras 50 and 60.

In the codification process, not only the requirements contained in Article 27(2) but also the requirements contained in Article 28(1) of the Citizenship Directive should be used as a reference point for an SIS alert. Article 28(1) requires that considerations such as the duration of the foreigner's residence on the territory, his or her age, 'state of health, family and economic situation, social and cultural integration into the host Member State and the extent of his/her links with the country of origin' have to be assessed.[49] These factors would provide a better structure to the balancing process and have the advantage of accommodating the conditions for expulsion decisions against long-term resident third-country nationals that are contained in Article 12(3) of the LTR Directive.

Even though Article 24(1) of the SIS Regulation prescribes an individual assessment, the explicit mentioning of specific balancing factors of Article 28(1) of the Citizenship Directive such as the 'family and economic situation, social and cultural integration into the host Member State' can improve compliance with the requirements of Article 7 of the Charter, which provides for the right to respect for private and family life.

III. Likelihood of a Harmonisation of the Criteria for National Expulsion Decisions

Indications regarding the likelihood of harmonisation can be drawn from different sources, such as comments in the literature, reactions to proposed legislation and the differences between draft legislation and the finally adopted version of that legislation.

The European Commission's Green Paper on a Community Return Policy tabled in April 2002 clarified that the Commission strove for a greater level of harmonisation. The paper stated that Directive 2001/40/EC on the mutual recognition of decisions on expulsion of third-country nationals sets 'initial standards for expulsion' and proposed that 'on the basis of these general definitions more detailed, specific statutory grounds for an expulsion decision could be developed'.[50] Further, it suggested that a distinction 'between mandatory reasons for expulsion decisions on the grounds of extraordinary danger and other legitimate reasons' could be drawn.

The Council, by contrast, was more reserved. The Presidency Note from November 2002 regarding the 'Proposal for a Return Action Programme' addresses the preconditions for expulsion decisions, points to the rules on expulsion contained in Articles 5, 23 and 96 of the Schengen Convention and states that Directive 2001/40/EC further elaborated these rules. Regarding Directive 2001/40/EC,

[49] Article 28(1) of Directive 2004/38/EC.
[50] COM(2002) 175 final, p 13.

the Council noted that the 'implementation of these initial standards provided for in the Directive should create the foundation for further considerations on harmonisation in this field'.[51]

Comparing the Commission's and the Council's wording regarding the function of Directive 2001/40/EC for further harmonisation, it stands out that the Commission considers it to be a general basis upon which 'more detailed, specific statutory grounds for an expulsion decision could be developed', whereas the Council considers it a 'foundation for further considerations on harmonisation'. It is a small difference, but a foundation for further consideration is less specific and also weaker than the wording chosen by the Commission.

Moreover, the Council stated that it

> might be examined whether it would be appropriate to make a distinction between the reasons for expulsion decisions on the grounds of a serious threat to public order or to national security and other legitimate reasons which would normally lead to an expulsion decision.[52]

Again, the Council's reaction to the Commission's proposal to differentiate between mandatory reasons for expulsion decisions and other reasons was rather restrained as it merely stated that it 'might be examined'.

Further indications regarding the likelihood of a harmonisation can be drawn from the developments and reactions to the proposal for a Return Directive. The Commission Staff Working Paper from 2005 acknowledged that 'the common return policy should not be seen as a self-standing policy but as part of a complex European immigration policy' which comprises not only the immigration of third-country nationals, but also the termination of legal stay.[53] The Commission proposal for a Return Directive from the same day clarified that the Directive does not aim at harmonising or setting common standards for expulsion on grounds of public policy or public security, 'even if there was a case for further harmonizing the issue'.[54] Even though the Commission initially considered a broader approach and still acknowledges that there might be 'a case for further harmonising this issue', it excludes this harmonisation from the scope of the Directive. According to the Council, 'there is no need to include the subject matter dealt with in Directive 2001/40/EC' into the scope of the Return Directive.[55] Lutz points out that the harmonisation of the reasons leading to expulsion was excluded from the proposal

[51] Council of the European Union, Note from the Presidency, 'Proposal for a Return Action Programme', 25 November 2002, doc 14673/02, p 23.

[52] ibid.

[53] SEC(2005)1057, Commission Staff Working Document, Annex to the Proposal for a European Parliament and Council Directive on common standards on procedures in Member States for returning illegally staying third-country nationals – Impact Assessment, p 10.

[54] COM(2005) 391 final, Proposal for a Directive of the European Parliament and of the Council on common standards and procedures in Member States for returning illegally staying third-country nationals, p 5.

[55] Council Document 6624/07 of 28 February 2007, p 5.

for the Return Directive because 'legal migration Directives as well as instruments in the asylum acquis already contained provisions on 'public order/security' which allow Member States to withdraw' residence permits.[56] Another reason was, according to Lutz, that the expulsion of a 'criminal or a suspected criminal, may not always be in the interest of a Member State, as it may sometimes be preferable to … keep him or her under surveillance in a Member State'.[57]

Prior to the adoption of the Return Directive, different opinions were voiced regarding the level of harmonisation. Most Member States were of the opinion that the Commission had gone too far regarding the level of harmonisation sought.[58]

IV. Likelihood of a Further Specification of the Criteria for Entering Alerts into the SIS

In 1999 Steenbergen observed that, considering the sensitivity of Member States regarding the harmonisation of criteria for reporting an individual into the SIS, 'there is little chance that consensus can be reached on clear and precise common criteria to report a person into such a computer system'.[59] She argued that the 'limitation of the reporting grounds' would already be a step forward.[60] The Council held in 2006 that even though the Parliament would prefer to set out common criteria for SIS alerts regarding the refusal of entry or stay, 'it is generally accepted that this will be impossible in the short term and definitely not before the deadline of mid-2006'.[61] A year later the House of Lords called for a harmonisation of the substantial rules for entering an alert into the SIS and suggested that Member States publish a list in the Official Journal 'of the different national laws and practices concerning the creation of an immigration alert'.[62] Similarly, Groenendijk argued that a registration in the SIS which is limited to certain, specific crimes would be much clearer.[63]

Initial indications regarding the likelihood of a further specification of the requirements for entering alerts into the SIS can be drawn from a comparison

[56] F Lutz, 'Prologue: The Genesis of the EU's Return Policy' in M Moraru, G Cornelisse and P De Bruycker (eds), *Law and Judicial Dialogue on Return of Irregular Migrants from the European Union* (Oxford, Hart Publishing, 2020) 9.

[57] ibid.

[58] Council Document 6624/07 of 28 February 2007, p 1.

[59] J Steenbergen, 'All the King's Horses …: Probabilities and Possibilities for the Implementation of the New Title IV EC Treaty' (1999) 1 *European Journal of Migration and Law* 29, 50.

[60] ibid.

[61] Council of the European Union, Note from the Presidency, 'Selected issues concerning the legal basis for SIS II' 20 April 2006, doc. 8537/06, p 6.

[62] House of Lords, Schengen Information System II (SIS II): Report with Evidence, 9th Report of Session 2006–2007, p 24.

[63] House of Lords, Schengen Information System II (SIS II): Report with Evidence, 9th Report of Session 2006–2007, Minutes of Evidence by K Groenendijk, 11 October 2006, p 25.

between the draft and the final version of the (now repealed) SIS II Regulation (Regulation (EC) 2006/1987). The draft SIS II Regulation[64] from 2005 contained a reference to the offences listed in Article 2(2) of Council Framework decision 2002/584/JHA on the European arrest warrant, which would have limited the grounds for entering an alert at least to some degree and would have made the requirements for an alert more specific.[65] This reference, however, was deleted from the final version of the Regulation. In 2011 Brouwer pointed out that even if

> in the long-term the EU legislator considers closer harmonization a prerequisite to justify mutual recognition of SIS alerts, in practice the current use of the SIS is still based on the discretionary power of the Schengen states. Since 1995, the year the SIS became operational, no serious proposals have been submitted for further harmonization of the national criteria for a SIS alert for the purpose of refusing entry.[66]

However, Article 24(5) of the now repealed SIS II Regulation afforded the European Commission powers to specify the criteria for SIS alerts, by stipulating that

> [t]he Commission shall review the application of this Article three years after the date referred to in Article 55(2). On the basis of that review, the Commission shall, using its right of initiative in accordance with the Treaty, make the necessary proposals to modify the provisions of this Article to achieve a greater level of harmonisation of the criteria for entering alerts.

In 2012 the Meijers Committee held that 'it would be far too late if the European Commission would await the period of three years'.[67] Nonetheless, the European Commission awaited the three-year period and published its report on the evaluation of SIS II in 2016. The Commission Staff Working Document[68] accompanying the Commission report highlighted that the wording of Article 24(3) of the SIS II Regulation 'is unhelpful in that it proposes that an alert "may" be entered'.[69] The Staff Working Document noted that 'Different national interpretations of this text have resulted in some Member States entering alerts whilst others do not'.[70] This shortcoming has been remedied by the current SIS Regulation as the optional ground ('may') for issuing an alert has been deleted. This deletion demonstrates

[64] COM(2005) 236 final.

[65] S Peers, 'The Schengen Information System and EC Immigration and Asylum Law' in J de Zwaan and F Goudappel (eds), *Freedom, Security and Justice in the European Union* (The Hague, T.C.M. Asser Press, 2006) 183.

[66] E Brouwer, 'Mutual Trust in Migration Law: the SIS and Alerts on Admissible Aliens' in H Battjes, E Brouwer, P de Morree and J Ouwerkerk (eds), *The Principle of Mutual Trust in European Asylum, Migration and Criminal Law* (Utrecht, Forum, 2011) 22.

[67] Commissie Meijers, 'Note on the coordination of the relationship between the Entry Ban and the SIS-alert: an urgent need for legislative measures' CM 1203, 8 February 2012.

[68] SWD(2016) 450 final, Commission Staff Working Document accompanying the document report from the Commission to the European Parliament and the Council on the evaluation of the second generation Schengen Information System (SIS II).

[69] ibid, 7.4.

[70] ibid.

Member States' willingness to limit their discretion and constitutes a specification of the grounds for entering an alert into the SIS.

In 2017 the European Parliament submitted a report on the draft SIS Regulation and proposed an amendment of Article 24(1). This amendment envisaged under *litera* (a) that 'the alert shall be issued only if … (i) a third-country national has been convicted in a Member State of an offence carrying a penalty involving the deprivation of liberty of at least three years …'.[71] If implemented, it would have limited the number of criminal convictions that can precipitate an SIS alert. However, this amendment did not find its way into the final version of the 2018 Regulation, according to which 'an offence carrying a penalty involving the deprivation of liberty of at least one year' is sufficient to trigger an SIS alert.[72]

The rejection of the amendment to increase the required term of imprisonment from at least one year to at least three years also demonstrates that Member States wish to retain their wide discretion. Moreover, the attempt to limit the crimes that can precipitate an SIS alert to those that are listed in Article 2(2) of Council Framework decision 2002/584/JHA on the European arrest warrant has found its way neither into the 2006 SIS II Regulation nor the 2018 SIS Regulation. Interestingly, the review powers that were granted to the Commission by Article 24(5) of the repealed SIS II Regulation are no longer contained in the 2018 Regulation. This deletion suggests that the Commission's powers to make proposals 'to achieve a greater level of harmonisation of the criteria for entering alerts' have come to an end and that future harmonisations of the criteria for entering an alert into the SIS have become less likely.

V. Final Remarks and Outlook

Member States' wide margin of discretion regarding the grounds for entering an alert into the SIS was the most pressing weakness of the pre-2018 system. The 2018 SIS Regulation and the Court's case law, in particular the *Zh* and *O* case[73] concerning the interpretation of the notion of public policy in the context of the Return Directive, have limited Member States' discretion. The principles that were established in the *Zh* and *O* case were confirmed in subsequent judgments[74] and should be codified in both the Return Directive and the SIS Regulation to enhance clarity and legal certainty.

[71] European Parliament Committee on Civil Liberties, Justice and Home Affairs, Report on the proposal for a regulation on the establishment, operation and use of the Schengen Information System (SIS) in the field of border checks, amending Regulation (EU) No 515/2014 and repealing Regulation (EC) No 1987/2006 (COM(2016)0882 – C8-0533/2017–2016/0408(COD)), A8-0347/2017, p 63.

[72] Article 24(2)(a) of Regulation (EU) 2018/1861.

[73] *Zh* and *O*, para 60.

[74] *H. T.*, para 79; *J. N.*, paras 65, 65; *E.*, para 49; *WM*, para 45.

Moreover, it would be advisable if both instruments contained a clear reference to human rights obligations. Even though an explicit reference to the CFR is unnecessary, as Member States are bound by the Charter when they are applying the Return Directive or the SIS Regulation,[75] a reminder can only be useful.

While the Return Directive contains a reference to human rights obligations in Article 1, the ECHR is only mentioned in Recital 22 of the Preamble and a reference to the Charter is absent from the Directive, which was adopted before the Charter came into force. The SIS Regulation does not contain any reference to the ECHR but provides in Recital 56 of the Preamble that 'This regulation respects fundamental rights and observes the principles recognised in particular by the Charter of Fundamental Rights' and in particular 'the protection of personal data in accordance with Article 8 of the Charter'. While the protection of personal data is certainly relevant, a reference to Article 7 (respect for private and family life) and Article 24 (the rights of the child) of the Charter should also be added.

Both the ECHR and the CFR require that the interests of the individual be balanced against those of the state. Even though Article 24(1) of the SIS Regulation explicitly provides for an individual assessment, such an assessment is not foreseen by the text of the Return Directive. While both instruments contain a reference to the interests of the state (public policy, public security),[76] the Return Directive does not sufficiently address the interests of the individual. The SIS Regulation refers to 'an assessment of the personal circumstances of the third-country national concerned and the consequences of refusing him or her entry and stay' but it does not contain an explicit reference to the right to respect for private and family life. The Return Directive contains a reference to family life[77] and state of health[78] but does not mention the foreigner's private life.

Moreover, the balancing factors of Article 28(1) of the Citizenship Directive should be incorporated into both instruments to provide for a better structure of the balancing process between the interests of the foreigner and the interests of the state. The incorporation of the balancing factors of Article 28(1) has the advantage that it covers all balancing factors of Article 12(3) of the LTR Directive that have to be considered before expelling a long-term resident third-country national. This can help avoiding situations where a long-term resident third-country national is subject to an SIS alert even if s/he could not be expelled. Moreover, the explicit mentioning of the specific balancing factors of Article 28(1), such as the foreigner's 'family and economic situation, social and cultural integration into the host Member State', serve as a reminder to take Article 7 of the Charter into account.

Despite the limitation of Member States' discretion through both the 2018 SIS Regulation and the Court's case law, Member States still enjoy discretion in certain

[75] Article 51(1) CFR.

[76] See, for example, Article 11(2) Return Directive and Article 24(1)(a) and (2) SIS Regulation.

[77] Article 5(1)(b) Return Directive.

[78] Article 5(1)(c) Return Directive.

situations, as demonstrated by Article 24(2)(b) of the SIS Regulation. Provided that the requirements of Article 24(1)(a) are met, Member States shall enter an alert into the SIS if

> there are serious grounds for believing that a third-country national has committed a serious criminal offence, including a terrorist offence, or there are clear indications of his or her intention to commit such an offence in the territory of a Member State.

The vagueness of this provision leaves sufficient room for interpretation and allows Member States to interpret this provision in line with their national priorities. In the legislative process of the SIS Regulation, the European Parliament proposed an amendment to Article 24, which referred to a third-country national's conviction 'in a Member State of an offence referred to in Directive (EU) 2017/541 with a custodial sentence or detention order of at least five years, ….'[79] If only the crimes listed in Directive (EU) 2017/541[80] on combating terrorism were capable of triggering an alert pursuant to Article 24(1)(a) in conjunction with Article 24(2)(b) of the SIS Regulation, the wide discretion currently afforded to the Member States under this provision would be limited. A further specification of Article 24(2)(b) could be reached by requiring a specific minimum prison term.

Another problem that needs to be addressed is the vague wording of Article 24(2)(b), in particular the low threshold of 'serious grounds for believing that a third-country national has committed a serious criminal offence' or 'clear indications of his or her intention to commit such an offence' and its compatibility with the specific requirement of 'a genuine, present and sufficiently serious threat affecting one of the fundamental interests of society' that has been established by the CJEU in the *Zh* and *O* case.[81] Moreover, the compatibility of the wording of Article 24(2)(b) of the SIS Regulation with the Court's statement in the *Zh* and *O* case 'that the fact that a third-country national is suspected, or has been criminally convicted, of an act punishable as a criminal offence under national law cannot, in itself, justify a finding that that national poses a risk to public policy'[82] requires clarification.

Finally, the duration of the entry ban/SIS alert needs to be clarified. In order to achieve greater coherence, more specific criteria for determining the duration of the entry ban/SIS alert should be established, together with a binding upper

[79] European Parliament Committee on Civil Liberties, Justice and Home Affairs, Report on the proposal for a regulation on the establishment, operation and use of the Schengen Information System (SIS) in the field of border checks, amending Regulation (EU) No 515/2014 and repealing Regulation (EC) No 1987/2006 (COM(2016)0882 – C8-0533/2017–2016/0408(COD)), A8-0347/2017, p 64, amendment 126.

[80] Directive (EU) 2017/541 of the European Parliament and of the Council of 15 March 2017 on combating terrorism and replacing Council Framework Decision 2002/475/JHA and amending Council Decision 2005/671/JHA [2017] OJ L 88/6.

[81] *Zh* and *O*, para 60.

[82] ibid, para 50.

maximum duration. The 2020 European Parliamentary Research Service study on the Return Directive highlighted discrepancies regarding the length of entry bans and found that 'some countries do not clarify the length of an entry ban related to public order' while other countries sometimes have 'various thresholds'.[83] Differences between the Member States regarding the duration of the entry ban, and thus also the SIS alert,[84] result in differences of third-country nationals' return options to the Schengen area and undermine a common European approach.

[83] Eisele (ed), European Parliamentary Research Service, 'The Return Directive 2008/115/EC, European Implementation Assessment' 80.

[84] See Article 24(1)(b) of Regulation (EU) 2018/1861.

Final Summary and Conclusions

The focus of this book rests on the margin of discretion in transnational administrative acts and more specifically on expulsion decisions and entry bans following a criminal conviction. In a first step the research assessed the effects of the European level on the national level and in a second step the effects of the national level on the European level. Using this two-tiered approach, the first part provided an overview of the European system, by outlining the criteria that national expulsion decisions have to comply with. It introduced the applicable legal instruments and discussed the interpretation of the criteria contained in these instruments by the CJEU and the ECtHR. The focus rested on the balancing process between the interests of the individual and the interests of the state that must be conducted before an expulsion decision can be taken, the criteria that guide this balancing process, and the weight that is attached to these criteria. The identification of the European criteria that national decisions have to comply with simultaneously outlined the margin of discretion granted by the European level to the national level. The more specific the European standard, the smaller the state's margin of discretion or appreciation is regarding the issuance of expulsion decisions and the imposition of entry bans.

The various groups of foreigners were addressed in 'declining' order, starting with foreigners covered by the strictest European requirements and thereby enjoying the most far-reaching protection against expulsion. The analysis started with EU law, which imposes the strictest requirements regarding the expulsion of EU citizens, with the consequence that the margin of discretion of the Member States is the smallest as regards this group.[1] Third-country national family members of EU citizens have a level of protection similar, but not equal, to EU citizens.[2]

Next to EU citizens and their family members, the analysis focused on Turkish citizens covered by the EEC–Turkey Association Agreement and long-term resident third-country nationals who can rely on the LTR Directive.[3] These groups of foreigners have been chosen as the requirements for expulsion decisions

[1] See Chapter 1.

[2] The strongest protection against expulsion is granted by Article 28(3) of Directive 2004/38/EC of the European Parliament and of the Council of 29 April 2004 on the right of citizens of the Union and their family members to move and reside freely within the territory of the Member States amending Regulation (EEC) No 1612/68 and repealing Directives 64/221/EEC, 68/360/EEC, 72/194/EEC, 73/148/EEC, 75/34/EEC, 75/35/EEC, 90/364/EEC, 90/365/EEC and 93/96/EEC [2004] OJ L 158/77, which is inapplicable to third-country national family members of EU citizens.

[3] Council Directive 2003/109/EC of 25 November 2003 concerning the status of third-country nationals who are long-term residents [2004] OJ L 16/44.

concerning these groups of foreigners are those most regulated,[4] or most specified by the CJEU's case law.[5]

Regarding EU citizens, the focus rested on Articles 27 and 28 of the Citizenship Directive, which set out the principles that have to be observed when restricting EU citizens' free movement rights on grounds of public policy and public security. These articles contain three main features. First, Article 27 contains general principles and 'prohibitions', such as the need to adhere to the principle of proportionality and the prohibition to invoke public policy or public security grounds for economic ends.[6] Second, Article 28(1) establishes a non-exhaustive list of factors that have to be considered in the balancing process between the interests of the individual and the interests of the state. Third, Article 28 provides for a layered protection against expulsion depending on the duration of lawful residence. The longer the EU citizens and their family members lawfully reside on the territory of the host Member State, the stronger their protection against expulsion will be. Three stages of protection can be distinguished in relation to the duration of lawful residence: residence for up to five years,[7] residence between five and 10 years,[8] and residence of at least 10 years.[9] The layered protection against expulsion provided for by Article 28 of the Citizenship Directive already attaches a certain weight to the respective interests. Article 28(3)(a), for instance, stipulates that an EU citizen with more than 10 years of residence may not be expelled unless the Member State can invoke imperative grounds of public security, which implies that public policy grounds are no longer sufficient. However, while the CJEU previously strengthened EU citizens' protection by restricting Member States' powers to take expulsion decisions, a shift in the Court's case law can be noticed after the codification of its case law in the 2004 Citizenship Directive. In a series of judgments concerning the interpretation of Article 28(3) of the Citizenship Directive,[10] the Court strengthened Member States' power to expel EU citizens.

Turkish nationals' protection against expulsion is determined by Article 14 of Association Council Decision 1/80, which has been interpreted by the Court in analogy to the safeguards that are applicable to nationals of the Member States.[11] Even though the Court clarified in its *Ziebell* judgment that Turkish nationals

[4] See in particular the requirements for the expulsion of EU citizens in the LTR Directive.

[5] See in particular the CJEU's case law regarding Turkish citizens covered by the Association Agreement and Association Council Decision 1/80.

[6] Articles 27(1) and (2) Citizenship Directive.

[7] Articles 27 and 28(1) Citizenship Directive are applicable.

[8] Articles 27 and 28(1) and (2) Citizenship Directive are applicable.

[9] Articles 27 and 28(1) and (3) Citizenship Directive are applicable.

[10] Case C-145/09 *Tsakouridis* ECLI:EU:C:2010:708, [2010] ECR I-11979; Case C-348/09 *P.I.* ECLI:EU:C:2012:300, [2012]; Case C-400/12 *M.G.* ECLI:EU:C:2014:9; Joined Cases C-316/16 and C-424/16 *B* and *Franco Vomero* ECLI:EU:C:2018:256, [2018].

[11] Case C-303/08 *Bozkurt* ECLI:EU:C:2010:800, [2010] ECR I-13445, para 55; Case C-349/06 *Polat* ECLI:EU:C:2007:581, [2007] ECR I-08167, para 30; Case C-136/03 *Dörr* and *Ünal* ECLI:EU:C:2005:340, [2005] ECR I-04759, para 63; Case C-467/02 *Cetinkaya* ECLI:EU:C:2004:708, [2004] ECR I-10895, para 43; Case C-340/97 *Nazli* ECLI:EU:C:2000:77, [2000] ECR I-00957, para 56.

cannot rely on Article 28(3) of the Citizenship Directive,[12] which is unsurprising given that this provision cannot even be invoked by third-country national family members of EU citizens, the judgment did not affect the previously established principles and safeguards of Turkish nationals' protection against expulsion. Those safeguards, which reflect the foundational principles of EU citizens' protection against expulsion, continue to apply to Turkish nationals.[13]

Long-term resident third-country nationals' protection against expulsion is determined by Article 12 of the LTR Directive. In *López Pastuzano* the Court provided an interpretation of this provision and transferred the principles that determine Turkish nationals' protection against expulsion to long-term resident third-country nationals.[14] The Court thereby synchronised Turkish nationals' and long-term resident third-country nationals' protection against expulsion and aligned it to the general principles that govern EU citizens' protection against expulsion. This alignment limited Member States' margin of discretion to expel these two groups of third-country nationals and led to an approximation of the standards of protection against expulsion that are available to EU citizens and their family members, Turkish nationals and long-term resident third-country nationals.

The focus at the ECHR level rested on Article 8 ECHR (the right to respect for private and family life), the requirements of justification for an interference with this right, and the ECtHR's case law, which is highly casuistic.[15]

The criteria that guide the balancing process between the interests of the delinquent foreigner and the interests of a state, to determine whether the interference with Article 8 ECHR is necessary in a democratic society, were only established by the ECtHR in the *Boultif*[16] and *Üner*[17] judgments. Neither in the *Boultif* case nor in later judgments did the Court ascribe an abstract weight to the respective criteria in the balancing process, which makes it difficult for national courts to adjust their balancing process to the ECtHR's case law. The ECtHR also refrained from introducing a hierarchy among these criteria. Even though the Court often attaches a greater weight to the fact that the foreigner committed a drug-related crime[18] or the fact that the expulsion affects a second-generation immigrant or a migrant who spent the majority of his childhood in the host state,[19] the weight ascribed to

[12] Case C-371/08 *Ziebell* ECLI:EU:C:2011:809, [2011] ECR I-12735, para 86.

[13] ibid, paras 81–84.

[14] Case C-636/16 *López Pastuzano* ECLI:EU:C:2017:949, [2017], para 27.

[15] See Chapter 2.

[16] *Boultif v Switzerland* App no 54273/00 (ECHR, 2 August 2001).

[17] *Üner v The Netherlands* App no 46410/99 (ECHR, 18 October 2006).

[18] In *Dalia v France* App no 26102/95 (ECHR, 19 February 1998), para 54; *Baghli v France* App no 34374/97 (ECHR, 30 November 1999), para 48: 'In view of the devastating effects of drugs on people's lives, the Court understands why the authorities show great firmness with regard to those who actively contribute to the spread of this scourge.'

[19] *Maslov v Austria* App no 1638/03 (ECHR, 23 June 2008), para 75: regarding a 'migrant who has lawfully spent all or the majority of his or her childhood and youth in the host country very serious reasons are required to justify expulsion.'

the criteria can differ from case to case. This was acknowledged by the Court when it stated that the weight attached to these criteria will 'inevitably vary according to the specific circumstances of each case'.[20]

Even though the Court's approach reduces predictability, it enhances flexibility and must be seen in the context of the ECHR and the ECtHR's subsidiary position and the politically sensitive area of its jurisdiction. Moreover, three features which distinguish the ECHR from EU law might provide a further explanation as to why the ECtHR refrains from attaching a specific weight to the criteria in the balancing process.

First, while the Citizenship Directive contains general principles and prohibitions that have to be observed when expelling beneficiaries of this Directive,[21] comparable prohibitions are not contained in the ECHR. Second, the Citizenship Directive provides a non-exhaustive list of criteria that guide the balancing process,[22] while these criteria first had to be established by the ECtHR in the *Boultif* and *Üner* judgments. Third, the Citizenship Directive attaches a specific weight to the interests of the state and the interests of the foreigner, respectively,[23] while such weight is not provided for by the ECHR. It is to be welcomed that the ECtHR established the *Boultif* and *Üner* balancing criteria, but Judge Turković rightly emphasised the need for clarification. In her dissenting opinion in the *Ndidi* case she stated that 'an overly casuistic approach to the matter fails to achieve consistency in decision making and to bring certainty to the decision-making process, both at the national and European level'.[24] Moreover, she pointed out that 'the inconsistencies in application of the *Üner*, *Maslov* and *A.A.* principles, … may warrant their further clarification and/or elaboration'.[25]

After outlining the European standards in the first part, the analysis zoomed into the national level and assessed the termination of residence following a criminal conviction and the imposition of entry bans in Germany, the Netherlands and the United Kingdom.[26]

The three states under scrutiny take different approaches concerning the margin of discretion granted by the legislature to the executive. The Dutch legislature grants a considerable margin of discretion in the Vreemdelingenwet 2000.[27] This discretion is further specified by the Vreemdelingenbesluit (Decree on Foreign Nationals) and the Vreemdelingencirculair, which are not Acts of Parliament.

The German legislature provides for more specific rules in the Residence Act by stipulating that the decision maker has to conduct a balancing process

[20] ibid, para 70; *A.A. v The United Kingdom* App no 8000/08 (ECHR, 20 September 2011), para 57.

[21] Article 27(1) and (2) Citizenship Directive.

[22] Article 28(1) Citizenship Directive.

[23] Article 28(2) and (3) Citizenship Directive.

[24] *Ndidi v The United Kingdom* App no 41215/14 (ECHR, 14 September 2017), dissenting opinion of Judge Turković, para 6.

[25] ibid, para 7.

[26] Part II.

[27] Article 19 in conjunction with Article 18(1)(e); Article 22(2)(c) and (d) Vw 2000.

between the interests of the foreigner and the interests of the state.[28] If this balancing process leads to the conclusion that the interests of the state take precedence over the interests of the foreigner, the foreigner must be expelled.[29] Moreover, the statutory system provides for a non-exhaustive list of considerations that guide the balancing process[30] and attaches a specific weight to certain factors in the balancing process.[31]

The UK legislature has established even more specific rules by providing for automatic deportation.[32] The Secretary of State is under an obligation to 'make a deportation order in respect of a foreign criminal'.[33] This obligation is not absolute but is supplemented by a list of exceptions.[34]

Moreover, none of the three systems provides for an absolute security of residence for certain groups of long-term resident foreigners. The Dutch system previously exempted certain long-term resident foreigners from expulsion, but abolished this protection in 2012.

The structure of the national provisions has an effect on the way in which the interests of the state and the interests of the individual are considered. The Dutch sliding scale, which is provided for in Article 3.86 Vb 2000, directly relates the duration of the foreigner's lawful stay to the seriousness of the criminal offence, which is determined by the crime that has been committed and the prison term that has been imposed.[35] The German system[36] also addresses the interests of the state and the interests of the individual at the same level of assessment by requiring a balancing process.[37] In the United Kingdom, by contrast, the deportation of a foreign criminal is the rule,[38] and therefore the Secretary of State must make a deportation order[39] unless an exception applies.[40] The interests of the foreigner are only addressed in a second step as possible exceptions to the rule of deportation.[41]

The structure of the national provisions and the (lack of a) margin of discretion granted to the decision maker also has an effect on legal certainty. In the Netherlands, the sliding scale provides for a relatively high level of legal certainty in those cases in which the duration of the foreigner's lawful residence outweighs the criminal offence. In such a situation, residence can no longer be terminated.

[28] Residence Act, s 53(1).
[29] Residence Act, s 53(1).
[30] Residence Act, s 53(2).
[31] Residence Act, ss 54–55.
[32] Borders Act 2007, s 32.
[33] Borders Act 2007, s 32(5).
[34] Borders Act 2007, s 33.
[35] See Chapter 6.
[36] See Chapter 5.
[37] Residence Act, s 53(1).
[38] Borders Act 2007, s 32(4).
[39] Borders Act 2007, s 32(5).
[40] Borders Act 2007, s 32(5) in conjunction with s 33.
[41] Chapter 7.

Notably, the reverse situation, that is, cases in which the interests of the state per se trump the interests of the foreigner and take priority over the latter, is not envisaged. In the remaining cases, where the foreigner's lawful residence does not outweigh the criminal offence, a balancing process has to be conducted which has to take the *Üner* and *Boultif* criteria into account.

The German legislature provides for an increased level of legal certainty by establishing a non-exhaustive list of criteria that must be considered in the balancing process[42] and by attaching a specific weight to certain balancing factors.[43]

The UK statutory provisions provide for a very high level of legal certainty by limiting the discretion of the executive and by prescribing the deportation of a criminal foreigner unless an exception applies. Even if a foreigner can have recourse to the Article 8 ECHR exception, the relevant statutory provisions stipulate in a very detailed manner when the Article 8 exception can successfully be invoked where the foreigner has been sentenced to a term of imprisonment of less than four years[44] or to a term of imprisonment of more than four years.[45]

The analysis focused, in particular, on the differences between the Netherlands and Germany.[46] Both countries can give a European effect to their expulsion decisions and national entry bans by entering an alert regarding a third-country national into the SIS for the purpose of refusing entry. Differences can occur at three points. First, the termination of residence in these two countries has certain common features while following slightly different mechanisms. Both states consider the interests of the individual and the interests of the state at the same stage of assessment and thereby create a level playing field. Moreover, both states strongly focus on, on the one hand, the duration of the foreigner's residence on their territory and, on the other, the crime s/he committed and the term of imprisonment that has been imposed. However, the Netherlands operates a sliding scale, which bars the termination of the foreigner's residence where the duration of lawful residence outweighs the seriousness of the crime s/he has committed, as specified by the different categories of the sliding scale. The German statutory system, by contrast, does not provide for a sliding scale. It requires a balancing process between the interests of the state and the interests of the individual[47] but does not establish a system that bars expulsion if the duration of the foreigner's residence outweighs the seriousness of the offence. The balancing process is guided to some extent by the legislature as the relevant provisions attach a specific weight to certain balancing factors, such as the type of residence permit held by

[42] Residence Act, s 53(2).
[43] Residence Act, ss 54–55.
[44] Nationality, Immigration and Asylum Act 2002 (NIAA), s 117C(3); the exceptions are listed in s 117C(4) and (5) NIAA.
[45] NIAA, s 117C(6).
[46] See Chapters 8 and 10.
[47] Residence Act, s 53(1).

the foreigner,[48] the existence of family ties with German nationals,[49] the prison term imposed,[50] or the crime committed.[51] The differences between both systems can manifest themselves in situations where the foreigner's residence outweighs, according to the Dutch sliding scale, the seriousness of the crime, with the consequence that residence can no longer be terminated. In Germany, where a sliding scale does not operate, a balancing process has to be conducted, which could lead to the conclusion that the state's interests outweigh the interests of the individual, in which case the foreigner has to be expelled.[52]

A second difference between the two systems concerns the question of whether a national entry ban and an SIS alert will be imposed. The German Residence Act stipulates that 'entry or residence bans are to be issued to foreigners who have been expelled'.[53] An expulsion decision consequently triggers a national entry ban, but it does not necessarily lead to an SIS alert. The relevant provision grants discretion regarding the entry of an alert into the SIS and therefore requires a balancing process between the competing interests, which bars any automatism.[54] In the Netherlands the relevant provision stipulates that a national entry ban – the *inreisverbod*, which is only applicable to third-country nationals – is mandatory in two situations[55] and may be imposed in other situations.[56] The national entry ban is mandatory if the individual is not granted a period for voluntary return since s/he is deemed a risk to public policy.[57] In the *Zh* and *O* judgment, the CJEU clarified that Member States must 'assess the concept of "risk to public policy" … on a case-by-case basis, in order to ascertain whether the personal conduct of the third-country national concerned poses a genuine and present risk to public policy'.[58] Hence, neither the denial of a period for voluntary return nor the imposition of a national entry ban can constitute the automatic consequence of a criminal conviction. Moreover, a national entry ban cannot be imposed if it would result in a violation of the ECHR or the CFR. In contrast to a German entry ban, a Dutch entry ban shall also lead to the entry of an alert into the SIS.[59]

The third area of differentiation relates to the duration of the entry ban. While both countries provide for a maximum duration of 20 years for the entry ban, the two systems display several differences. The Dutch Vb provides for a more nuanced system than the German Residence Act. First, it establishes more detailed time limits by providing for entry bans of one, two, three, five, 10 and 20 years.[60]

[48] Residence Act, s 55(1) nos 1–3 and 5.
[49] Residence Act, s 55(1) no 4.
[50] Residence Act, s 54(1) no 1 and (2) nos 1 and 2.
[51] Residence Act, ss 54(1) nos 1a–5 and 54(2) nos 3–6.
[52] Residence Act, s 53(1).
[53] Residence Act, s 11(1).
[54] Residence Act, s 50(6).
[55] Article 66a(1) (a) and (b) Vw 2000.
[56] Article 66(2) Vw 2000.
[57] Article 66a(1)(a) in conjunction with Article 62(2)(c) Vw 2000.
[58] Case C-554/13 *Zh* and *O* ECLI:EU:C:2015:377, [2015], para 50.
[59] Article 66a(3) Vw 2000.
[60] Article 6.5a(1)–(6) Vb 2000.

The German system, by contrast, only differentiates between entry bans of five, 10 and 20 years.

Additionally, the Dutch provisions are more specific than the German provisions as they link the maximum duration of the entry ban to the duration of the criminal conviction. If the foreigner has been sentenced to a period of imprisonment of less than six months, the maximum duration of the entry ban shall be three years.[61] If a prison term of six months or more has been imposed, the duration of the entry ban can be up to five years.[62] An entry ban with a maximum duration of 10 years can be imposed, among other reasons, if the foreigner has been sentenced to a prison term for a violent or drug-related crime.[63]

The German Residence Act, by contrast, provides that an entry ban shall not exceed 10 years if the foreigner was expelled on grounds of a criminal conviction or if the foreigner poses a serious threat to public policy or public security,[64] thereby allowing greater discretion to the decision maker than the Dutch provisions do. In the Netherlands the entry ban can be up to 20 years where the foreigner poses a serious threat to national security or if serious reasons require an entry ban that exceeds 10 years.[65] Interestingly, a 20-year entry ban in Germany shall be imposed if the foreigner has committed crimes that are listed in Article 1 F Geneva Refugee Convention, which comprise crimes against peace, war crimes, and crimes against humanity.[66] These crimes can lead to an entry ban of a maximum duration of 10 years in the Netherlands.[67]

In light of the differences between these two national systems, the third part focused on the effects of national decisions on the European level. It introduced the concept of the transnational administrative act, which is defined as a public decision and which aims to have effects outside the territory of the state whose administration issued the act.[68] Examples of legal regimes in migration law that can attach a transnational effect to national decisions are the Dublin Regulation,[69] the LTR Directive, Directive 2001/40/EC on mutual recognition of decisions on the expulsion of third-country nationals, the Return Directive,[70] and the SIS.[71]

[61] Article 6.5a(3) Vb 2000.

[62] Article 6.5a (4)(a) Vb 2000.

[63] Article 6.5a(5) Vb 2000.

[64] Residence Act, s 11(5).

[65] Article 6.5a(6) Vb 2000.

[66] Residence Act, s 11(5a).

[67] Article 6.5a (5)(c) Vb 2000.

[68] A Gerontas, *Europäisierung und Internationalisierung des Verwaltungshandelns* (Baden-Baden, Nomos, 2011) 41, 42.

[69] Regulation (EU) No 604/2013 of the European Parliament and of the Council of 26 June 2013 establishing the criteria and mechanisms for determining the Member State responsible for examining an application for international protection lodged in one of the Member States by a third-country national or a stateless person [2013] OJ L 180/31.

[70] Directive 2008/115/EC of the European Parliament and of the Council of 16 December 2008 on common standards and procedures in Member States for returning illegally staying third-country nationals [2008] OJ L 348/98.

[71] J Bast, 'Transnationale Verwaltung des europäischen Migrationsraums' (2007) 46 *Der Staat* 1, 16; Gerontas, *Europäisierung und Internationalisierung des Verwaltungshandelns* 132, 185; M Laas, *Die Entstehung eines europäischen Migrationsverwaltungsraumes* (Baden-Baden, Nomos, 2008) 106, 107, 222.

The analysis focused on the Return Directive and on the SIS Regulation.[72] The SIS Regulation 'establishes the conditions and procedures for the entry and processing of alerts in SIS on third-country nationals … for the purpose of refusing entry into and stay on the territory of the Member States'.[73] The SIS Regulation can attach a transnational effect to national expulsion decisions and entry bans. A third-country national in respect of whom an alert for the purpose of refusing entry and stay has been entered into the SIS must be refused entry by all Schengen States unless an exception applies. States shall enter an alert into the SIS, among other reasons, if 'a third-country national has been convicted in a Member State of an offence carrying a penalty involving the deprivation of liberty of at least one year',[74] provided that further conditions are met.[75] Even though Member States' discretion has already been curtailed by the SIS Regulation, compared to its predecessor it still affords states a certain discretion.[76]

A second instrument that can attach a transnational effect to a national expulsion decision and entry ban is the Return Directive. According to Article 11(1) of the Return Directive, an entry ban shall be issued in two cases,[77] even though the CJEU clarified that 'the principle of proportionality must be observed throughout all the stages of the return procedure established by that directive',[78] which in turn bars any automatism. Moreover, the Return Directive stipulates that 'return decisions may be accompanied by an entry ban',[79] which grants considerable discretion to the Member States. A return decision is defined by Article 3(4) of the Return Directive as 'an administrative or judicial decision or act, stating or declaring the stay of a third-country national to be illegal and imposing or stating an obligation to return'. The illegality of stay is primarily determined by national law. A return decision is taken on the basis of national criteria and can be linked to an entry ban. In the Netherlands the withdrawal of a residence permit (for example after a criminal conviction) is a return decision[80] and can comprise an entry ban[81] in terms of the Return Directive. In Germany the expulsion decision (sections 53–55 Residence Act) as such is said not to be covered by the notion of return decision in terms of Article 3(4) of the Return Directive,[82] while the national entry and residence ban (section

[72] Regulation (EU) 2018/1861 on the establishment, operation and use of the Schengen Information System (SIS) in the field of border checks, and amending the Convention implementing the Schengen Agreement, and amending and repealing Regulation (EC) No 1987/2006 [2018] OJ L 312/14.

[73] Article 2 SIS Regulation.

[74] Article 24(2)(a) SIS Regulation.

[75] Article 24(1)(a) SIS Regulation.

[76] Chapter 9.

[77] Article 11(1)(a) and (b) Return Directive.

[78] *Zh* and *O*, para 49.

[79] Article 11(1) Return Directive.

[80] Article 27(2)(c) in conjunction with Article 27(1) Vw 2000.

[81] Article 27(4) Vw 2000. The entry ban (*inreisverbod*) is addressed by Article 66a Vw 2000 and was further discussed above, Chapter 6.

[82] Higher Administrative Court Baden-Württemberg, decision of 15 October 2013, 11 S 2114/13, para 8 with further references; F Dollinger, '§ 11 AufenthG' in J Bergmann and K Dienelt (eds), *Ausländerrecht*, 13th edn (Munich, C.H. Beck, 2020), paras 23, 24.

11(1) Residence Act), which is precipitated by an expulsion decision, is covered by the scope of the Return Directive.[83] An entry ban according to Article 11(1) of the Return Directive shall lead to an SIS alert,[84] even though both legal instruments exhibit several differences.[85] Both the SIS Regulation and the Return Directive grant Member States discretion, which can abet divergences. Mutual recognition of possibly diverging decisions is problematic in light of the negative repercussions on the individual and on the common European approach to migration.

Given that the comparison between Germany and the Netherlands demonstrated differences, in particular regarding the termination of residence, the imposition of national entry bans and SIS alerts and the duration of the entry ban, several options to remedy the existing divergences were discussed.[86]

First, the introduction of EU-wide rules for expulsion decisions was proposed. If expulsion decisions were adopted on the basis of harmonised rules, and if these expulsion decisions then led to SIS alerts, a greater coherence could be achieved. Such a system should refrain from providing for mandatory expulsion decisions given the disadvantages they engender, and they should specify the grounds for an expulsion decision by listing specific crimes and/or a specific minimum prison term that could lead to an expulsion decision.

Nevertheless, even if the rules for adopting expulsion decisions were harmonised in such a manner across all EU Member States, diverging expulsion decisions could still occur. The penal frameworks of the Member States differ, leading to different prison terms, which can have an impact on the question of whether an expulsion decision will be taken. Moreover, in the absence of mandatory expulsion decisions, a balancing process between the interests of the individual and the interests of the state has to be conducted. This balancing process could lead to diverging outcomes as different states attach a different weight to the factors in the balancing process. Additionally, such a system would have to clarify whether lawful residence can be terminated on grounds other than a criminal conviction as the current SIS Regulation and its predecessors provide for the possibility to enter alerts for the purpose of refusing entry even in the absence of a criminal conviction.

However, the harmonisation of national rules regarding expulsion does not seem realistic. The comparison between Germany and the Netherlands has already highlighted the differences between these two states, and a harmonisation of all participating states' systems seems inconceivable. Decisions on foreigners' entry, residence and removal from the national territory are inextricably linked to national sovereignty, which is why Member States wish to retain discretion in this area, making complete harmonisation unlikely. Moreover, complete harmonisation would affect Member States' competence to decide on their internal public

[83] Dollinger, '§ 11 AufenthG', para 28.
[84] Article 24(1)(b) SIS Regulation.
[85] Chapter 9.
[86] Chapter 11.

policy rules. According to Article 72 TFEU, the European Union is barred from exhaustively regulating the content and consequences of Member States' internal public policy in areas covered by Title V TFEU. Finally, it was pointed out that even if it was possible to harmonise Member States' rules on expulsions, there is a risk that Member States with the strictest rules would refuse to commit to such a system unless their rules were reflected at EU level, which ultimately might lead to a deterioration of the legal position of third-country nationals.

Second, the introduction of two types of entry bans was suggested, a binding and a non-binding entry ban. A non-binding entry ban would be similar to an extension of the currently existing exceptions that allow a state to depart from an SIS alert. However, such a system might not lead to significant change as Member States might be inclined to reject access to third-country nationals who are subject to a non-binding entry ban. Moreover, the high administrative burden that this system involves might trigger opposition from Member States.

A third proposal drew on the structure of expulsion decisions in the German *Reich*,[87] which consisted of several federal states (*Bundesstaaten*). Federal states were entitled to expel a foreigner from the territory of the *Reich* if the foreigner committed crimes listed in the Criminal Code or criminal provisions of the *Reich*.[88] Moreover, federal states had the power to expel foreigners from their territory, even though this expulsion did not entail the termination of residence in the *Reich*. In practice, however, most federal states were not willing to accept a foreigner who was subject to an expulsion decision by another federal state.[89] If transferred to the current European framework, this would enable Member States to expel foreigners from the territory of the European Union, a power that Member States currently do not possess, and link this expulsion decision to an EU-wide entry ban, a power Member States do possess. Member States would have to agree on a list of crimes that can trigger an expulsion decision from the territory of the European Union. In the remaining cases, Member States could issue an expulsion decision against a third-country national that obliges the foreigner to leave the territory of the respective Member State but not the territory of the European Union, which mirrors the currently existing national entry ban. This proposal would have the disadvantage that expelled foreigners could return to the expelling state in the absence of intra-EU border checks.

A fourth option is the further clarification of the notion of public policy in both the Return Directive and the SIS Regulation. The CJEU has already limited

[87] G Renner, 'Staatliche Souveränität und die Verweigerung des weiteren Aufenthalts, Zur Geschichte des deutschen Ausweisungsrechts' in K Barwig, G Brinkmann, B Huber, K Lörcher and C Schumacher (eds), *Ausweisung im demokratischen Rechtsstaat, Hohenheimer Tage zum Ausländerrecht 1995* (Baden-Baden, Nomos, 1996) 23–28.

[88] The competence to issue an expulsion decision from the *Reich* rested with the higher police authority, s 39(2) Criminal Code 1871.

[89] Renner, 'Staatliche Souveränität und die Verweigerung des weiteren Aufenthalts' 29. Renner points out that in certain situations a *Bundesstaat* was obliged to take back a foreigner.

Member States' discretion in the *Zh* and *O* case,[90] where it specified the notion of public policy in the context of the Return Directive, by aligning it to the definition provided by Article 27(2) of the Citizenship Directive. However, in order to enhance clarity and legal certainty, the requirements that have been established by the CJEU should be codified in both the Return Directive and the SIS Regulation. Moreover, it would be advisable for the balancing criteria that are contained in Article 28(1) of the Citizenship Directive to be reflected in the Return Directive and the SIS Regulation to provide better structure to the balancing process.

Finally, the likelihood of a harmonisation of the criteria for national expulsion decisions and the likelihood of a further specification of the criteria for entering alerts into the SIS were examined, based on Member States' reactions to European Commission proposals. These reactions point to a low likelihood of both a harmonisation of the criteria for national expulsion decisions and a specification of the criteria for entering alerts into the SIS.

The analysis mapped the development of Member States' margin of discretion to expel foreigners[91] and to impose entry bans and SIS alerts.[92] Even though EU Member States' margin of discretion to remove foreigners from their territory has been limited by human rights law and by EU law, Member States are keen to retain and assert their power to remove foreigners from their territory, given that it constitutes a fundamental expression of their sovereignty. This is vividly underpinned by the reactions to the proposal made by the European Commission in the drafting process of the Citizenship Directive. The Commission proposed that EU citizens and their family members who had resided on the territory of the host Member State for five years, as well as family members who are minors, should enjoy an absolute protection against expulsion. The European Parliament supported this approach and stated that an absolute protection from expulsion after five years of lawful residence 'puts an end to the historic sovereignty of the Member States in this area'.[93] The historic sovereignty still exists as Member States almost unanimously rejected this proposal in the Council.[94] Even though the European Union has granted the nationals of its Member States the fundamental status of EU citizenship, this status does not put EU citizens and nationals on an

[90] *Zh* and *O*, paras 50 and 60.

[91] Chapter 1.

[92] Chapter 9.

[93] European Parliament legislative resolution on the proposal for directive on the right of citizens of the Union and their family members to move and reside freely within the territory of the Member States (COM(2001) 257 – C5-0336/2001–2001/0111(COD)), p 55.

[94] Common Position (EC) No 6/2004 of 5 December 2003 adopted by the Council, acting in accordance with the procedure referred to in Article 251 of the Treaty establishing the European Community, with a view to adopting a directive of the European Parliament and of the Council on the right of citizens of the Union and their family members to move and reside freely within the territory of the Member States amending Regulation (EEC) No 1612/68 and repealing Directives 64/221/EEC, 68/360/EEC, 72/194/EEC, 73/148/EEC, 75/34/EEC, 75/35/EEC, 90/364/EEC, 90/365/EEC and 93/96/EEC [2004] OJ C 54 E/12.

equal footing as the former can still be expelled from the territory of Member States other than their Member State of nationality.

While Member States' power to expel EU citizens from their territory highlights one of the weaknesses of the status of EU citizenship, three aspects, which are closely linked to each other, urgently need to be addressed. First, de facto natives, that is, foreigners who were born in the host Member State or who have spent the majority of their life there, should no longer be expellable. The legally non-binding recommendations that were adopted two decades ago already called for an enhanced security of residence of long-term residents.[95] It is high time for the Contracting States to accept their responsibility and to acknowledge that these individuals are de facto natives with a foreign passport, who often slipped into criminality in the state's society. This needs to be reflected in their protection against expulsion.

Second, the best chances of rehabilitation must be considered in the balancing process. In the context of EU citizens, AG Bot stipulated that the Member State that expels a foreigner must explain precisely 'in what way the decision does not prejudice the offender's rehabilitation'.[96] This important aspect was taken up by the CJEU, which pointed out that social rehabilitation of an EU citizen in the Member State in which s/he has become genuinely integrated is not only in the interest of the individual, but also in the interest of the Union.[97] Consequently, it stated that the risk of compromising social rehabilitation has to be considered in the balancing process.[98] However, the best chances of rehabilitation are not only relevant in the context of EU citizens' expulsion: they must be considered in every foreigner's expulsion, in particular when assessing long-term residents' situations.

Third, the structure of the balancing process, that is, a balancing of the interests of the foreigner against the interests of the state, must be reconsidered. This binary structure is not only visible in the three national systems that have been assessed, but it is also applied by the CJEU and the ECtHR. Judge Turković warned in her dissenting opinion in the *Ndidi* case that 'it is of utmost importance to balance wisely society's impulse to attach greater weight to the public interest than to private and family life claims under Article 8 of the Convention' and that 'it is impossible to make a sharp distinction between the two'.[99] Moreover, she rightly argued that 'It is in the public interest to protect the private- and family-life claims of long-term migrants'.[100] Therefore, the binary structure of the balancing process needs to be replaced by a multifaceted assessment.

[95] Council of Europe, Committee of Ministers, Recommendation Rec (2000)15, concerning the security of residence of long-term migrants, adopted on 13 September 2000 at the 720th meeting of the Ministers' Deputies; Council of Europe, Parliamentary Assembly's Committee on Migration, Refugees and Demography, Recommendation 1504, Non-expulsion of long-term immigrants, adopted by the Standing Committee, acting on behalf of the Assembly, on 14 March 2001.

[96] Case C-145/09 *Tsakouridis* ECLI:EU:C:2010:322, [2010] ECR I-11979, Opinion of AG Bot, para 95.

[97] *Tsakouridis*, para 50.

[98] ibid.

[99] *Ndidi*, dissenting opinion of Judge Turković, para 7.

[100] ibid.

BIBLIOGRAPHY

Books, Chapters, Articles

Aarrass, B, 'Artikel 8 EVRM als middel tegen uitzetting: de moeizame integratie van "privéleven" in migratiezaken' (2010) *Asiel & Migrantenrecht* 176

Aas, KF, '"Crimmigrant" Bodies and Bona Fide Travelers: Surveillance, Citizenship And Global Governance' (2011) 15 *Theoretical Criminology* 331

Acosta Arcarazo, D, 'The Good, The Bad And The Ugly in EU Migration Law: Is The European Parliament Becoming Bad And Ugly? (The Adoption of Directive 2008/15: The Returns Directive)' (2009) 11 *European Journal of Migration and Law* 19

—— 'The Returns Directive' in S Peers, E Guild, D Acosta Arcarazo, K Groenendijk and V Moreno-Lax (eds), *EU Immigration and Asylum Law (Text and Commentary), Volume 2: EU Immigration Law* (Leiden, Martinus Nijhoff, 2012) 483

—— *Latin American Reactions to the Adoption of the Returns Directive* (CEPS, 2009)

—— *The Long-Term Resident Status as a Subsidiary Form of EU Citizenship* (The Hague, Martinus Nijhoff, 2011)

Alexy, H, 'Subsumtion oder Abwägung – Was gilt im Ausweisungsrecht?' (2011) 126 *Deutsches Verwaltungsblatt* 1185

Alfenaar, K, 'De toegang tot het grondgebied van de Europese Unie en de toegang tot Nederland' in E Brouwer and K Groenendijk (eds), *Derdelanders in de Europese Unie* (Utrecht, Forum, 2001) 17

Alleweldt, R, 'Ausweisung und Abeschiebungsschutz' in K Barwig, G Brinkmann and K Hailbronner (eds), *Neue Regierung – Neue Ausländerpolitik?, Hohenheimer Tage zum Ausländerrecht* (Baden-Baden, Nomos, 1999) 275

Anagnostaras, G, 'Enhanced Protection of EU Nationals Against Expulsion and the Concept of Internal Public Security: Comment on the PI Case' (2012) 37 *EL Rev* 627

Anderson, B, Gibney, M and Paoletti, E, 'Citizenship, Deportation and the Boundaries of Belonging' (2011) 15 *Citizenship Studies* 547

Arai-Takahashi, Y, *The Margin of Appreciation Doctrine and the Principle of Proportionality in the Jurisdiction of the ECHR* (Antwerp, Intersentia, 2001)

Arnardóttir, OM, '*Res Interpretata, Erga Omnes* Effect and Role of the Margin of Interpretation in Giving Domestic Effect to the Judgments of the European Court of Human Rights' (2017) 28 *European Journal of International Law* 819

Azoulai, L, 'The (Mis)Construction of the European Individual, Two Essays on Union Citizenship Law' (2014) no 14 *EUI Department of Law Research Paper*

Azoulai, L and Coutts, S, 'Restricting EU Citizens' Residence Rights on Grounds of Public Security. Where EU Citizenship and the AFSJ Meet: P.I.' (2013) 50 *CML Rev* 553

Baldaccini, A, 'The Return and Removal of Irregular Migrants under EU Law: An Analysis of the Returns Directive' (2009) 11 *European Journal of Migration and Law* 1

Barak, A, *Proportionality: Constitutional Rights and their Limitations* (Cambridge, CUP, 2012)

Barkhuysen, T, 'Een revolutie in het bestuursrecht?' (2015) 24 *Nederlands Juristenblad* 1583

Barnard, C, *The Substantive Law of the EU, The Four Freedoms*, 2nd edn (Oxford, OUP, 2007)

—— *The Substantive Law of the EU*, 6th edn (Oxford, OUP, 2019)

Bast, J, 'Internationalisierung und De-Internationalisierung der Migrationsverwaltung' in C Möllers, A Voßkuhle and C Walter (eds), *Internationales Verwaltungsrecht* (Tübingen, Mohr Siebeck, 2007) 279

—— 'Transnationale Verwaltung des europäischen Migrationsraums' (2007) 46 *Der Staat* 1
—— *Aufenthaltsrecht und Migrationssteuerung* (Tübingen, Mohr Siebeck, 2011)
Bauer, I, 'Vor §§ 53-56 AufenthG' in J Bergmann and K Dienelt (eds), *Ausländerrecht* 13th edn (Munich, C.H. Beck, 2020)
Bauer, I and Beichel-Benedetti, S, 'Das neue Ausweisungsrecht' (2016) *Neue Zeitschrift für Verwaltungsrecht* 416
Beichel, S, *Ausweisungsschutz und Verfassung* (Berlin, Mensch & Buch, 2001)
—— 'Das deutsche Ausweisungsrecht auf dem Prüfstand' (2002) 24 *Informationsbrief Ausländerrecht* 457
Bergmann, M and Hörich, C, 'Besonders schwerwiegende Ausweisungsrechtsfehler – Kritische Anmerkungen zur jüngsten Reform des Ausweisungsrechts' (2016) 36 *Zeitschrift für Ausländerrecht und Ausländerpolitik* 269
Berneri, C, *Family Reunification in the EU* (Oxford, Hart Publishing, 2017)
Boelaert-Suominen, S, 'Non-EU Nationals and Council Directive 2003/109/EC on the Status of Third-Country Nationals Who Are Long-Term Residents: Five Paces Forward and Possibly Three Paces Back' (2005) 42 *CML Rev* 1011
Boeles, P, 'De aanval op de gezinshereniging en de rol van het international recht' (2005) *Migrantenrecht* 116
—— 'Noot bij ABRvS (17 December 2004)' (2005) *Jurisprudentie Vreemdelingenrecht* 65
—— 'Het gezin als de hoeksteen van de wereld' (2007) *Migrantenrecht* 4
—— 'Wat betekent de Terugkeerrichtlijn voor ongewenstverklaring?' (2010) *Asiel & Migrantenrecht* 531
—— 'Is een oude ongewenstverklaring onder de Terugkeerrichtlijn nog geldig?' (2012) 8 *Asiel & Migrantenrecht* 371
—— 'Criminalisering van illegaal verblijf' (2013) *Journaal Vreemdelingenrecht* 17
—— 'Strafbaarstelling van illegaal verblijf en het Unierecht' (2013) *Asiel & Migrantenrecht* 66
—— 'Residence Rights of Turkish Nationals under the Association Agreement' in P Boeles, M den Heijer, G Lodders and K Wouters (eds), *European Migration Law*, 2nd edn (Cambridge, Intersentia, 2014) 97
Bombeke, A and Franssen, K, 'De Terugkeerrichtlijn: over de normen voor de terugkeer van illegaal verblijvende derdelanders' (2010) *Asiel & Migrantenrecht* 257
Bouma, M, 'Terugkeerrichtlijn: nationale en Europese uitspraken over inreisverbod en ongewenstverklaring' (2012) 16 *Journaal Vreemdelingenrecht* 172
Bowling, B and Westenra, S, '"A Really Hostile Environment": Adiaphorization, Global Policing and the Crimmigration Control System' (2020) 24 *Theoretical Criminology* 163
Brems, E and Gerards, J, *Shaping Rights in the ECHR: The Role of the European Court of Human Rights in Determining the Scope of Human Rights* (Cambridge, CUP, 2014)
Brouwer, E, *Digital Borders and Real Rights* (Leiden, Brill Martinus Nijhoff, 2008)
—— 'Legal Boundaries and the Use of Migration Technology' in H Dijstelbloem and A Meijer (eds), *Migration and the New Technological Borders of Europe* (London, Palgrave Macmillan, 2011) 134
—— 'Mutual Trust in Migration Law: the SIS and Alerts on Admissible Aliens' in H Battjes, E Brouwer, P de Morree and J Ouwerkerk (eds), *The Principle of Mutual Trust in European Asylum, Migration and Criminal Law* (Utrecht, Forum, 2011) 19
Bryan, I and Langford, P, 'Impediments to the Expulsion of Non-Nationals: Substance and Coherence in Procedural Protection under the European Convention on Human Rights' (2010) 79 *Nordic Journal of International Law* 457
Callewaert, J, 'The European Convention on Human Rights and European Union Law: A Long Way to Harmony' (2009) 6 *European Human Rights Law Review* 768
Caroni, M, *Privat- und Familienleben zwischen Menschenrecht und Migration* (Berlin, Duncker & Humblot, 1999)
Chlebny, J, 'Public Order, National Security and the Rights of Third-Country Nationals in Immigration Cases' (2018) 20 *European Journal of Migration and Law* 115

Cholewinski, R, 'Mutual Recognition of Expulsion Decisions' in S Peers and N Rogers (eds), *EU Immigration and Asylum Law, Text and Commentary* (Leiden, Martinus Nijhoff, 2006) 787

—— 'The Criminalisation of Migration Policy in EU Law and Policy' in A Baldaccini, E Guild and H Toner (eds), *Whose Freedom, Security, and Justice?* (Oxford, Hart Publishing, 2007) 301

—— 'The EU *Acquis* on Irregular Migration Ten Years On: Still Reinforcing Security at the Expense of Rights?' in E Guild and P Minderhoud (eds), *The First Decade of EU Migration and Asylum Law* (Leiden/Boston, Martinus Nijhoff, 2012) 127

Choudhury, T, 'The Radicalisation of Citizenship Deprivation' (2017) 37 *Critical Social Policy* 225

Collinson, J, 'Suspended Deportation Orders: A Proposed Law Reform' (2020) 40 *Oxford Journal of Legal Studies* 291

Coutts, S, 'Union Citizenship as Probationary Citizenship: Onuekwere' (2015) 52 *CML Rev* 531

Craig, P, *EU Administrative Law*, 3rd edn (Oxford, OUP, 2018)

Davy, U, 'Aufenthaltssicherheit: Ein verlässliches Versprechen?' (2007) 27 *Zeitschrift für Ausländerrecht und Ausländerpolitik* 169

de la Rasilla del Moral, I, 'The Increasingly Marginal Appreciation of the Margin-of-Appreciation Doctrine' (2006) 6 *German Law Journal* 611

de Morree, P, 'Mutual Trust in Migration Law: The Returns Directive and Mutual Recognition of Entry Bans' in H Battjes, E Brouwer, P de Morree and J Ouwerkerk (eds), *The Principle of Mutual Trust in European Asylum, Migration and Criminal Law* (Utrecht, Forum, 2011) 28

Deibel, K, 'Die Ausweisung von Ausländern unter Berücksichtigung der Rechtsprechung des Europäischen Gerichtshofes für Menschenrechte' (2009) 29 *Zeitschrift für Ausländerrecht und Ausländerpolitik* 121

Dembour, M-B, 'Human Rights Law and National Sovereignty in Collusion: The Plight of Quasi-Nationals at Strasbourg' (2003) 21 *Netherlands Quarterly of Human Rights* 63

Dienelt, K, 'Die Aufenthaltsrechtliche Bedeutung des Diskriminierungsverbots nach Art. 37 des Zusatzprotokolls' (2003) 22 *Neue Zeitschrift für Verwaltungsrecht* 54

Dollinger, F, '§ 11 AufenthG' in J Bergmann and K Dienelt (eds), *Ausländerrecht*, 13th edn (Munich, C.H. Beck, 2020)

Drobak, JN and North, DC 'Understanding Judicial Decision-Making: The Importance of Constraints on Non-Rational Deliberations' (2008) 26 *Washington University Journal of Law & Policy* 131

Dubinsky, L, *Foreign National Prisoners: Law and Practice* (Legal Action Group, 2012)

Duff, A, 'Inclusion and Exclusion: Citizens, Subjects and Outlaws' (1998) 51 *Current Legal Problems* 241

Düsterhaus, D, 'Judicial Coherence in the Area of Freedom, Security and Justice – Squaring Mutual Trust with Effective Judicial Protection' (2015) 8 *Review of European Administrative Law* 151

Egter van Wissekerke, HG, *Regulier Verblijfsrecht* (The Hague, Boom Juridische Uitgevers, 2011)

Eicke, T, 'Paradise Lost? Exclusion and Expulsion from the EU' in K Groenendijk, E Guild and P Minderhoud (eds), *In Search of Europe's Borders* (The Hague, Kluwer Law International, 2003) 147

Farahat, A, 'Enhancing Constitutional Justice by Using External References: The European Court of Human Rights' Reasoning on the Protection Against Expulsion' (2015) 28 *Leiden Journal of International Law* 303

—— 'The Exclusiveness of Inclusion: On the Boundaries of Human Rights in Protecting Transnational and Second Generation Migrants' (2009) 11 *European Journal of Migration and Law* 253

Fennelly, N, 'The European Union and Protection of Aliens from Expulsion' (1999) 1 *European Journal of Migration and Law* 313

Fornalé, E, 'The European Returns Policy and the Re-Shaping of the National: Reflections on the Role of Domestic Courts' (2012) 31 *Refugee Survey Quarterly* 134

Franken, A, *Detention and the Re-entry Ban in the Returns Directive – A Race to the Bottom?* (Masters Thesis, Tilburg University, 2010)

Franßen-de la Cerda, B, 'Die Vergemeinschaftung der Rückführungspolitik – das Inkrafttreten der EU-Rückführungsrichtlinie' (2008) 28 *Zeitschrift für Ausländerrecht und Ausländerpolitik* 377

Franz, F, 'Der Gesetzesentwurf der Bundesregierung zur Neuregelung des Ausländerrechts' (1990) 10 *Zeitschrift für Ausländerrecht und Ausländerpolitik* 3

Frenz, W, 'Differenzierter Ausweisungsschutz von Unionsbürgern nach dem Urteil Tsakouridis' (2011) 31 *Zeitschrift für Ausländerrecht und Ausländerpolitik* 174

Fritzsch, F, *Der Schutz sozialer Bindungen von Ausländern* (Baden-Baden, Nomos, 2009)

—— 'Die Auswirkungen des Rechtes auf Achtung des Privat- und Familienlebens auf Ausweisung und andere Rückführungsentscheidungen' (2011) *Zeitschrift für Ausländerrecht und Ausländerpolitik* 297

—— 'Die Grenzen des völkerrechtlichen Schutzes sozialer Bindungen von Ausländern nach Art. 8 EMRK' (2010) 30 *Zeitschrift für Ausländerrecht und Ausländerpolitik* 14

Frowein, J and Peukert, W, *Europäische Menschenrechtskonvention* (Kehl am Rhein, N. P. Engel Verlag, 1985)

Gatta, F, 'The Problematic Management of Migratory Flows in Europe and its Impact on Human Rights: the Prohibition of Collective Expulsion of Aliens in the Case-law of the European Court of Human Rights' in G Bruno, F Palombino and A Di Stefano (eds), *Migration Issues before International Courts and Tribunals* (Rome, CNR edizioni, 2019) 119

Geertsema, K, 'Noot bij ABRvS (1 April 2010)' (2010) *Jurisprudentie Vreemdelingenrecht* 195

Gerontas, A, *Europäisierung und Internationalisierung des Verwaltungshandelns* (Baden-Baden, Nomos, 2011)

Glas, L and Krommendijk, J, 'From *Opinion 2/13* to *Avotiņš*: Recent Developments in the Relationship between the Luxembourg and Strasbourg Courts' (2017) 17 *Human Rights Law Review* 567

Greer, S, 'The Interpretation of the European Convention on Human Rights: Universal Principle or Margin of Appreciation' (2010) 3 *UCL Human Rights Review* 1

Griffiths, M, 'Foreign, Criminal: A Doubly Damned Modern British Folk-devil' (2017) 21 *Citizenship Studies* 527

Groenendijk, CA, 'Noot bij ABRvS (18 June 2013)' (2013) *Jurisprudentie Vreemdelingenrecht* 379

Groenendijk, K, 'Long-term Immigrants and the Council of Europe' in E Guild and P Minderhoud (eds), *Security of Residence and Expulsion* (The Hague, Kluwer Law International, 2001) 7

—— 'Long-Term Residents' in S Peers, E Guild, D Acosta Arcarazo, K Groenendijk and V Moreno-Lax (eds), *EU Immigration and Asylum Law (Text and Commentary) Volume 2: Immigration Law*, 2nd edn (Leiden, Martinus Nijhoff Publishers, 2012) 287

—— 'Reinstatement of Controls at the Internal Borders of Europe: Why and Against Whom?' (2004) 10 *European Law Journal* 150

—— 'The Directive on Mutual Recognition of Expulsion Decisions: Symbolic or Unbalanced Politics' in P De Bruycker (ed), *The Emergence of a European Immigration Policy* (Brussels, Bruylant, 2003) 447

Grupp, K and Stelkens, U, 'Zur Berücksichtigung der Europäischen Menschenrechtskonvention bei der Auslegung deutschen Rechts' (2005) 120 *Deutsches Verwaltungsblatt* 133

Guild, E, 'Restrictions on the Right of Entry and the Rights of Residence on Grounds of Public Policy, Public Security, or Public Health' in E Guild, S Peers and J Tomkin (eds), *The EU Citizenship Directive, A Commentary*, 2nd edn (Oxford, OUP, 2019) 253

—— 'Security of Residence and Expulsion of Foreigners: European Community Law' in E Guild and P Minderhoud (eds), *Security of Residence and Expulsion* (The Hague, Kluwer Law International, 2001) 59

Gutmann, R, 'Anmerkung zum Urteil des Hessischen Verwaltungsgerichtshofs, Urteil vom 4.3.2002, 12 UE 200/02' (2002) 24 *Informationsbrief Ausländerrecht* 346

—— 'Assoziationsrechtliche Schranken gesetzgeberischer Gestaltungsbefugnis im Ausländerrecht' (2003) 23 *Zeitschrift für Ausländerrecht und Ausländerpolitik* 60

—— 'Ausländerrecht: Die Befristung der Ausweisung' (2009) 62 *Neue Juristische Wochenschrift* 2657

—— 'Die neue Unionsbürger-Richtlinie 2004/38/EG und ihr Verhältnis zu Art. 14 Abs. 1 ARB 1 /80' (2005) 27 *Informationsbrief Ausländerrecht* 401

—— 'Menschenrechtliche Fragen an das Ausländergesetz' (2000) 23 *Informationsbrief Ausländerrecht* 1

Hailbronner, K, 'Ausweisung und Abschiebung straffälliger Ausländer, The Expulsion of Criminal Aliens' in K Hailbronner and E Klein (eds), *Einwanderungskontrolle und Menschenrechte – Immigration Control and Human Rights, Beiträge anläßlich des Symposiums am 29.30. Juni 1998 in Potsdam* (Heidelberg, C.F. Müller Verlag, 1999) 169

—— 'Einreise und Aufenthalt türkischer Staatsangehöriger im Assoziationsrecht EWG-Türkei – Anmerkungen zur Rechtsprechung des EuGH' (2011) 31 *Zeitschrift für Ausländerrecht und Ausländerpolitik* 322

—— 'Langfristig aufenthaltsberechtigte Drittstaatsangehörige' (2004) 24 *Zeitschrift für Ausländerrecht und Ausländerpolitik* 163

—— 'Neue Entwicklungen im Personenverkehr für Unionsbürger und Angehörige assoziierter Staaten' (2002) 22 *Zeitschrift für Ausländerrecht und Ausländerpolitik* 7

Harvey, C, 'Promoting Insecurity: Public Order, Expulsion and the European Convention on Human Rights' in E Guild and P Minderhoud (eds), *Security of Residence and Expulsion* (The Hague, Kluwer Law International, 2001) 41

Hauschild, C, 'Neues europäisches Einwanderungsrecht: Das Daueraufenthaltsrecht von Drittstaatsangehörigen' (2003) 23 *Zeitschrift für Ausländerrecht und Ausländerpolitik* 350

Heringa, R, 'Ongewenstverklaring en verblijfsbeëindiging: een gemiste kans' (2001) *Migrantenrecht* 144

Hirsch, G, 'Auf dem Weg zum Richterstaat? Vom Verhältnis des Richters zum Gesetzgeber in unserer Zeit' (2007) 62 *Juristen Zeitung* 853

—— 'Zwischenruf: Der Richter wird's schon richten' (2006) 39 *Zeitschrift für Rechtspolitik* 161

Hirsch Ballin, E, 'Dynamiek in de bestuursrechtspraak' in E Hirsch Ballin, R Ortlep and A Tollenaar, *Rechtsontwikkeling door de bestuursrechter* (Den Haag, Boom Juridische uitgevers, 2015) 7

Hutchinson, M, 'The Margin of Appreciations Doctrine in the European Court of Human Rights' (1999) 48 *ICLQ* 638

Imkamp, R, 'Terugkeerrichtlijn beschermt tegen dubbel inreisverbod' (2012) *Asiel & Migrantenrecht* 491

Janssens, C, *The Principle of Mutual Recognition in EU Law* (Oxford, OUP, 2013)

Kabera Karanja, S, *Transparency and Proportionality in the Schengen Information System and Border Control Co-operation* (Leiden, Martinus Nijhoff, 2008)

Kälin, W, 'Aliens, Expulsion and Deportation' in R Wolfrum (ed), *The Max Planck Encyclopedia on Public International Law* (2008)

Kanstroom, D, 'Deportation, Social Control, and Punishment: Some Thoughts about Why Hard Laws Make Bad Cases' (2000) 113 *Harvard Law Review* 1890

Kempees, P, '"Legitimate Aims" in the Case Law of the European Court of Human Rights' in P Mahoney, F Matscher, H Petzold and L Wildhaber (eds), *Protection des droits de l'homme: la perspective européenne* (Cologne, Carl Heymanns Verlag KG, 2000) 659

Kießling, A, 'Fremdenpolizeirecht im Rechtsstaat (?) – Zu Herkunf und Zukunft des Ausweisungsrechts' (2016) 36 *Zeitschrift für Ausländerrecht und Ausländerpolitik* 45

Kirkagac, N, *Verdachtsausweisungen im deutschen Rechtsstaat* (Frankfurt, Peter Lang, 2011)

Kluth, W, 'Reichweite und Folgen der Europäisierung des Ausländer- und Asylrechts' (2006) 26 *Zeitschrift für Ausländerrecht und Ausländerpolitik* 1

Kochenov, D and Pirker, B, 'Deporting the Citizens within the European Union: A Counter-Intuitive Trend in Case C-348/09, P.I. v Oberbürgermeisterin der Stadt Remscheid' (2013) 19 *Columbia Journal of European Law* 369

Koprolin, E, 'Introduction' in E Guild and P Minderhoud (eds), *Security of Residence and Expulsion* (The Hague, Kluwer Law International, 2001) 3

Kostakopoulou-Douchery, D and Ferreira, N, 'Testing Liberal Norms: The Public Policy and Public Security Derogations and the Cracks in European Union Citizenship' (2014) 20 *Columbia Journal of European Law* 167

Koutrakos, P, 'Public Security Exceptions and EU Free Movement Law' in P Koutrakos, N Nic Shuibhne and P Sypris (eds), *Exceptions from EU Free Movement Law* (Oxford, Hart Publishing, 2016) 190

Laas, M, *Die Entstehung eines europäischen Migrationsverwaltungsraumes* (Baden-Baden, Nomos, 2008)

Lambert, H, *The Position of Aliens in Relation to the European Convention on Human Rights* (Strasbourg, Council of Europe Publishing, 2007)

Landau, H, 'Die Entwicklung der Menschenrechte in der Rechtsprechung des Bundesverfassungsgerichts und des Europäischen Gerichtshofs für Menschenrechte' (2008) 133 *Deutsches Verwaltungsblatt* 1269

Langenfeld, C, 'Menschenrecht auf Aufenthalt?' in M Herdegen, H Klein, H-J Papier and R Scholz (eds), *Staatsrecht und Politik, Festschrift für Roman Herzog* (Munich, C.H. Beck, 2009) 247

Leboeuf, L and Carlier, J-Y, 'The Prohibition of Collective Expulsion as an Individualisation Requirement' in M Moraru, G Cornelisse and P De Bruycker (eds), *Law and Judicial Dialogue on Return of Irregular Migrants from the European Union* (Oxford, Hart Publishing, 2020) 455

Legomsky, S, 'Ausweisung und Abschiebung straffälliger Ausländer. The Expulsion of Criminal Aliens' in K Hailbronner and E Klein (eds), *Einwanderungskontrolle und Menschenrechte – Immigration Control and Human Rights, Beiträge anlässlich des Symposiums am 29-30 Juni 1998 in Potsdam* (Heidelberg, C.F. Müller Verlag, 1999) 163

Lenaerts, K, 'La vie après l'avis: Exploring the Principle of Mutual (Yet Not Blind) Trust' (2017) 54 *CML Rev* 805

Lester, A, 'The European Court of Human Rights After 50 Years' (2009) 4 *European Human Rights Law Review* 461

Lodders, G, 'Movement and Residence Rights of Third-Country Nationals' in P Boeles, M den Heijer, G Lodders and K Wouters (eds), *European Migration Law*, 2nd edn (Cambridge, Intersentia, 2014) 127

Lutz, F, 'Prologue: The Genesis of the EU's Return Policy' in M Moraru, G Cornelisse and P De Bruycker (eds), *Law and Judicial Dialogue on Return of Irregular Migrants from the European Union* (Oxford, Hart Publishing, 2020) 1

Mahony, P, 'Marvellous Richness of Diversity or Invidious Cultural Relativism?' (1998) 19 *Human Rights Law Journal* 1

Maiani, F and Migliorini, S, 'One Principle to Rule Them All? Anatomy of Mutual Trust in the Law of the Area of Freedom, Security and Justice' (2020) 57 *CML Rev* 7

Manthey, L and Unseld, C, 'Der Mythos vom contra-legem Verbot: Vom Umgang des EuGH mit einem Verfassungsprinzip' (2011) 64 *Die Öffentliche Verwaltung* 921

Marauhn, T and Thorn, J, 'Privat- und Familienleben' in O Dörr, R Grote and T Marauhn (eds), *EMRK/GG Konkordanzkommentar, Volume 1*, 2nd edn (Tübingen, Mohr Siebeck, 2013)

Marx, R, 'Aktuelle Entwicklungen im gemeinschaftsrechtlichen Ausweisungsschutz' (2007) *Zeitschrift für Ausländerrecht und Ausländerpolitik* 142

Mayer, K-G, 'Systemwechsel im Ausländerrecht – der Schutz "faktischer Inländer" mit und ohne familiäre Bindungen nach dem Grundgesetz und der Europäischen Menschenrechtskonvention (EMRK)' (2010) 101 *Verwaltungsarchiv* 482

McHarg, A, 'Reconciling Human Rights and the Public Interest' (1999) 62 *Modern Law Review* 671

Meduna, M, '"Scelestus Europeus Sum": What Protection against Expulsion Does EU Citizenship Offer to European Offenders?' in D Kochenov (ed), *EU Citizenship and Federalism: The Role of Rights* (Cambridge, CUP, 2017) 394

Meyer, W, 'Die Ausweisung nach dem Ausländergesetz in der Rechtsprechung des Bundesverwaltungsgerichts' (1984) 3 *Neue Zeitschrift für Verwaltungsrecht* 13

Mielitz, C, 'Die aufenthaltsrechtlichen Rechtsfolgen der Ausweisung' (2009) 29 *Zeitschrift für Ausländerrecht und Ausländerpolitik* 264

Mitsilegas, V, 'The Symbiotic Relationship Between Mutual Trust and Fundamental Rights in Europe's Area of Criminal Justice' (2015) 6 *New Journal of European Criminal Law* 457

Morano-Foadi, S and Andreadakis, S, 'The Convergence of the European Legal System in the Treatment of Third-Country Nationals in Europe: The ECJ and ECtHR Jurisprudence' (2011) 22 *EJIL* 1071.

Naumann, K, 'Die Prüfung der Verhältnismäßigkeit im Rahmen gebundener Entscheidungen' (2011) 64 *Die Öffentliche Verwaltung* 96

Nic Shuibhne, N, 'Limits Rising, Duties Ascending: The Changing Legal Shape of Union Citizenship' (2015) 52 *CML Rev* 889

Nicolaïdis, K, 'Trusting the Poles? Constructing Europe through mutual recognition' (2007) 14 *Journal of European Public Policy* 682

O'Donnell, T, 'The Margin of Appreciation Doctrine' (1982) 4 *Human Rights Quarterly* 474

Okresek, W, 'Die Umsetzung der EGMR-Urteile und ihre Überwachung' (2003) 31 *Europäische Grundrechte-Zeitschrift* 168

Oosterom-Staples, H, 'Adjudicating the External Schengen Border' in K Groenendijk, E Guild and P Minderhoud (eds), *In Search of Europe's Borders* (The Hague, Kluwer Law International, 2002) 215

—— 'Adjudicating the Schengen Agreement in the Netherlands' (2000) 2 *European Journal of Migration and Law* 53

—— 'Botsende openbare-ordebegrippen in het Europese Migratierecht' (2006) 8/9 *Nederlands Tijdschrift voor Europees Recht* 169

—— 'Naar een Europese glijdende openbare ordeschaal voor het personenverkeer' (2012) 18 *Nederlands tijdschrift voor Europees recht* 265

Ortleb, R and Zorg, W, 'Marginale rechterlijke toetsing onder druk: een voortgaande trend vooruit?' in R Ortleb, F Groothuijse, J Kiewiet, R Nehmelman (eds), *De rechter onder vuur* (Oisterwijk, Wolf Legal Publishers, 2016) 1

Ottaviano, M, *Der Anspruch auf rechtzeitigen Rechtsschutz im Gemeinschaftsprozessrecht* (Tübingen, Mohr Siebeck, 2009)

Otto, KE, 'The Foreign National Prisoner's Dilemma in the United Kingdom: The Human Rights Implications of Restricting Article 8 Claims' (2015) 24 *Transnational Law & Contemporary Problems* 431

Ovey, C, 'The Margin of Appreciation and Article 8 of the Convention' (1998) 19 *Human Rights Law Journal* 10

Papagianni, G, *Institutional and Policy Dynamics of EU Migration Law* (Leiden/Boston, Martinus Nijhoff, 2006)

Parkin, J, *The Difficult Road to the Schengen Information System II* (CEPS, 2011)

Peers, S, 'Implementing Equality? The Directive on Long-term Resident Third-country Nationals' (2004) 29 *EL Rev* 437

—— 'Key Legislative Developments on Migration in the European Union: SIS II' (2008) 10 *European Journal of Migration and Law* 89

—— 'Schengen Information System' in S Peers, E Guild and J Tomkins (eds), *EU Immigration and Asylum Law (Text and Commentary), Volume 1: Visas and Border Controls* (Leiden, Martinus Nijhoff, 2012) 77

—— 'The Schengen Information System and EC Immigration and Asylum Law' in J de Zwaan and F Goudappel (eds), *Freedom, Security and Justice in the European Union* (The Hague, T.C.M. Asser Press, 2006) 172

Pistoia, E, 'The Unbearable Lightness of a Piecemeal Approach. Moving Public Policy or Public Security Offenders in Europe' (2014) 420 *European Public Law* 745

Pollet, K, 'The Negotiations on the Return Directive: Challenges, Outcomes and Lessons Learned from an NGO Perspective' in K Zwaan (ed), *The Returns Directive: Central Themes, Problem Issues, and Implementation in Selected Member States* (Nijmegen, Wolf Legal Publishers, 2011) 25

Renner, G, *Ausländerrecht in Deutschland* (Munich, C.H. Beck, 1998)

—— 'Staatliche Souveränität und die Verweigerung des weiteren Aufenthalts, Zur Geschichte des deutschen Ausweisungsrechts' in K Barwig, G Brinkmann, B Huber, K Lörcher and C Schumacher (eds), *Ausweisung im demokratischen Rechtsstaat, Hohenheimer Tage zum Ausländerrecht 1995* (Baden-Baden, Nomos, 1996) 23

Ress, G, 'Wirkung und Beachtung der Urteile und Entscheidungen der Straßburger Konventionsorgane' (1996) 24 *Europäische Grundrechte-Zeitschrift* 350

Roagna, I, *Protecting the Right to Respect for Private and Family Life under the European Convention on Human Rights* (Strasbourg, Council of Europe, 2012)

Roelofs, S, 'De maatregel tot ongewenstverklaring (deel 1)' (2002) *Migrantenrecht* 248

—— 'De maatregel tot ongewenstverklaring (deel 2)' (2002) *Migrantenrecht* 284

Rubel, J, *Entscheidungsfreiräume in der Rechtsprechung des Europäischen Gerichtshofes für Menschenrechte und des Europäischen Gerichtshofes* (Hamburg, Verlag Dr. Kovač, 2005)

Ruffert, M, 'Der transnationale Verwaltungsakt' (2001) 34 *Die Verwaltung* 453

—— 'Die Europäische Menschenrechtskonvention und innerstaatliches Recht' (2007) 35 *Europäische Grundrechte-Zeitschrift* 245

Rupp-Swienty, A, *Die Doktrin von der margin of appreciation in der Rechtsprechung des Europäischen Gerichtshofs für Menschenrechte* (Munich, VVF, 1999)

Rüthers, B, 'Zwischenruf aus der methodischen Wüste: "Der Richter wird's schon richten"(?)' (2006) 61 *Juristen Zeitung* 958

s.n., 'Part C: Deportation, Removal, Exclusion' in E Fripp (ed), *The Law and Practice of Expulsion and Exclusion from the United Kingdom* (Oxford, Hart Publishing, 2015) 229

Sander, D, *Der Schutz des Aufenthalts durch Artikel 8 der Europäischen Menschenrechtskonvention* (Berlin, Duncker & Humblot, 2008)

Schmid-Drüner, M, Der Begriff der öffentlichen Sicherheit und Ordnu*ng im Einwanderungsrecht ausgewählter EU-Mitgliedstaaten* (Baden-Baden, Nomos, 2007)

Schmidt-Aßmann, E, 'Verwaltungskooperation und Verwaltungskooperationsrecht in der Europäischen Gemeinschaft' (1996) 31 *Europarecht* 270

Schmitt Glaeser, A, 'Individualgerechtigkeit im Ausländerrecht' (2003) 23 *Zeitschrift für Ausländerrecht und Ausländerpolitik* 176

Schokkenbroek, J, 'The Basis, Nature and Application of the Margin-of-Appreciation Doctrine in the Case-Law of the European Court of Human Rights' (1998) 19 *Human Rights Law Journal* 30

Schuback, M, *Die Ausweisung nach dem Ausländergesetz in der Rechtsprechungskonzeption der Gerichte* (Frankfurt, Peter Lang, 2003)

Schuck, PH, 'The Transformation of Immigration Law' (1984) 84 *Columbia Law Review* 1

Schüller, F, 'Wakker worden! Verblijf na opheffing ongewenstverklaring' (2010) *Asiel & Migrantenrecht* 185

Schwarze, J, 'Der Beitrag des Europarates zur Entwicklung von Rechtsschutz und Verfahrensgarantien im Verwaltungsrecht' (1993) 21 *Europäische Grundrechte-Zeitschrift* 377

Sennekamp, C, 'Ist-Ausweisung menschenrechtswidrig?' (2002) 22 *Zeitschrift für Ausländerrecht und Ausländerpolitik* 136

Siess-Scherz, I, 'Die Bedeutung des Subsidiaritätsprinzips für den Reformprozess des EGMR' in W Karl and F Matscher (eds), *Internationale Gerichtshöfe und nationale Rechtsordnung* (Kehl am Rhein, N.P. Engel Verlag, 2005) 83

Sieveking, K, 'Security of Residence and Expulsion: The German Experience' in E Guild and P Minderhoud (eds), *Security of Residence and Expulsion* (The Hague, Kluwer Law International, 2001) 105

Spielmann, D, 'Allowing the Right Margin: The European Court of Human Rights and the National Margin of Appreciation Doctrine: Waiver of Subsidiarity of European Review?' (2012) 14 *Cambridge Yearbook of European Legal Studies* 381

Spijkerboer, TP, 'Noot bij ABRvS (18 October 2004)' (2004) *Jurisprudentie Vreemdelingenrecht* 468

Steenbergen, J, 'All the King's Horses ...: Probabilities and Possibilities for the Implementation of the New Title IV EC Treaty' (1999) 1 *European Journal of Migration and Law* 29

Steinebach, A and Güneş, L, 'Prekärer Aufenthaltsstatus? Ausweisungsschutz von Unionsbürgern und Drittstaatsangehörigen in der EU – ein Überblick' (2010) 31 *Zeitschrift für Ausländerrecht und Ausländerpolitik* 97

Steinorth, C, '*Üner v. The Netherlands*: Expulsion of Long-term Immigrants and the Right to Respect for Private and Family Life' (2008) 8 *Human Rights Law Review* 185

Stoyanova, V, 'Populism, Exceptionality and the Right of Migrants to Family Life Under the European Convention on Human Rights' (2018) 10 *European Journal of Legal Studies* 83

Strieder, B, 'Wann "gebieten" Belange des Ausländers im Ausweisungsrecht eine Ermessensentscheidung?' (2009) 31 *Informationsbrief Ausländerrecht* 371

Stronks, M, 'Een bijna ongebreidelde beteugeling van de tijd, Een analyse van aanscherpingen van de glijdende schaal' (2013) 34 *Nederlands Juristenblad* 2306

Sydow, G, 'Vollzug des europäischen Unionsrechts im Wege der Kooperation nationaler und europäischer Behörden' (2006) 59 *Die Öffentliche Verwaltung* 66

Tezcan-Idriz, N, 'Free Movement of Persons Between Turkey and the EU: To Move or Not to Move? The Response of the Judiciary' (2009) 46 *CML Rev* 1625

Thym, D, 'Directive 2003/109/EC' in K Hailbronner and D Thym (eds), *EU Immigration and Asylum Law, A Commentary*, 2nd edn (Munich, C.H. Beck, 2016)

—— 'Humanitäres Bleiberecht zum Schutz des Privatlebens?' (2007) 29 *Informationsbrief Ausländerrecht* 133

—— 'Menschenrecht auf Legalisierung des Aufenthalts?' (2006) 34 *Europäische Grundrechte-Zeitschrift* 541

—— *Migrationsverwaltungsrecht* (Tübingen, Mohr Siebeck, 2010)

—— 'Respect for Private and Family Life under Article 8 ECHR in Immigration Cases: A Human Right to Regularize Illegal Stay?' (2008) 57 *ICLQ* 87

—— 'Schutz des Aufenthalts zwischen polizeilicher Herkunft und menschenrechtlicher Neuausrichtung' in F Arndt, N Betz, A Farahat, M Goldmann, M Huber, R Keil, P Láncos, J Schaefer, M Smrkolj, F Sucker and S Valta (eds), *Freiheit – Sicherheit – Öffentlichkeit, 48. Assistententagung Öffentliches Recht* (Baden-Baden, Nomos, 2009) 221

—— 'Towards a Contextual Conception of Social Integration in EU Immigration Law. Comments on P & S and K & A' (2016) 18 *European Journal of Migration and Law* 89

Tomuschat, C, 'The Effects of Judgments of the European Court of Human Rights according to the German Constitutional Court' (2010) 11 *German Law Journal* 513

Toner, H, 'Article 8 ECHR – Full Judicial Scrutiny?' (2007) 1–2 *Migrantenrecht* 48

Trechsel, S, 'Artikel 3 EMRK als Schranke der Ausweisung' in K Barwig (ed), *Ausweisung im demokratischen Rechtsstaat* (Baden-Baden, Nomos, 1996) 223

Tridimas, T, *General Principles of EU Law*, 2nd edn (Oxford, Oxford EU Law Library, 2006)

Tümay, M, 'The "Margin of Appreciation Doctrine" Developed by the European Court of Human Rights' (2008) 5 *Ankara Law Review* 201

Turnbull, S and Hasselberg, I, 'From Prison to Detention: The Carceral Trajectories of Foreign National Prisoners in the United Kingdom' (2017) 19 *Punishment & Society* 135

van Dijk, P, 'Protection of "Integrated" Aliens Against Expulsion under the European Convention on Human Rights' in E Guild and P Minderhoud (eds), *Security of Residence and Expulsion* (The Hague, Kluwer Law International, 2001) 23

van Riel, M, 'Nieuwe wetgeving ter implementatie van de Terugkeerrichtlijn' (2012) *Asiel & Migrantenrecht* 68

van Walsum, S, 'Jurisprudentie over migratierecht en gezinsleven. Deel II: Artikel 8 EVRM' (2010) *Asiel & Migrantenrecht* 520

van Wijk, H, Konijnenbelt, W and van Male, R, *Hoofdstukken van bestuursrecht* (Deventer, Kluwer, 2014)

Verschaeren, N and Peeters, M, 'Vreemdelingenrechtelijke verweren in een strafzaak' (2013) *Journaal Vreemdelingenrecht* 165

Vondung, J, *Die Architektur des europäischen Grundrechtsschutzes nach dem Beitritt der EU zur EMRK* (Tübingen, Mohr Siebeck, 2012)

Voßkuhle, A, 'Theorie und Praxis der verfassungskonformen Auslegung von Gesetzen durch Fachgerichte' (2000) 125 *Archiv des öffentlichen Rechts* 177

Waite, L, 'Asylum Seekers and the Labour Market: Spaces of Discomfort and Hostility' (2017) 16 *Social Policy & Society* 669

Warbrick, C, 'The Structure of Article 8 ECHR' (1998) 1 *European Human Rights Law Review* 32

Wegner, J, 'Die Behandlung straffällig gewordender Einwanderer im neuen Ausweisungsrecht' (1993) 46 *Die Öffentliche Verwaltung* 1031

Weiß, W, 'Human Rights in the EU: Rethinking the Role of the ECHR After Lisbon' (2011) 7 *European Constitutional Law Review* 64

Wischmeyer, T, 'Generating Trust Through Law? Judicial Cooperation in the European Union and the "Principle of Mutual Trust"' (2016) 17 *German Law Journal* 339

Wollenschläger, M and Schraml, A, 'Zum Recht der Ausweisung im neuen Ausländergesetz' (1992) 12 *Zeitschrift für Ausländerrecht und Ausländerpolitik* 66
Zedner, L, 'Citizenship Deprivation, Security and Human Rights' (2016) 18 *European Journal of Migration and Law* 222
Zeichen, S, 'Ausweisungsschutz für integrierte Fremde' (2002) 57 *Zeitschrift für Öffentliches Recht* 413

Official Documents

Advies Raad van State, W 04.11.0396/I, 28 November 2011, Staatscourant 2012, no 14035
Bundesministerium des Innern, für Bau und Heimat, 'Polizeiliche Kriminalstatistik 2018 Ausgewählte Zahlen im Überblick' (Innenminister Konferenz 2019)
COM(94) 23 final, Communication from the Commission to the Council and the European Parliament on Immigration and Asylum Policies
COM(2001) 257 final, Proposal for a European Parliament and Council Directive on the right of citizens of the Union and their family members to move and reside freely within the territory of the Member States
COM(2002) 175 final, Opinion on the Green Paper on a Community return policy on illegal residents
COM(2002) 564 final, Opinion of the European Economic and Social Committee on the Communication from the Commission to the Council and the European Parliament on a Community return policy on illegal residents
COM(2005) 236 final, Proposal for a Regulation of the European Parliament and of the Council on the establishment, operation and use of the second generation Schengen information system (SIS II)
COM(2005) 391 final, Proposal for a Directive of the European Parliament and of the Council on common standards and procedures in Member States for returning illegally staying third-country nationals
COM(2008) 840 final, Report from the Commission to the European Parliament and the Council on the application of Directive 2004/38/EC on the right of citizens of the Union and their family members to move and reside freely within the territory of the Member States
COM(2009) 313 final, Communication from the Commission to the European Parliament and the Council on guidance for better transposition and application of Directive 2004/38/EC on the right of citizens of the Union and their family members to move and reside freely within the territory of the Member States
COM(2011) 585 final, Report from the Commission to the European Parliament and the Council on the application of Directive 2003/109/EC concerning the status of third-country nationals who are long-term residents
COM(2016) 880 final, Report from the Commission to the European Parliament and the Council on the evaluation of the second generation Schengen Information System (SIS II) in accordance with artt 24 (5), 43 (3) and 50 (5) of Regulation (EC) No 1987/2006 and artt 59 (3) and 66 (5) of Decision 2007/533/JHA
COM(2019) 161 final, Report from the Commission to the European Parliament and the Council on the implementation of Directive 2003/109/EC concerning the status of third-country nationals who are long-term residents
Committee on Citizens' Freedoms and Rights and Justice and Home Affairs of the European Parliament, European Parliament legislative resolution on the proposal for a European Parliament and Council Directive on the right of citizens of the Union to and their family members to move and reside freely within the territory of the Member States, PE 319.238, A5-0009/2003 of 23 January 2003
Common Position (EC) No 6/2004 of 5 December 2003 adopted by the Council, acting in accordance with the procedure referred to in Article 251 of the Treaty establishing the European Community, with a view to adopting a directive of the European Parliament and of the Council on the right of citizens of the Union and their family members to move and reside freely within the territory

of the Member States amending Regulation (EEC) No 1612/68 and repealing Directives 64/221/EEC, 68/360/EEC, 72/194/EEC, 73/148/EEC, 75/34/EEC, 75/35/EEC, 90/364/EEC, 90/365/EEC and 93/96/EEC [2004] OJ C 54 E/12

Council Document 6624/07 of 28 February 2007

Council Framework Decision 2004/757/JHA of 25 October 2004, laying down minimum provisions on the constituent elements of criminal acts and penalties in the field of illicit drug trafficking [2004] OJ L 335/8

Council of Europe, Committee of Ministers, Recommendation Rec (2000)15, concerning the security of residence of long-term migrants, adopted on 13 September 2000 at the 720th meeting of the Ministers' Deputies

Council of Europe, Committee of Ministers, Recommendation Rec (2002)4 on the legal status of persons admitted for family reunification, adopted by the Committee of Ministers on 26 March 2002 at the 790th meeting of the Ministers' Deputies

Council of Europe, Explanatory Report to Protocol No 7 to the Convention for the Protection of Human Rights and Fundamental Freedoms, ETS no 117

Council of Europe, Parliamentary Assembly's Committee on Migration, Refugees and Demography, Recommendation 1504, Non-expulsion of long-term immigrants, adopted by the Standing Committee, acting on behalf of the Assembly, on 14 March 2001

Council of the European Union, Note from the Presidency, 'Proposal for a Return Action Programme', 25 November 2002, doc 14673/02

Council of the European Union, Note from the Presidency, 'Selected issues concerning the legal basis for SIS II' 20 April 2006, doc. 8537/06

European Parliament Committee on Civil Liberties, Justice and Home Affairs, Report on the proposal for a regulation on the establishment, operation and use of the Schengen Information System (SIS) in the field of border checks, amending Regulation (EU) No 515/2014 and repealing Regulation (EC) No 1987/2006 (COM(2016)0882 – C8-0533/2017–2016/0408(COD)), A8-0347/2017

European Parliament legislative resolution on the proposal for directive on the right of citizens of the Union and their family members to move and reside freely within the territory of the Member States (COM(2001) 257 – C5-0336/2001–2001/0111(COD))

European Parliament resolution on the report from the Commission to the Council and the European Parliament on the implementation of Directives 90/364, 90/365 and 93/96 (right of residence) and on the communication from the Commission on the special measures concerning the movement and residence of citizens of the Union which are justified on grounds of public policy, public security or public health (COM(1999)127, COM(99)372 – C5-0177/1999, C5-0178/1999–1999/2157(COS))

European Union Agency for the Operational Management of Large-Scale IT Systems in the Area of Freedom, Security and Justice, SIS II – 2020 statistics, March 2021

Explanatory Report to Protocol No 4 to the Convention for the Protection of Human Rights and Fundamental Freedoms, securing certain rights and freedoms other than those already included in the Convention and in the first Protocol thereto, ETS no 46 (Strasbourg, 16 September 1963)

Gesetzentwurf der Abgeordneten Memet Kilic, Josef Philip Winkler, Dr. Konstantin von Notz, Volker Beck (Köln), Jerzy Montag, Claudia Roth (Augsburg), Wolfgang Wieland und der Fraktion BÜNDNIS 90/DIE GRÜNEN, 'Gesetzentwurf zur Klarstellung des assoziationsrechtlichen Rechtsstatus Staatsangehöriger der Türkei im Aufenthalts-, Beschäftigungserlaubnis- und Beamtenrecht' (2013) Bundestagsdrucksache 17/12193

Gesetzentwurf der Bundesregierung, 'Entwurf eines Gesetzes zur Neubestimmung des Bleiberechts und der Aufenthaltsbeendigung' (2015) Bundestagsdrucksache 18/4097

Gesetzentwurf der Bundesregierung, 'Entwurf eines Gesetzes zur Neubestimmung des Bleiberechts und der Aufenthaltsbeendigung' (2015) Bundestagsdrucksache 18/5420

Gesetzentwurf der Bundesregierung, 'Entwurf eines Gesetzes zur Umsetzung aufenthalts- und asylrechtlicher Richtlinien der Europäischen Union' (2007) Bundestagsdrucksache 16/5065

Gesetzentwurf der Fraktionen der CDU/CSU und FDP, 'Entwurf eines Gesetzes zur Umsetzung aufenthaltsrechtlicher Richtlinien der Europäischen Union und zur Anpassung nationaler Rechtsvorschriften an den EU-Visakodex' (2011) Bundestagsdrucksache 17/5470

Gesetzentwurf der Fraktionen der CDU/CSU und SPD, 'Entwurf eines Gesetzes zur erleichterten Ausweisung von straffälligen Ausländern und zum erweiterten Ausschluss der Flüchtlingsanerkennung bei straffälligen Asylbewerbern'(2016), Bundestagsdrucksache 18/7537

House of Lords, Schengen Information System II (SIS II): Report with Evidence, 9th Report of Session 2006–2007

House of Lords, Schengen Information System II (SIS II): Report with Evidence, 9th Report of Session 2006–2007, Minutes of Evidence by K Groenendijk, 11 October 2006

International Law Commission, Draft Articles on the Expulsion of Aliens, with Commentaries, (2014) UN Doc. A/69/10

International Law Commission, Expulsion of Aliens: Memorandum by the Secretariat, UN Doc. A/CN.4/565 of 10 July 2006

Opinion of the Joint Supervisory Authority on the proposed legal basis for SIS II, 27 September 2005

Presidency Conclusions, Tampere European Council, 15 and 16 October 1999, SN 200/99

Steering Committee for Human Rights, CDDH Report on the Longer-Term Future of the System of the European Convention on Human Rights (CDDH Report), Doc CDDH(2015)R 84, Addendum I, 11 December 2015

SWD(2016) 450 final, Commission Staff Working Document accompanying the document report from the Commission to the European Parliament and the Council on the evaluation of the second generation Schengen Information System (SIS II)

Other Sources

Adviescommissie voor Vreemdelingenzaken (ACVZ), Advies 'Gewogen gevaar', uitgebracht aan de staatssecretaris van Justitie en Veiligheid (2018)

Besselink, L, 'Acceding to the ECHR notwithstanding the Court of Justice Opinion 2/13' (*Verfassungsblog*, 23 December 2014)

Commissie Meijers, 'Note on the coordination of the relationship between the Entry Ban and the SIS-alert: an urgent need for legislative measures' CM 1203, 8 February 2012

Commissie Meijers, 'Strafbaarstelling overtreding inreisverbod' (TK 2010-2011, 32 420, nr. 9) CM 1018, 24 December 2010

Commissie Meijers, 'Wijziging van de Vreemdelingenwet 2000 ter implementatie van de Terugkeerrichtlijn' (TK 32 420) CM 1013, of 3 September 2010

Eisele, K (ed), European Parliamentary Research Service, 'The Return Directive 2008/115/EC, European Implementation Assessment'

European Commission, 'Expulsion' (Glossary of the EU Commission)

European Migration Network Ad-Hoc Query on Entry Bans Entered into the SIS and Consultation Procedures in Member States, requested by COM on 13th February 2015, Query No 2015.662

Immigratie- en Naturalisatiedienst, WI 2020/16 Richtlijnen voor de toepassing van artikel 8 EVRM, Werkinstructie 2020/16 (SUA), 18 November 2020

Migration Policy Group, 'ILPA/MPG Amsterdam Proposals' (London/Brussels, 2000)

Pernice, I, 'The Charter of Fundamental Rights in the Constitution of the European Union', WHI Paper 14/02

Press release by the EU Commission, 'Free movement: Commission asks Austria, Germany and Sweden to uphold EU citizens' rights', 21 June 2012, IP/12/646

Press release, 'European Commission assesses recent developments in France, discusses overall situation of the Roma and EU law on free movement of EU citizens', 29 September 2010, IP/10/1207

Report of the Ministry of the Interior of North-Rhine-Westphalia, 10 January 2016, www.mik.nrw.de/fileadmin/user_upload/Redakteure/Dokumente/Themen_und_Aufgaben/Schutz_und_Sicherheit/160111ssia/160111berppkoeln.pdf

Rijksoverheid, '"Bruggen slaan", Regeerakkoord VVD-PvdA', 29 October 2012

Rijksoverheid, '"Vrijheid en verantwoordelijkheid", Regeerakkoord VVD-CDA', 30 September 2010

SEC(2005)1057, Commission Staff Working Document, Annex to the Proposal for a European Parliament and Council Directive on common standards on procedures in Member States for returning illegally staying third-country nationals – Impact Assessment

Statewatch, 'Three quarters of a million "illegal aliens" banned from Schengen area' (2005)

United Kingdom Home Office, *Statement of Intent: Family Migration* (June 2012), https://assets.publishing.service.gov.uk/government/uploads/system/uploads/attachment_data/file/257359/soi-fam-mig.pdf

INDEX

Lightning Source UK Ltd.
Milton Keynes UK
UKHW020136040522
402443UK00003B/79

9 781509 925988